If I were rain,
That joins sky and earth that otherwise never touch,
Could I join two hearts as well?

BLEACH 3

memories in the rain

Shonen Jump Graphic Novel

STARS AND

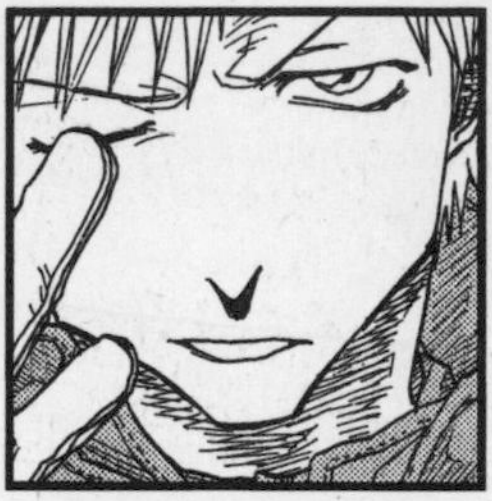

Ichigo Kurosaki

黒崎一護

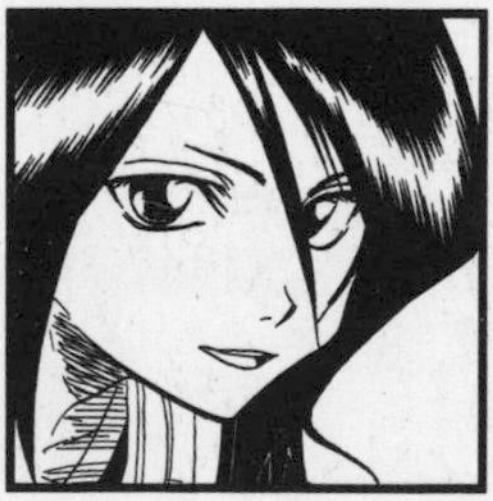

Rukia Kuchiki

朽木ルキア

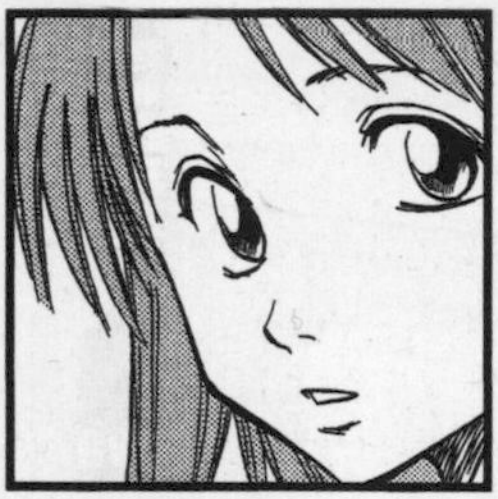

Orihime Inoue

井上織姫

plot

Ichigo Kurosaki, 15 years old. Except for being able to see ghosts, he is an ordinary (?) high school student. But when he meets the Soul Reaper Rukia Kuchiki, his life takes a dramatic turn for the bizarre, leading Ichigo to use his enormous spiritual energy to help Rukia do her job.

A Soul Reaper cleanses fallen souls called Hollows of their sins and guides them to the Soul Society. But as Ichigo fights an assortment of Hollows, he not only encounters souls who have lost their way in death, but one who had committed unforgivable crimes in life as well!

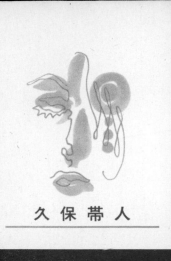

久保帯人

I tend to get worried about the seasons in *BLEACH* as opposed to the actual seasons in real life. The series started in the summer, but at that time, in was May in the book. That discrepancy has always bothered me. In this volume, the introduction of Ichigo, the main character, finally comes to an end. The setting is June. Unexpectedly, this all worked out quite well. If possible, please read this on a rainy night.
Tite Kubo

BLEACH is author Tite Kubo's second title. Kubo made his debut with *ZOMBIE POWDER*, a four-volume series for *WEEKLY SHONEN JUMP*. To date, *BLEACH* has sold nearly 7 million volumes and has been translated into seven different languages. Beginning its serialization in 2001, *BLEACH* is still a mainstay in the pages of *WEEKLY SHONEN JUMP*.

BLEACH
Vol. 3: memories in the rain
The SHONEN JUMP Graphic Novel Edition

STORY AND ART BY TITE KUBO

English Adaptation/Lance Caselman
Translation/Joe Yamazaki
Touch-Up Art & Lettering/Dave Lanphear
Cover, Graphics & Design/Sean Lee
Editor/Kit Fox

Managing Editor/Elizabeth Kawasaki
Director of Production/Noboru Watanabe
Editorial Director/Alvin Lu
Executive Vice President & Editor in Chief/Hyoe Narita
Sr. Director of Licensing & Acquisitions/Rika Inouye
Vice President of Sales/Joe Morici
Vice President of Marketing/Liza Coppola
Vice President of Strategic Development/Yumi Hoashi
Publisher/Seiji Horibuchi

Printed in the U.S.A.

Published by VIZ, LLC
P.O. Box 77010
San Francisco, CA 94107

SHONEN JUMP Graphic Novel Edition
10 9 8 7 6 5 4 3 2 1
First printing, September 2004

PARENTAL ADVISORY
BLEACH is rated T for Teen. It contains
fantasy violence and tobacco use. It is
recommended for ages 13 and up.

www.viz.com

THE WORLD'S
MOST POPULAR MANGA
SHONEN JUMP
GRAPHIC NOVEL
www.shonenjump.com

BLEACH ALL

黒崎真咲
Masaki Kurosaki

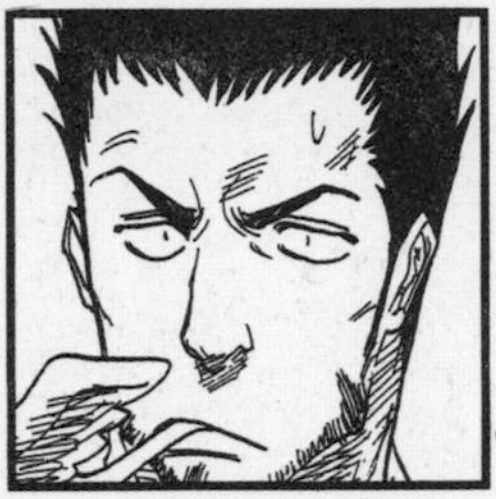

有沢竜貴
Tatsuki Arisawa

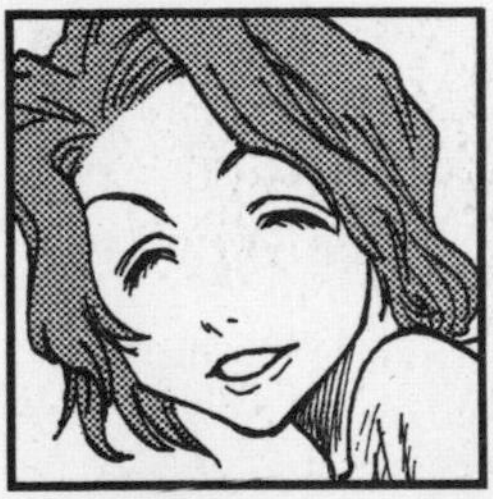

Isshin Kurosaki
黒崎一心

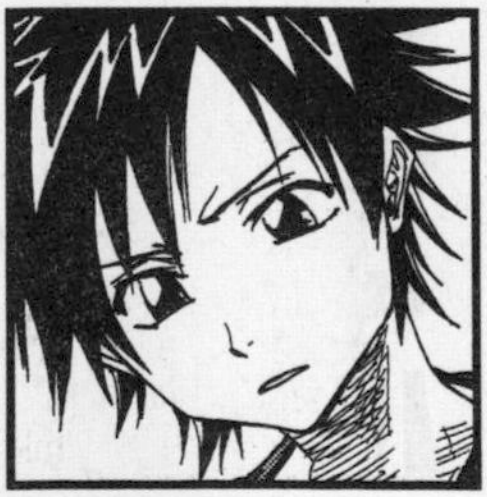

STORIES

BLEACH 3

memories in the rain

Contents

17. 6/17

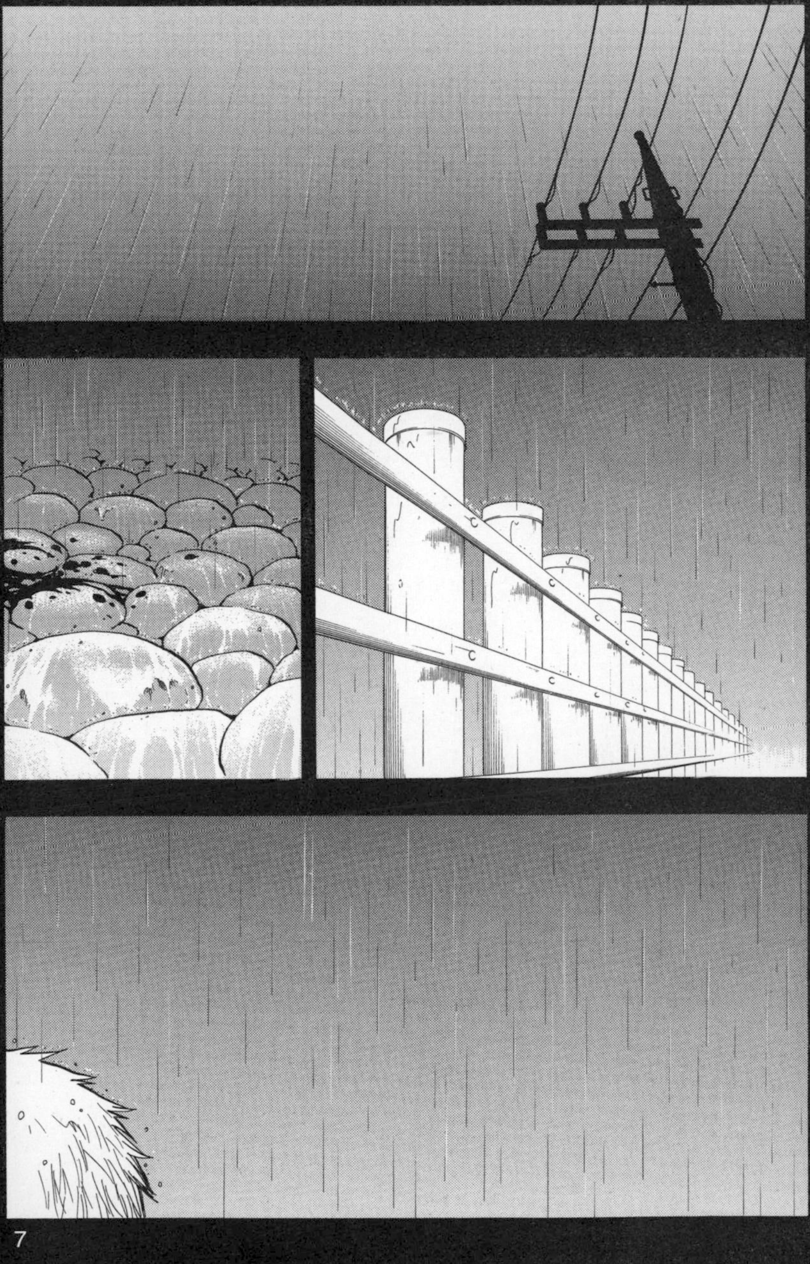

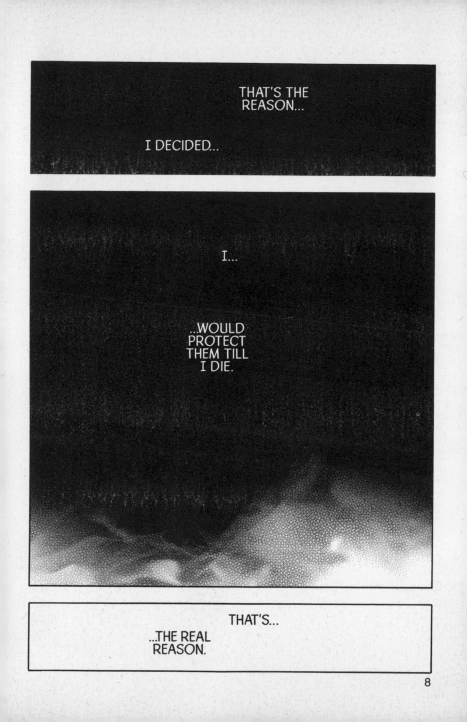

THAT'S THE
REASON...

I DECIDED...

I...

...WOULD
PROTECT
THEM TILL
I DIE.

THAT'S...

...THE REAL
REASON.

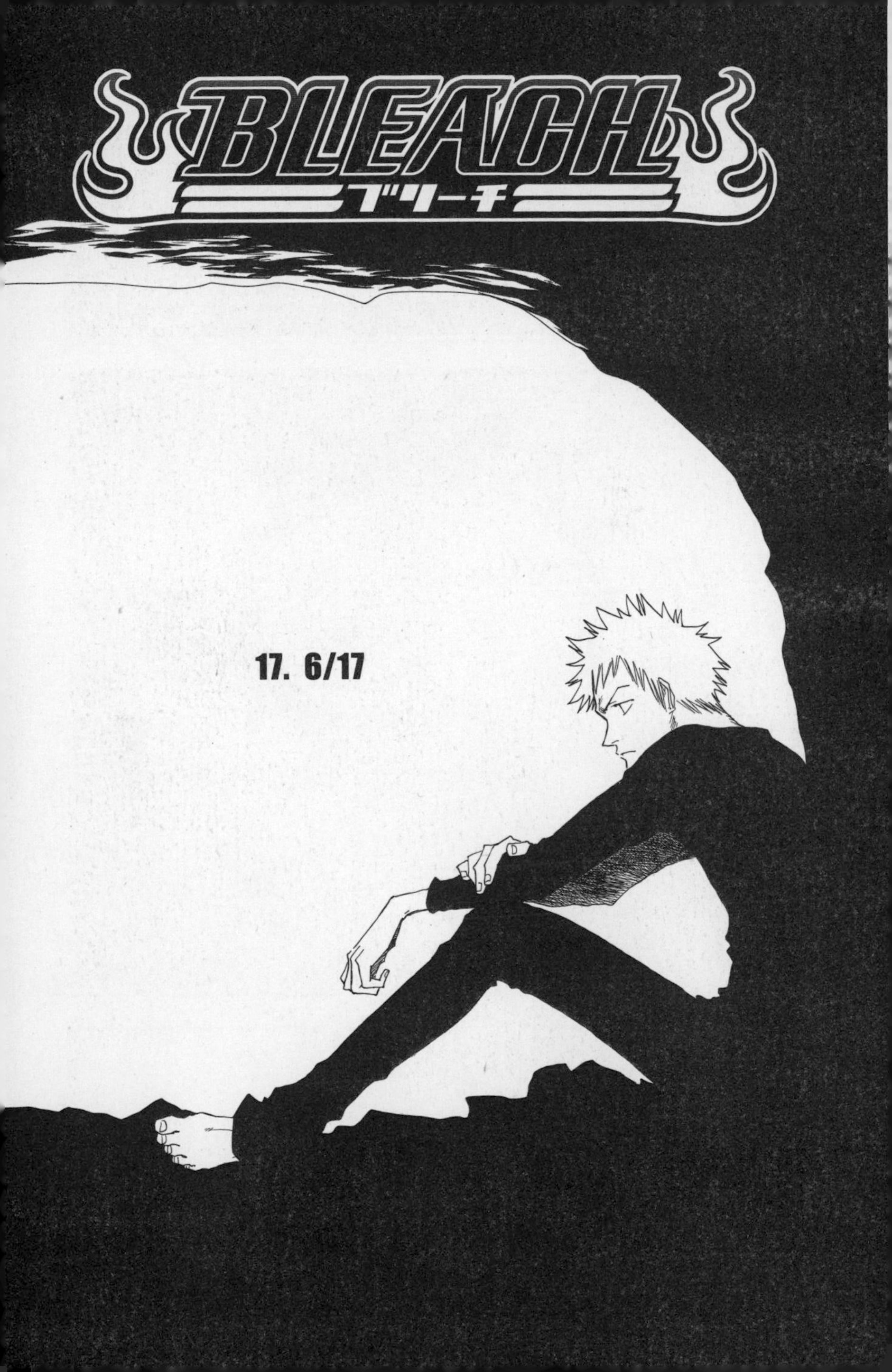
BLEACH
ブリーチ
17. 6/17

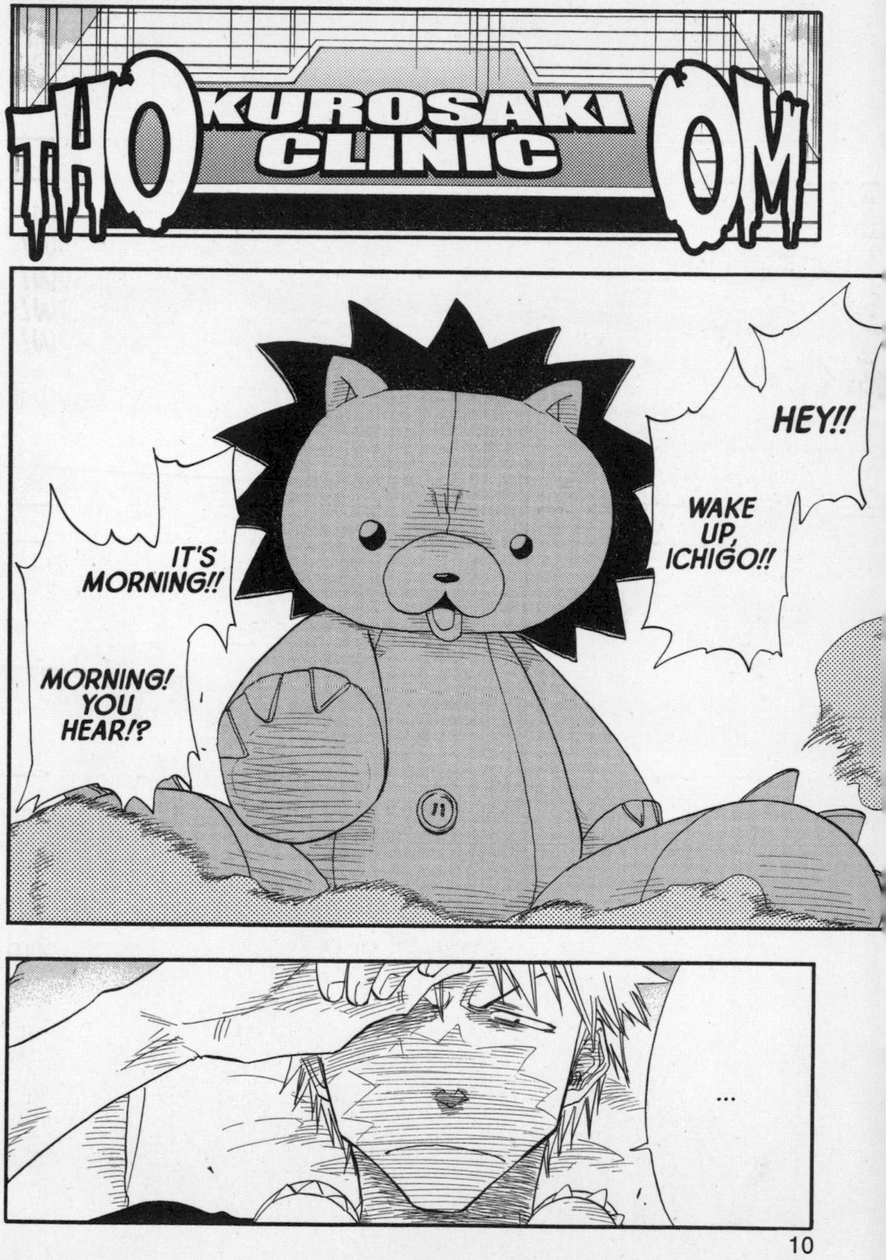
THO
KUROSAKI CLINIC
OM
HEY!!
WAKE UP, ICHIGO!!
IT'S MORNING!!
MORNING! YOU HEAR!?
...

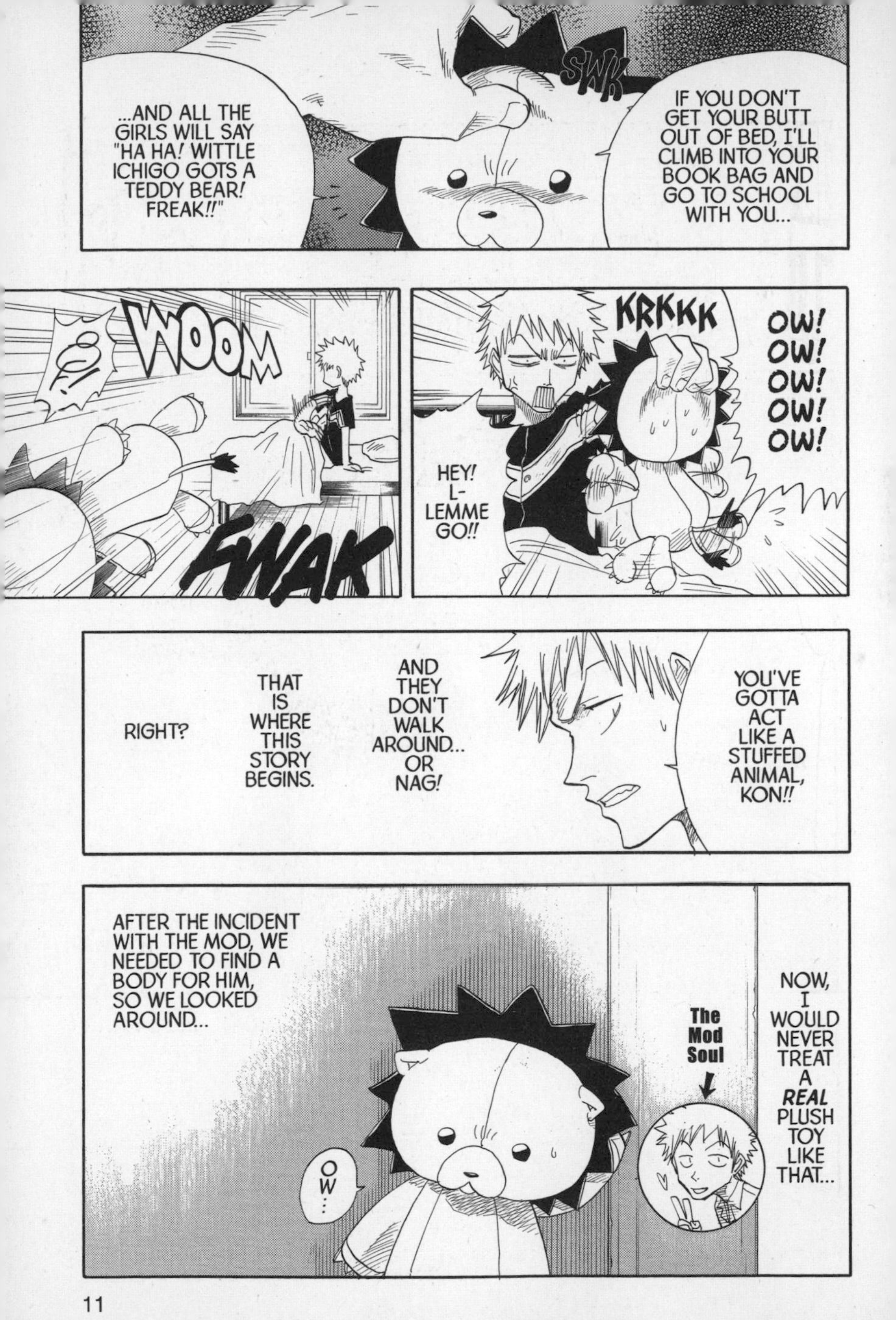

SWK
IF YOU DON'T GET YOUR BUTT OUT OF BED, I'LL CLIMB INTO YOUR BOOK BAG AND GO TO SCHOOL WITH YOU...
...AND ALL THE GIRLS WILL SAY "HA HA! WITTLE ICHIGO GOTS A TEDDY BEAR! FREAK!!"
KRKKK
OW! OW! OW! OW! OW!
HEY! L- LEMME GO!!
WOOM
FWAK
YOU'VE GOTTA ACT LIKE A STUFFED ANIMAL, KON!!
AND THEY DON'T WALK AROUND... OR NAG!
THAT IS WHERE THIS STORY BEGINS.
RIGHT?
NOW, I WOULD NEVER TREAT A *REAL* PLUSH TOY LIKE THAT...
The Mod Soul
AFTER THE INCIDENT WITH THE MOD, WE NEEDED TO FIND A BODY FOR HIM, SO WE LOOKED AROUND...
OW...

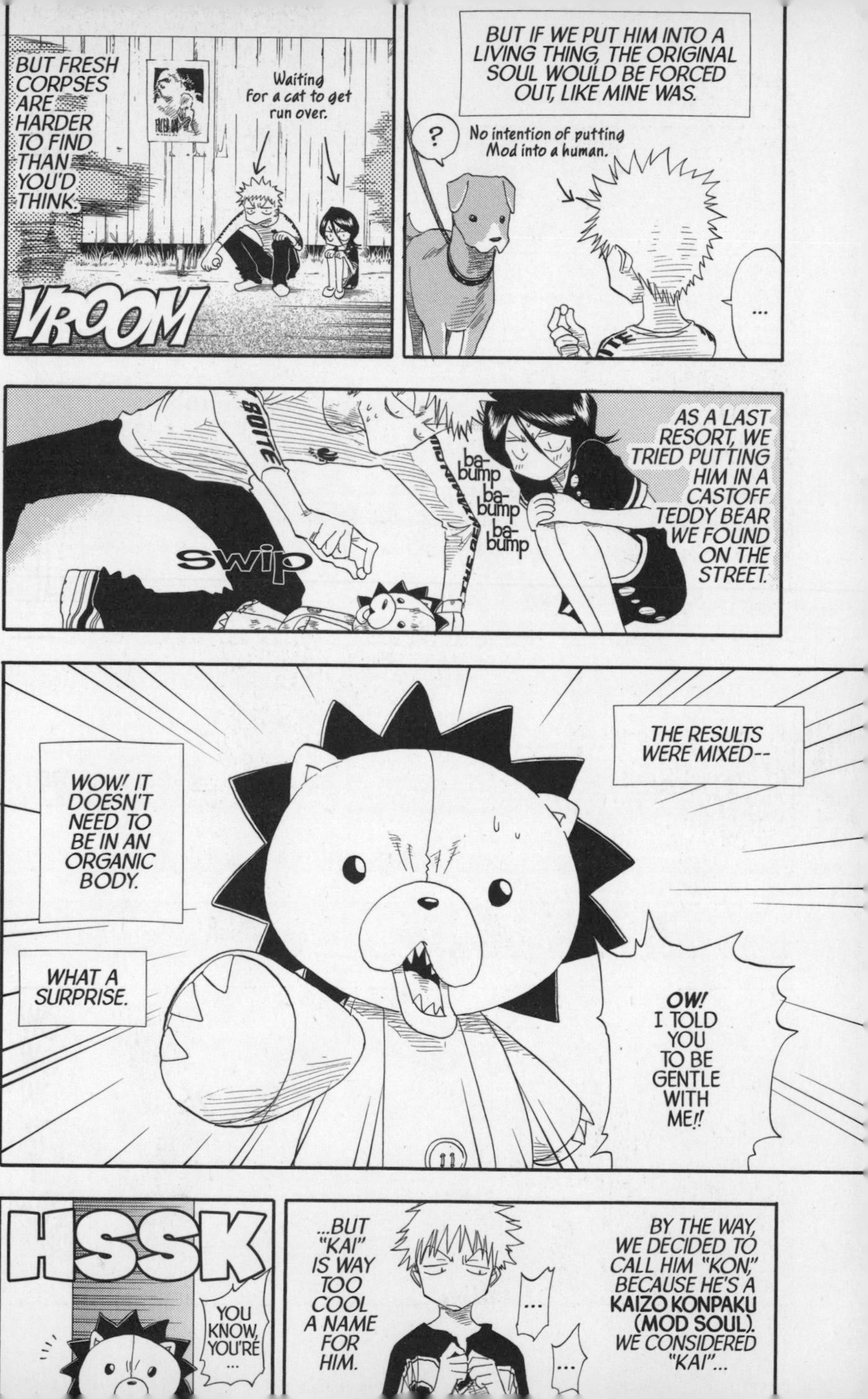
BUT IF WE PUT HIM INTO A LIVING THING, THE ORIGINAL SOUL WOULD BE FORCED OUT, LIKE MINE WAS.
?
No intention of putting Mod into a human.
...
BUT FRESH CORPSES ARE HARDER TO FIND THAN YOU'D THINK.
Waiting for a cat to get run over.
VROOM
AS A LAST RESORT, WE TRIED PUTTING HIM IN A CASTOFF TEDDY BEAR WE FOUND ON THE STREET.
ba-bump ba-bump ba-bump
swip
THE RESULTS WERE MIXED--
WOW! IT DOESN'T NEED TO BE IN AN ORGANIC BODY.
OW! I TOLD YOU TO BE GENTLE WITH ME!!
WHAT A SURPRISE.
BY THE WAY, WE DECIDED TO CALL HIM "KON," BECAUSE HE'S A KAIZO KONPAKU (MOD SOUL). WE CONSIDERED "KAI"...
...BUT "KAI" IS WAY TOO COOL A NAME FOR HIM.
...
...
HSSK
YOU KNOW, YOU'RE ...

READ THIS WAY

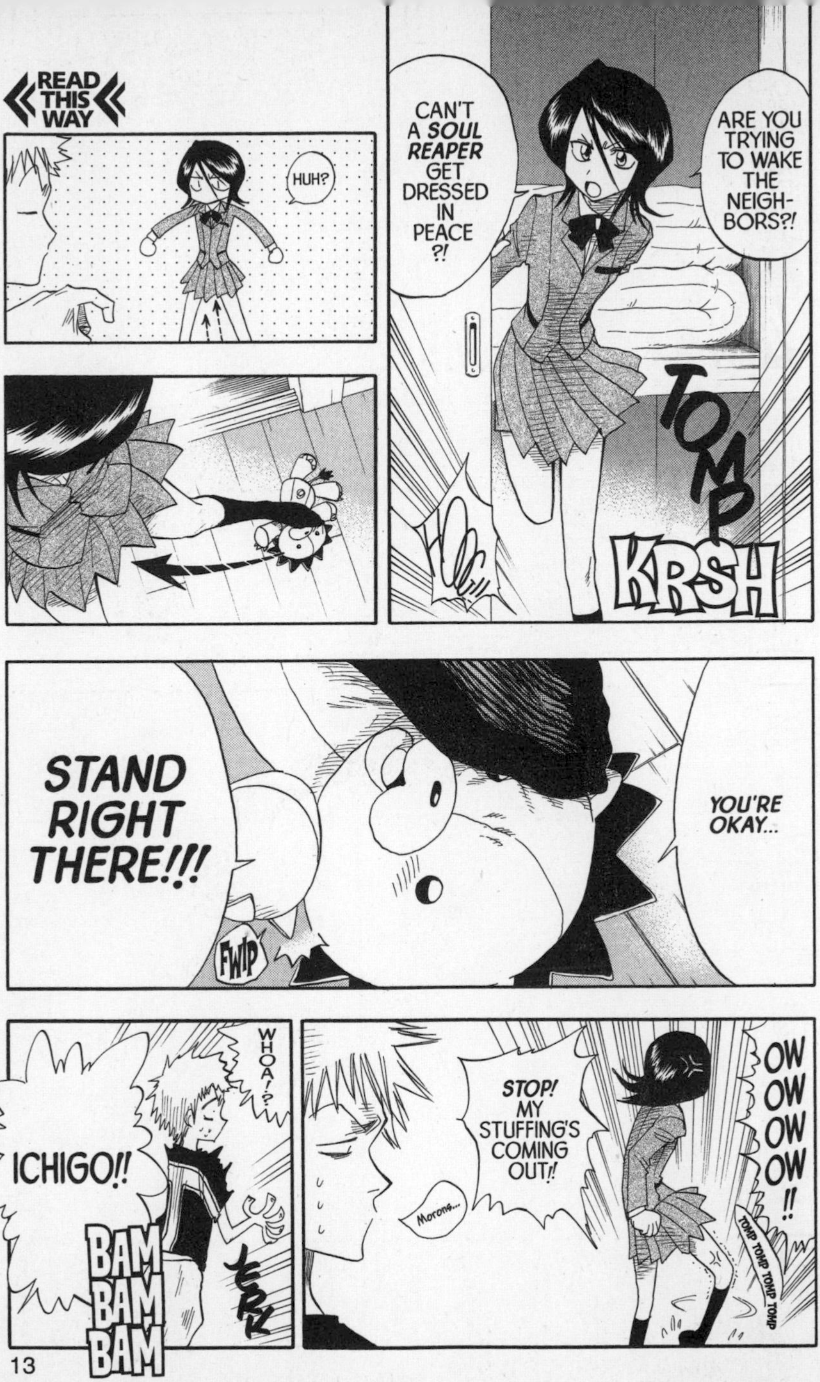

ARE YOU TRYING TO WAKE THE NEIGHBORS?!
CAN'T A ***SOUL REAPER*** GET DRESSED IN PEACE?!
TOMP
KRSH
HUH?
YOU'RE OKAY...
STAND RIGHT THERE!!!
FWIP
OW OW OW OW!!
TOMP TOMP TOMP TOMP
STOP! MY STUFFING'S COMING OUT!
Morons...
WHOA!?
ICHIGO!!
ERK
BAM BAM BAM

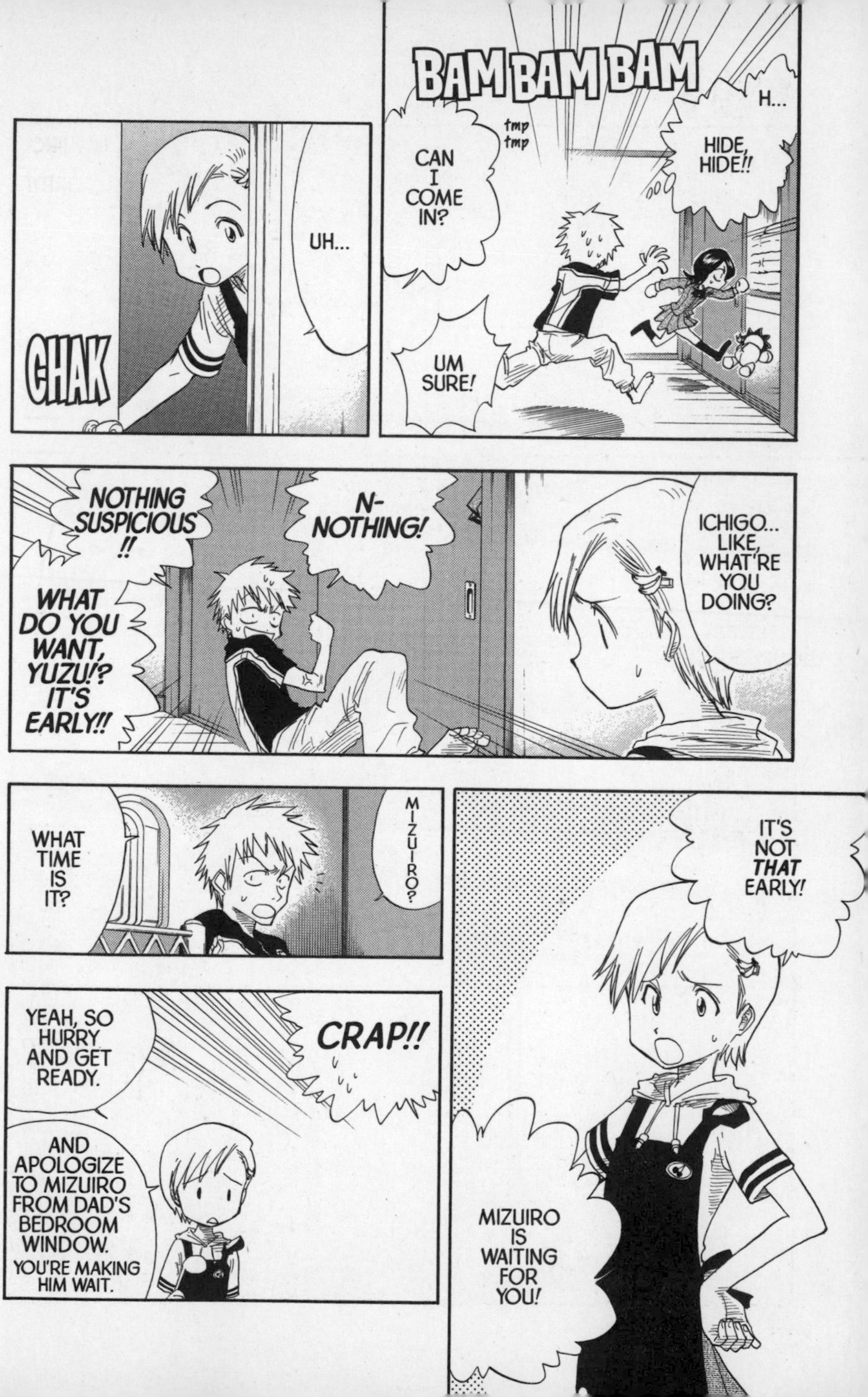
BAM BAM BAM
H...
HIDE, HIDE!!
tmp tmp
CAN I COME IN?
UM SURE!
UH...
CHAK
ICHIGO... LIKE, WHAT'RE YOU DOING?
N-NOTHING!
NOTHING SUSPICIOUS!!
WHAT DO YOU WANT, YUZU!? IT'S EARLY!!
IT'S NOT *THAT* EARLY!
MIZUIRO IS WAITING FOR YOU!
MIZUIRO?
WHAT TIME IS IT?
CRAP!!
YEAH, SO HURRY AND GET READY.
AND APOLOGIZE TO MIZUIRO FROM DAD'S BEDROOM WINDOW.
YOU'RE MAKING HIM WAIT.

READ THIS WAY

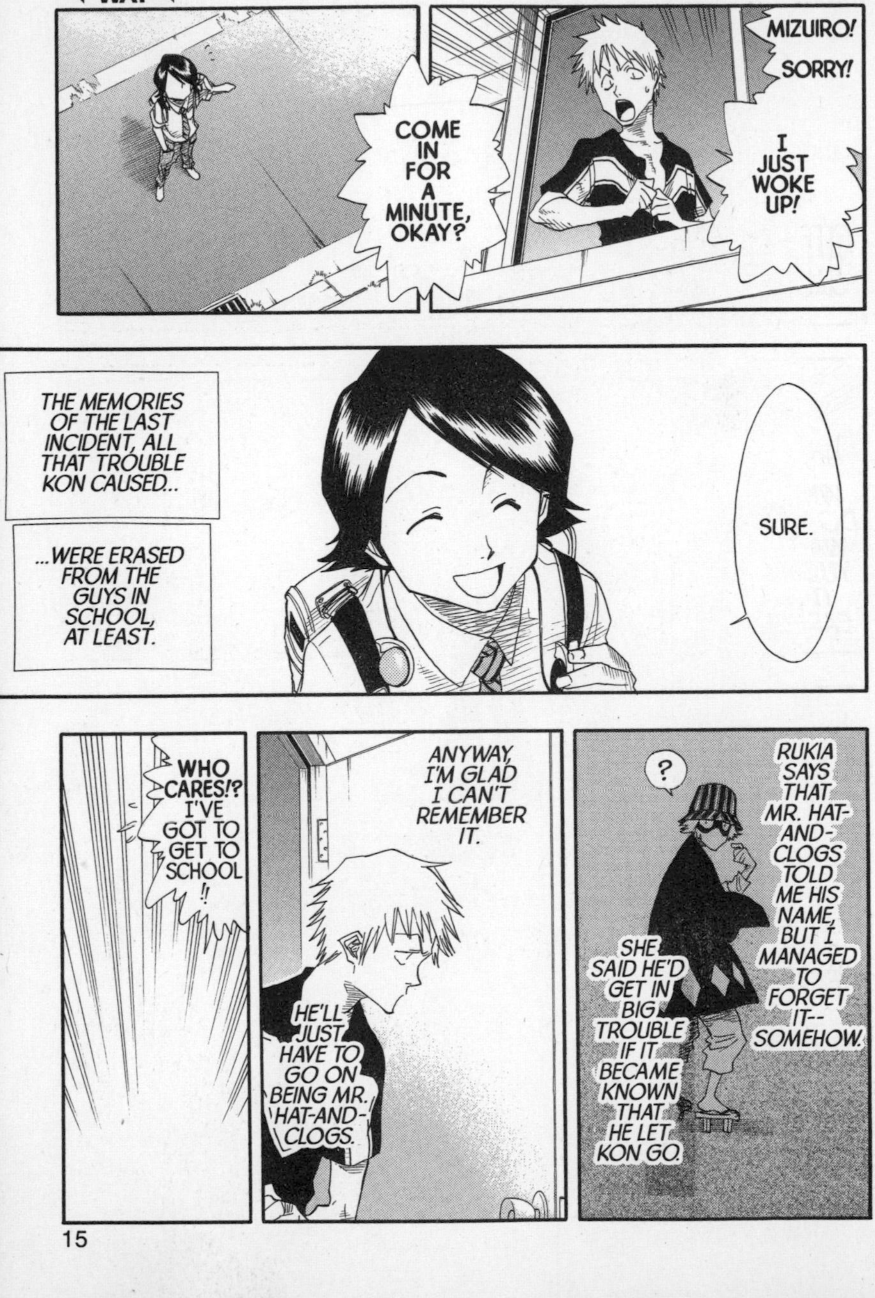
MIZUIRO!
SORRY!
I JUST WOKE UP!
COME IN FOR A MINUTE, OKAY?
SURE.
THE MEMORIES OF THE LAST INCIDENT, ALL THAT TROUBLE KON CAUSED...
...WERE ERASED FROM THE GUYS IN SCHOOL, AT LEAST.
?
RUKIA SAYS THAT MR. HAT-AND-CLOGS TOLD ME HIS NAME, BUT I MANAGED TO FORGET IT--SOMEHOW.
SHE SAID HE'D GET IN BIG TROUBLE IF IT BECAME KNOWN THAT HE LET KON GO.
ANYWAY, I'M GLAD I CAN'T REMEMBER IT.
HE'LL JUST HAVE TO GO ON BEING MR. HAT-AND-CLOGS.
WHO CARES!? I'VE GOT TO GET TO SCHOOL!!

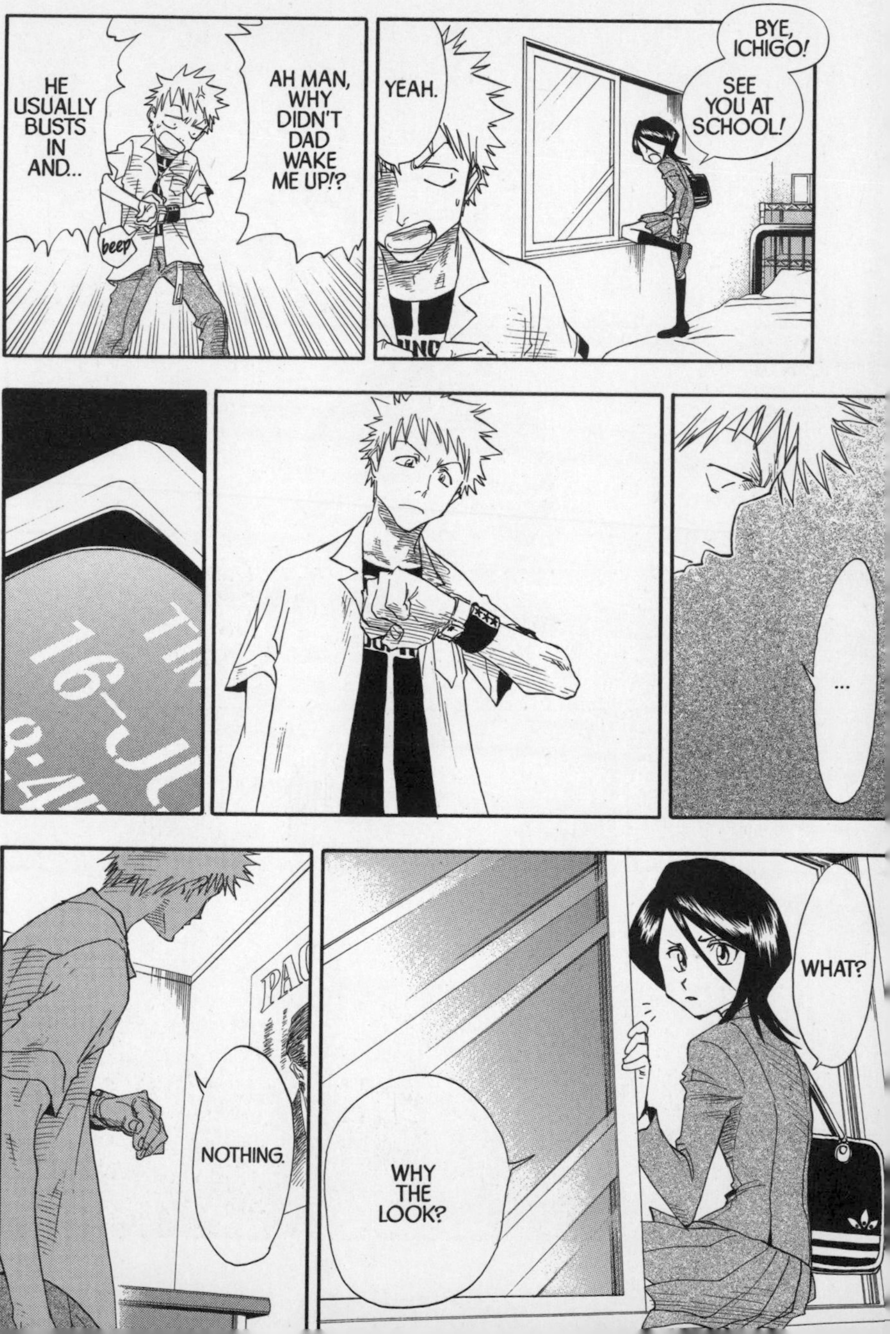
BYE, ICHIGO!
SEE YOU AT SCHOOL!
YEAH.
AH MAN, WHY DIDN'T DAD WAKE ME UP!?
HE USUALLY BUSTS IN AND...
beep
...
WHAT?
WHY THE LOOK?
NOTHING.

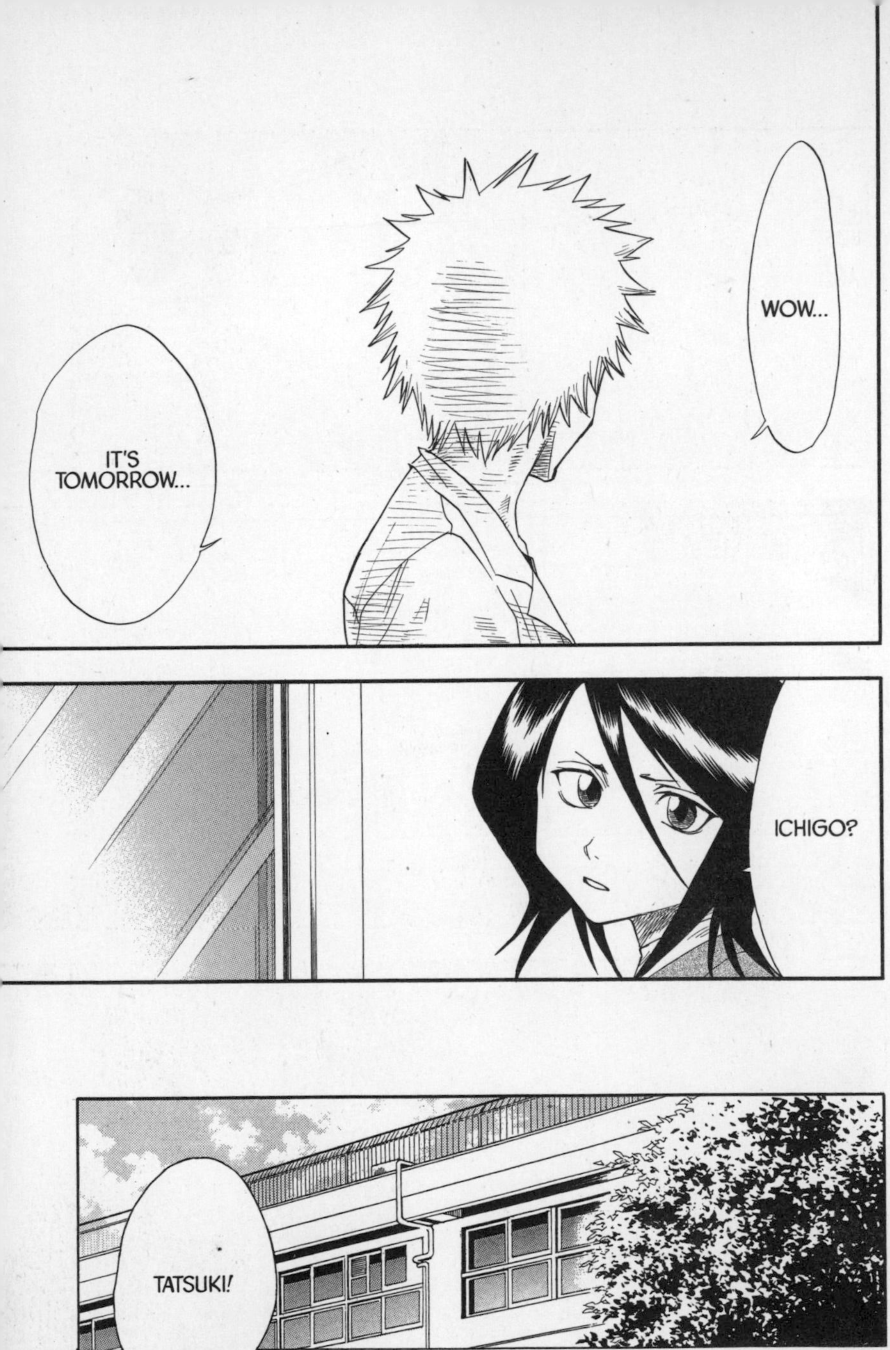
WOW...
IT'S TOMORROW...
ICHIGO?
TATSUKI!

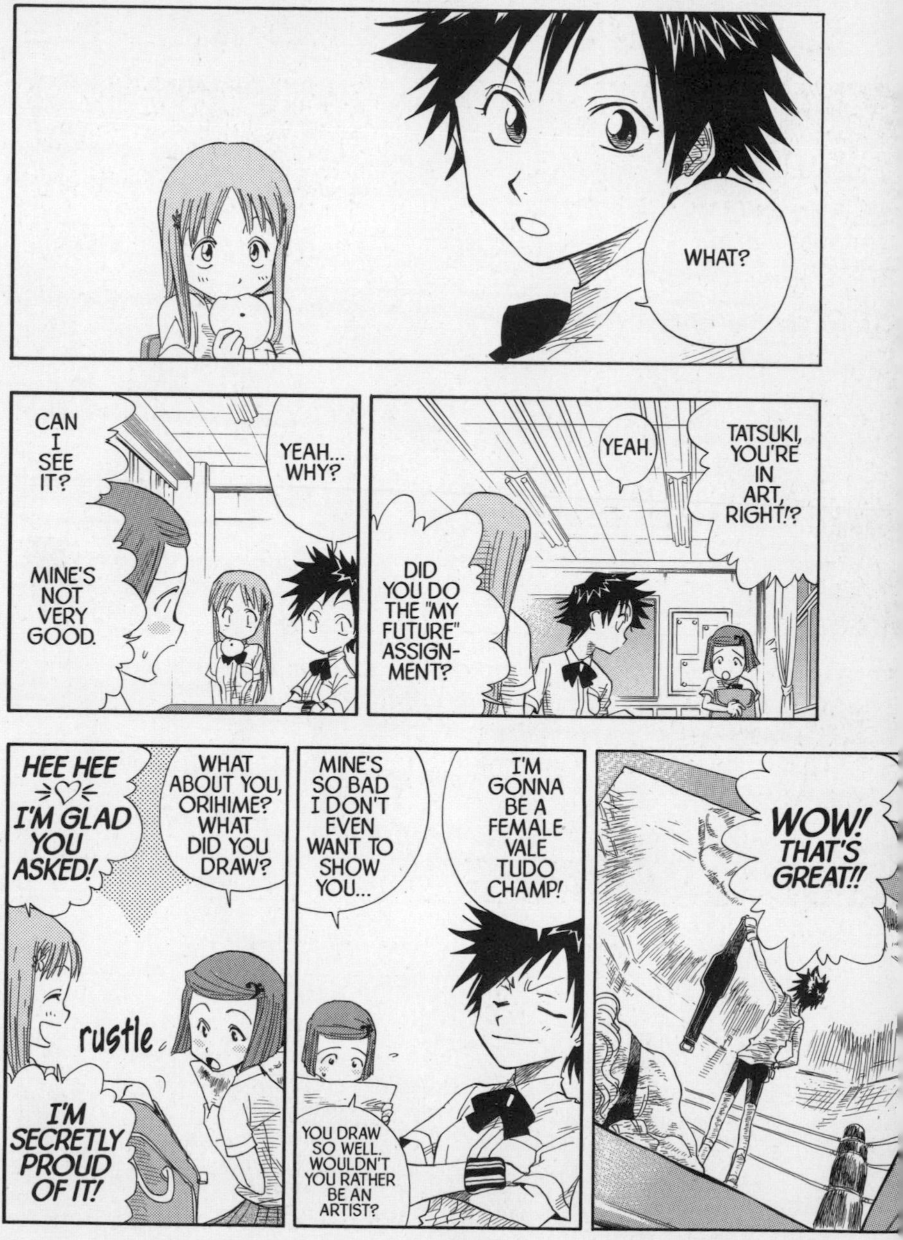
WHAT?
TATSUKI, YOU'RE IN ART, RIGHT!?
YEAH.
DID YOU DO THE "MY FUTURE" ASSIGNMENT?
YEAH... WHY?
CAN I SEE IT?
MINE'S NOT VERY GOOD.
WOW! THAT'S GREAT!!
I'M GONNA BE A FEMALE VALE TUDO CHAMP!
MINE'S SO BAD I DON'T EVEN WANT TO SHOW YOU...
YOU DRAW SO WELL. WOULDN'T YOU RATHER BE AN ARTIST?
WHAT ABOUT YOU, ORIHIME? WHAT DID YOU DRAW?
HEE HEE ♡ I'M GLAD YOU ASKED!
rustle
I'M SECRETLY PROUD OF IT!

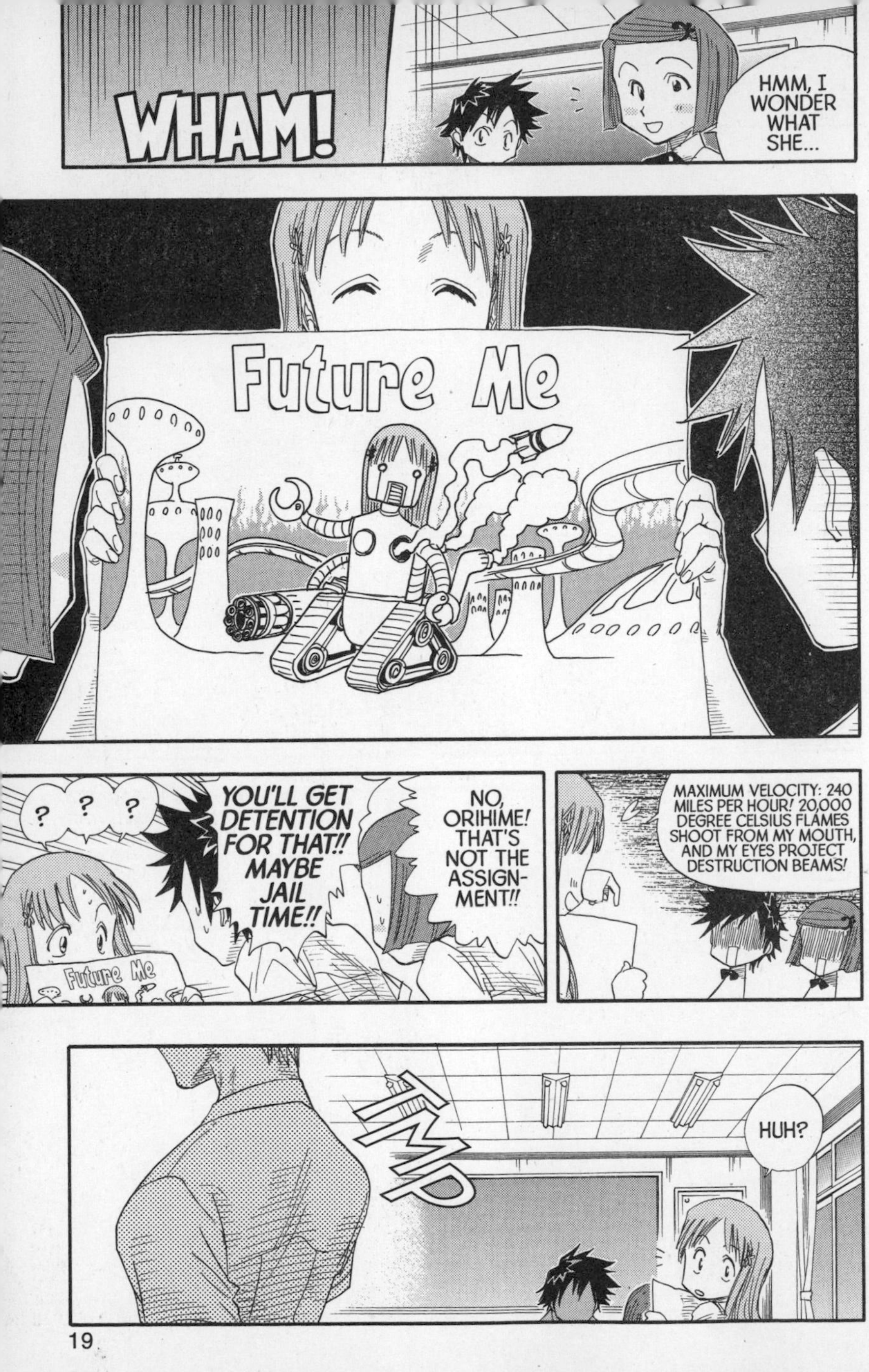
HMM, I WONDER WHAT SHE...
WHAM!
Future Me
MAXIMUM VELOCITY: 240 MILES PER HOUR! 20,000 DEGREE CELSIUS FLAMES SHOOT FROM MY MOUTH, AND MY EYES PROJECT DESTRUCTION BEAMS!
NO, ORIHIME! THAT'S NOT THE ASSIGNMENT!!
YOU'LL GET DETENTION FOR THAT!! MAYBE JAIL TIME!!
? ? ?
Future Me
HUH?
TMP

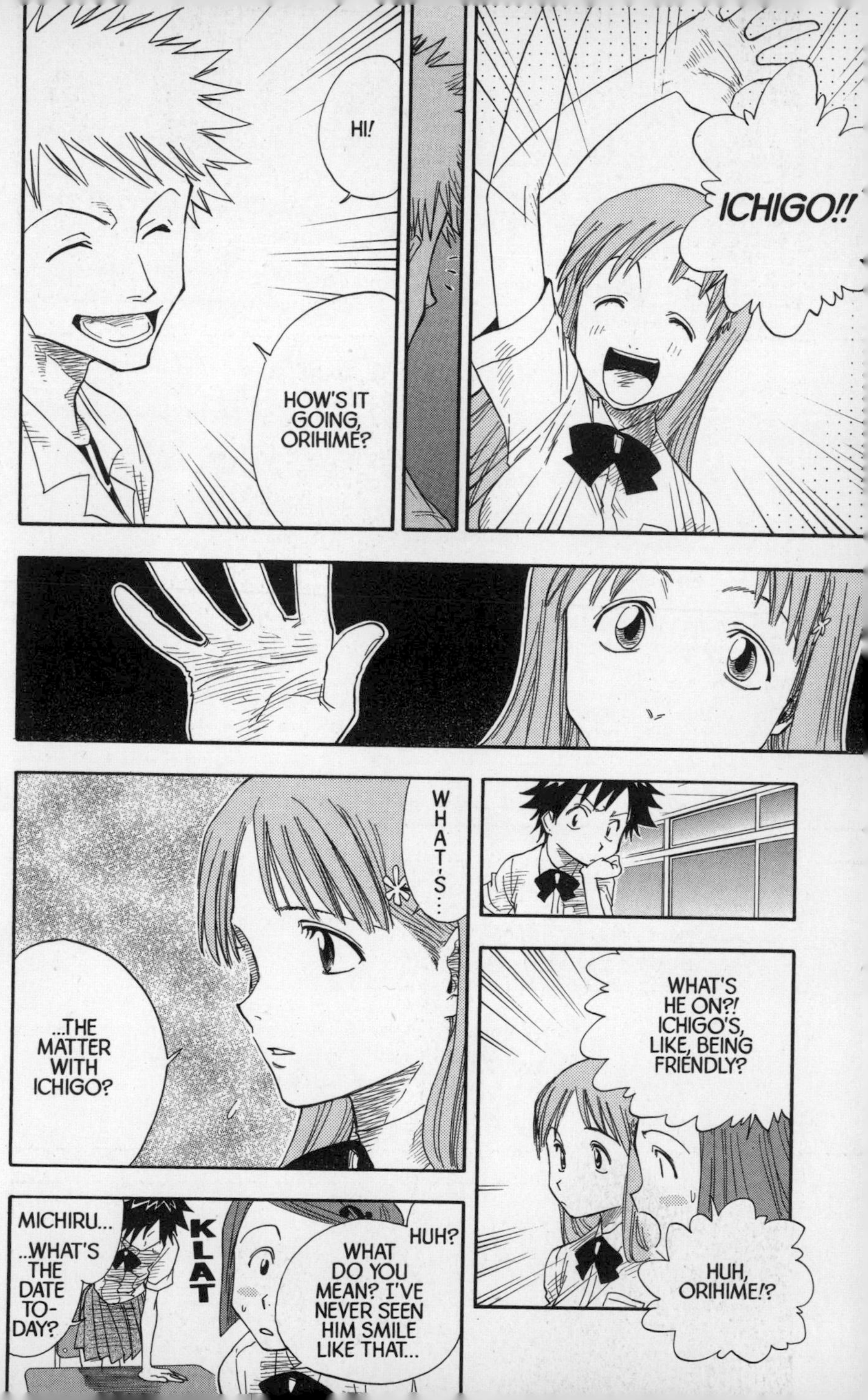
ICHIGO!!
HI!
HOW'S IT GOING, ORIHIME?
WHAT'S HE ON?! ICHIGO'S, LIKE, BEING FRIENDLY?
HUH, ORIHIME!?
WHAT'S...
...THE MATTER WITH ICHIGO?
HUH?
WHAT DO YOU MEAN? I'VE NEVER SEEN HIM SMILE LIKE THAT...
KLAT
MICHIRU...
...WHAT'S THE DATE TO-DAY?

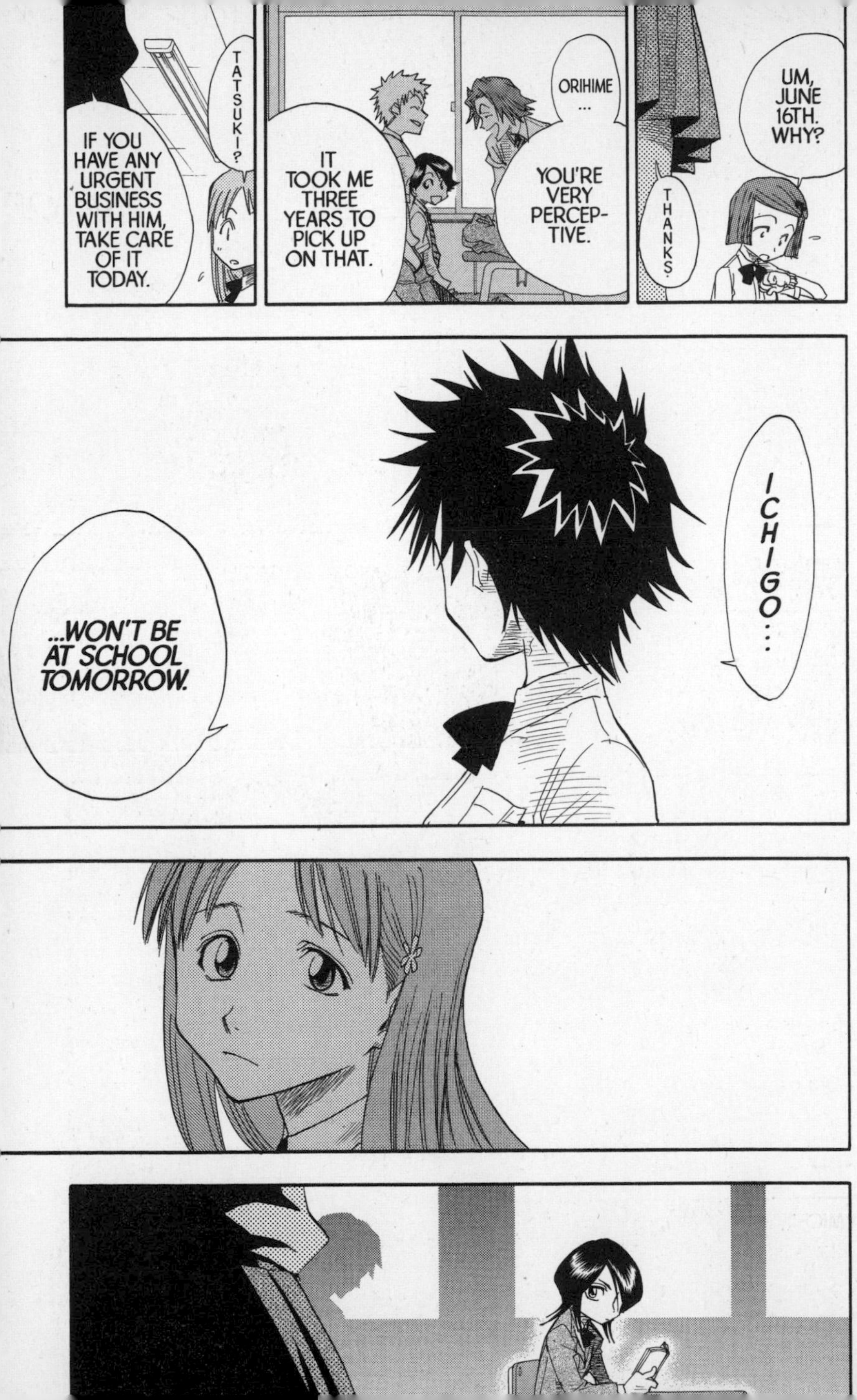
UM, JUNE 16TH. WHY?
THANKS.
ORIHIME ...
YOU'RE VERY PERCEP-TIVE.
IT TOOK ME THREE YEARS TO PICK UP ON THAT.
TATSUKI?
IF YOU HAVE ANY URGENT BUSINESS WITH HIM, TAKE CARE OF IT TODAY.
ICHIGO...
...WON'T BE AT SCHOOL TOMORROW.

READ THIS WAY

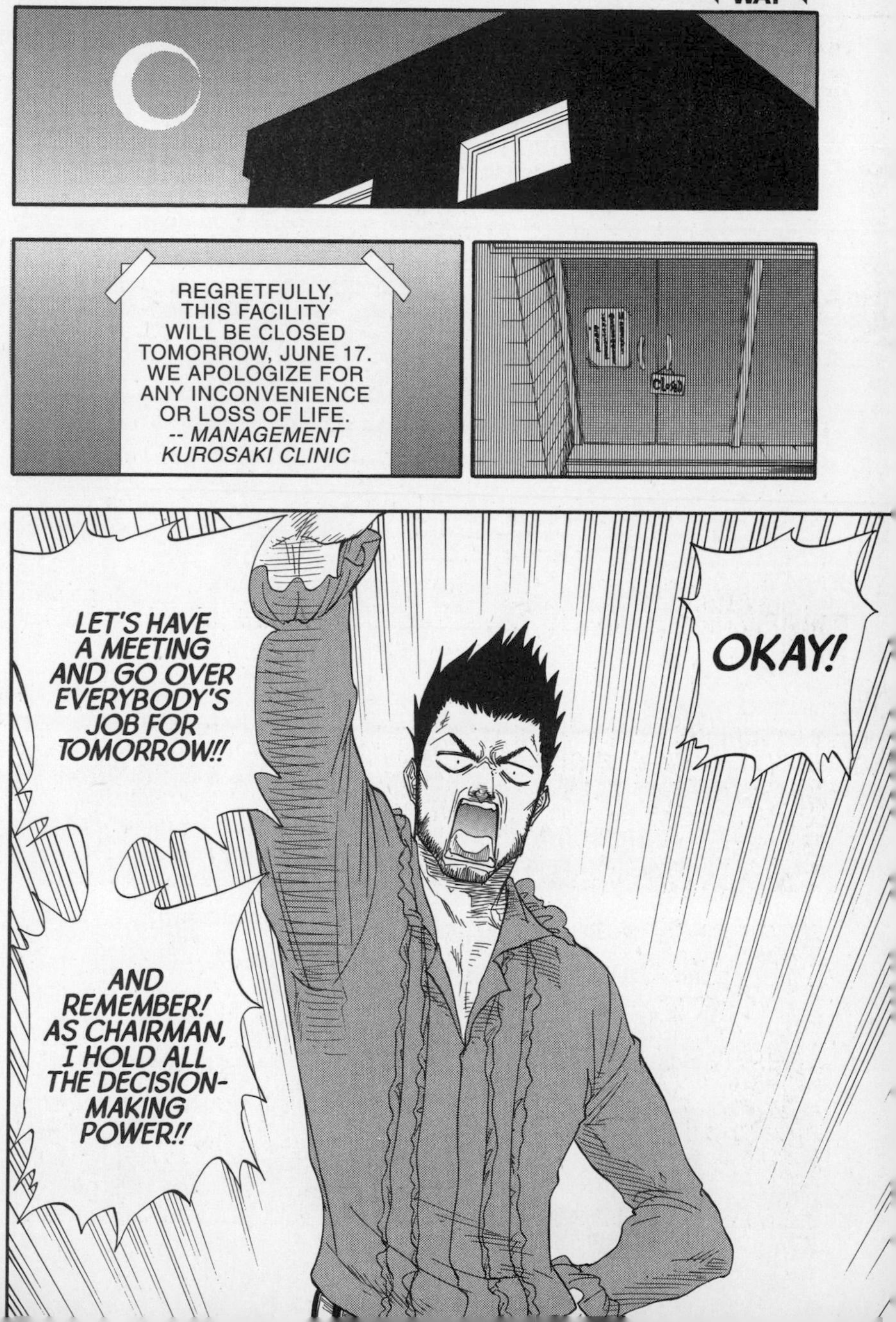
CLOSED
REGRETFULLY, THIS FACILITY WILL BE CLOSED TOMORROW, JUNE 17. WE APOLOGIZE FOR ANY INCONVENIENCE OR LOSS OF LIFE. -- MANAGEMENT KUROSAKI CLINIC
OKAY!
LET'S HAVE A MEETING AND GO OVER EVERYBODY'S JOB FOR TOMORROW!!
AND REMEMBER! AS CHAIRMAN, I HOLD ALL THE DECISION-MAKING POWER!!

READ THIS WAY

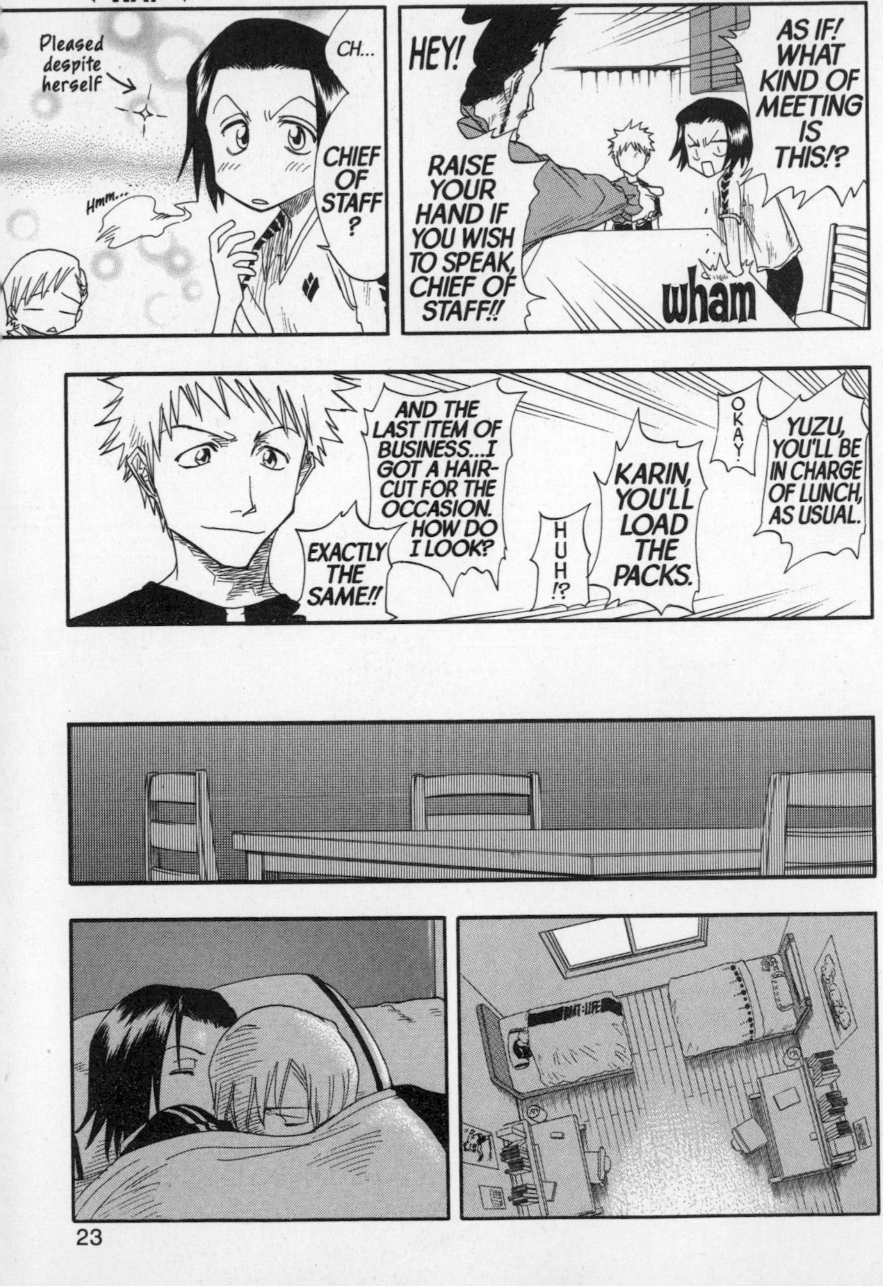

AS IF! WHAT KIND OF MEETING IS THIS!?
HEY!
RAISE YOUR HAND IF YOU WISH TO SPEAK, CHIEF OF STAFF!!
wham
CH...
CHIEF OF STAFF?
Pleased despite herself
Hmm...
YUZU, YOU'LL BE IN CHARGE OF LUNCH, AS USUAL.
OKAY!
KARIN, YOU'LL LOAD THE PACKS.
HUH!?
AND THE LAST ITEM OF BUSINESS...I GOT A HAIRCUT FOR THE OCCASION. HOW DO I LOOK?
EXACTLY THE SAME!!

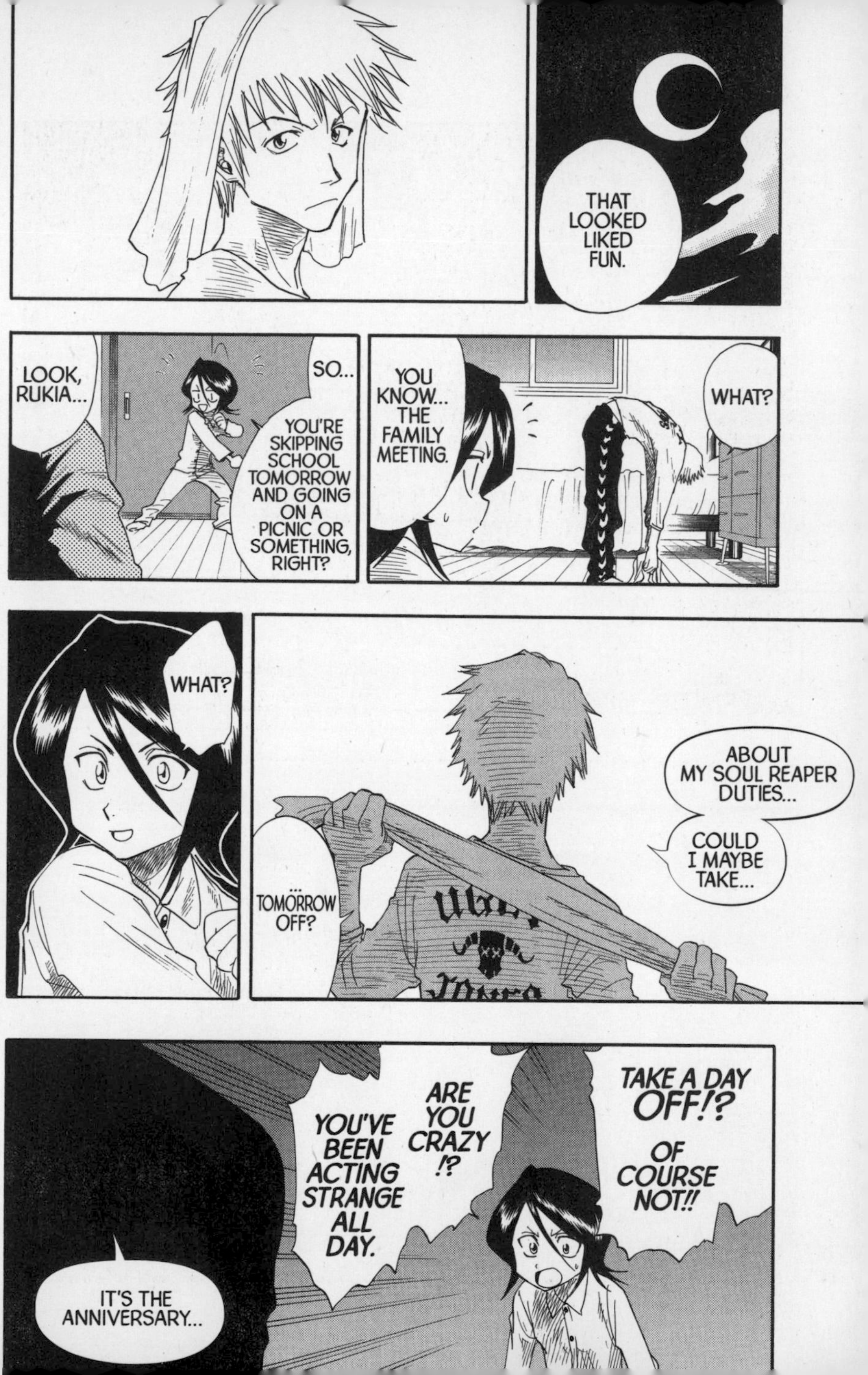
THAT LOOKED LIKED FUN.
WHAT?
YOU KNOW... THE FAMILY MEETING.
SO...
YOU'RE SKIPPING SCHOOL TOMORROW AND GOING ON A PICNIC OR SOMETHING, RIGHT?
LOOK, RUKIA...
ABOUT MY SOUL REAPER DUTIES...
COULD I MAYBE TAKE...
...TOMORROW OFF?
WHAT?
TAKE A DAY OFF!?
OF COURSE NOT!!
ARE YOU CRAZY!?
YOU'VE BEEN ACTING STRANGE ALL DAY.
IT'S THE ANNIVERSARY...

READ THIS WAY

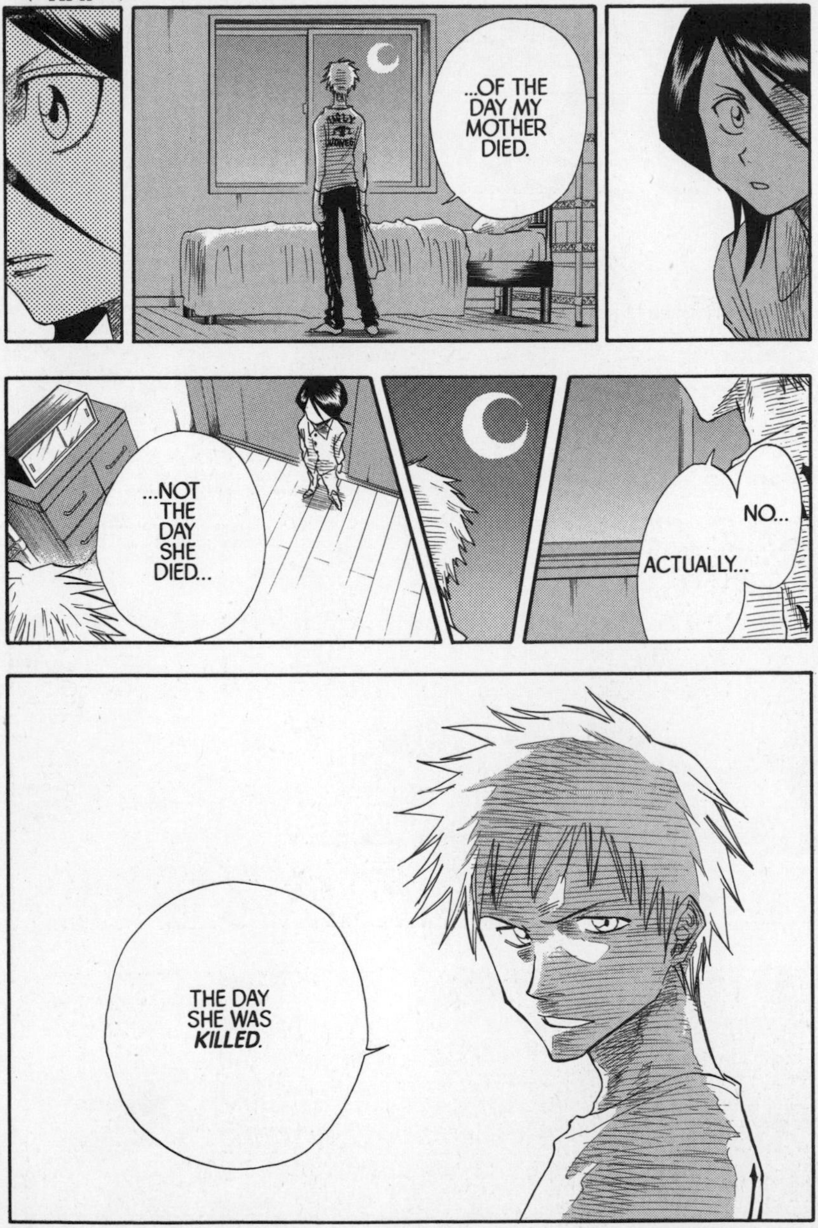
...OF THE DAY MY MOTHER DIED.
NO...
ACTUALLY...
...NOT THE DAY SHE DIED...
THE DAY SHE WAS *KILLED*.

18. 6/17 op. 2 Doesn't Smile Much Anymore

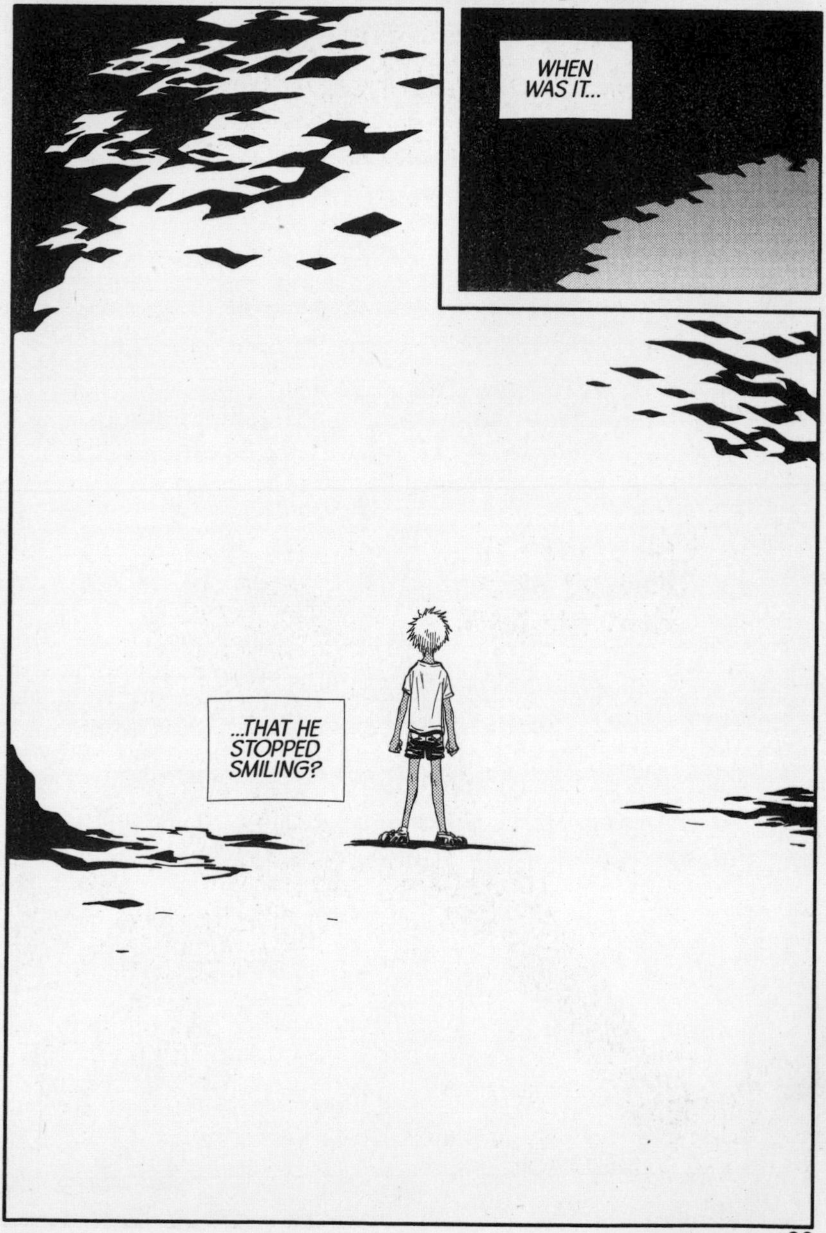
WHEN WAS IT...
...THAT HE STOPPED SMILING?

18. 6/17 op. 2
Doesn't Smile
Much Anymore

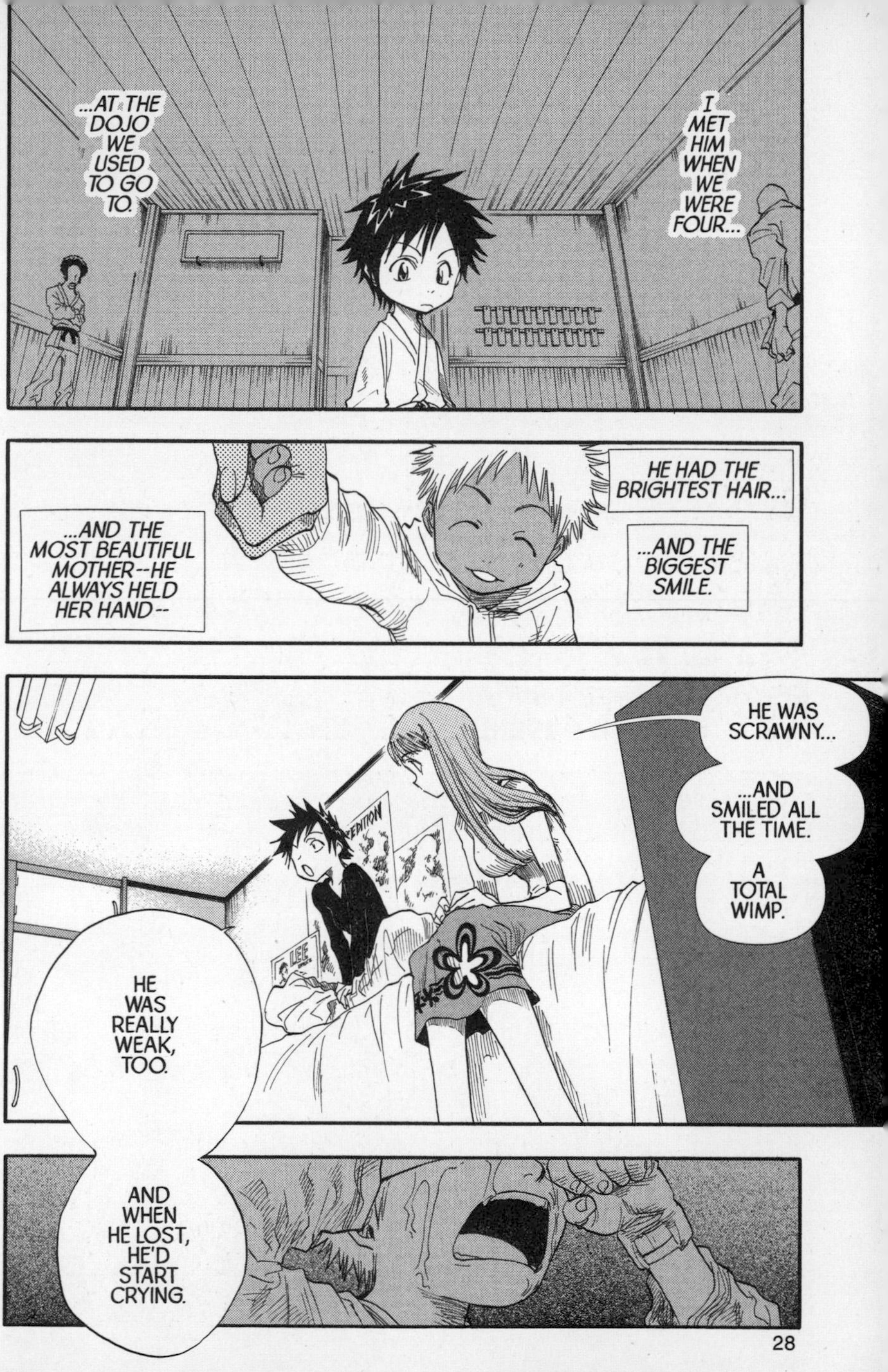
I MET HIM WHEN WE WERE FOUR...
...AT THE DOJO WE USED TO GO TO.
HE HAD THE BRIGHTEST HAIR...
...AND THE BIGGEST SMILE.
...AND THE MOST BEAUTIFUL MOTHER--HE ALWAYS HELD HER HAND--
HE WAS SCRAWNY...
...AND SMILED ALL THE TIME.
A TOTAL WIMP.
HE WAS REALLY WEAK, TOO.
AND WHEN HE LOST, HE'D START CRYING.

READ THIS WAY

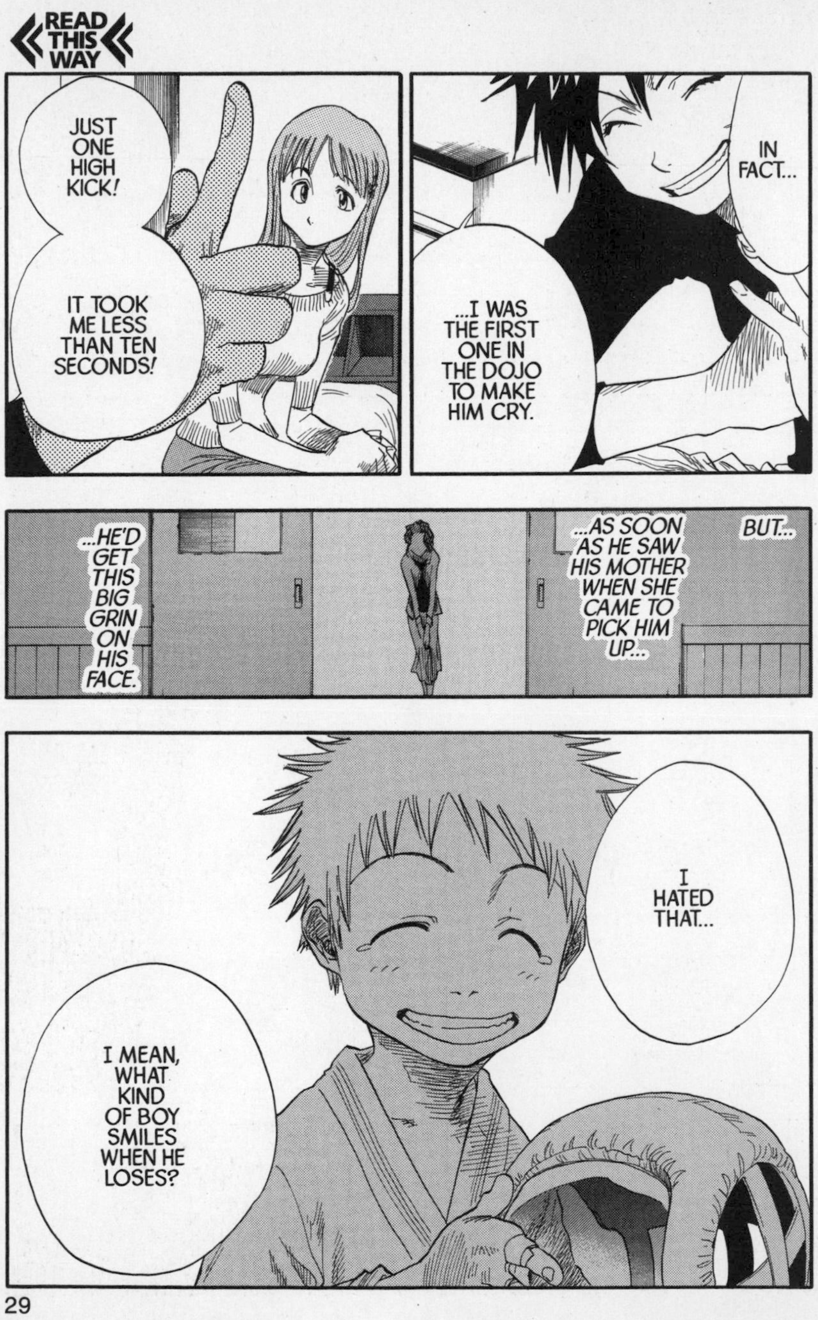

IN FACT...
...I WAS THE FIRST ONE IN THE DOJO TO MAKE HIM CRY.
JUST ONE HIGH KICK!
IT TOOK ME LESS THAN TEN SECONDS!
BUT...
...AS SOON AS HE SAW HIS MOTHER WHEN SHE CAME TO PICK HIM UP...
...HE'D GET THIS BIG GRIN ON HIS FACE.
I HATED THAT...
I MEAN, WHAT KIND OF BOY SMILES WHEN HE LOSES?

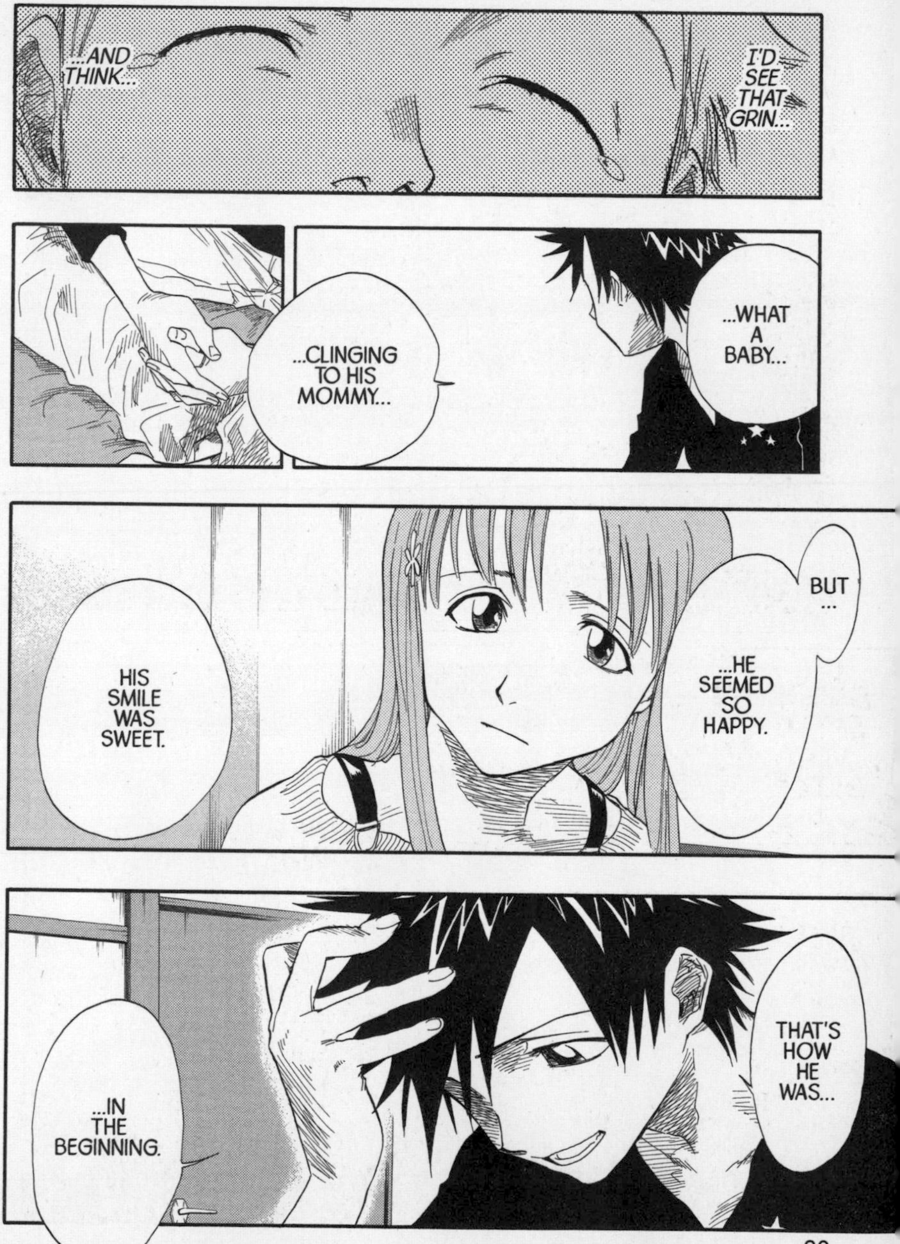
I'D SEE THAT GRIN...
...AND THINK...
...WHAT A BABY...
...CLINGING TO HIS MOMMY...
BUT...
...HE SEEMED SO HAPPY.
HIS SMILE WAS SWEET.
THAT'S HOW HE WAS...
...IN THE BEGINNING.

READ THIS WAY

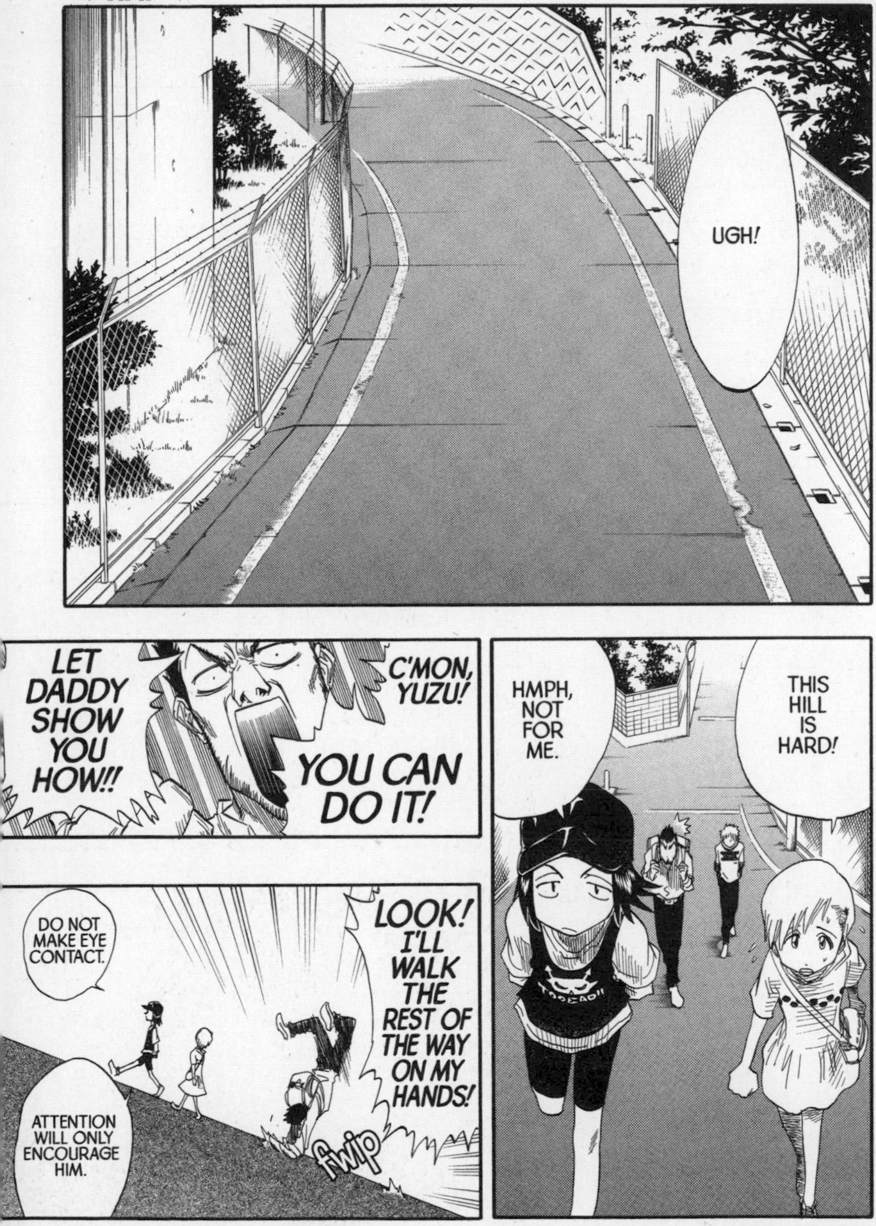
UGH!
THIS HILL IS HARD!
HMPH, NOT FOR ME.
C'MON, YUZU!
YOU CAN DO IT!
LET DADDY SHOW YOU HOW!!
LOOK! I'LL WALK THE REST OF THE WAY ON MY HANDS!
fwip
DO NOT MAKE EYE CONTACT.
ATTENTION WILL ONLY ENCOURAGE HIM.

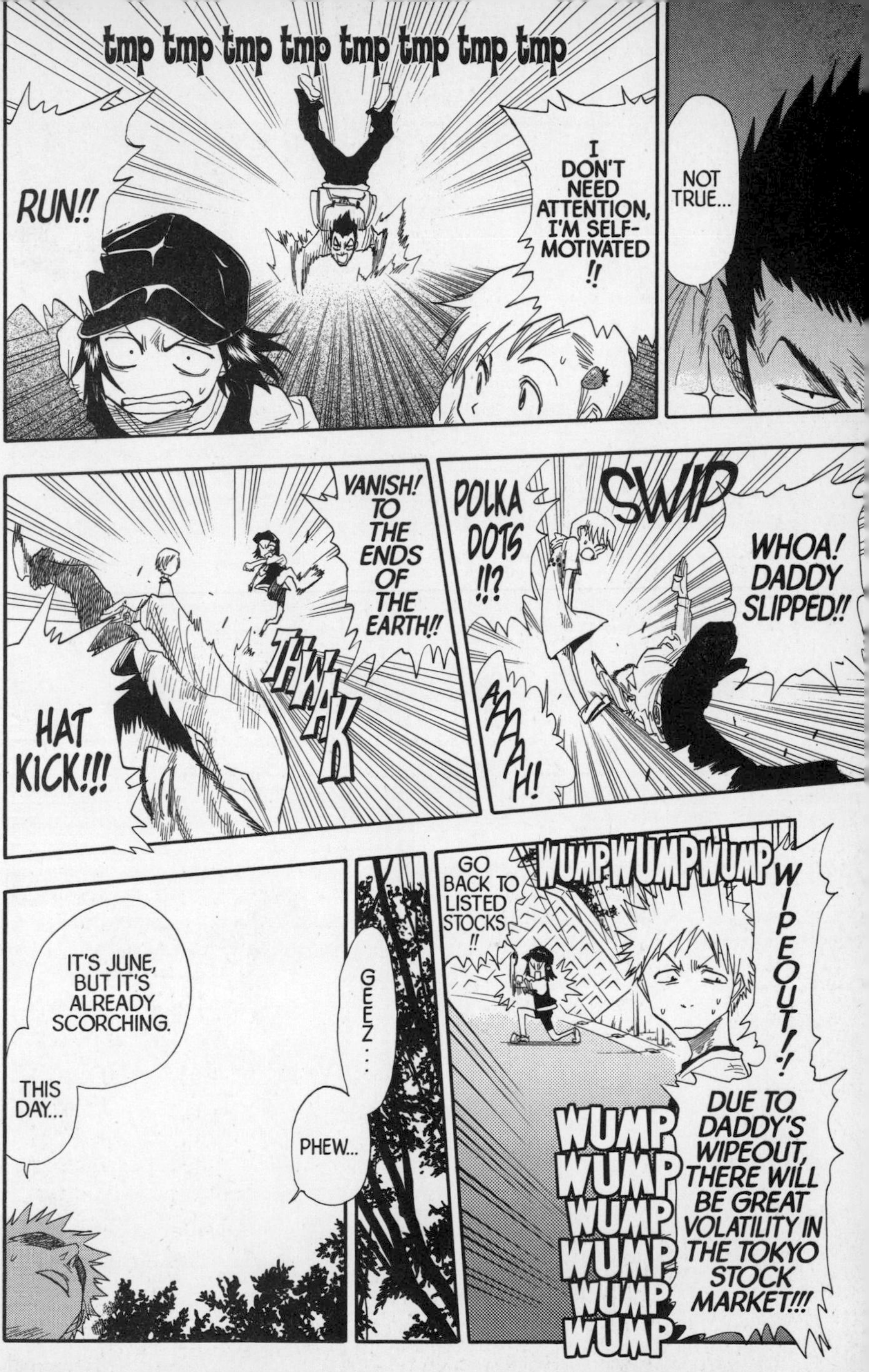
NOT TRUE...
tmp tmp tmp tmp tmp tmp tmp tmp
I DON'T NEED ATTENTION, I'M SELF-MOTIVATED!!
RUN!!
SWIP
WHOA! DADDY SLIPPED!!
POLKA DOTS!!?
AAAAAH!
VANISH! TO THE ENDS OF THE EARTH!!
THWAK
HAT KICK!!!
WUMPWUMPWUMP
WIPEOUT!!
GO BACK TO LISTED STOCKS!!
DUE TO DADDY'S WIPEOUT, THERE WILL BE GREAT VOLATILITY IN THE TOKYO STOCK MARKET!!!
WUMP WUMP WUMP WUMP WUMP WUMP
GEEZ...
PHEW...
IT'S JUNE, BUT IT'S ALREADY SCORCHING.
THIS DAY...

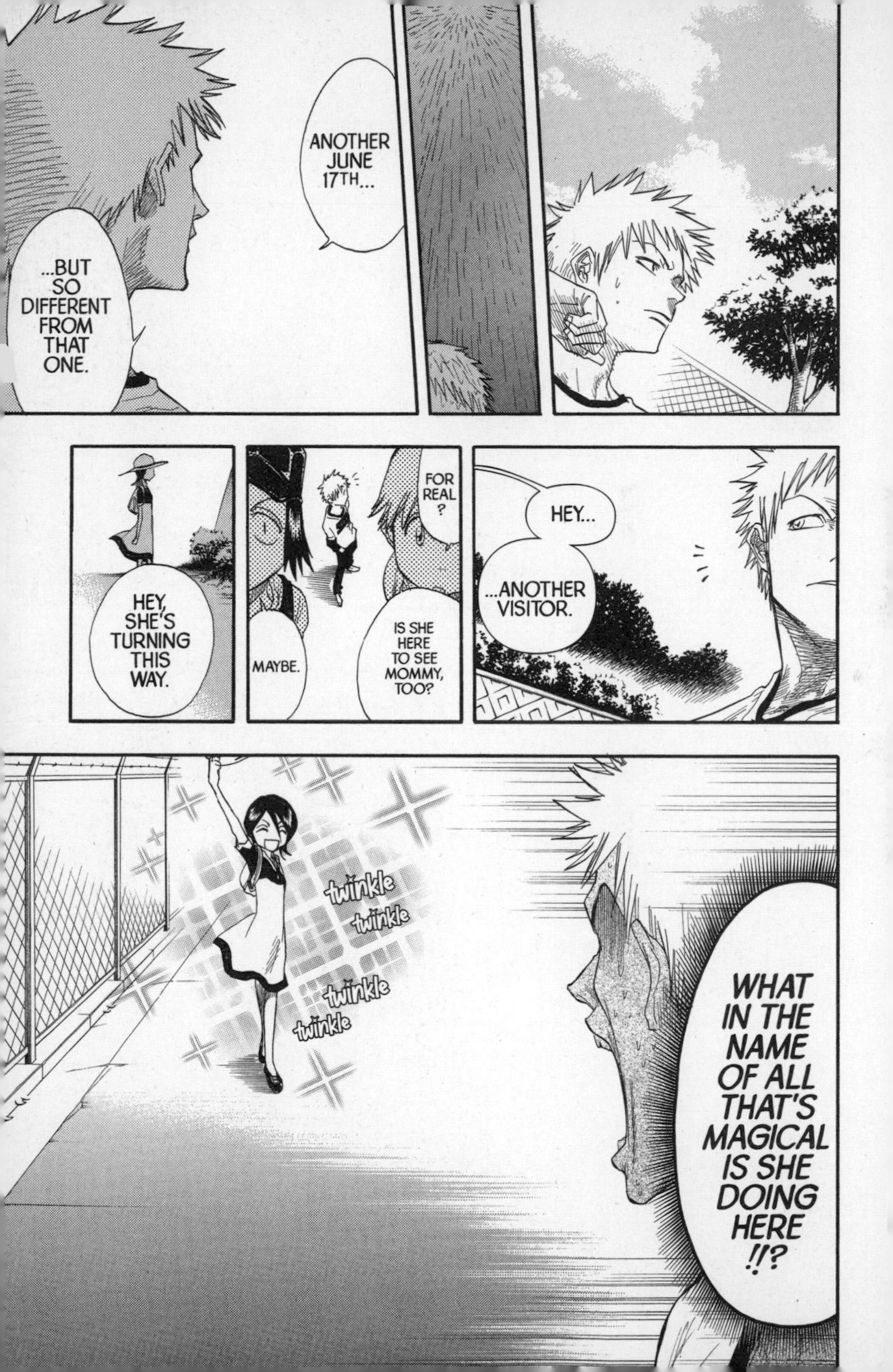
ANOTHER JUNE 17TH...
...BUT SO DIFFERENT FROM THAT ONE.
HEY...
...ANOTHER VISITOR.
FOR REAL?
IS SHE HERE TO SEE MOMMY, TOO?
MAYBE.
HEY, SHE'S TURNING THIS WAY.
WHAT IN THE NAME OF ALL THAT'S MAGICAL IS SHE DOING HERE!!?
twinkle
twinkle
twinkle
twinkle

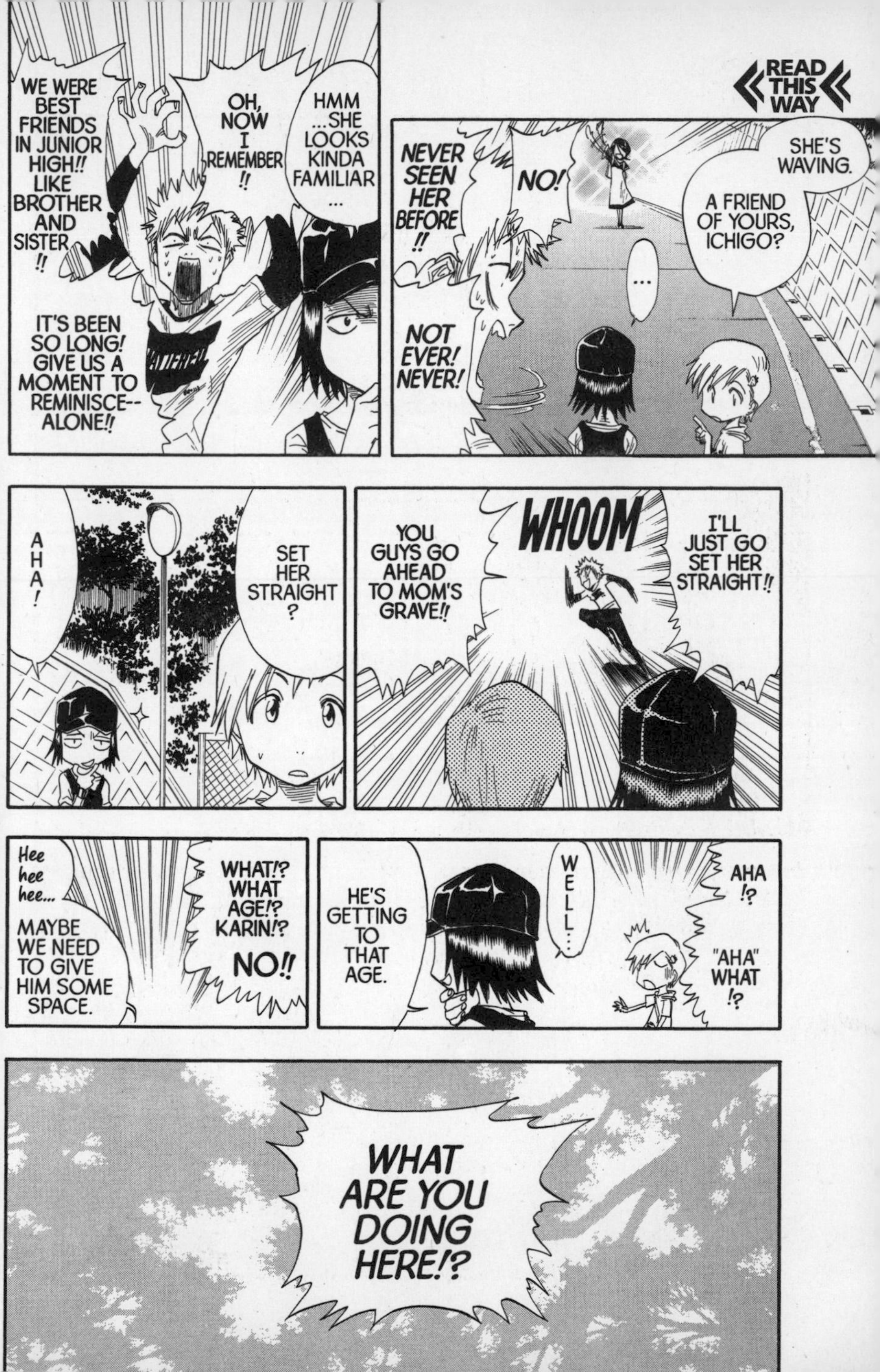
READ THIS WAY
SHE'S WAVING.
A FRIEND OF YOURS, ICHIGO?
...
NO!
NEVER SEEN HER BEFORE!!
NOT EVER! NEVER!
HMM ...SHE LOOKS KINDA FAMILIAR ...
OH, NOW I REMEMBER!!
WE WERE BEST FRIENDS IN JUNIOR HIGH!! LIKE BROTHER AND SISTER!!
IT'S BEEN SO LONG! GIVE US A MOMENT TO REMINISCE--ALONE!!
WHOOM
I'LL JUST GO SET HER STRAIGHT!!
YOU GUYS GO AHEAD TO MOM'S GRAVE!!
SET HER STRAIGHT?
AHA!
AHA!?
"AHA" WHAT!?
WELL...
HE'S GETTING TO THAT AGE.
WHAT!? WHAT AGE!? KARIN!?
NO!!
Hee hee hee...
MAYBE WE NEED TO GIVE HIM SOME SPACE.
WHAT ARE YOU DOING HERE!?

READ THIS WAY

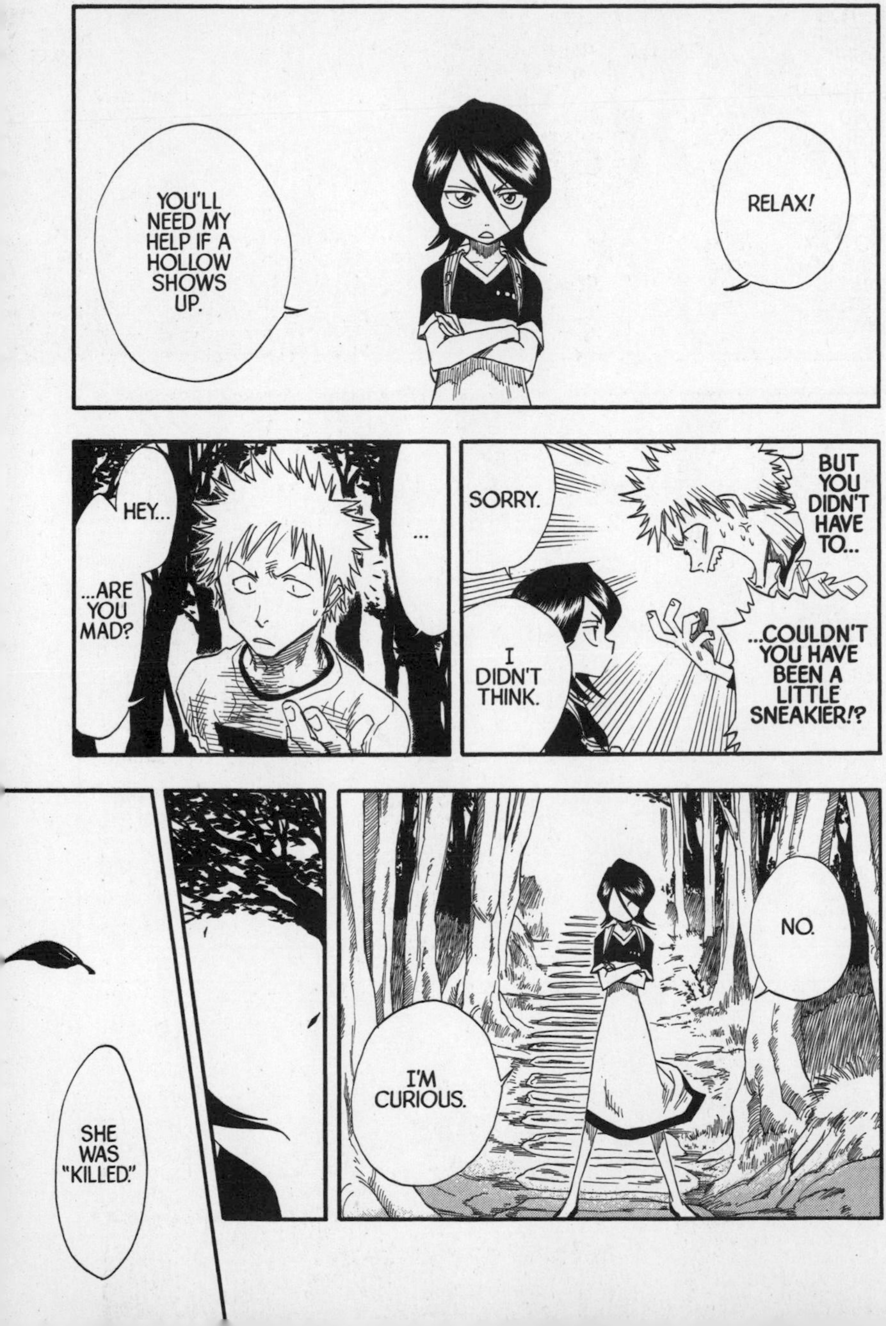
RELAX!
YOU'LL NEED MY HELP IF A HOLLOW SHOWS UP.
BUT YOU DIDN'T HAVE TO...
...COULDN'T YOU HAVE BEEN A LITTLE SNEAKIER!?
SORRY.
I DIDN'T THINK.
...
HEY...
...ARE YOU MAD?
NO.
I'M CURIOUS.
SHE WAS "KILLED."

READ THIS WAY

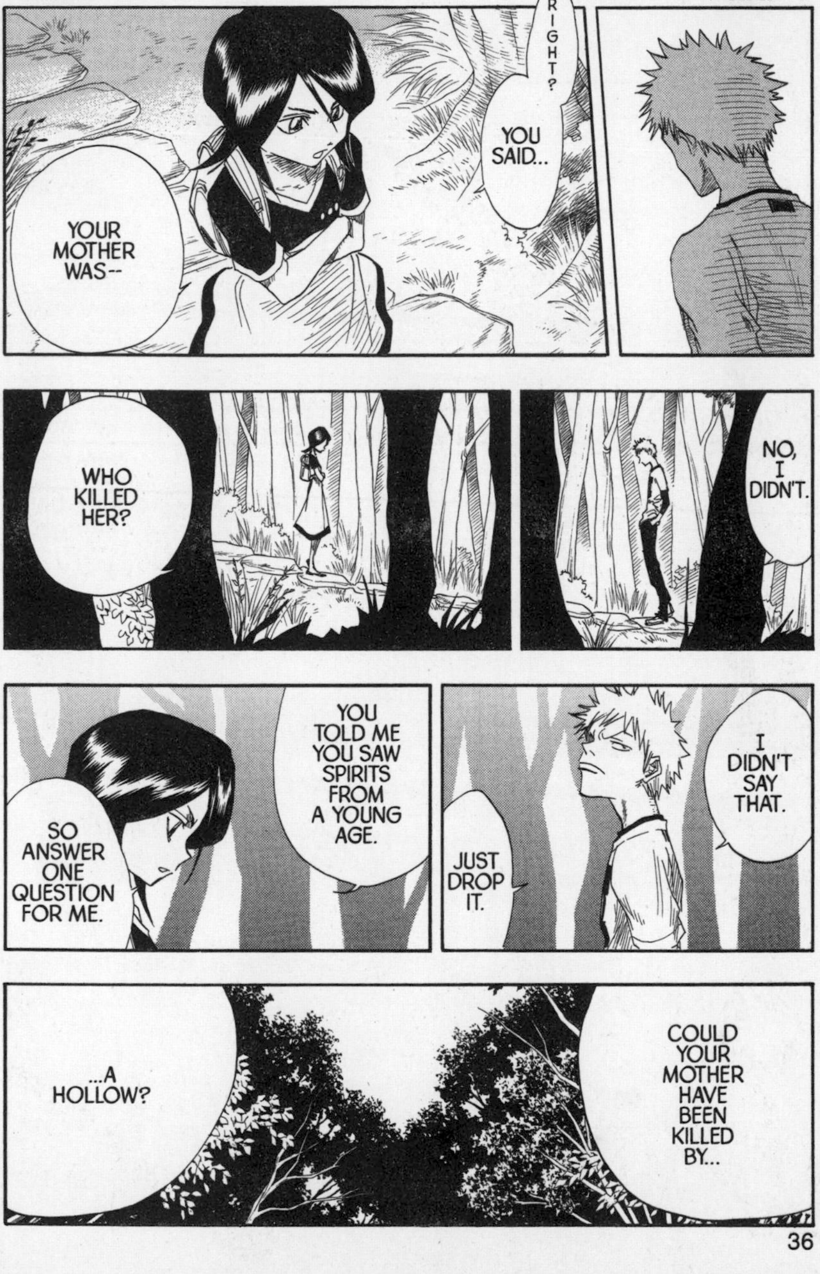
RIGHT? YOU SAID...
YOUR MOTHER WAS--
NO, I DIDN'T.
WHO KILLED HER?
I DIDN'T SAY THAT.
JUST DROP IT.
YOU TOLD ME YOU SAW SPIRITS FROM A YOUNG AGE.
SO ANSWER ONE QUESTION FOR ME.
COULD YOUR MOTHER HAVE BEEN KILLED BY...
...A HOLLOW?

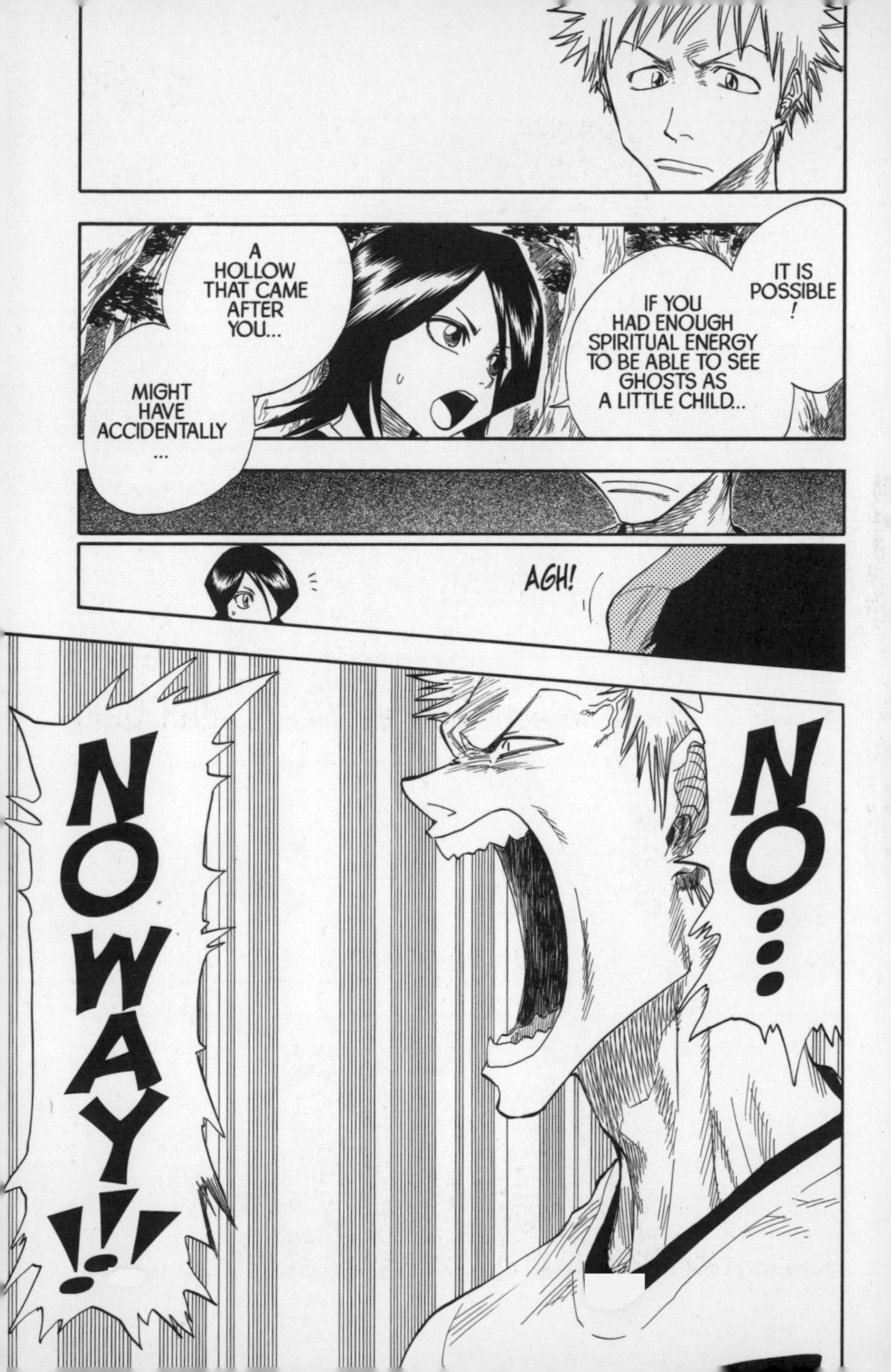
IT IS POSSIBLE!
IF YOU HAD ENOUGH SPIRITUAL ENERGY TO BE ABLE TO SEE GHOSTS AS A LITTLE CHILD...
A HOLLOW THAT CAME AFTER YOU...
MIGHT HAVE ACCIDENTALLY ...
AGH!
NO...
NO WAY!!

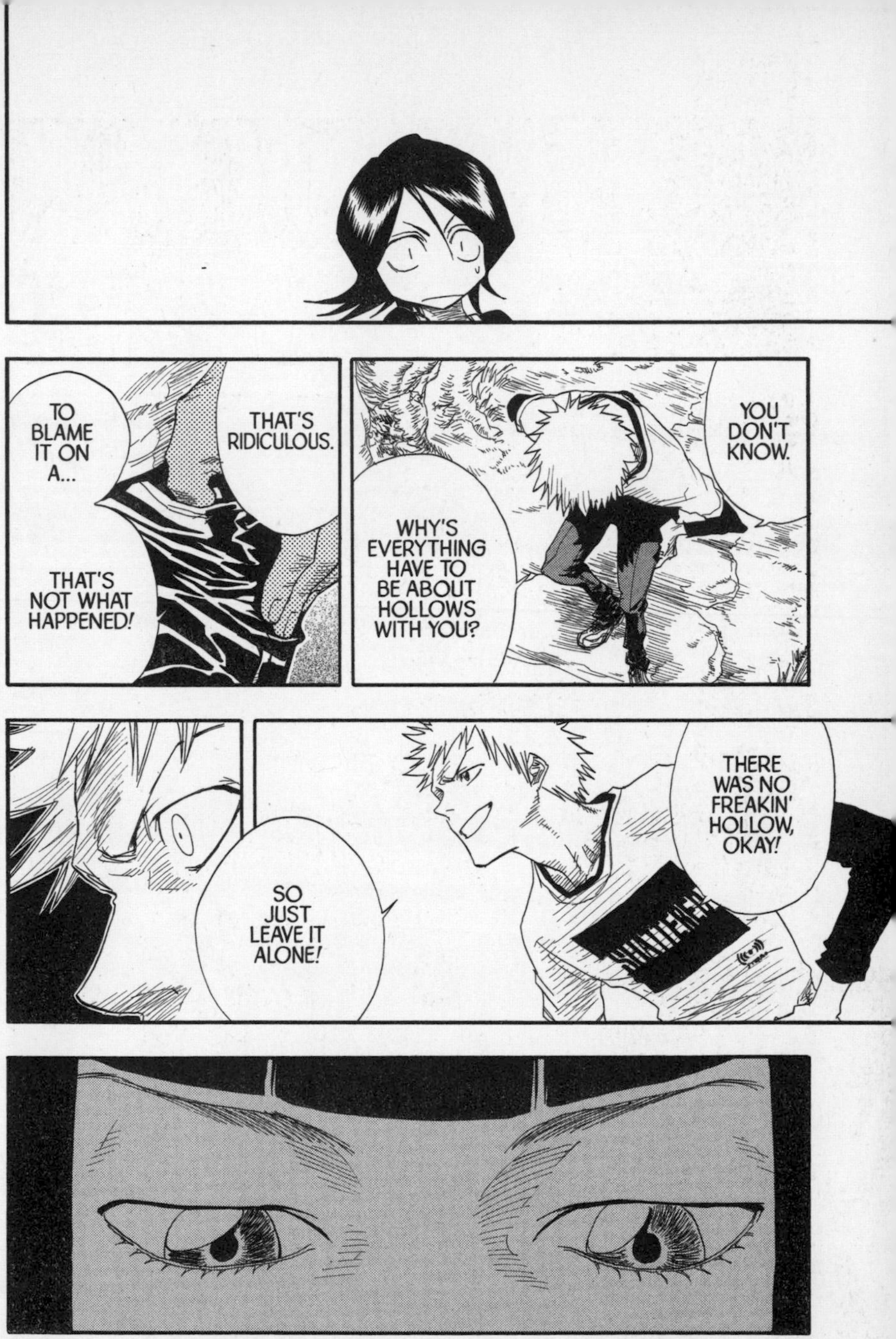
YOU DON'T KNOW.
WHY'S EVERYTHING HAVE TO BE ABOUT HOLLOWS WITH YOU?
THAT'S RIDICULOUS.
TO BLAME IT ON A...
THAT'S NOT WHAT HAPPENED!
THERE WAS NO FREAKIN' HOLLOW, OKAY!
SO JUST LEAVE IT ALONE!

READ THIS WAY

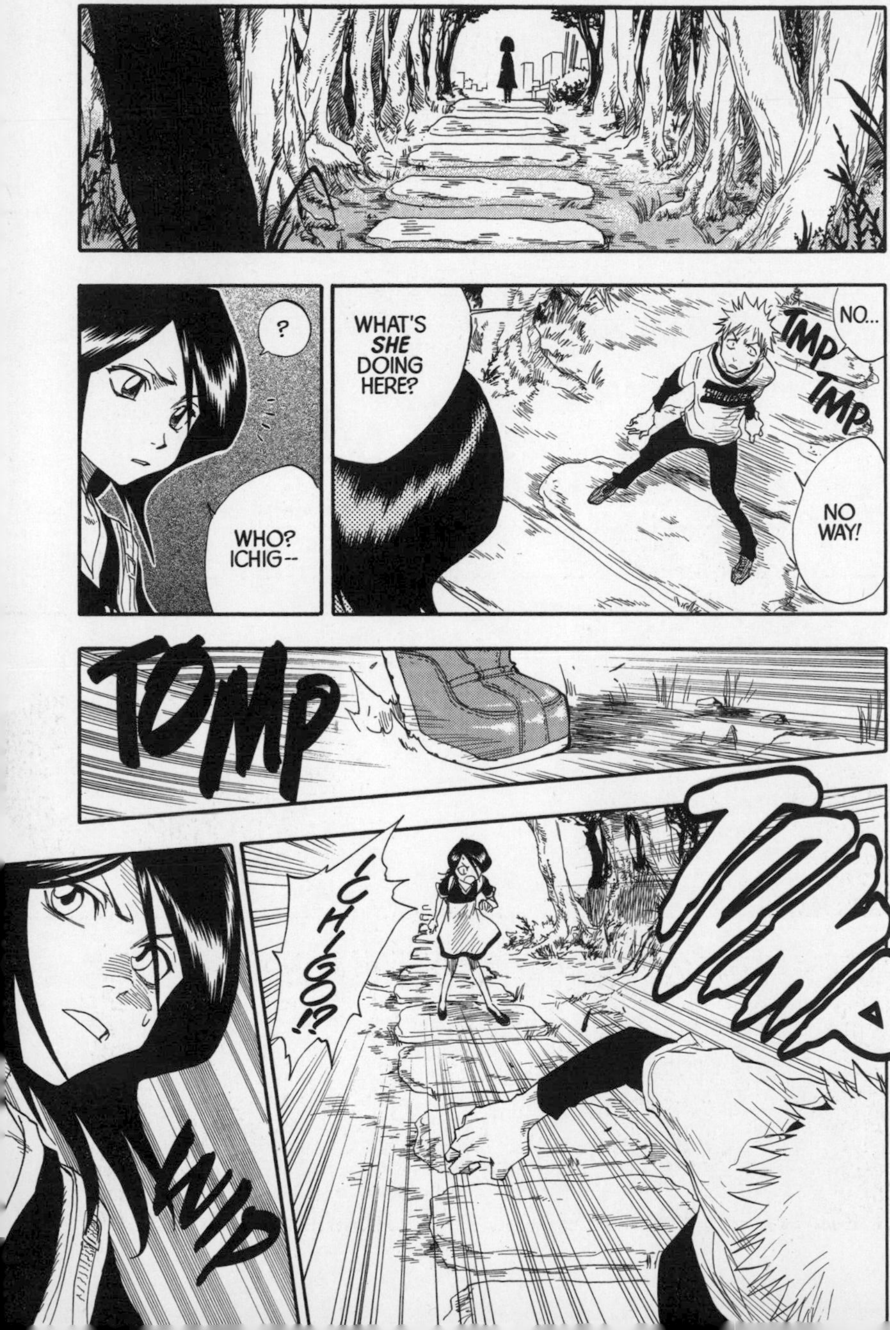

NO...
TMP
TMP
WHAT'S *SHE* DOING HERE?
NO WAY!
?
WHO? ICHIG--
TOMP
TOMP
ICHIGO!?
WHIP

READ THIS WAY

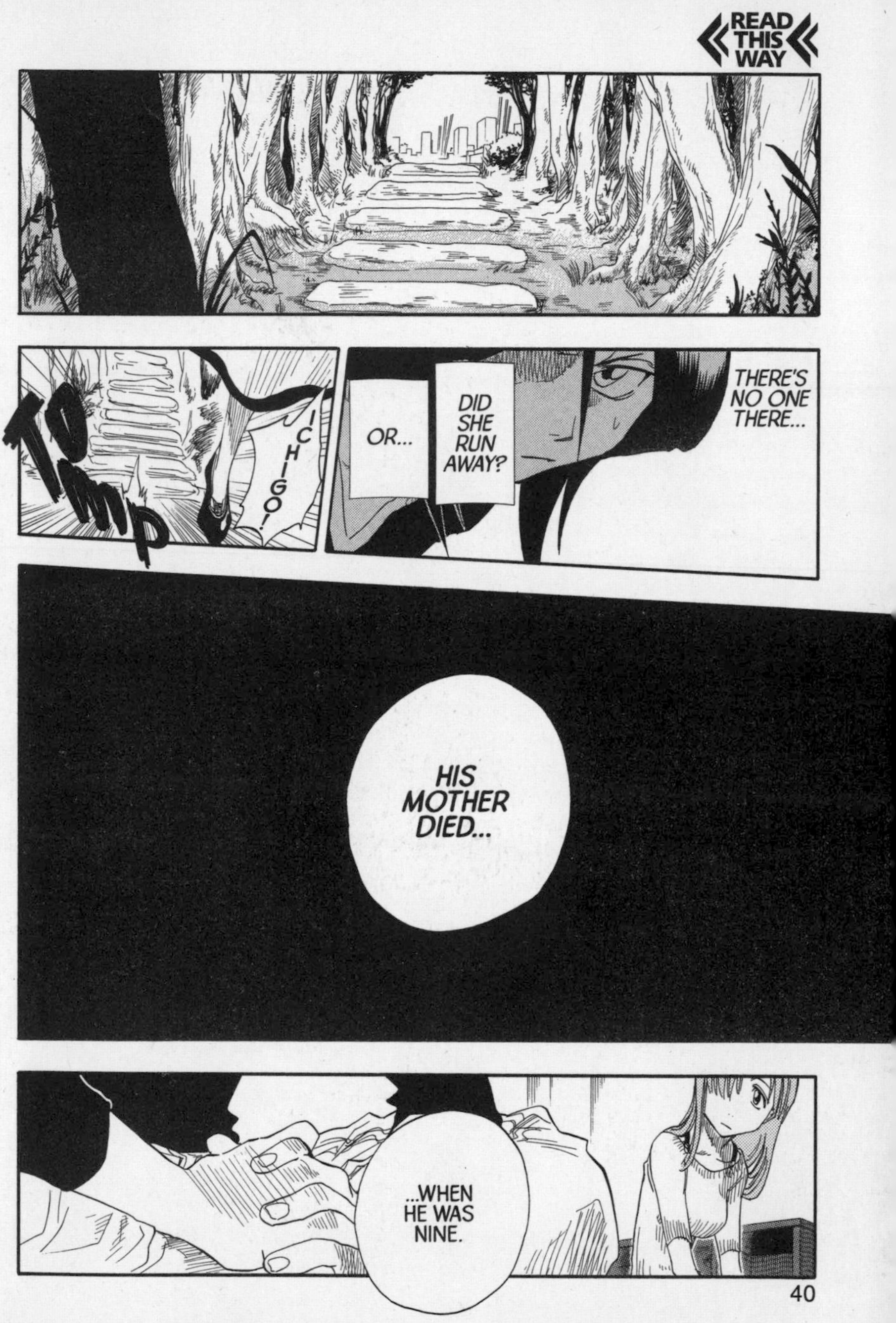
THERE'S NO ONE THERE...
DID SHE RUN AWAY?
OR...
ICHIGO!
TOMP
HIS MOTHER DIED...
...WHEN HE WAS NINE.

READ THIS WAY

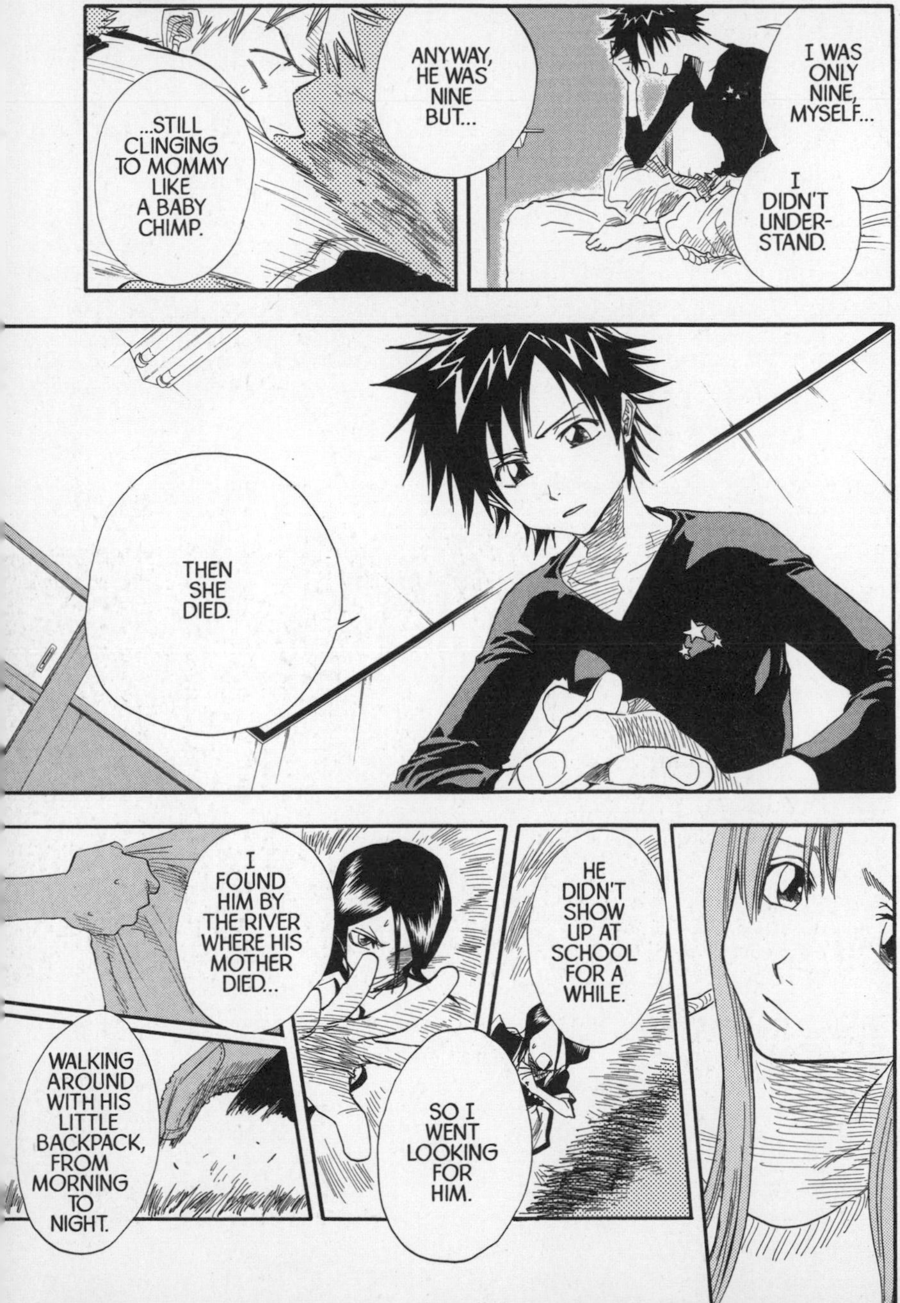
I WAS ONLY NINE, MYSELF...
I DIDN'T UNDER-STAND.
ANYWAY, HE WAS NINE BUT...
...STILL CLINGING TO MOMMY LIKE A BABY CHIMP.
THEN SHE DIED.
HE DIDN'T SHOW UP AT SCHOOL FOR A WHILE.
SO I WENT LOOKING FOR HIM.
I FOUND HIM BY THE RIVER WHERE HIS MOTHER DIED...
WALKING AROUND WITH HIS LITTLE BACKPACK, FROM MORNING TO NIGHT.

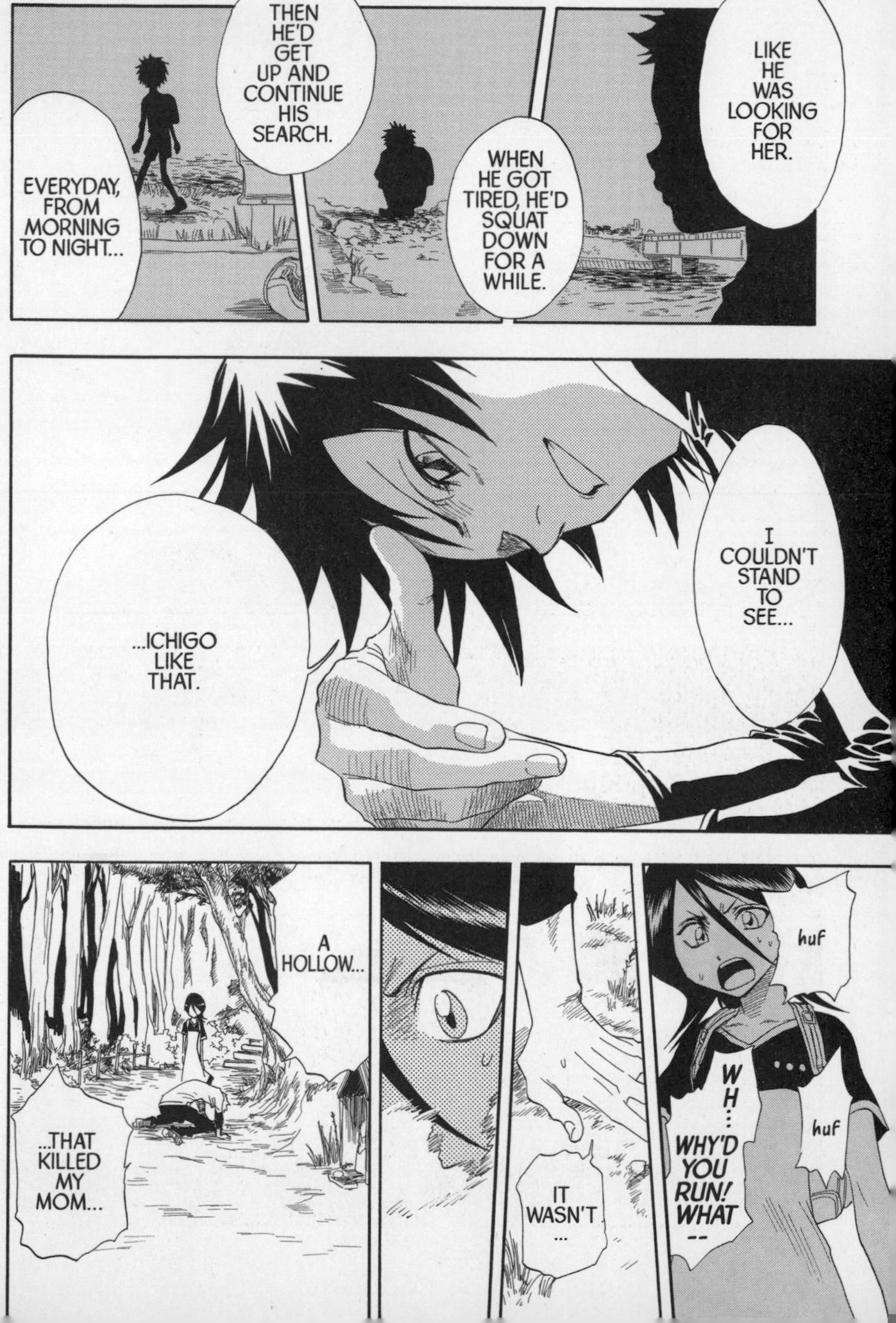
LIKE HE WAS LOOKING FOR HER.
WHEN HE GOT TIRED, HE'D SQUAT DOWN FOR A WHILE.
THEN HE'D GET UP AND CONTINUE HIS SEARCH.
EVERYDAY, FROM MORNING TO NIGHT...
I COULDN'T STAND TO SEE...
...ICHIGO LIKE THAT.
huf
WH...
WHY'D YOU RUN! WHAT --
huf
IT WASN'T ...
A HOLLOW...
...THAT KILLED MY MOM...

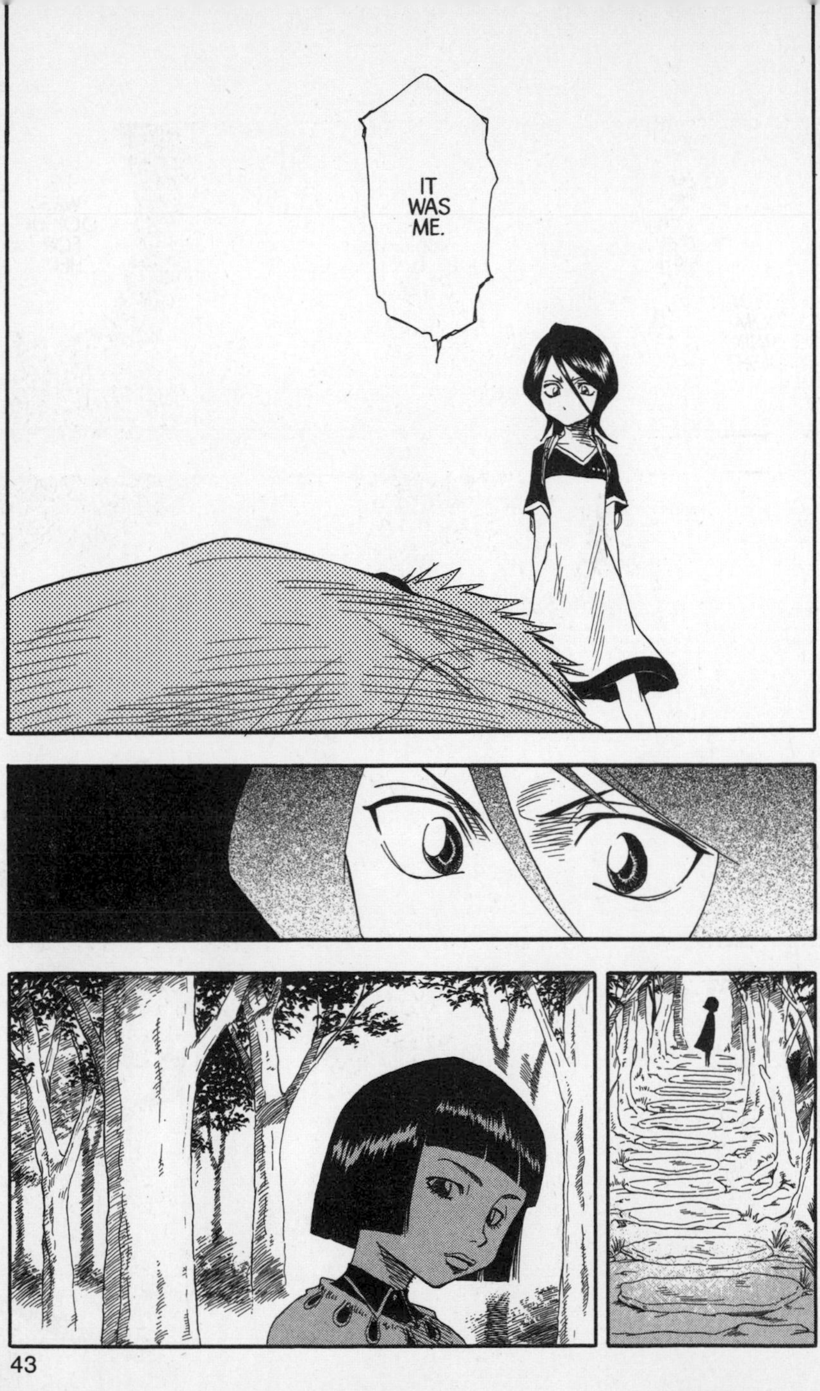
IT WAS ME.

Dressed
unusually plain
today.

Wonder
why?

You'll find
out in the last
episode of this
volume!!

19. 6/17 op. 3 memories in the rain

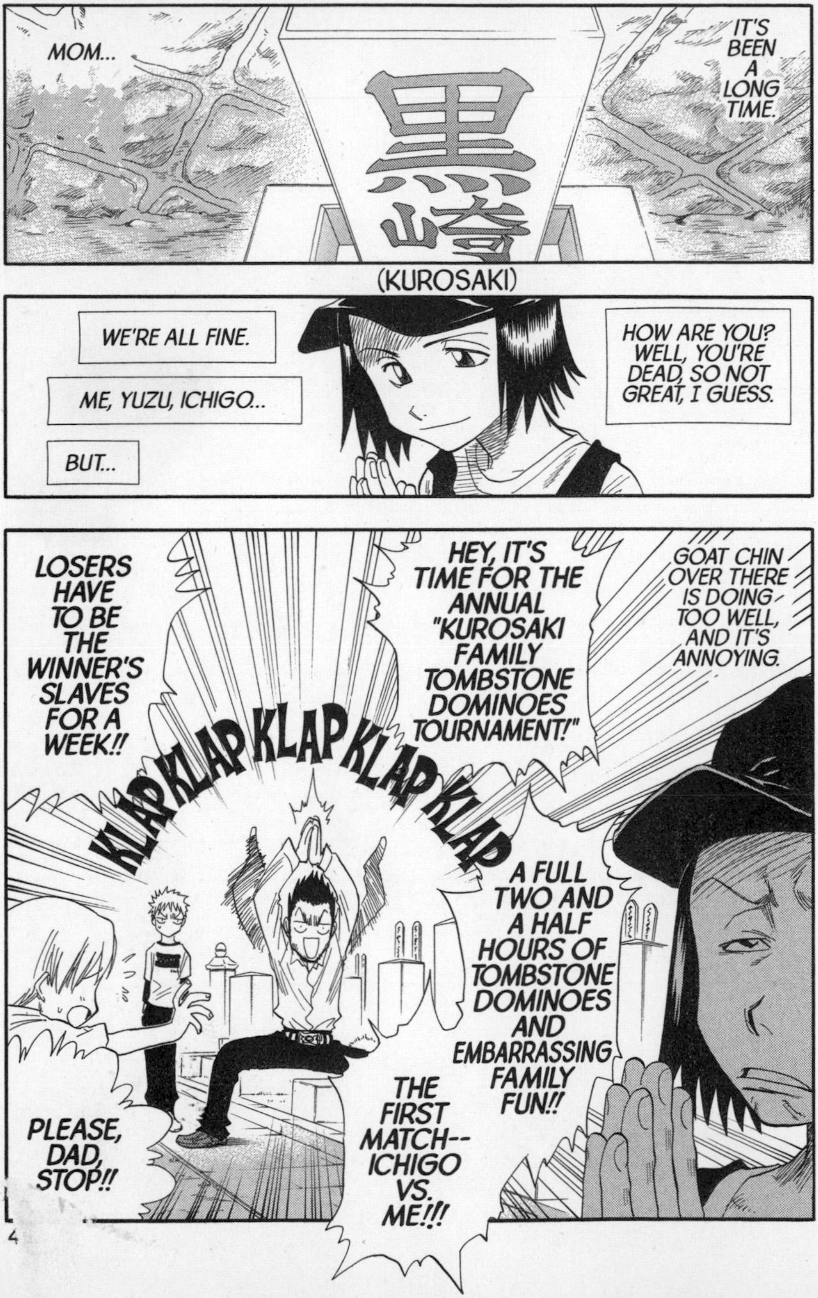
IT'S BEEN A LONG TIME.
MOM...
(KUROSAKI)
HOW ARE YOU? WELL, YOU'RE DEAD, SO NOT GREAT, I GUESS.
WE'RE ALL FINE.
ME, YUZU, ICHIGO...
BUT...
GOAT CHIN OVER THERE IS DOING TOO WELL, AND IT'S ANNOYING.
HEY, IT'S TIME FOR THE ANNUAL "KUROSAKI FAMILY TOMBSTONE DOMINOES TOURNAMENT!"
LOSERS HAVE TO BE THE WINNER'S SLAVES FOR A WEEK!!
KLAP KLAP KLAP KLAP KLAP KLAP
A FULL TWO AND A HALF HOURS OF TOMBSTONE DOMINOES AND EMBARRASSING FAMILY FUN!!
THE FIRST MATCH--ICHIGO VS. ME!!!
PLEASE, DAD, STOP!!

READ THIS WAY

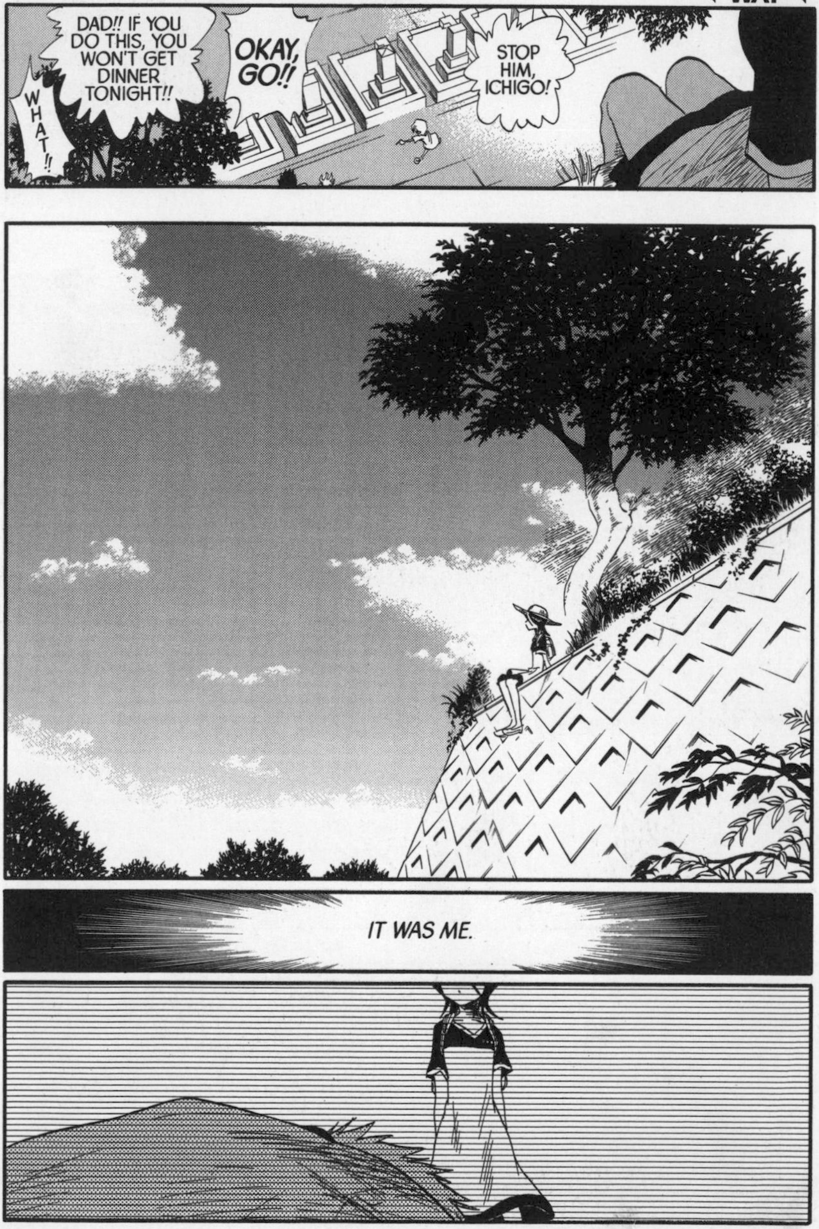
STOP HIM, ICHIGO!
OKAY, GO!!
DAD!! IF YOU DO THIS, YOU WON'T GET DINNER TONIGHT!!
WHAT!!
IT WAS ME.

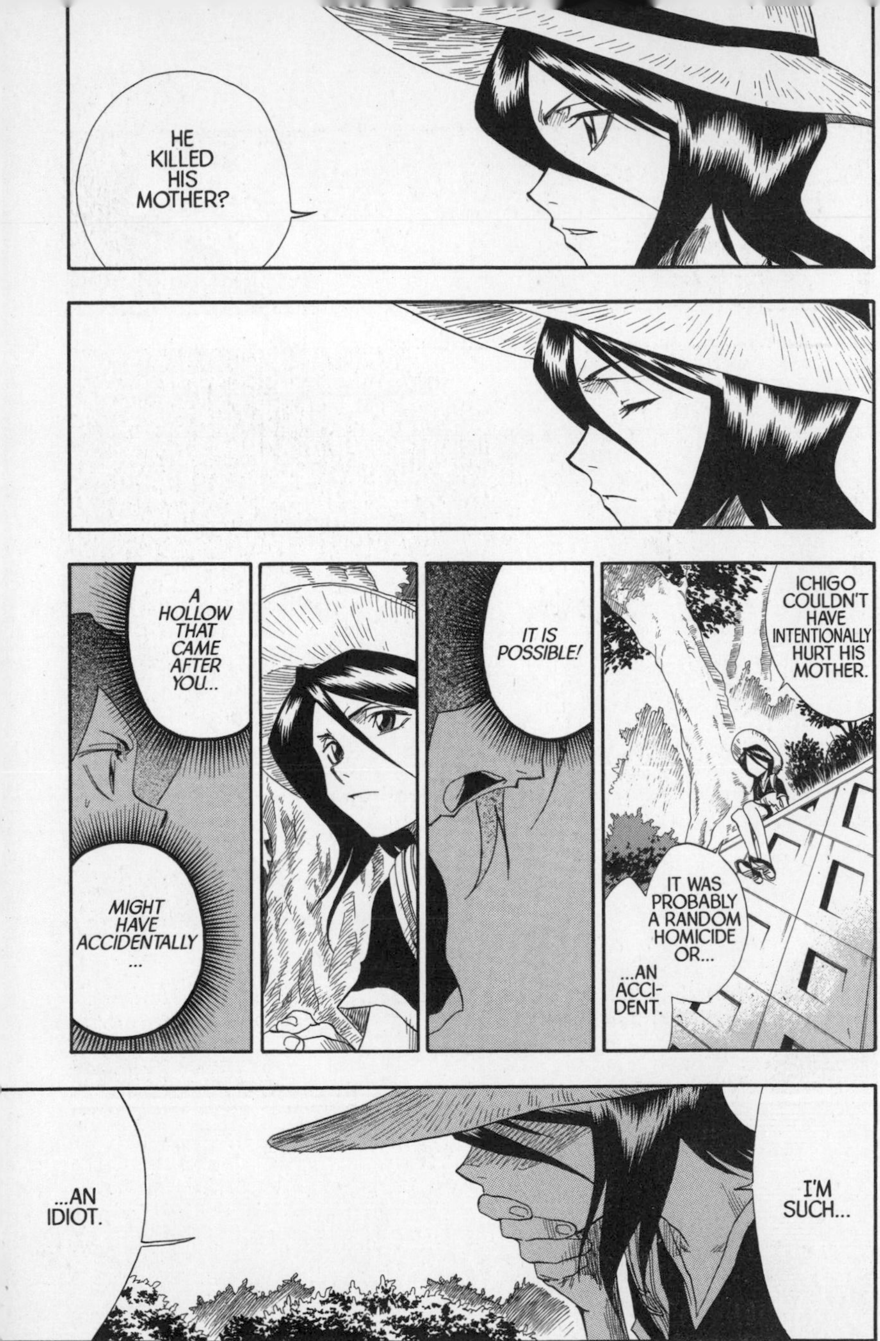
HE KILLED HIS MOTHER?
ICHIGO COULDN'T HAVE INTENTIONALLY HURT HIS MOTHER.
IT WAS PROBABLY A RANDOM HOMICIDE OR...
...AN ACCI-DENT.
IT IS POSSIBLE!
A HOLLOW THAT CAME AFTER YOU...
MIGHT HAVE ACCIDENTALLY ...
I'M SUCH...
...AN IDIOT.

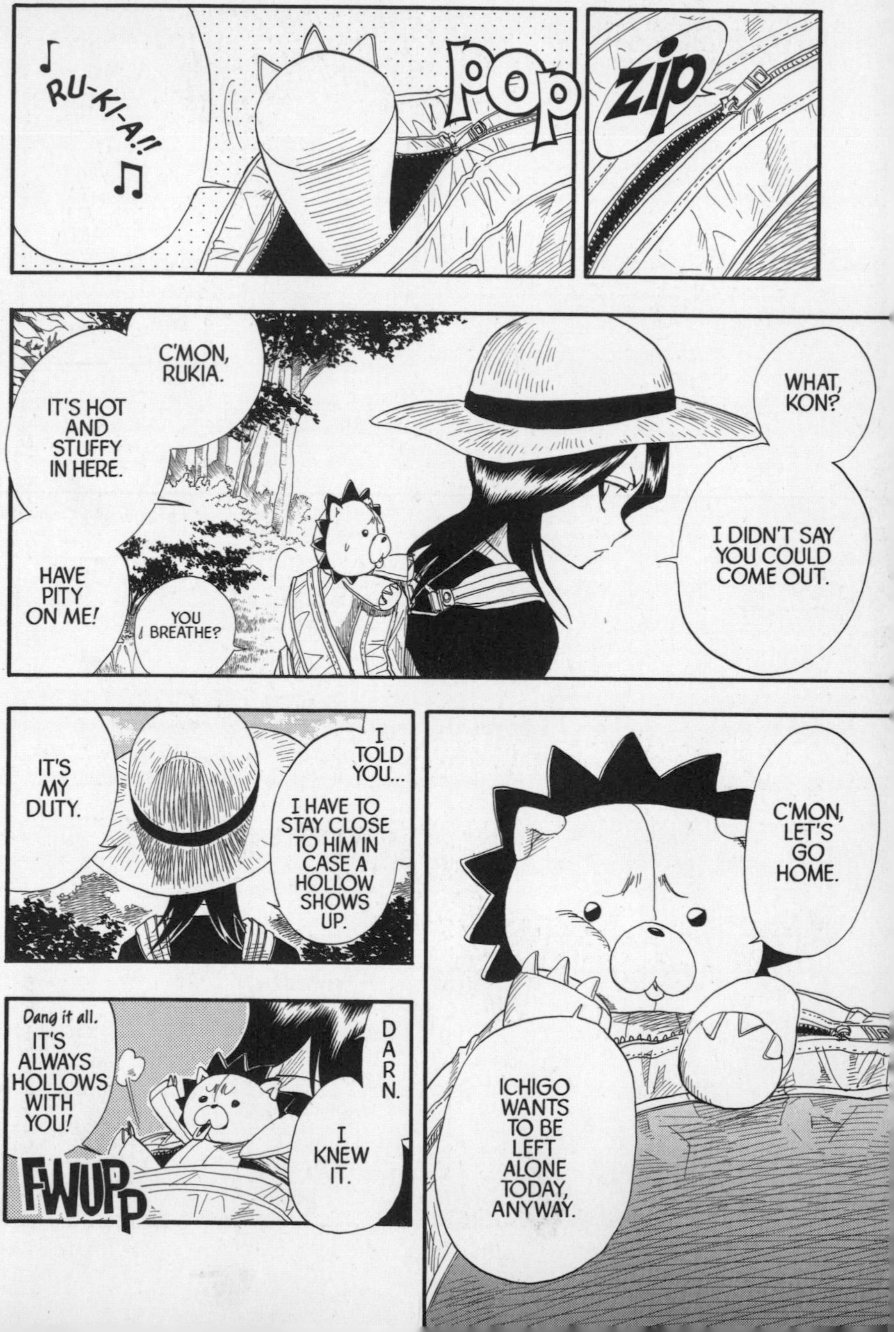
zip
♪ RU-KI-A!! ♫
POP
WHAT, KON?
I DIDN'T SAY YOU COULD COME OUT.
C'MON, RUKIA.
IT'S HOT AND STUFFY IN HERE.
YOU BREATHE?
HAVE PITY ON ME!
C'MON, LET'S GO HOME.
ICHIGO WANTS TO BE LEFT ALONE TODAY, ANYWAY.
I TOLD YOU...
I HAVE TO STAY CLOSE TO HIM IN CASE A HOLLOW SHOWS UP.
IT'S MY DUTY.
DARN.
I KNEW IT.
Dang it all.
IT'S ALWAYS HOLLOWS WITH YOU!
FWUPP

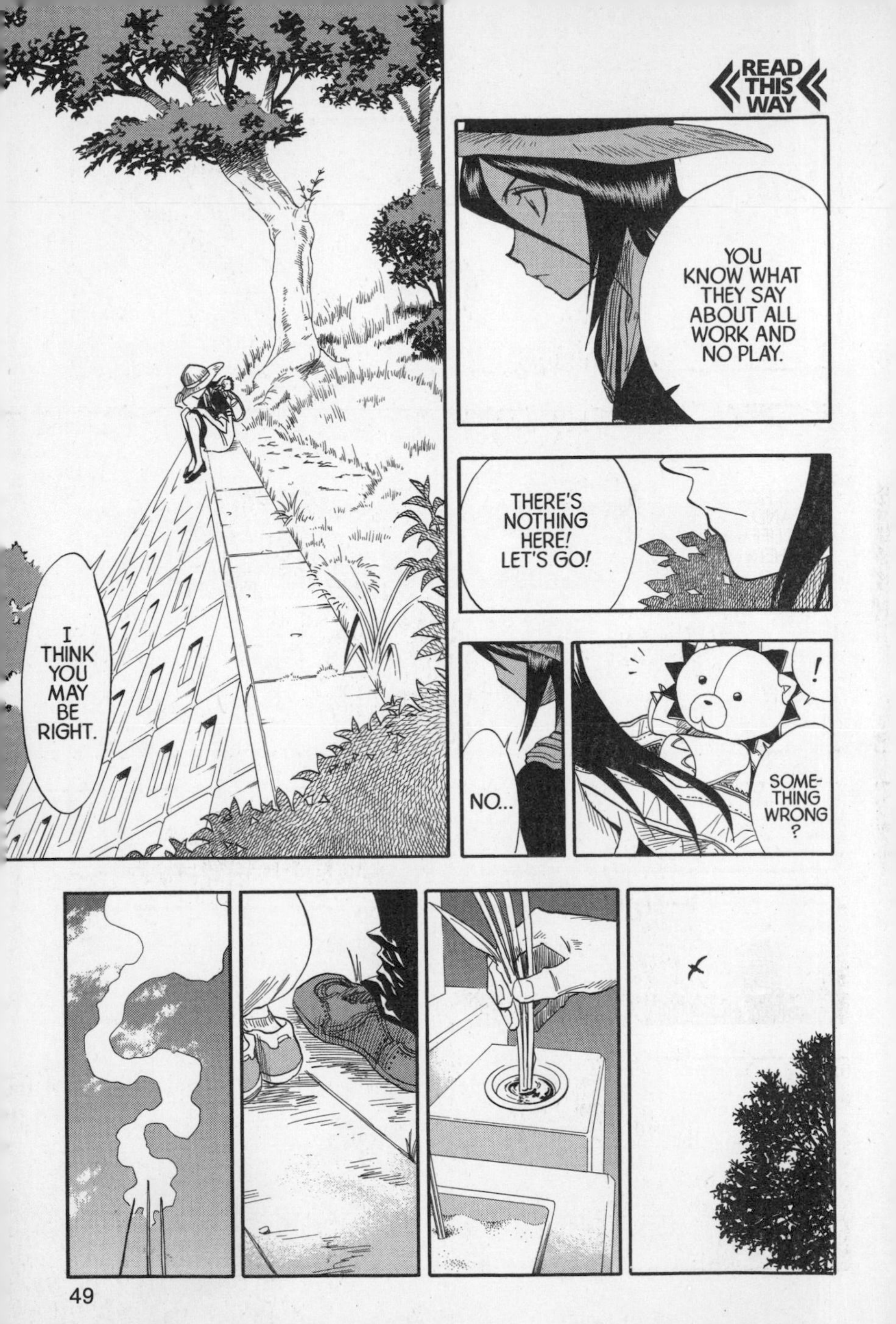
READ THIS WAY
YOU KNOW WHAT THEY SAY ABOUT ALL WORK AND NO PLAY.
THERE'S NOTHING HERE! LET'S GO!
!
SOME-THING WRONG?
NO...
I THINK YOU MAY BE RIGHT.

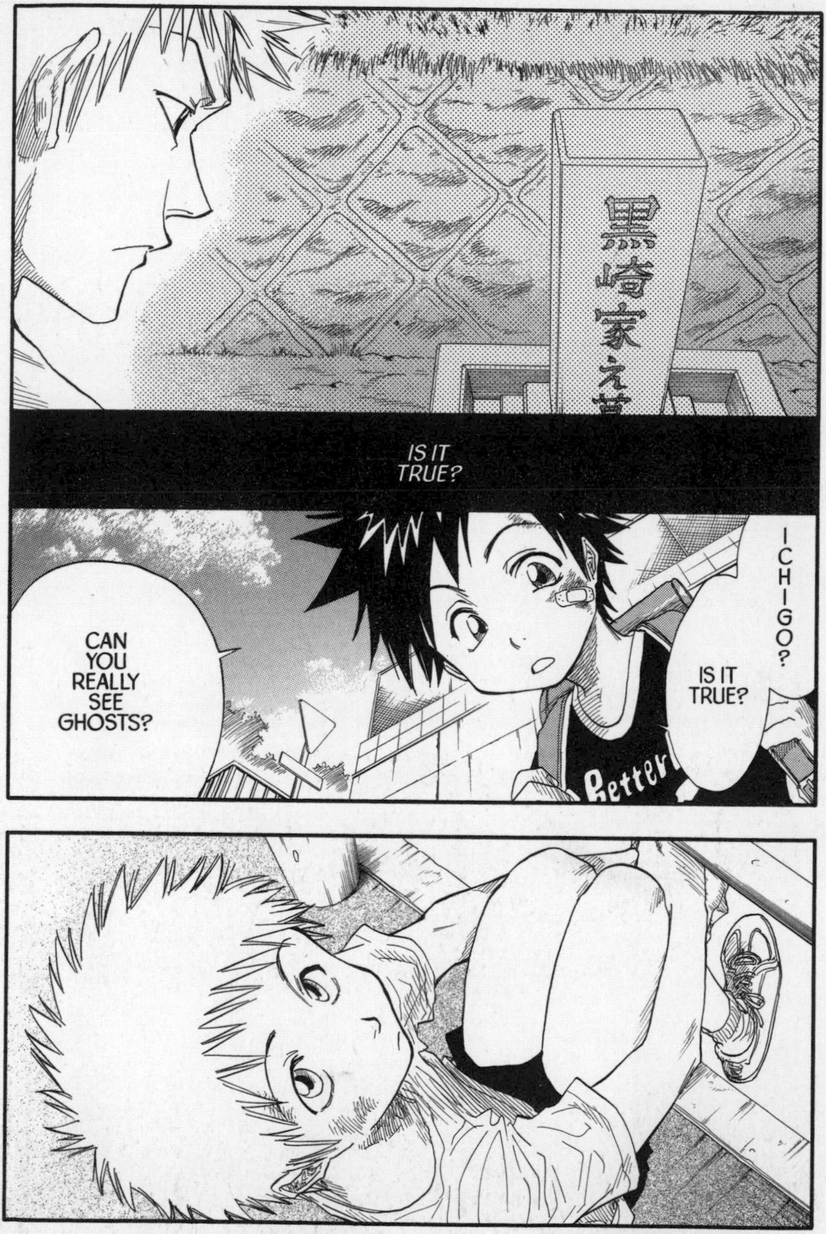
黒崎家之
IS IT TRUE?
ICHIGO?
IS IT TRUE?
CAN YOU REALLY SEE GHOSTS?
Better

READ THIS WAY

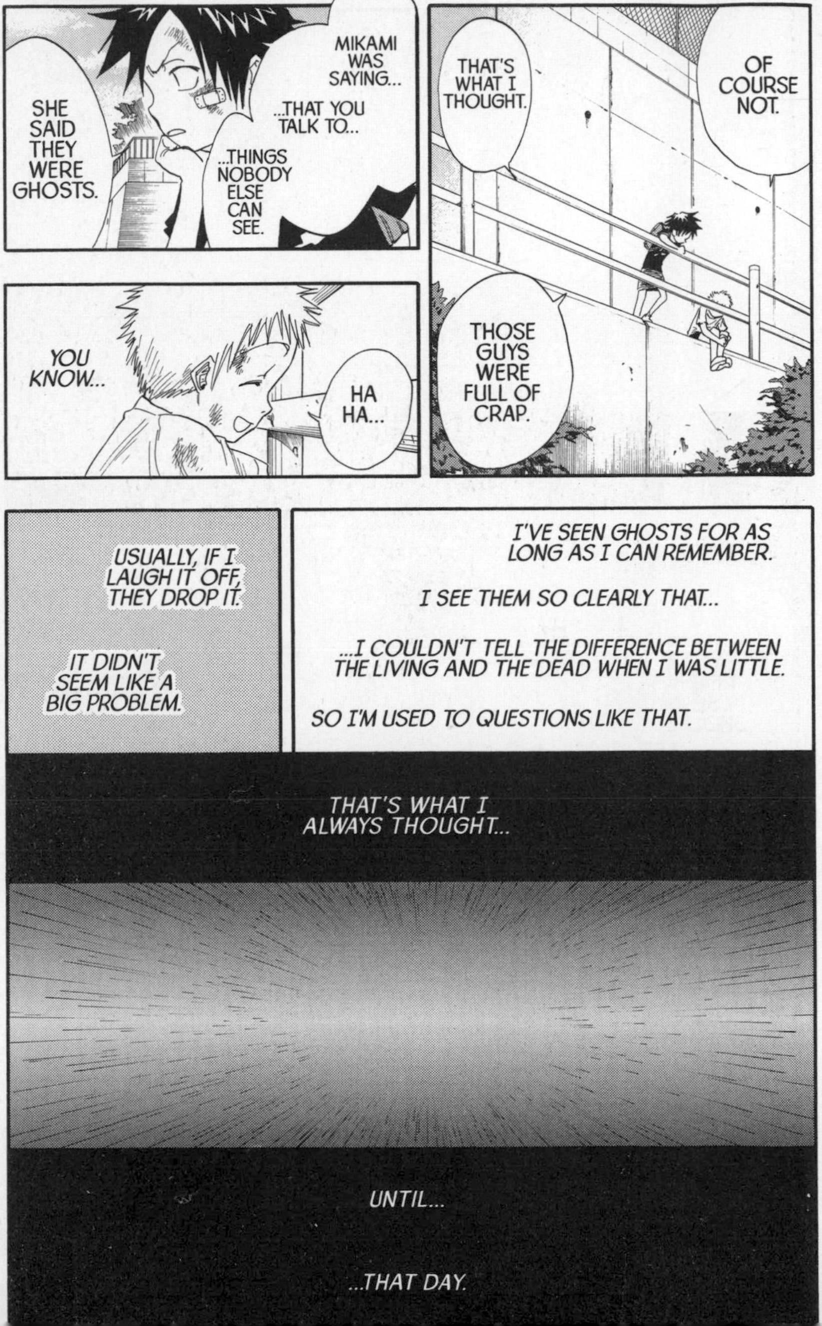
OF COURSE NOT.
THAT'S WHAT I THOUGHT.
THOSE GUYS WERE FULL OF CRAP.
MIKAMI WAS SAYING...
...THAT YOU TALK TO...
...THINGS NOBODY ELSE CAN SEE.
SHE SAID THEY WERE GHOSTS.
HA HA...
YOU KNOW...
I'VE SEEN GHOSTS FOR AS LONG AS I CAN REMEMBER.
I SEE THEM SO CLEARLY THAT...
...I COULDN'T TELL THE DIFFERENCE BETWEEN THE LIVING AND THE DEAD WHEN I WAS LITTLE.
SO I'M USED TO QUESTIONS LIKE THAT.
USUALLY, IF I LAUGH IT OFF, THEY DROP IT.
IT DIDN'T SEEM LIKE A BIG PROBLEM.
THAT'S WHAT I ALWAYS THOUGHT...
UNTIL...
...THAT DAY.

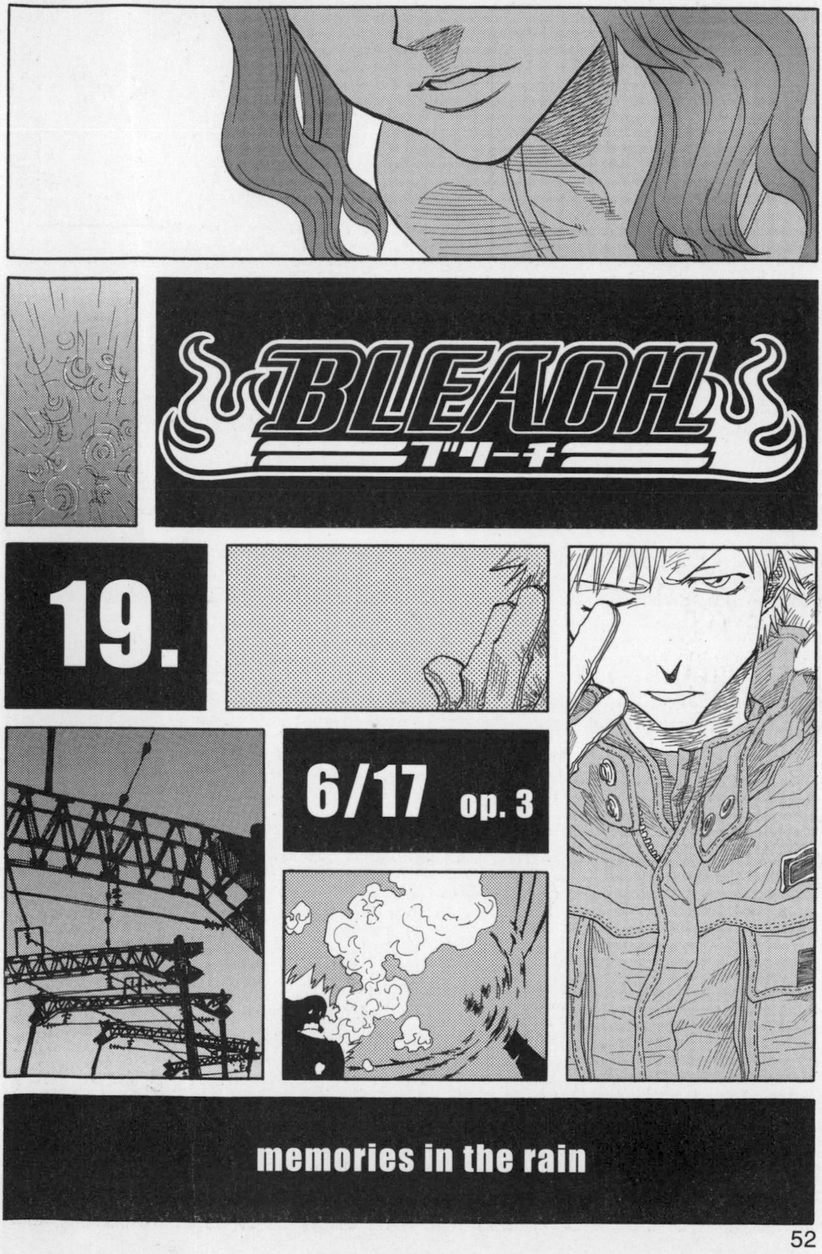
BLEACH
ブリーチ
19.
6/17 op. 3
memories in the rain

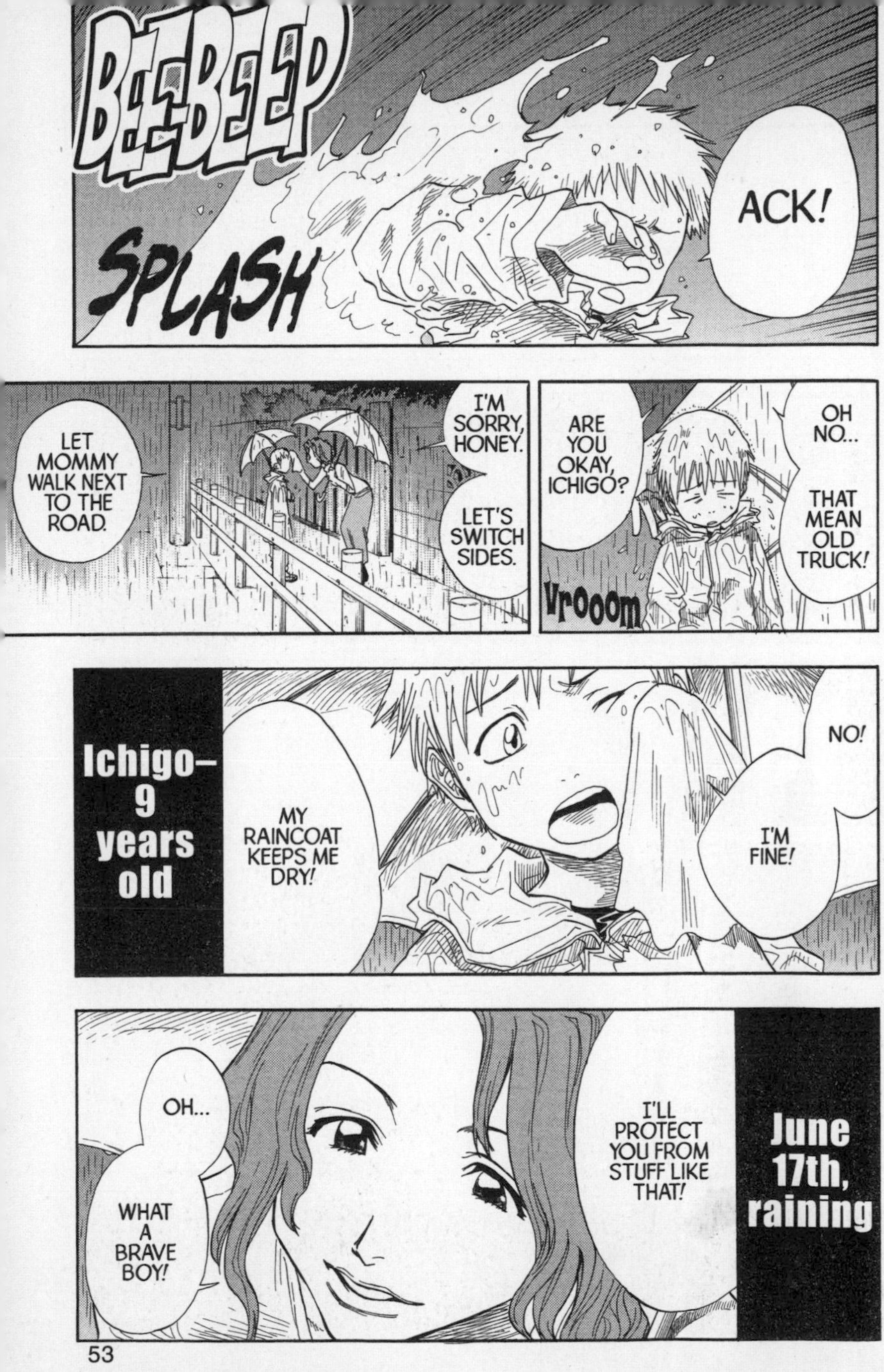
BEE-BEEP
ACK!
SPLASH
OH NO... THAT MEAN OLD TRUCK!
ARE YOU OKAY, ICHIGO?
Vrooom
I'M SORRY, HONEY.
LET'S SWITCH SIDES.
LET MOMMY WALK NEXT TO THE ROAD.
NO! I'M FINE!
MY RAINCOAT KEEPS ME DRY!
Ichigo–9 years old
June 17th, raining
I'LL PROTECT YOU FROM STUFF LIKE THAT!
OH...
WHAT A BRAVE BOY!

READ THIS WAY

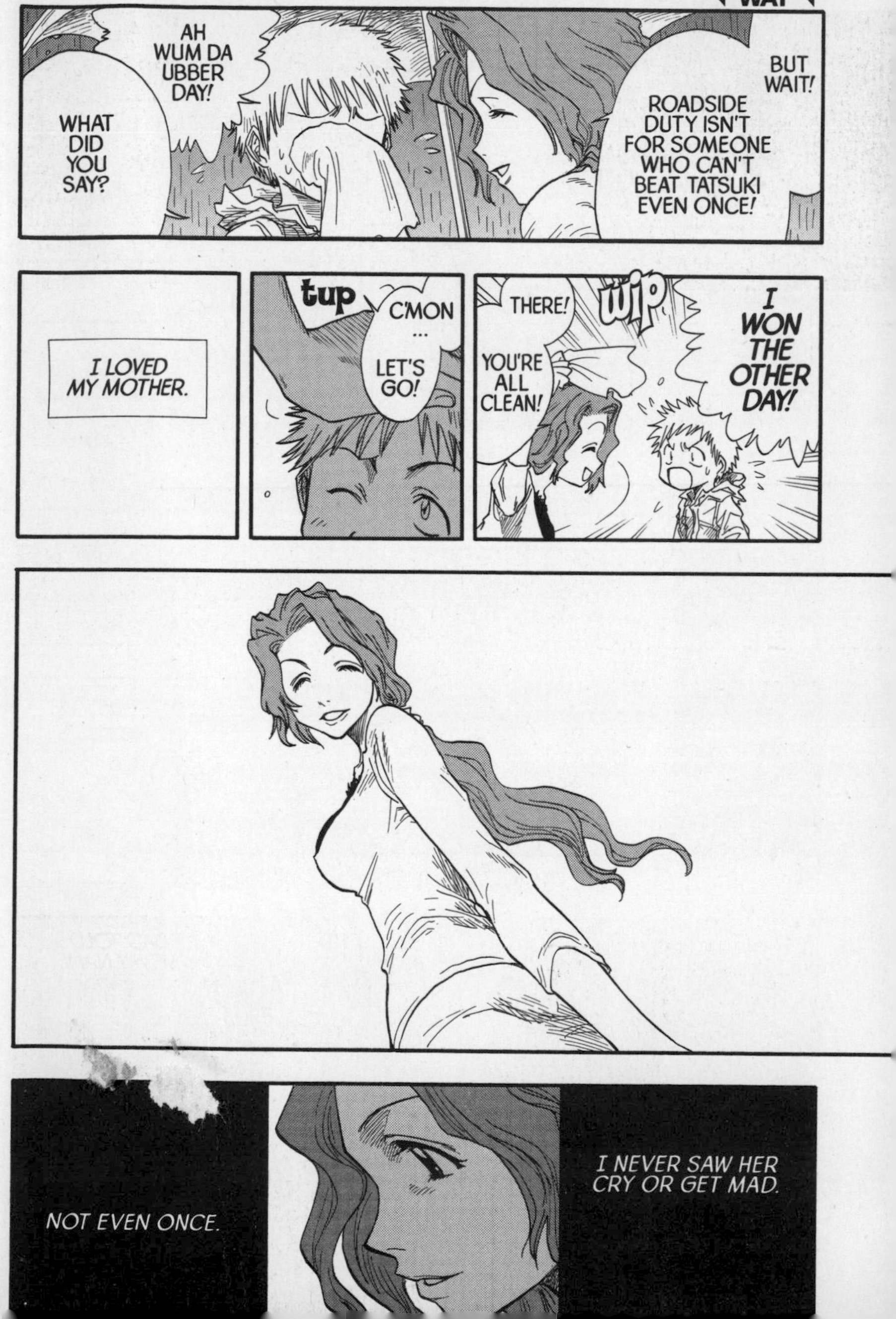

BUT WAIT!
ROADSIDE DUTY ISN'T FOR SOMEONE WHO CAN'T BEAT TATSUKI EVEN ONCE!
AH WUM DA UBBER DAY!
WHAT DID YOU SAY?
I WON THE OTHER DAY!
wip
THERE!
YOU'RE ALL CLEAN!
tup
C'MON ... LET'S GO!
I LOVED MY MOTHER.
I NEVER SAW HER CRY OR GET MAD.
NOT EVEN ONCE.

READ THIS WAY

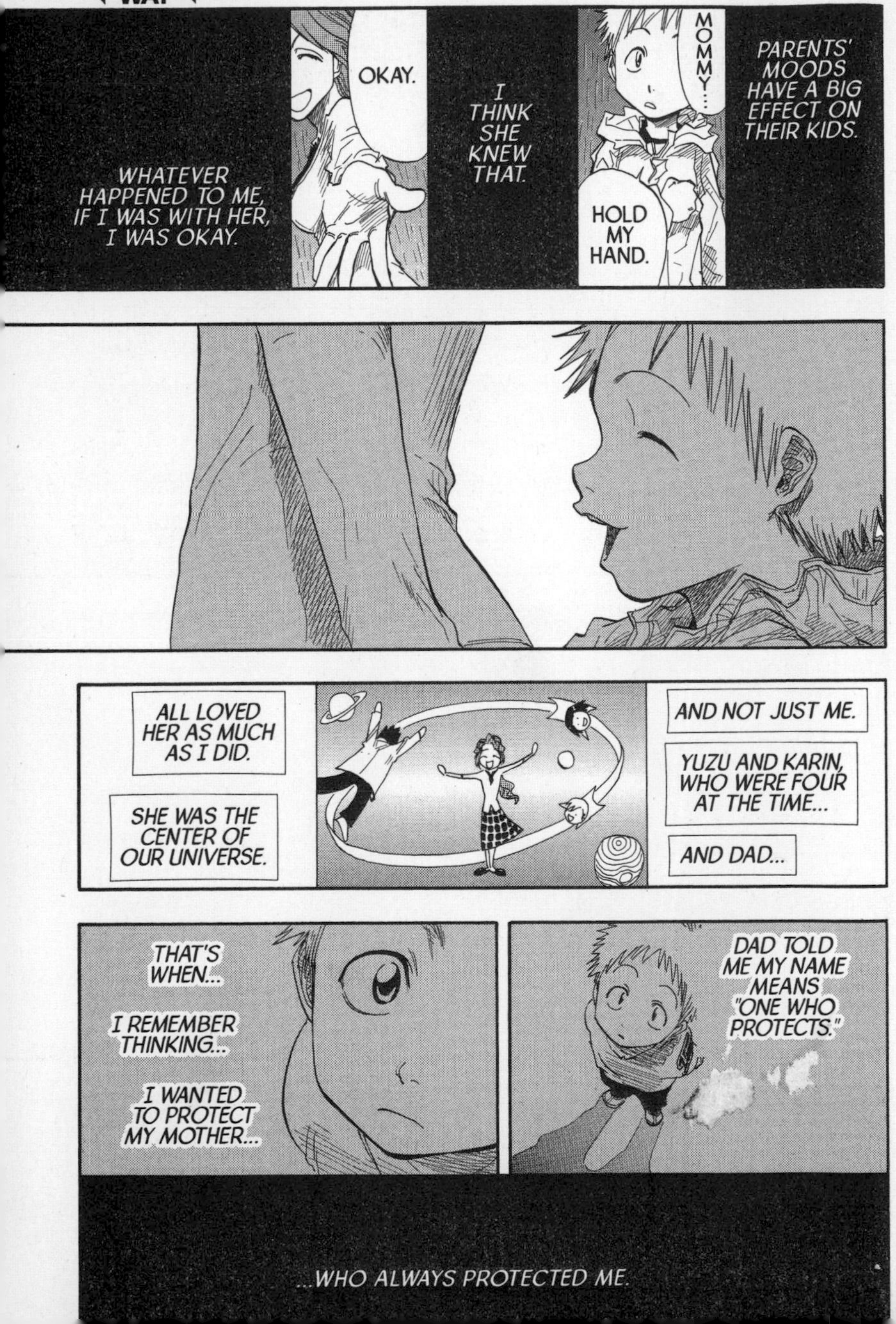
PARENTS' MOODS HAVE A BIG EFFECT ON THEIR KIDS.
MOMMY...
HOLD MY HAND.
I THINK SHE KNEW THAT.
OKAY.
WHATEVER HAPPENED TO ME, IF I WAS WITH HER, I WAS OKAY.
AND NOT JUST ME.
YUZU AND KARIN, WHO WERE FOUR AT THE TIME...
AND DAD...
ALL LOVED HER AS MUCH AS I DID.
SHE WAS THE CENTER OF OUR UNIVERSE.
DAD TOLD ME MY NAME MEANS "ONE WHO PROTECTS."
THAT'S WHEN...
I REMEMBER THINKING...
I WANTED TO PROTECT MY MOTHER...
...WHO ALWAYS PROTECTED ME.

READ THIS WAY

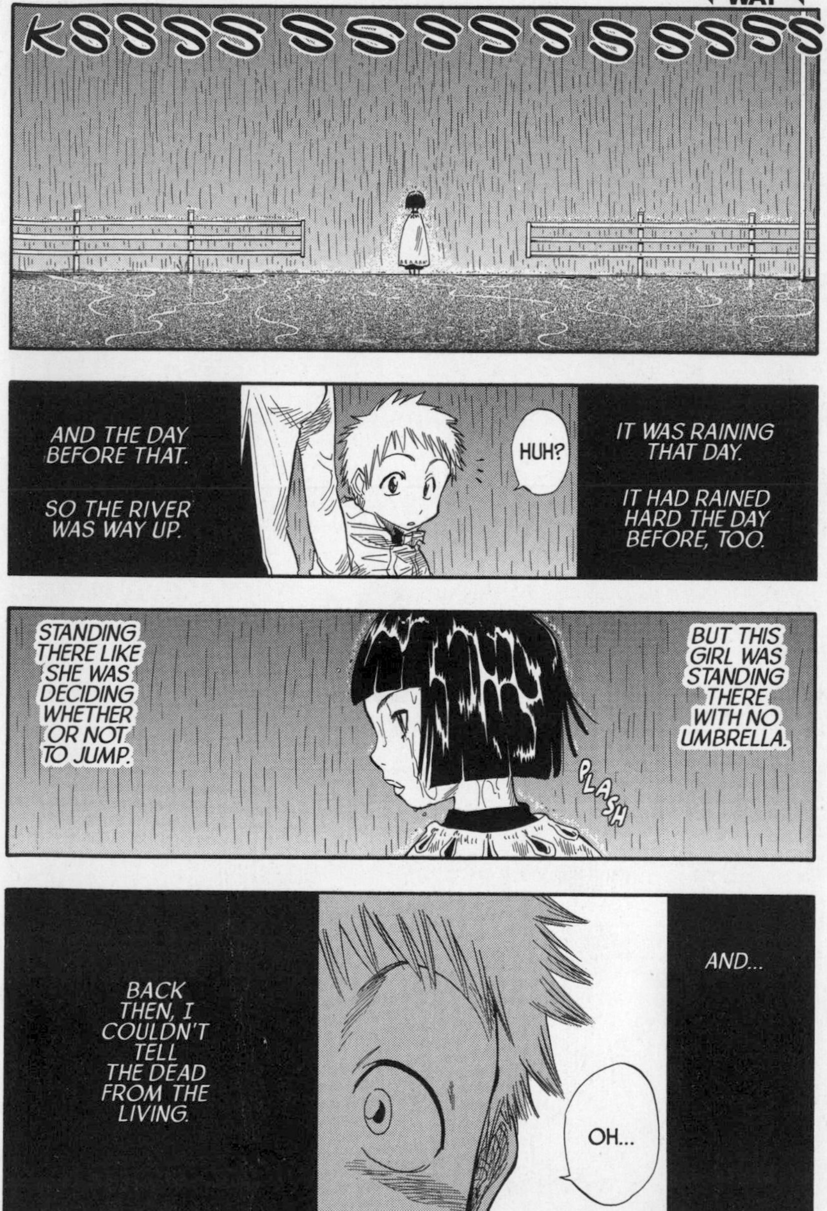
KSSSS SSSSSSSSSSS
IT WAS RAINING THAT DAY.
IT HAD RAINED HARD THE DAY BEFORE, TOO.
HUH?
AND THE DAY BEFORE THAT.
SO THE RIVER WAS WAY UP.
BUT THIS GIRL WAS STANDING THERE WITH NO UMBRELLA.
PLASH
STANDING THERE LIKE SHE WAS DECIDING WHETHER OR NOT TO JUMP.
AND...
OH...
BACK THEN, I COULDN'T TELL THE DEAD FROM THE LIVING.

READ THIS WAY

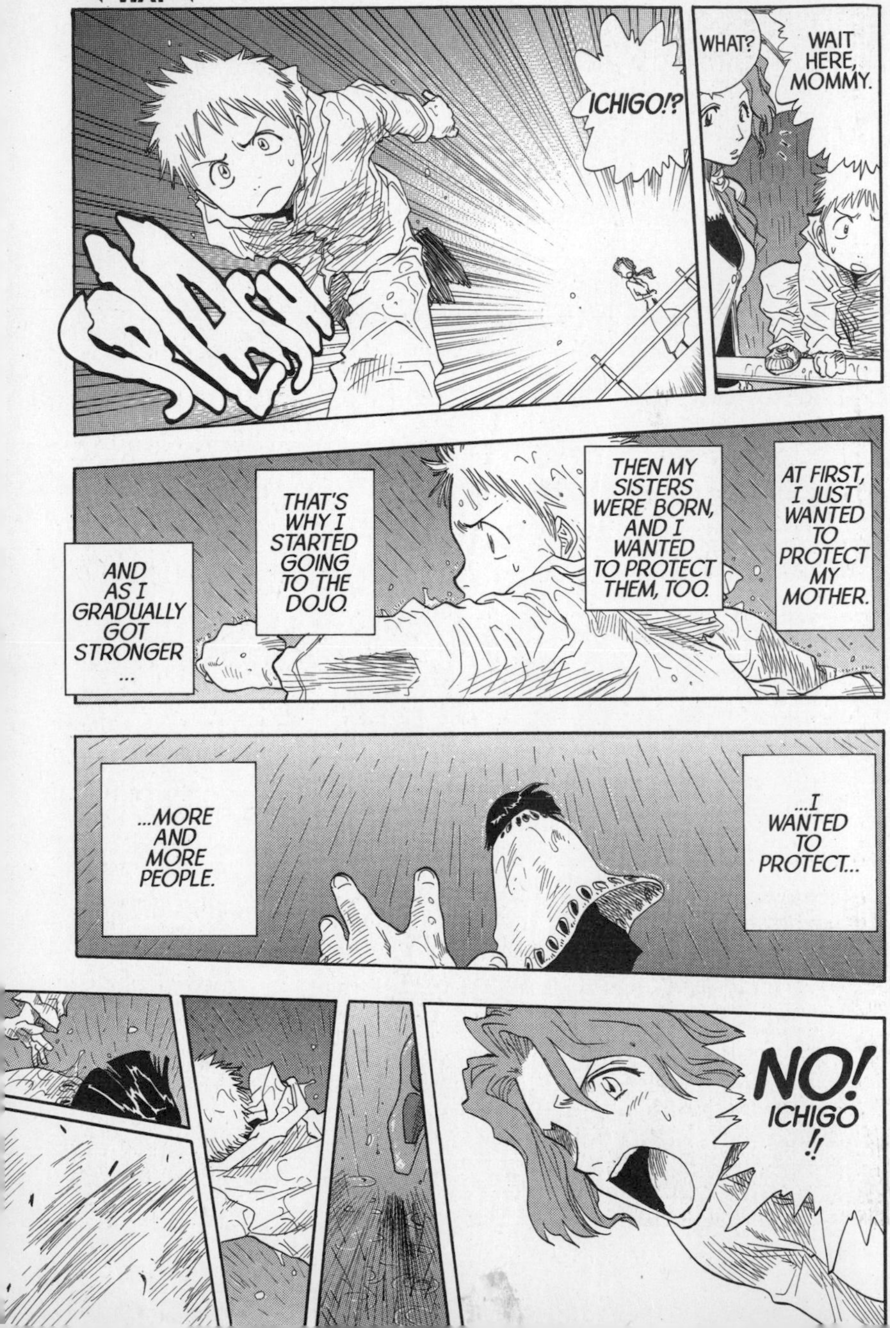
WAIT HERE, MOMMY.
WHAT?
ICHIGO!?
AT FIRST, I JUST WANTED TO PROTECT MY MOTHER.
THEN MY SISTERS WERE BORN, AND I WANTED TO PROTECT THEM, TOO.
THAT'S WHY I STARTED GOING TO THE DOJO.
AND AS I GRADUALLY GOT STRONGER ...
...I WANTED TO PROTECT...
...MORE AND MORE PEOPLE.
NO! ICHIGO!!

READ THIS WAY

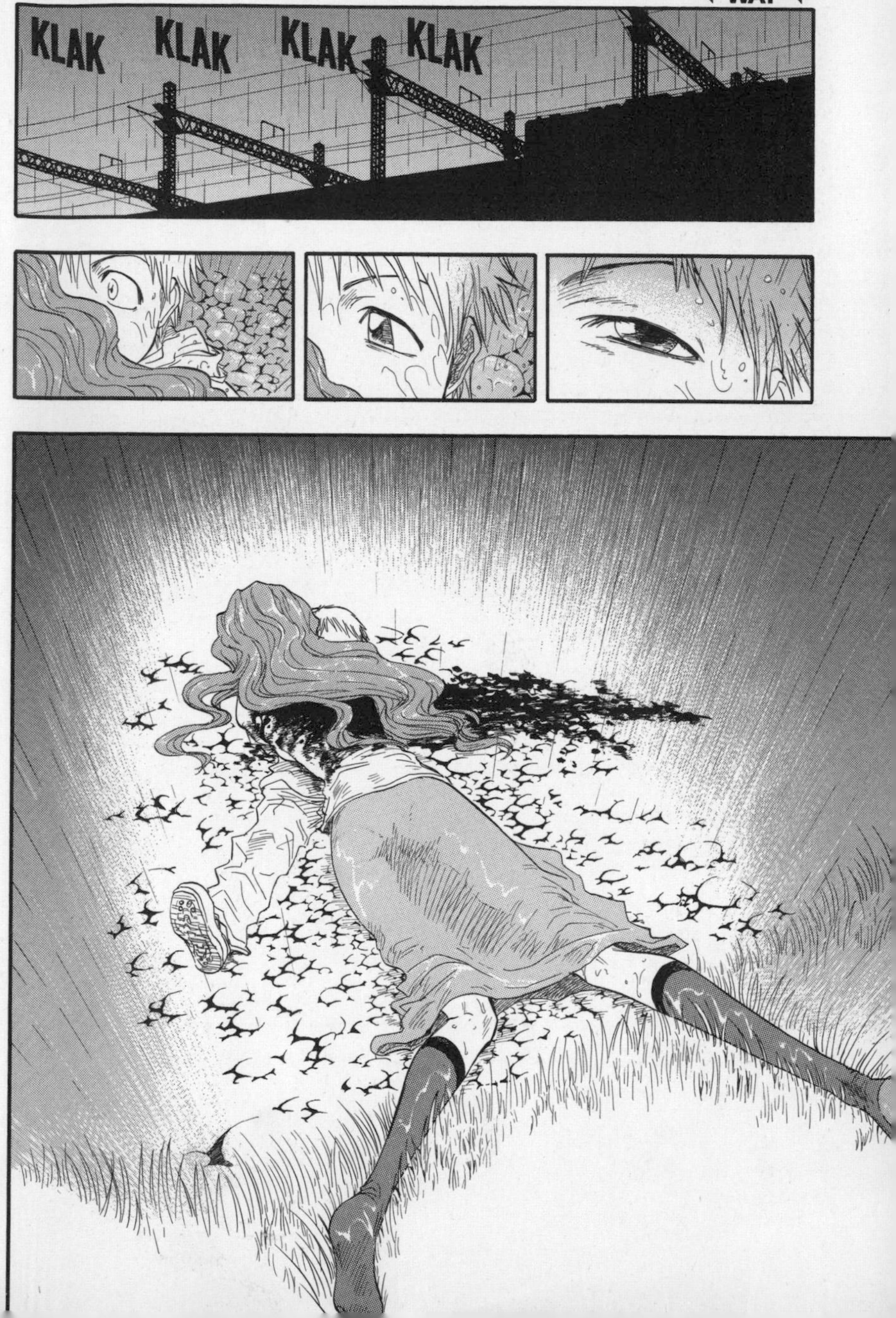
KLAK
KLAK
KLAK
KLAK

READ THIS WAY

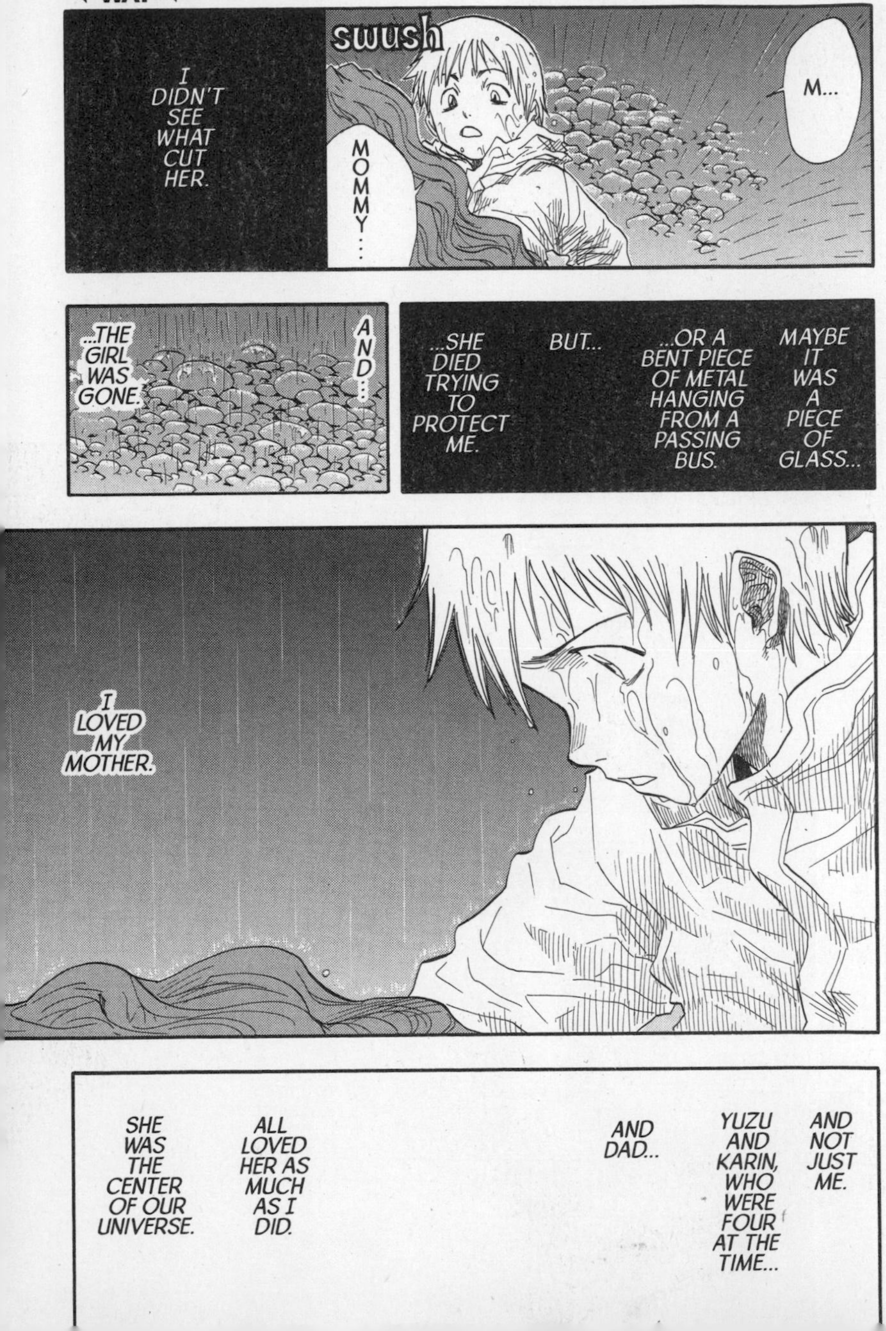
M...
swush
MOMMY...
I DIDN'T SEE WHAT CUT HER.
MAYBE IT WAS A PIECE OF GLASS...
...OR A BENT PIECE OF METAL HANGING FROM A PASSING BUS.
BUT...
...SHE DIED TRYING TO PROTECT ME.
AND...
...THE GIRL WAS GONE.
I LOVED MY MOTHER.
AND NOT JUST ME.
YUZU AND KARIN, WHO WERE FOUR AT THE TIME...
AND DAD...
ALL LOVED HER AS MUCH AS I DID.
SHE WAS THE CENTER OF OUR UNIVERSE.

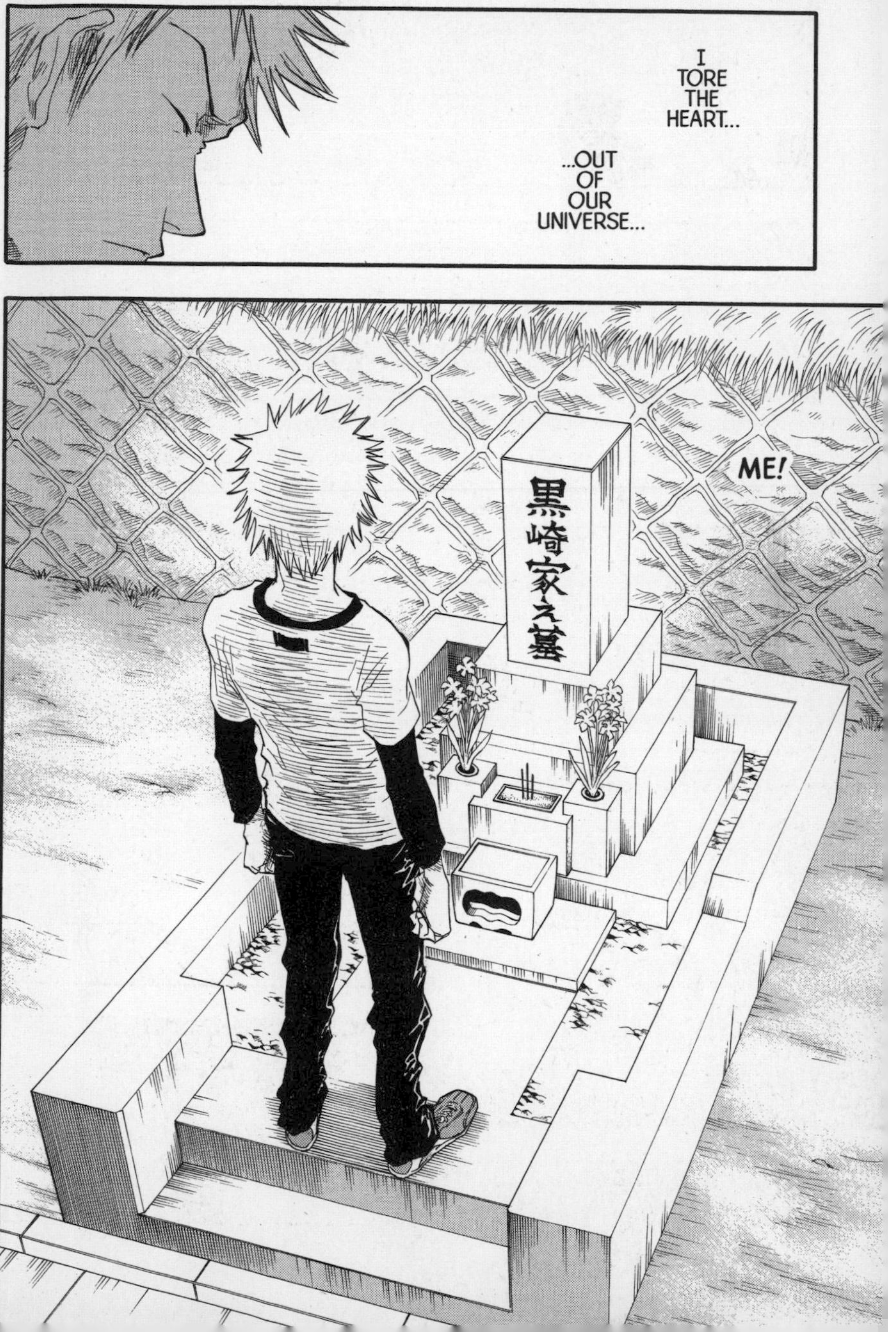
I TORE THE HEART...
...OUT OF OUR UNIVERSE...
黒崎家之墓
ME!

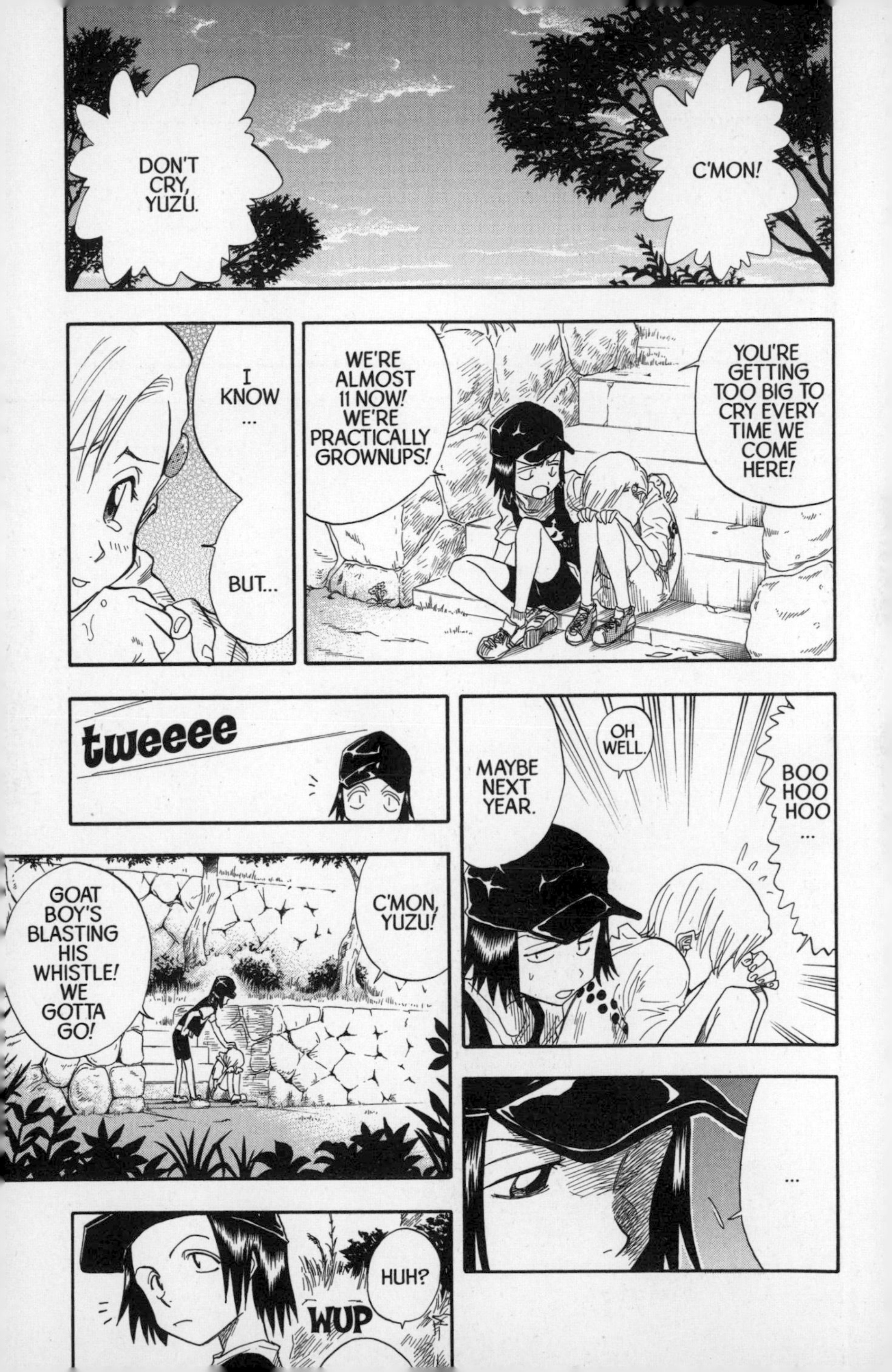
C'MON!
DON'T CRY, YUZU.
YOU'RE GETTING TOO BIG TO CRY EVERY TIME WE COME HERE!
WE'RE ALMOST 11 NOW! WE'RE PRACTICALLY GROWNUPS!
I KNOW ...
BUT...
BOO HOO HOO ...
OH WELL.
MAYBE NEXT YEAR.
tweeee
C'MON, YUZU!
GOAT BOY'S BLASTING HIS WHISTLE! WE GOTTA GO!
...
HUH?
WUP

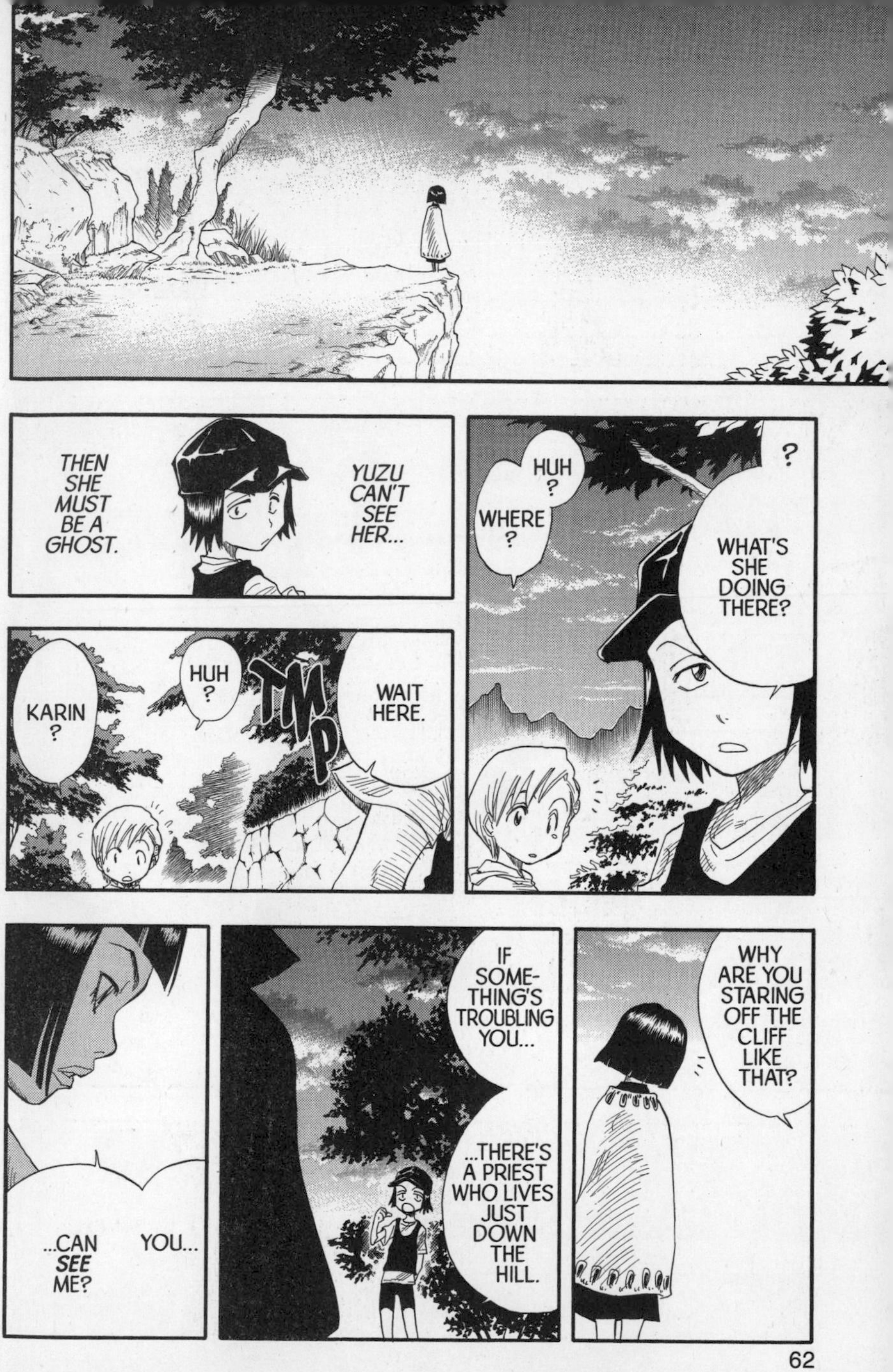
?
WHAT'S SHE DOING THERE?
HUH? WHERE?
YUZU CAN'T SEE HER...
THEN SHE MUST BE A GHOST.
WAIT HERE.
TMP
HUH?
KARIN?
WHY ARE YOU STARING OFF THE CLIFF LIKE THAT?
IF SOME-THING'S TROUBLING YOU...
...THERE'S A PRIEST WHO LIVES JUST DOWN THE HILL.
YOU...
...CAN *SEE* ME?

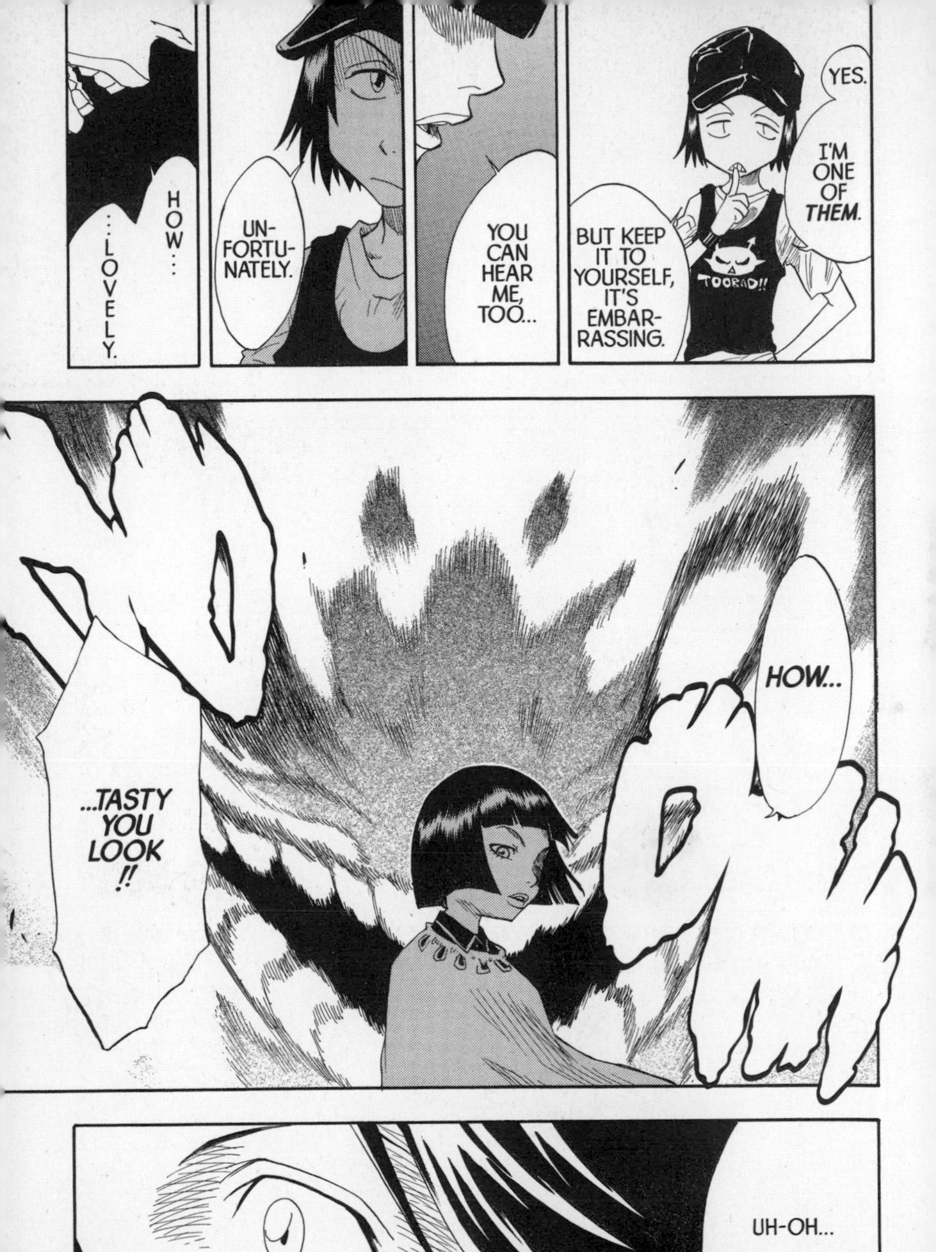
YES.
I'M ONE OF *THEM*.
TOOBAD!!
BUT KEEP IT TO YOURSELF, IT'S EMBARRASSING.
YOU CAN HEAR ME, TOO...
UN-FORTUNATELY.
HOW...
...LOVELY.
HOW...
...TASTY YOU LOOK!!
UH-OH...

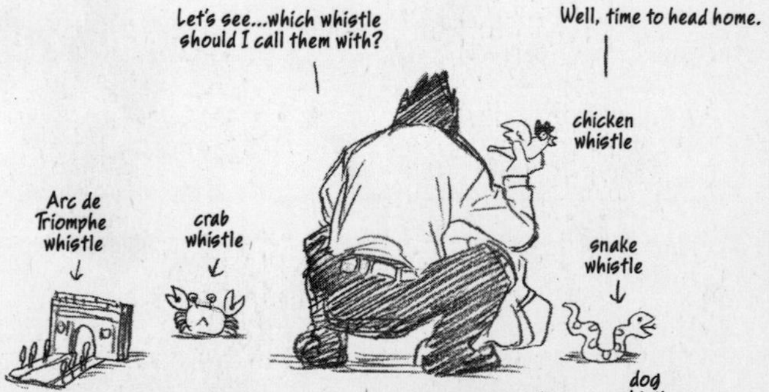
Well, time to head home.
Let's see...which whistle should I call them with?
chicken whistle
snake whistle
dog whistle
crab whistle
Arc de Triomphe whistle
coin purse whistle
lips whistle

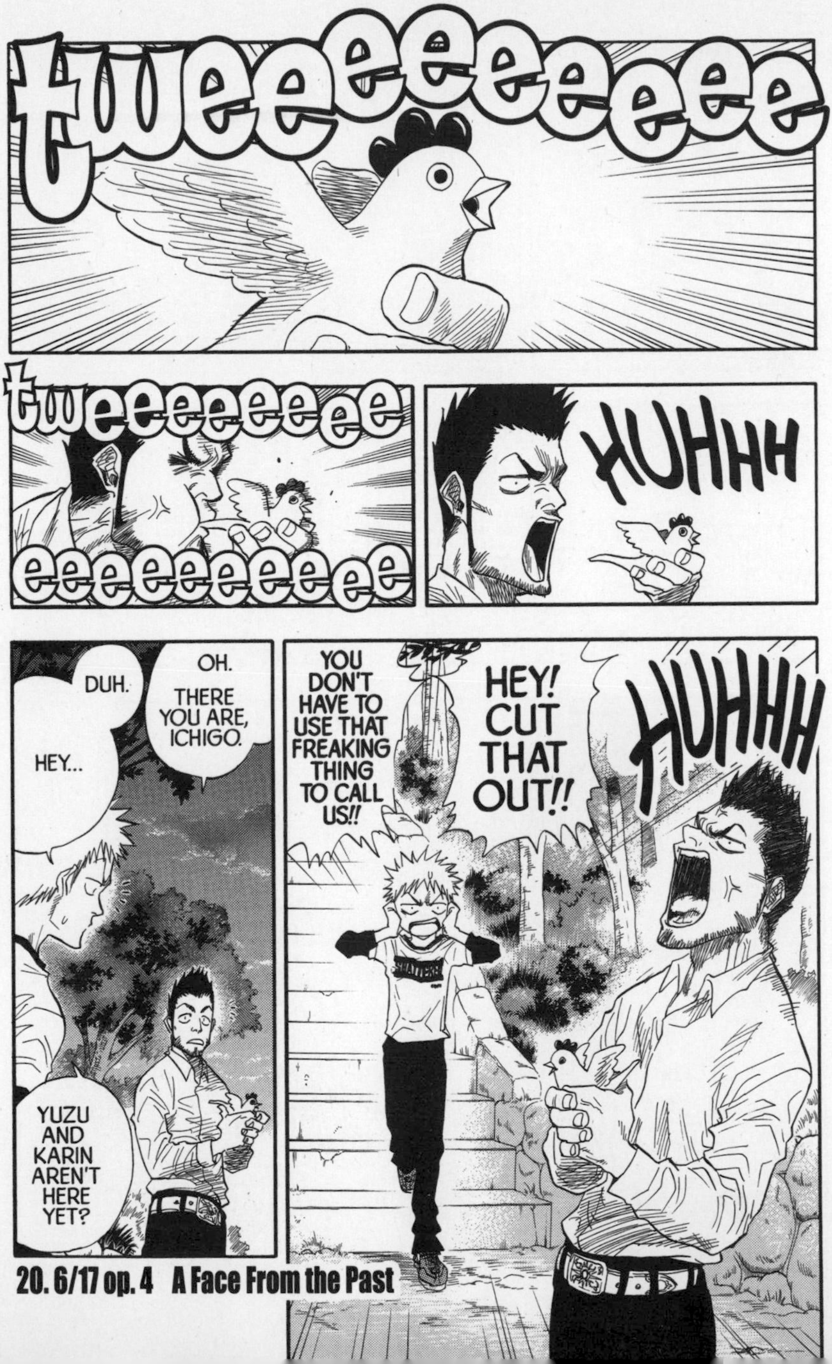
tweeeeeeeeee
HUHHH
tweeeeeeeee
eeeeeeeeeee
HUHHH
HEY! CUT THAT OUT!!
YOU DON'T HAVE TO USE THAT FREAKING THING TO CALL US!!
OH. THERE YOU ARE, ICHIGO.
DUH.
HEY...
YUZU AND KARIN AREN'T HERE YET?

20. 6/17 op. 4 A Face From the Past

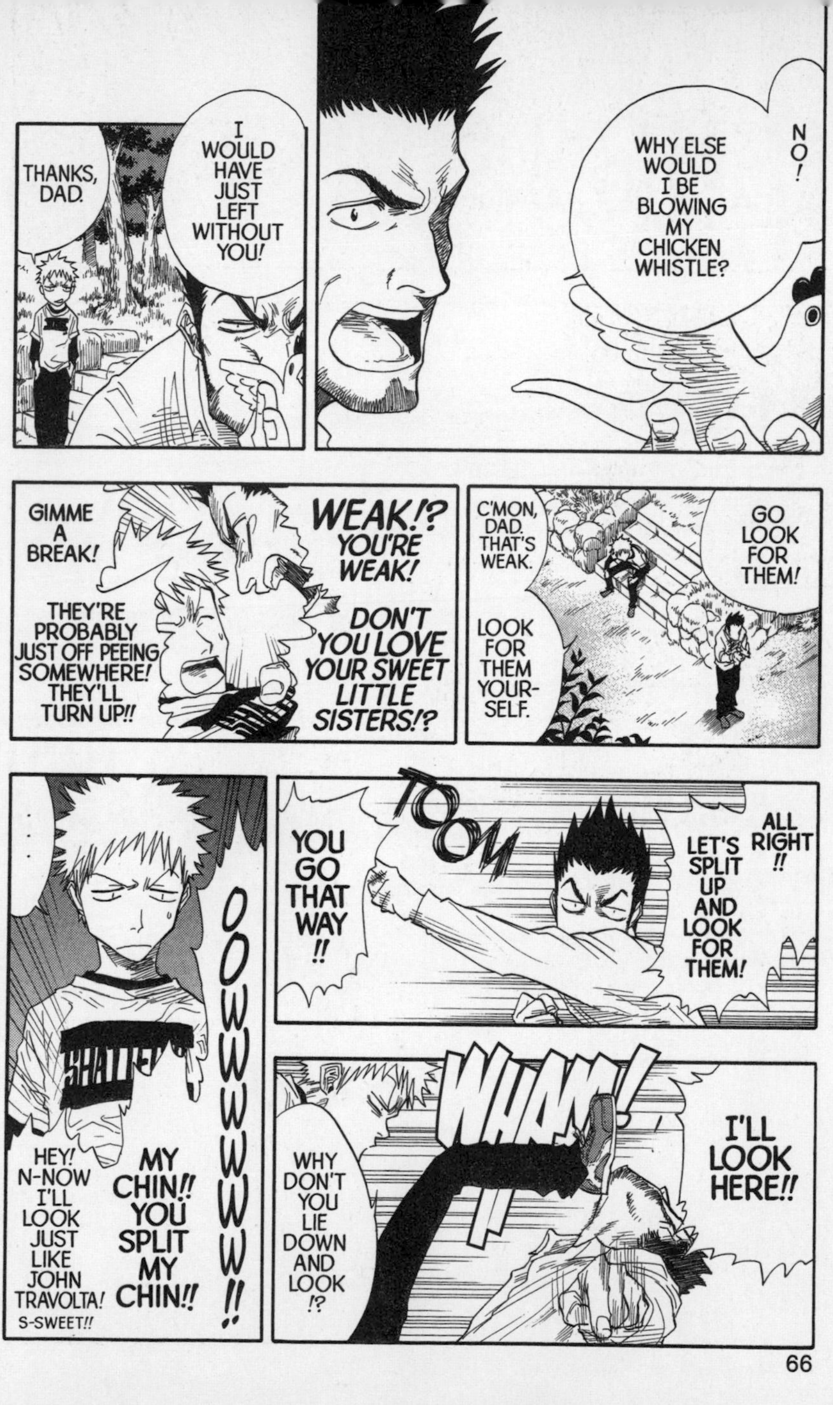
NO!
WHY ELSE WOULD I BE BLOWING MY CHICKEN WHISTLE?
I WOULD HAVE JUST LEFT WITHOUT YOU!
THANKS, DAD.
GO LOOK FOR THEM!
C'MON, DAD. THAT'S WEAK.
LOOK FOR THEM YOURSELF.
WEAK!? YOU'RE WEAK!
DON'T YOU LOVE YOUR SWEET LITTLE SISTERS!?
GIMME A BREAK!
THEY'RE PROBABLY JUST OFF PEEING SOMEWHERE! THEY'LL TURN UP!!
ALL RIGHT!!
LET'S SPLIT UP AND LOOK FOR THEM!
TOOM
YOU GO THAT WAY!!
WHAM!
I'LL LOOK HERE!!
WHY DON'T YOU LIE DOWN AND LOOK!?
...
OOWWWWWWWW!!
MY CHIN!! YOU SPLIT MY CHIN!!
HEY! N-NOW I'LL LOOK JUST LIKE JOHN TRAVOLTA!
S-SWEET!!

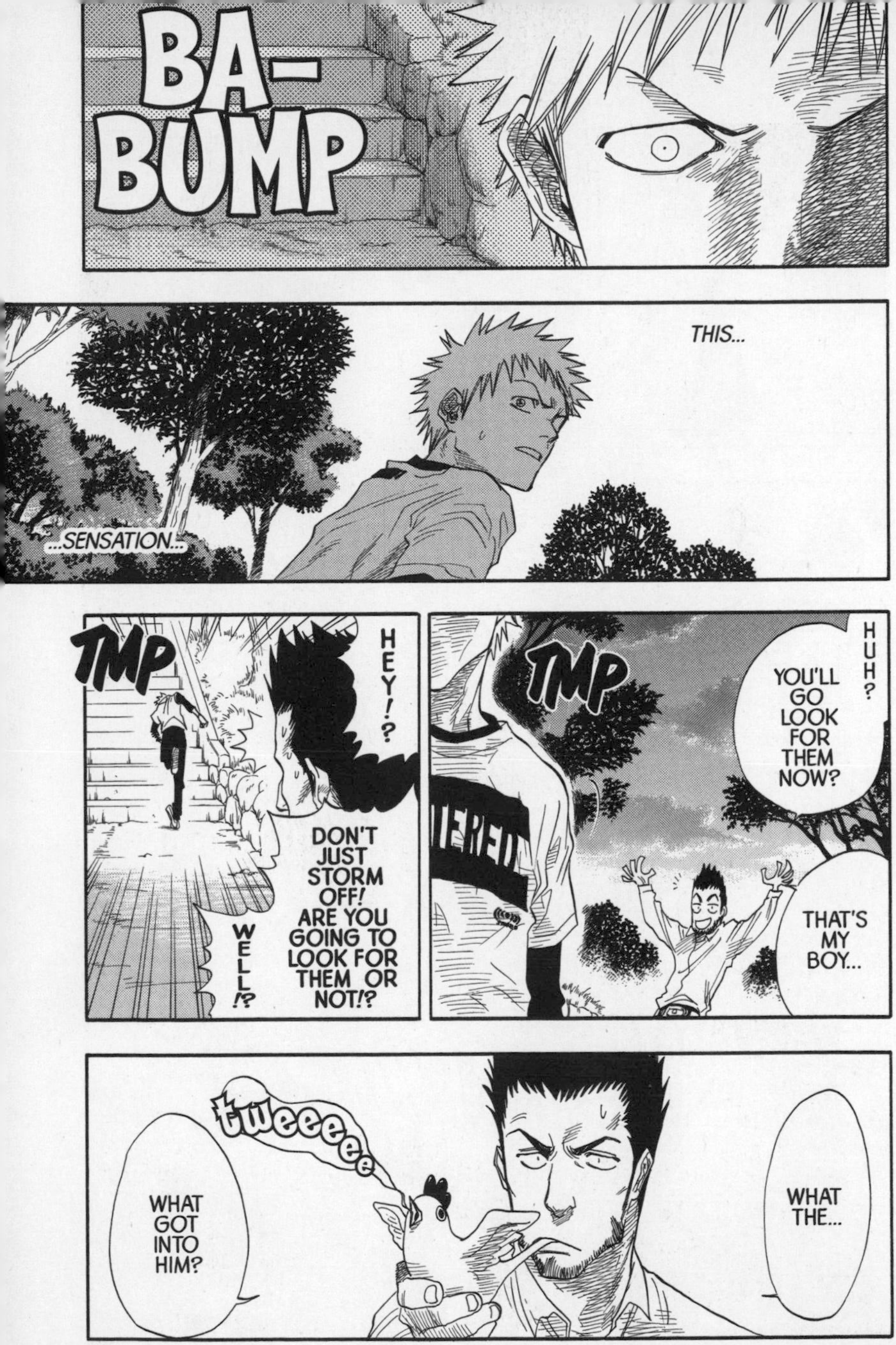
BA-BUMP
THIS...
...SENSATION...
HUH?
YOU'LL GO LOOK FOR THEM NOW?
TMP
THAT'S MY BOY...
HEY!?
TMP
DON'T JUST STORM OFF! ARE YOU GOING TO LOOK FOR THEM OR NOT!?
WELL!?
WHAT THE...
tweeeeeee
WHAT GOT INTO HIM?

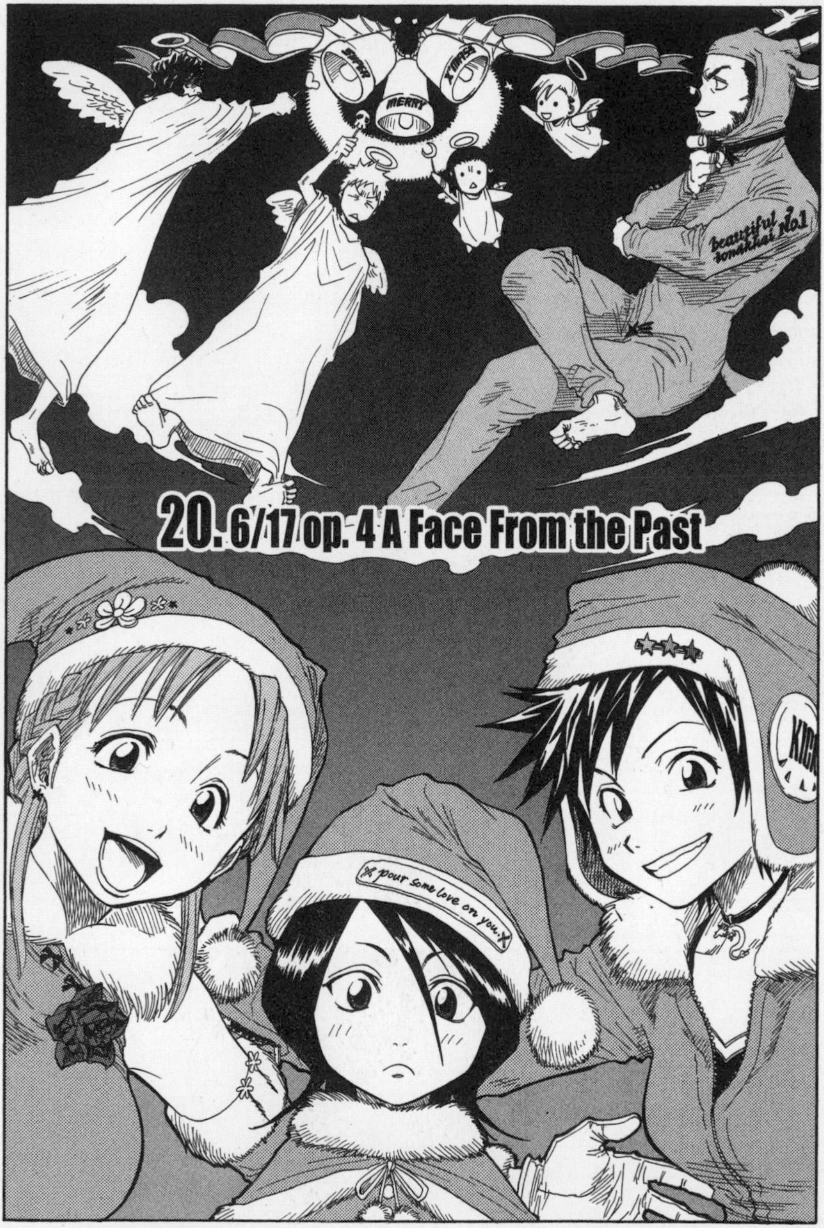
MERRY
X'MAS
20. 6/17 op. 4 A Face From the Past
pour some love on you.
KICK

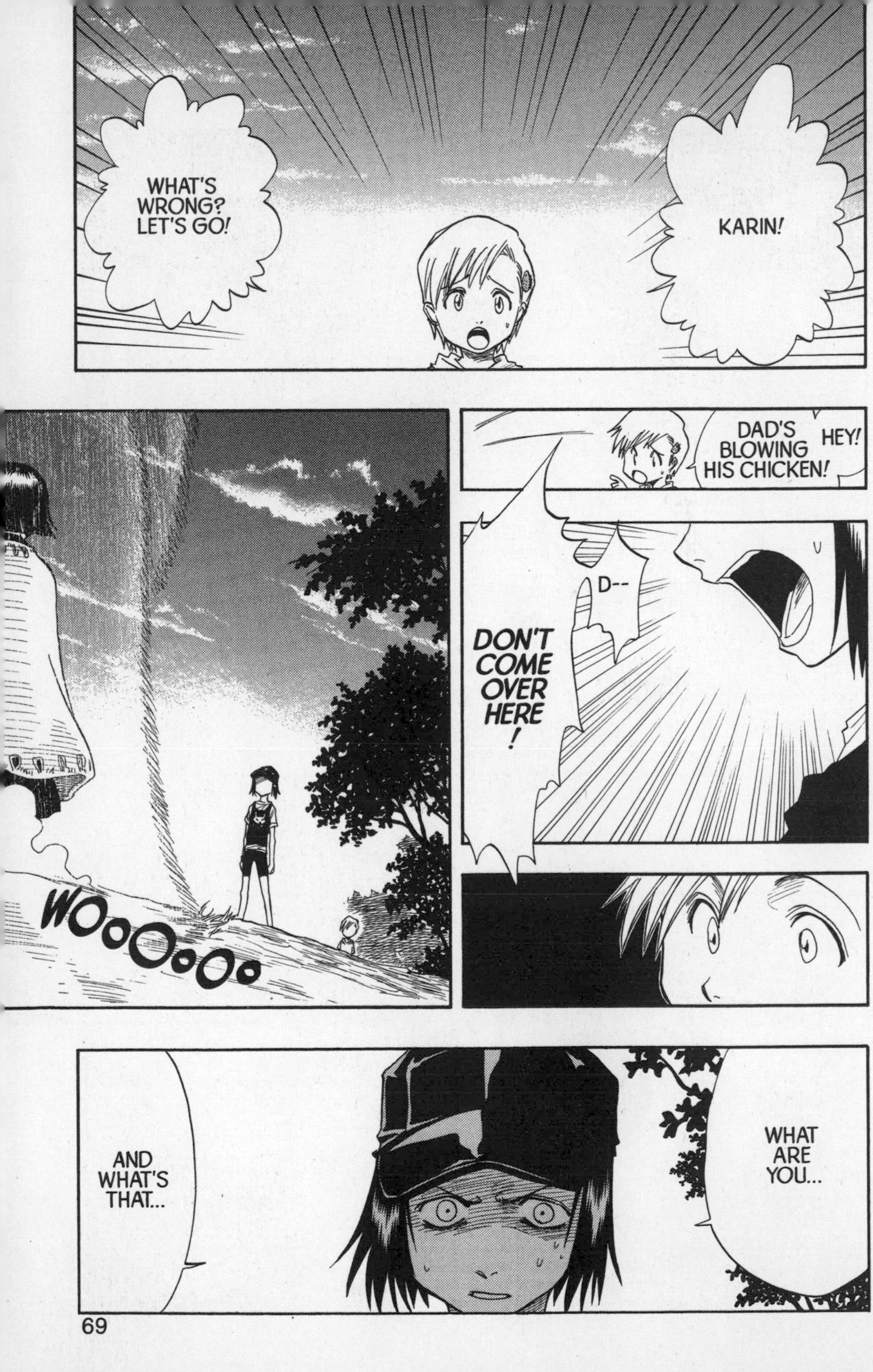
KARIN!
WHAT'S WRONG? LET'S GO!
HEY!
DAD'S BLOWING HIS CHICKEN!
D--
DON'T COME OVER HERE!
WOoOoOo
WHAT ARE YOU...
AND WHAT'S THAT...

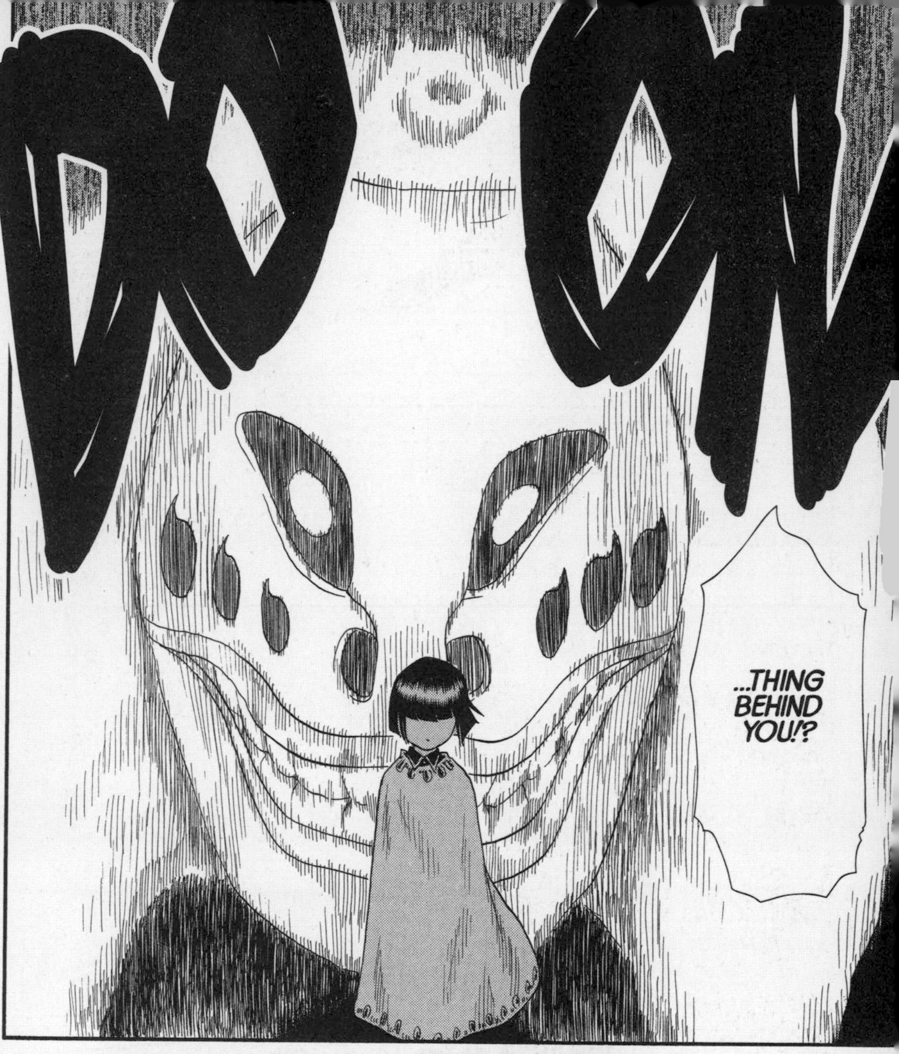
DOON
...THING BEHIND YOU!?

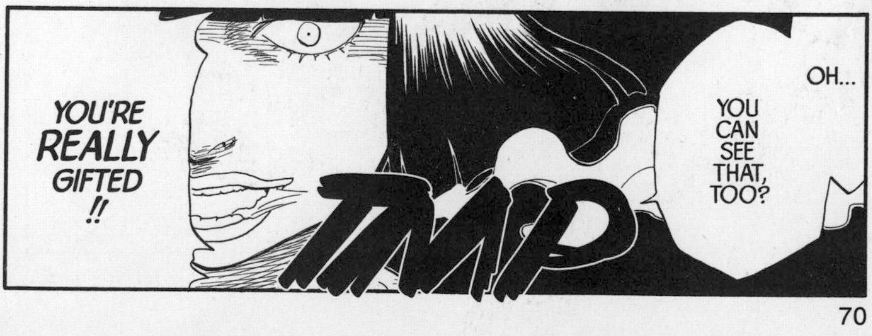
OH... YOU CAN SEE THAT, TOO?
TMP
YOU'RE REALLY GIFTED!!

READ THIS WAY

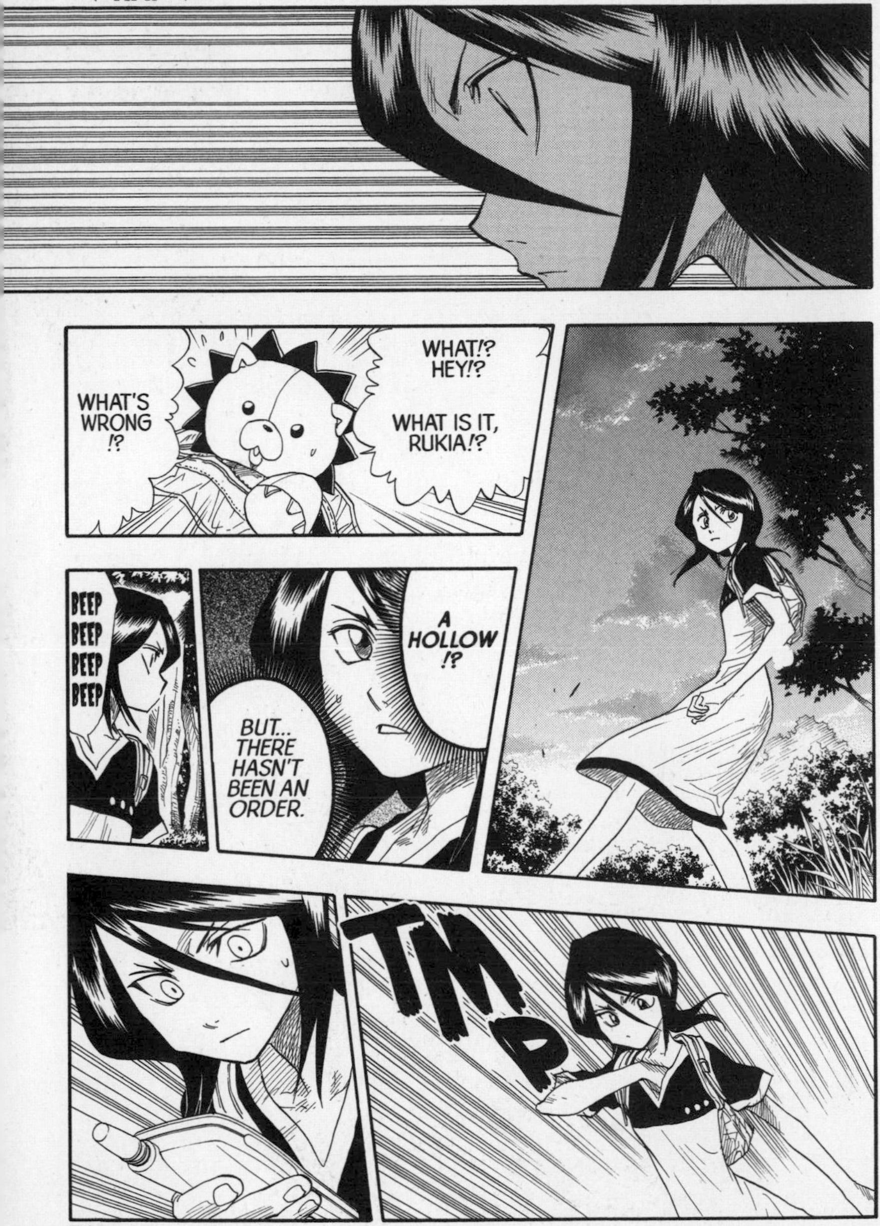
WHAT!? HEY!?
WHAT IS IT, RUKIA!?
WHAT'S WRONG !?
A HOLLOW !?
BUT... THERE HASN'T BEEN AN ORDER.
BEEP BEEP BEEP BEEP
TMP

READ THIS WAY

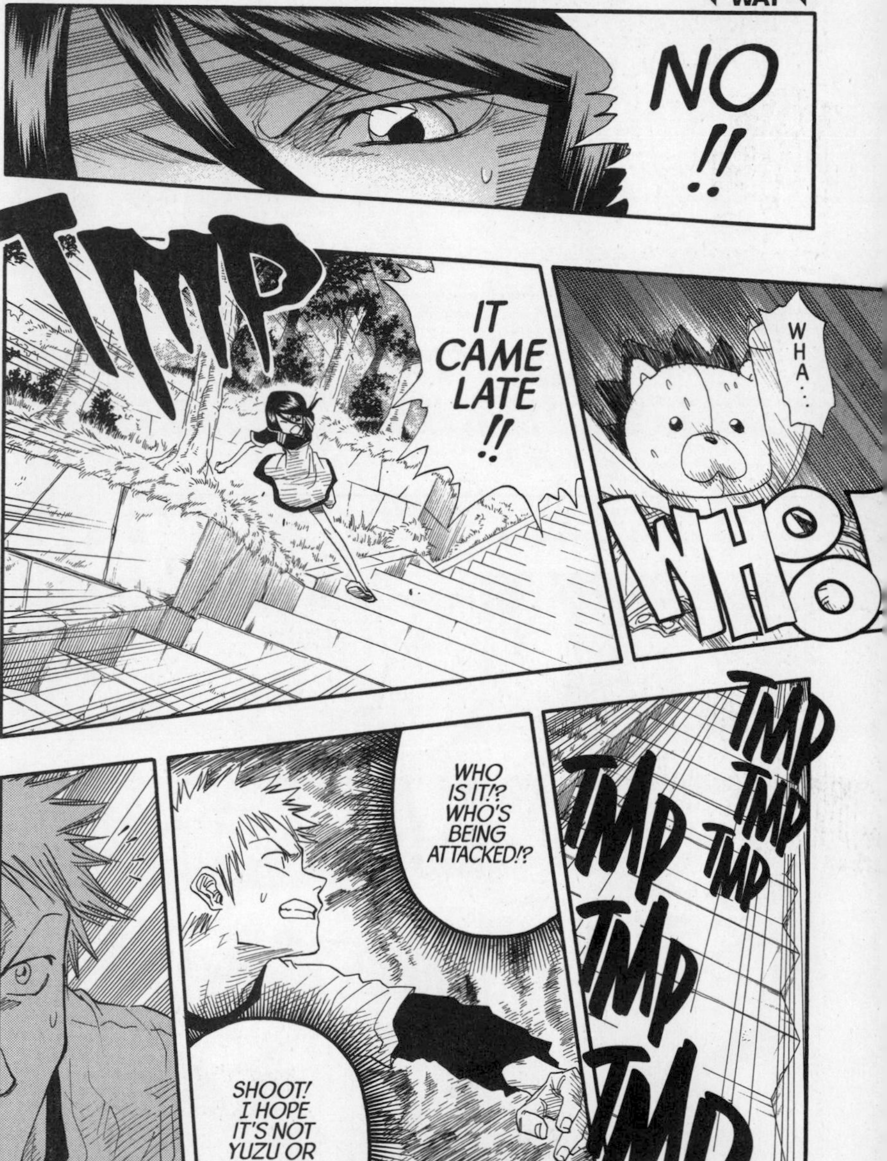
NO!!
WHA...
WHO
TMP
IT CAME LATE!!
TMP TMP TMP TMP TMP TMP TMP
WHO IS IT!? WHO'S BEING ATTACKED!?
SHOOT! I HOPE IT'S NOT YUZU OR KARIN!!

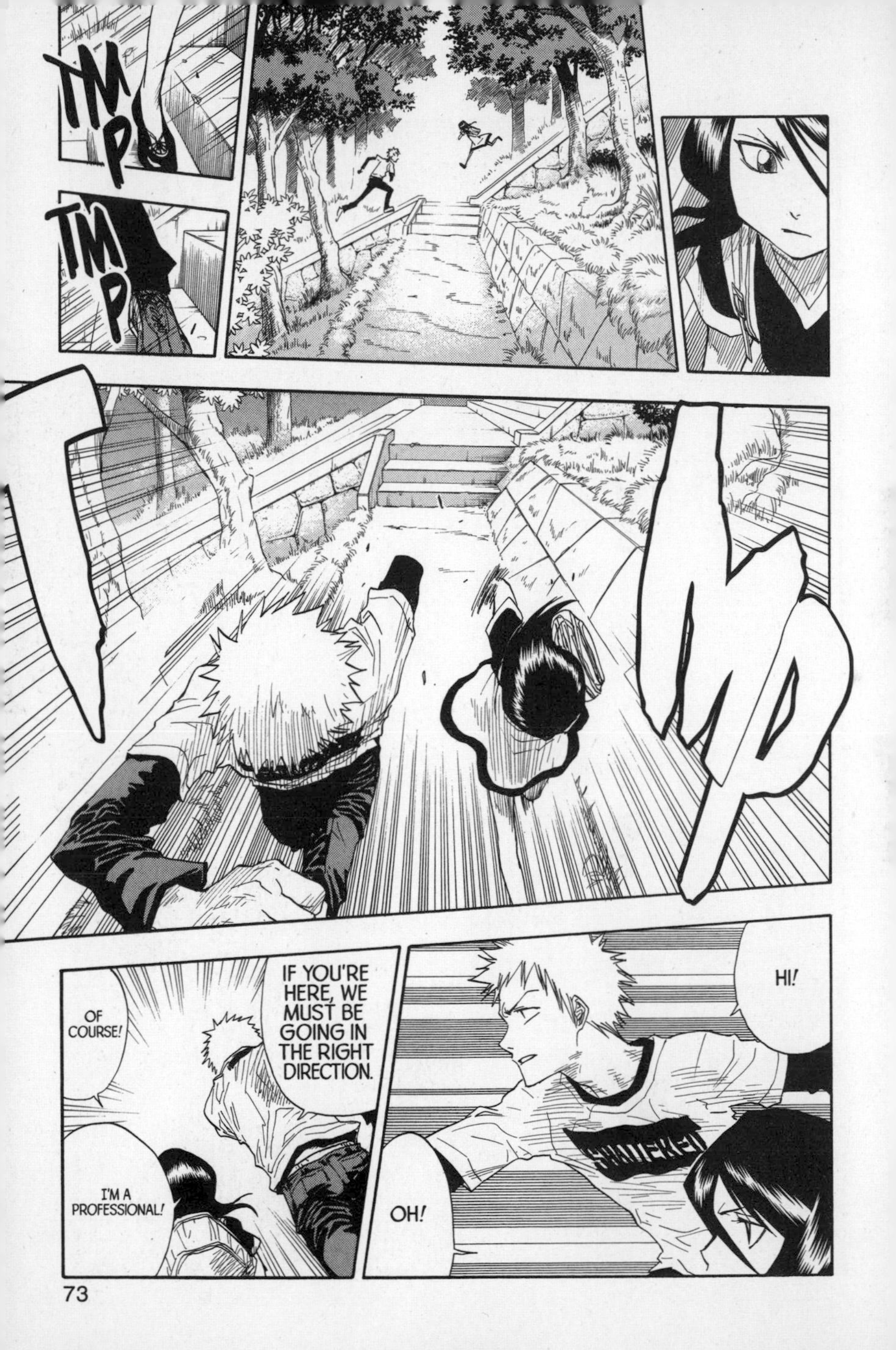
TMP
TMP
TMP
HI!
OH!
IF YOU'RE HERE, WE MUST BE GOING IN THE RIGHT DIRECTION.
OF COURSE!
I'M A PROFESSIONAL!

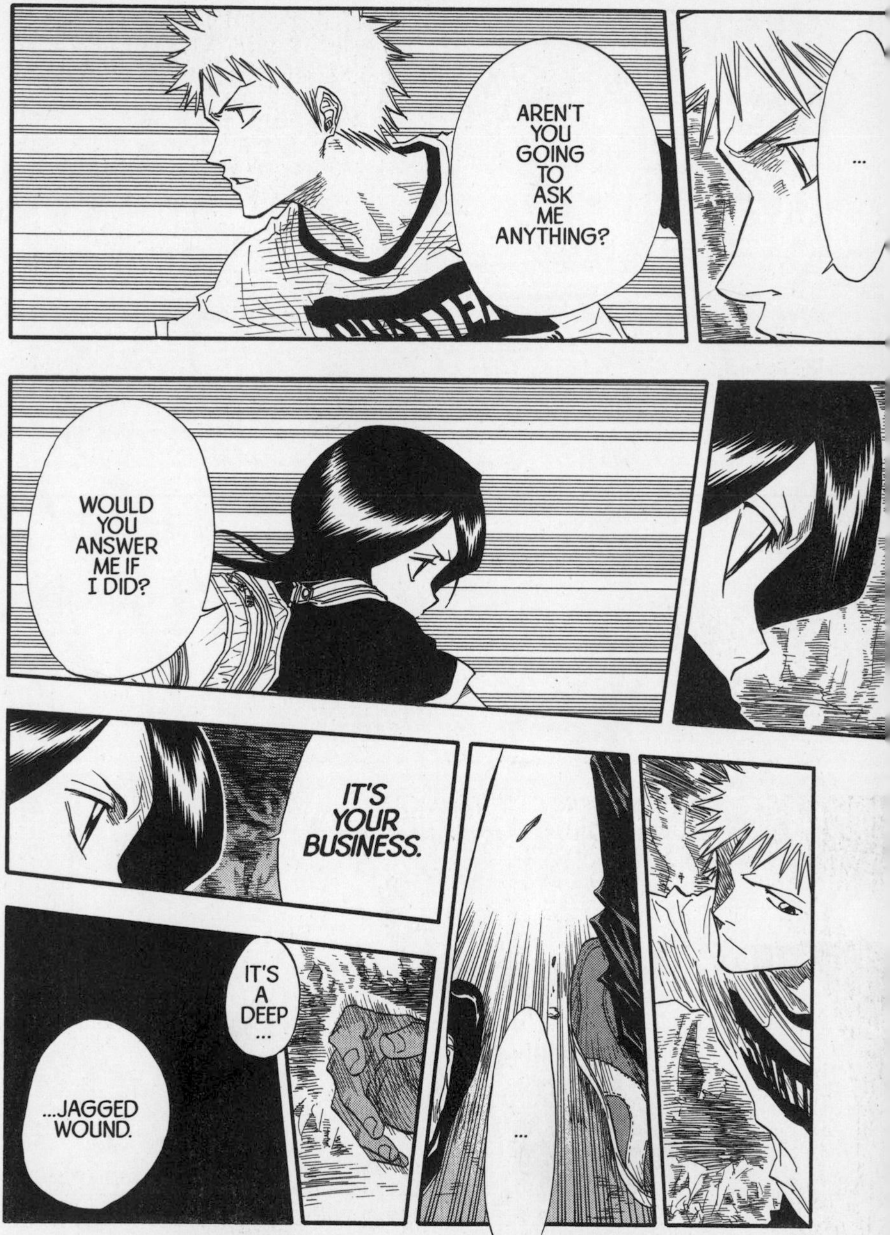
...
AREN'T YOU GOING TO ASK ME ANYTHING?
WOULD YOU ANSWER ME IF I DID?
...
IT'S YOUR BUSINESS.
IT'S A DEEP ...
...JAGGED WOUND.

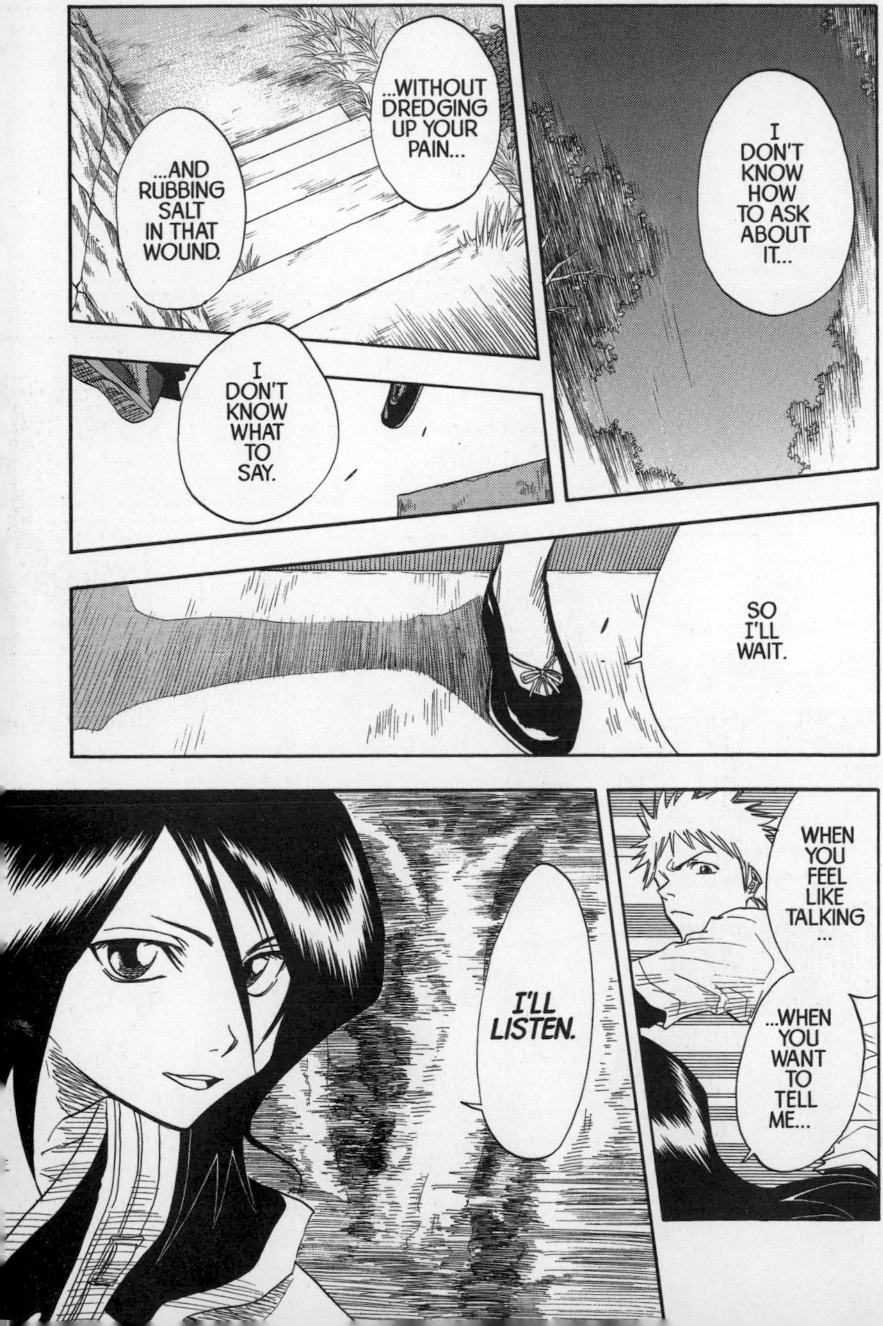
I DON'T KNOW HOW TO ASK ABOUT IT...
...WITHOUT DREDGING UP YOUR PAIN...
...AND RUBBING SALT IN THAT WOUND.
I DON'T KNOW WHAT TO SAY.
SO I'LL WAIT.
WHEN YOU FEEL LIKE TALKING...
...WHEN YOU WANT TO TELL ME...
I'LL LISTEN.

READ THIS WAY

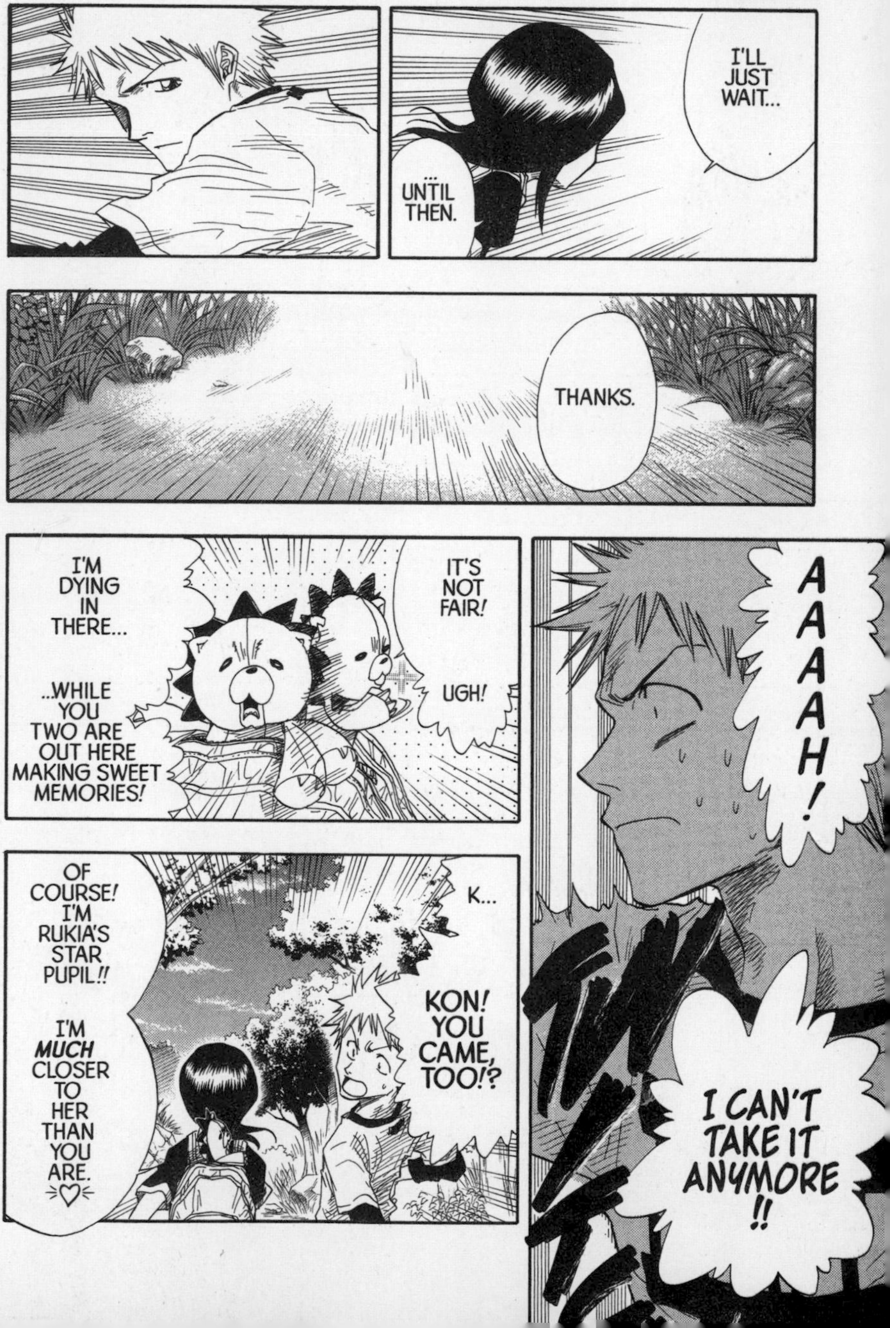
I'LL JUST WAIT...
...UNTIL THEN.
THANKS.
AAAAH!
I CAN'T TAKE IT ANYMORE!!
IT'S NOT FAIR!
I'M DYING IN THERE...
UGH!
...WHILE YOU TWO ARE OUT HERE MAKING SWEET MEMORIES!
K...
KON! YOU CAME, TOO!?
OF COURSE! I'M RUKIA'S STAR PUPIL!!
I'M *MUCH* CLOSER TO HER THAN YOU ARE. ♡

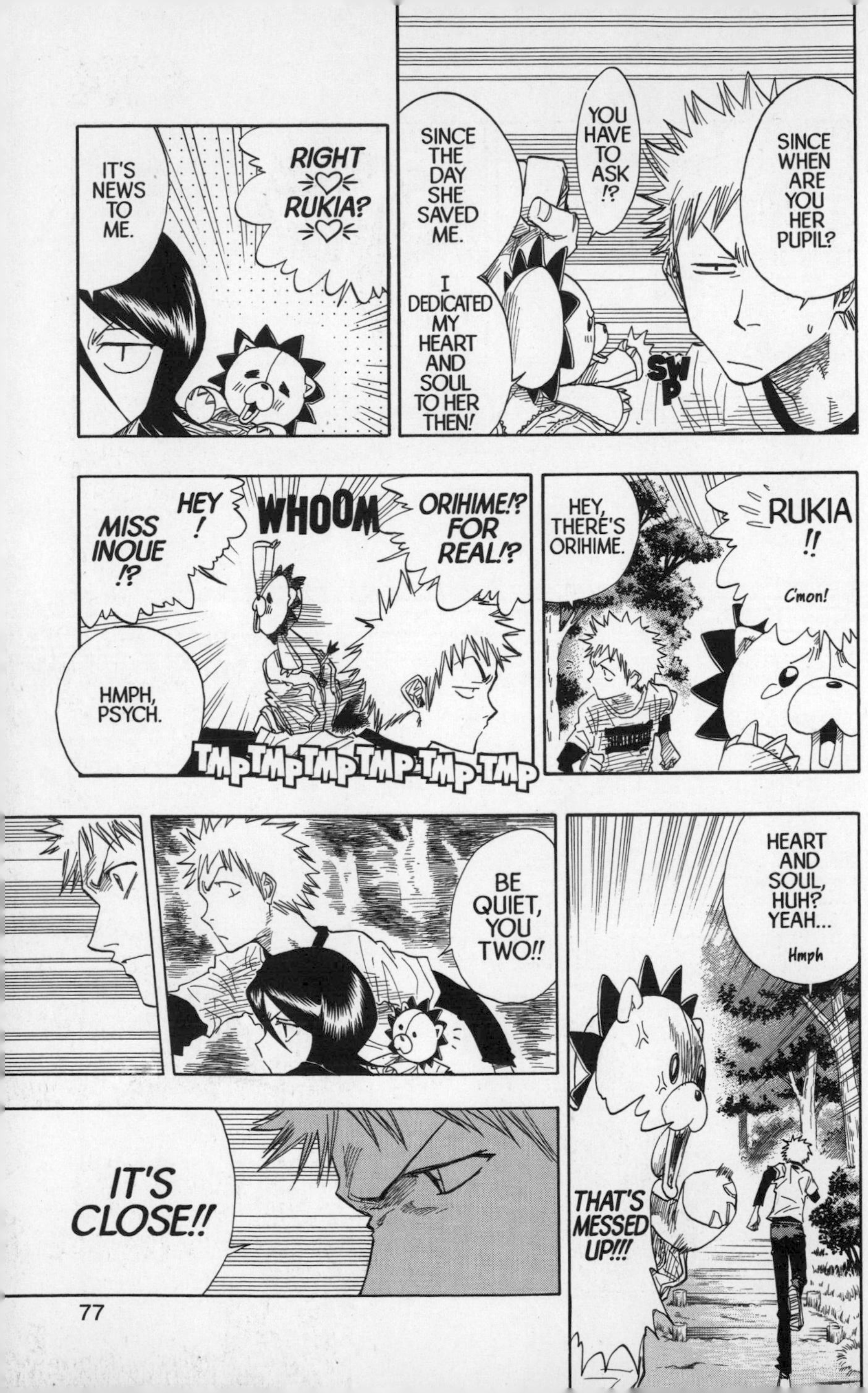
SINCE WHEN ARE YOU HER PUPIL?
YOU HAVE TO ASK!?
SINCE THE DAY SHE SAVED ME.
I DEDICATED MY HEART AND SOUL TO HER THEN!
SWP
RIGHT ♡ RUKIA? ♡
IT'S NEWS TO ME.
RUKIA!!
HEY, THERE'S ORIHIME.
C'mon!
ORIHIME!? FOR REAL!?
WHOOM
HEY!
MISS INOUE!?
HMPH, PSYCH.
TMP TMP TMP TMP TMP TMP
HEART AND SOUL, HUH? YEAH...
Hmph
THAT'S MESSED UP!!!
BE QUIET, YOU TWO!!
IT'S CLOSE!!

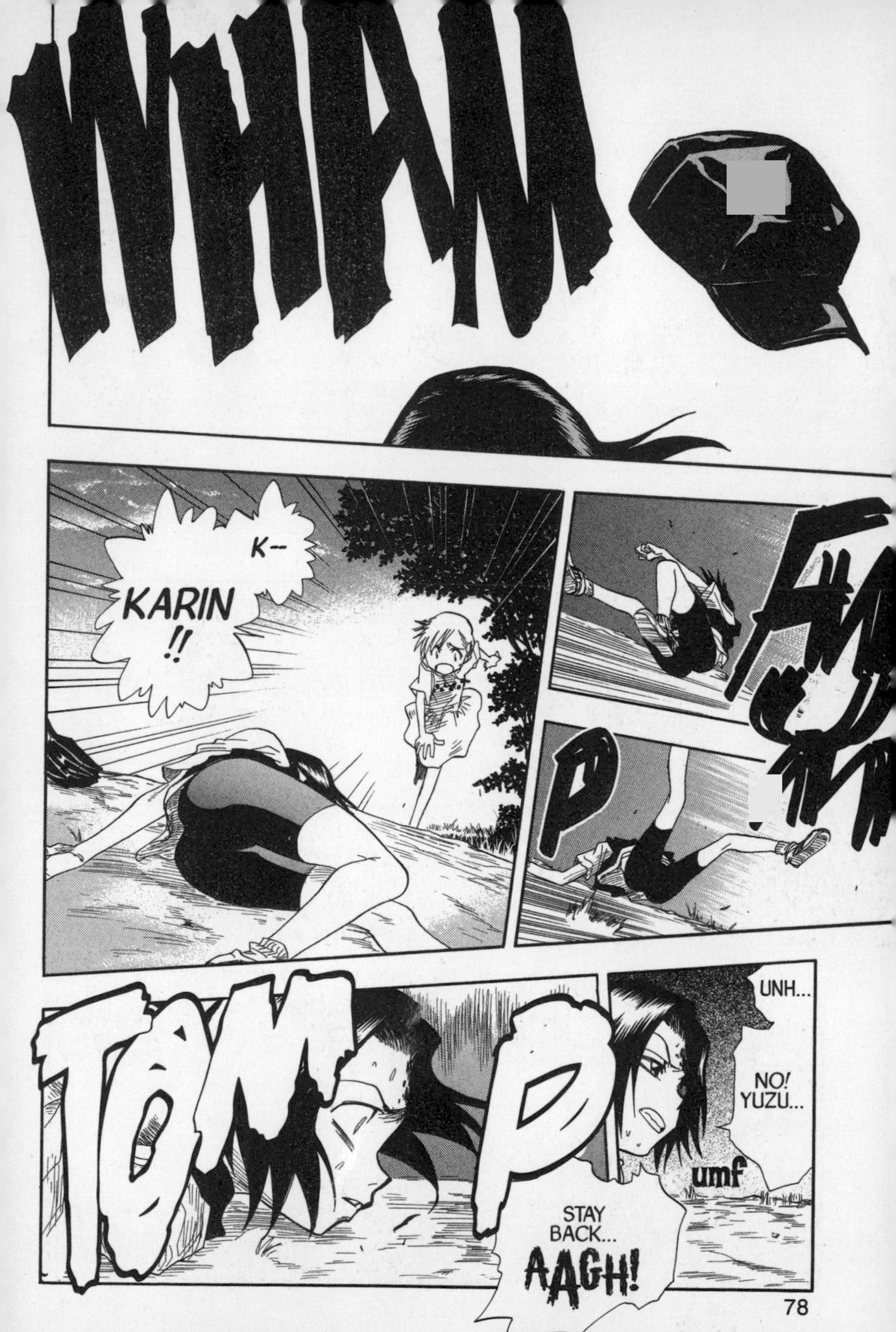
WHAM
K--
KARIN !!
UNH...
NO! YUZU...
umf
STAY BACK...
AAGH!
TOMP

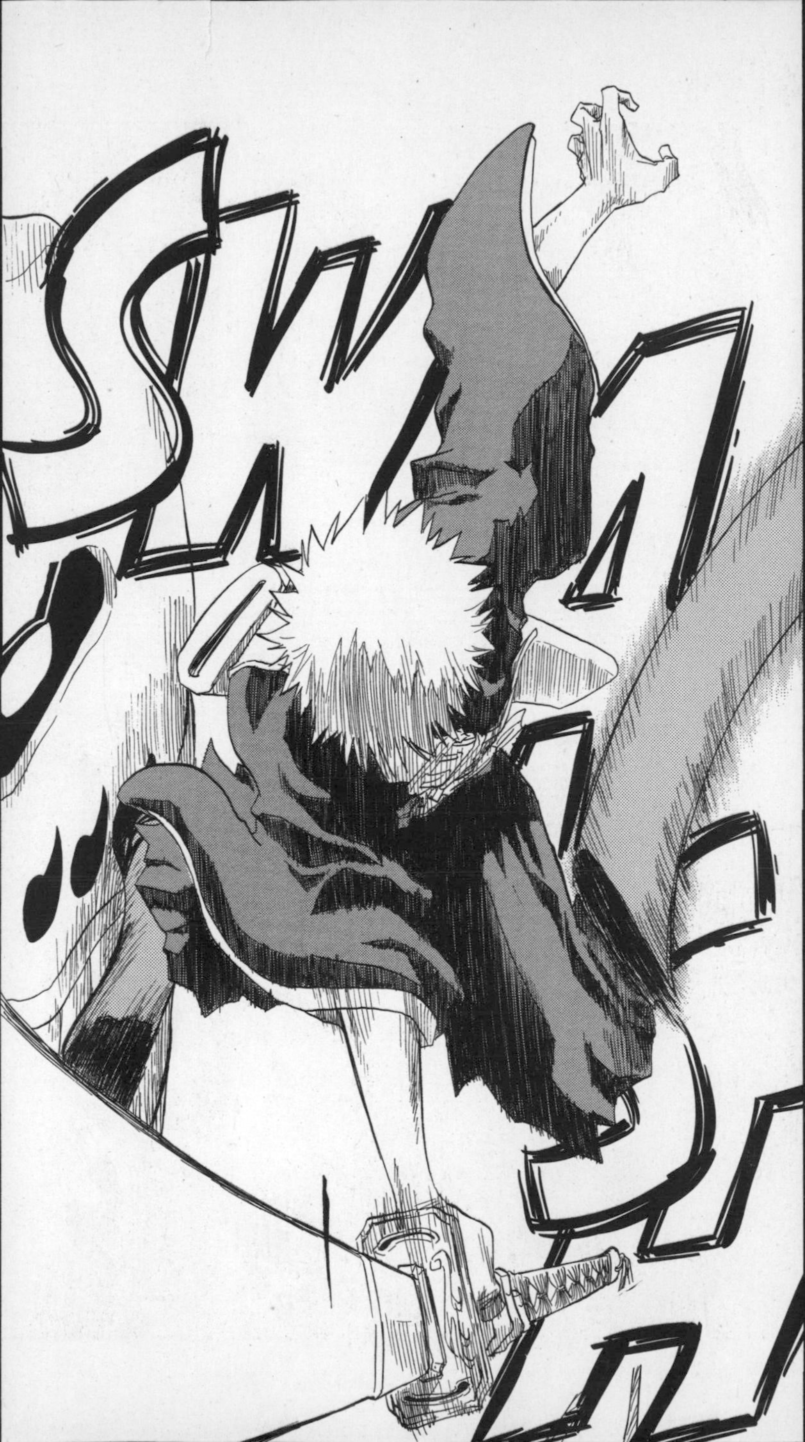

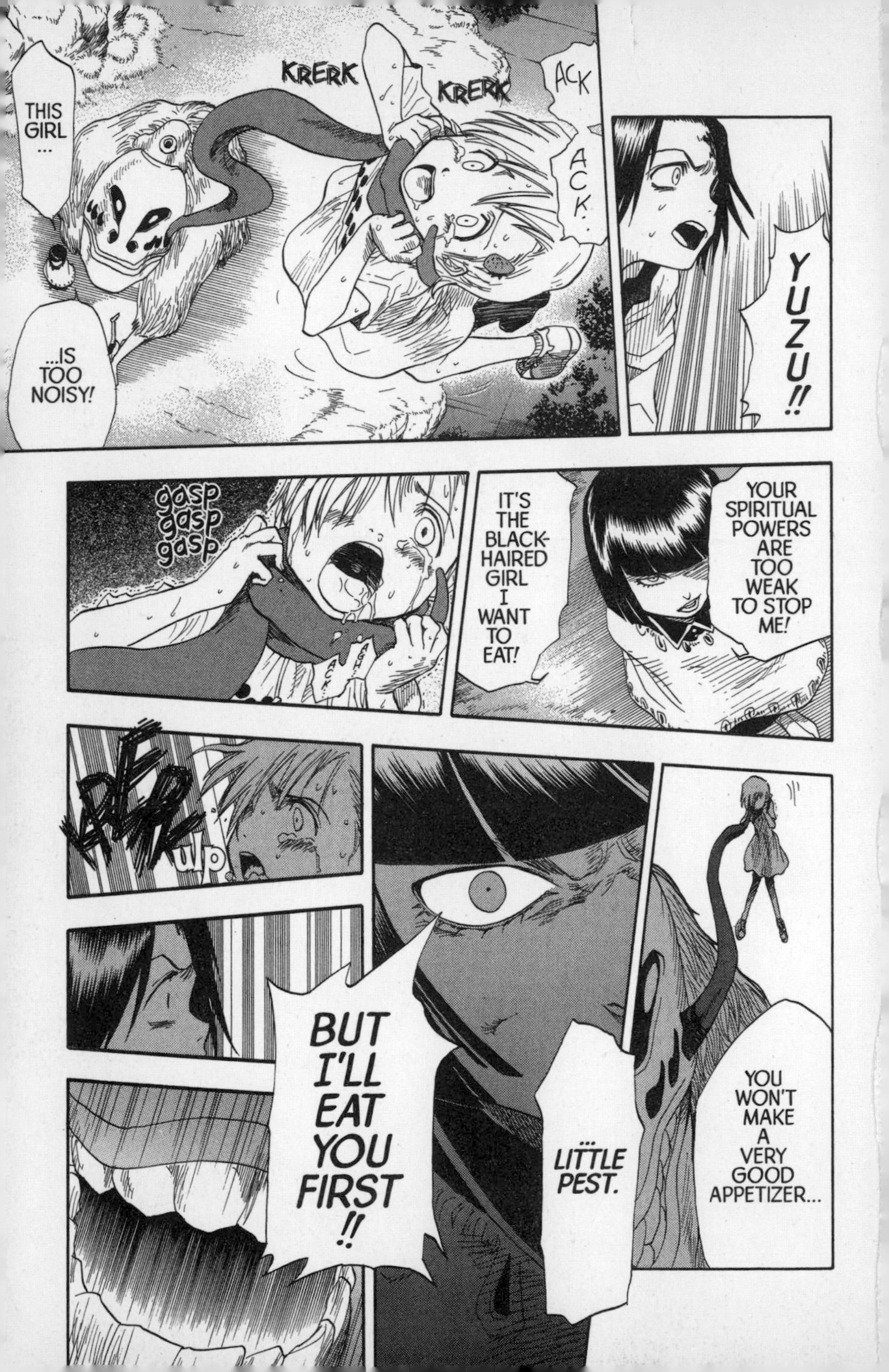
YUZU!!
ACK
ACK.
KRERK
KRERK
THIS GIRL...
...IS TOO NOISY!
YOUR SPIRITUAL POWERS ARE TOO WEAK TO STOP ME!
IT'S THE BLACK-HAIRED GIRL I WANT TO EAT!
gasp gasp gasp
ACK...
AGH...
YOU WON'T MAKE A VERY GOOD APPETIZER...
...LITTLE PEST.
BUT I'LL EAT YOU FIRST!!
ulp

READ THIS WAY

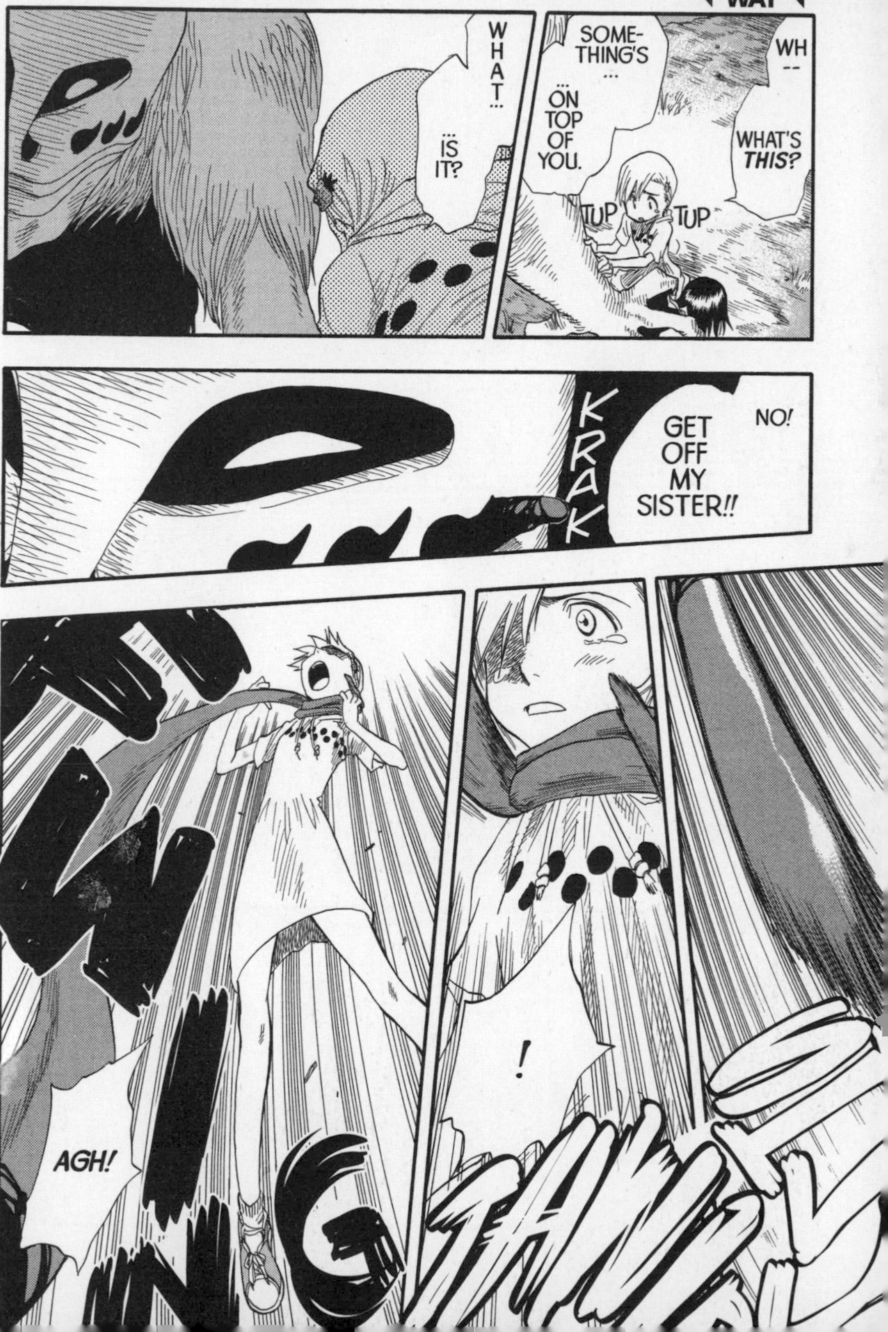
WH --
WHAT'S *THIS?*
SOME-THING'S ...
... ON TOP OF YOU.
TUP
TUP
WHAT...
... IS IT?
NO!
GET OFF MY SISTER!!
KRAK
!
AGH!

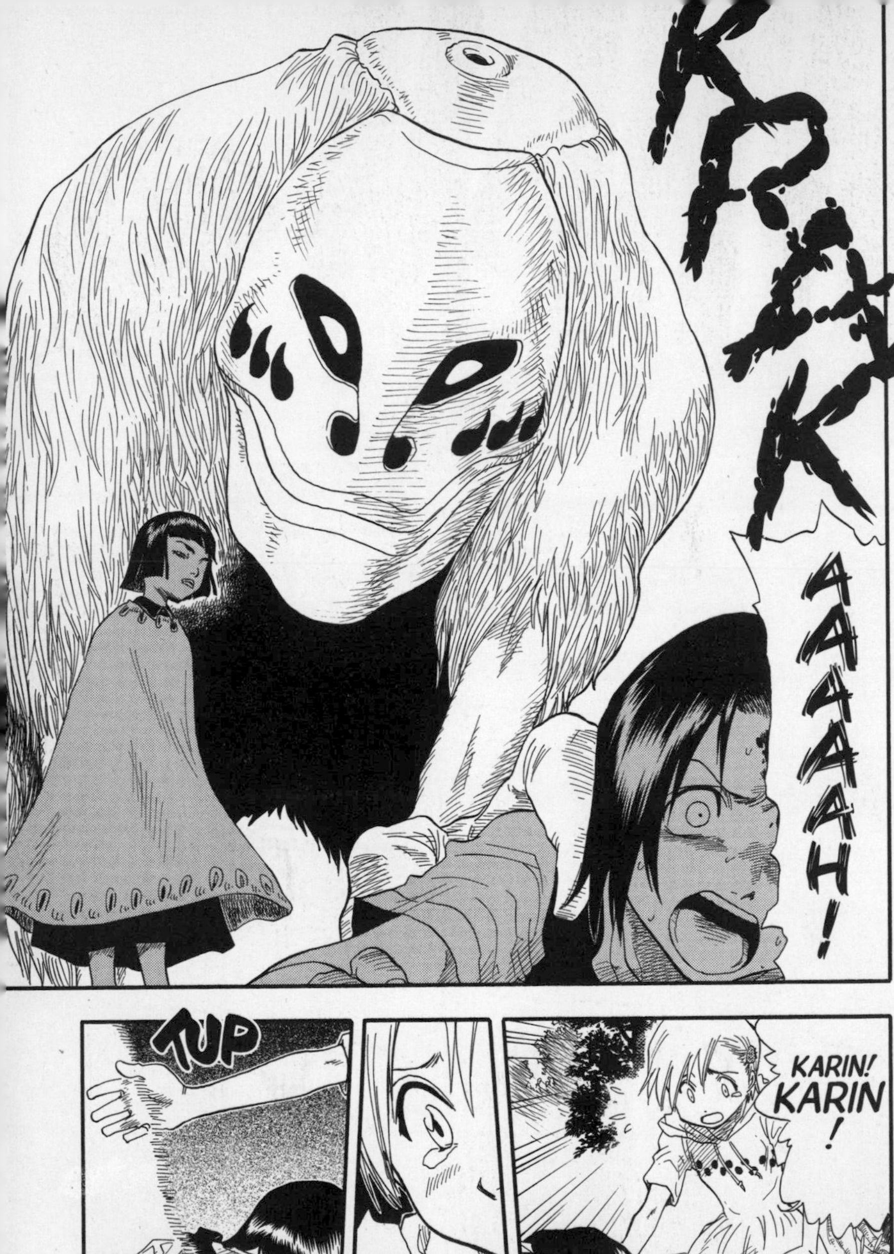
KRAK
AAAAAH!
KARIN! KARIN!
!!
TUP

READ THIS WAY

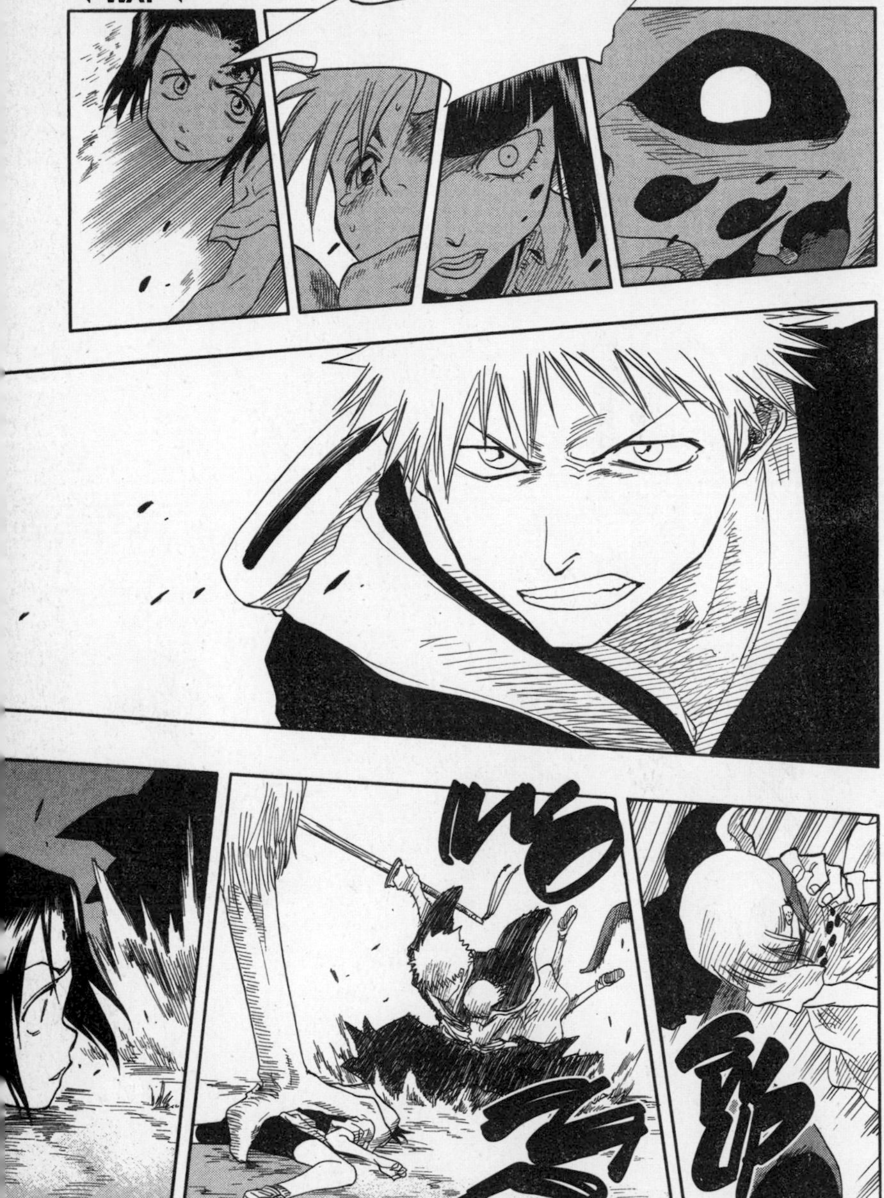

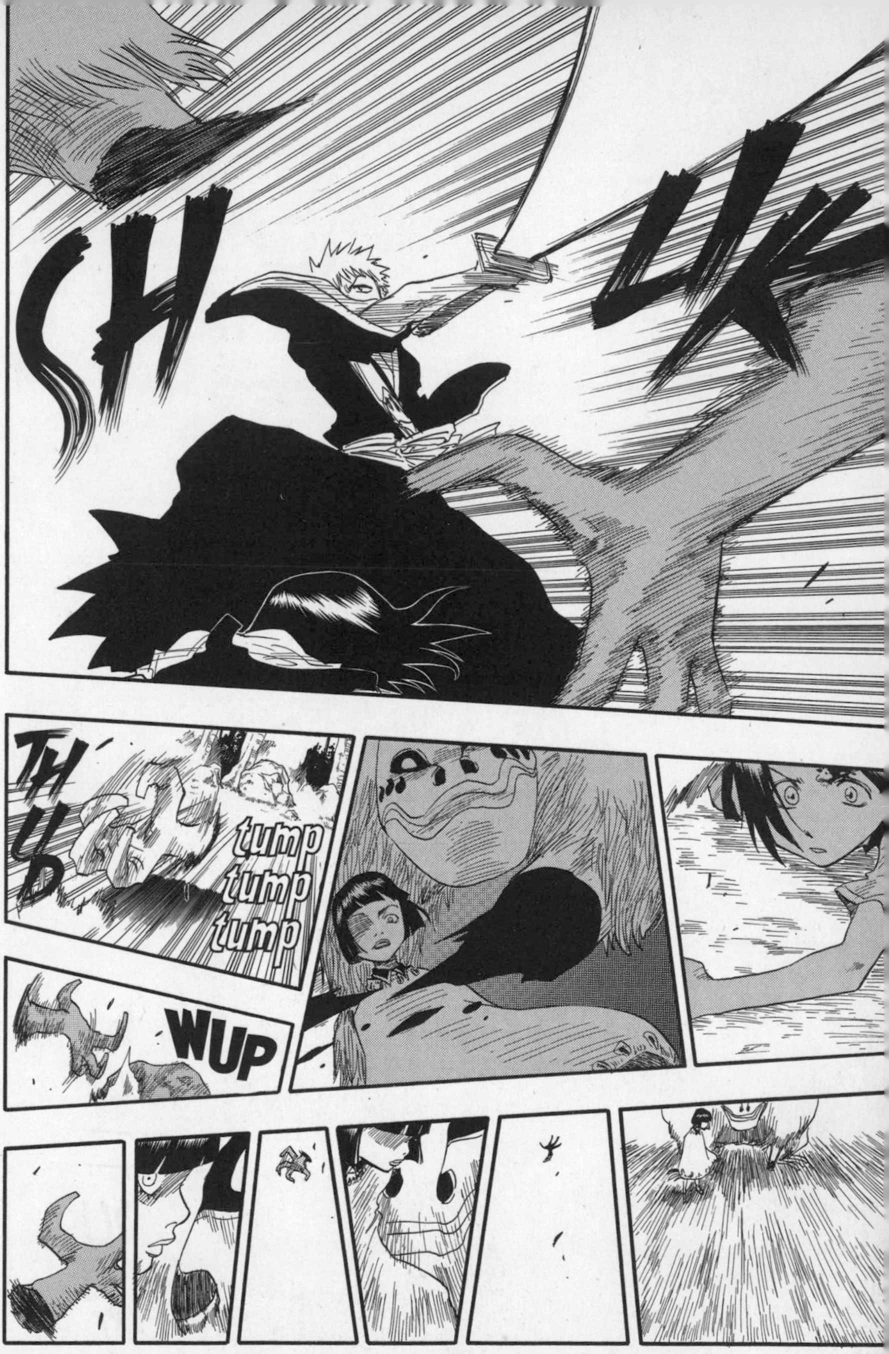
CHUK
THUD
tump
tump
tump
WUP

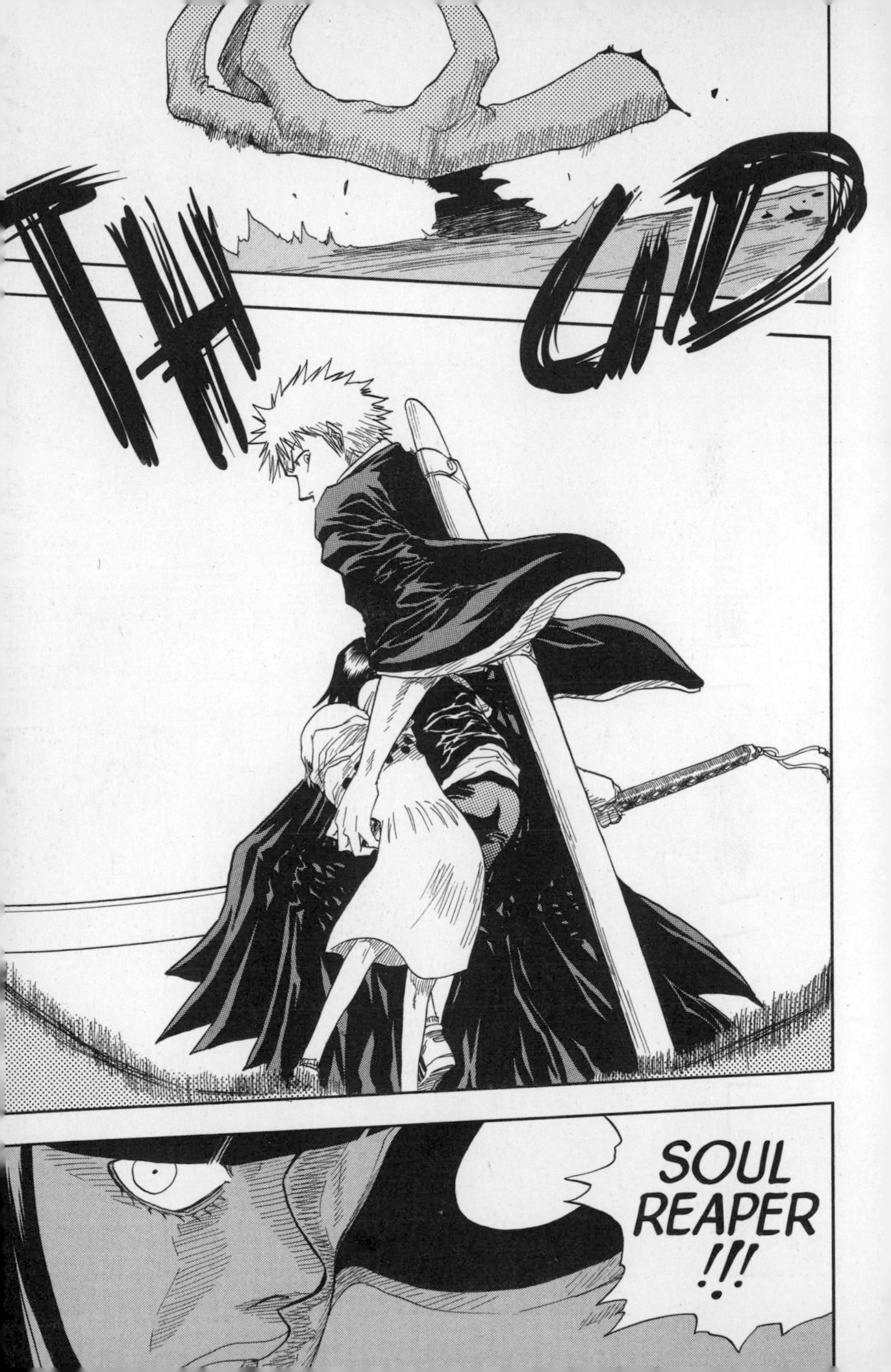
THUD
SOUL REAPER !!!

READ THIS WAY

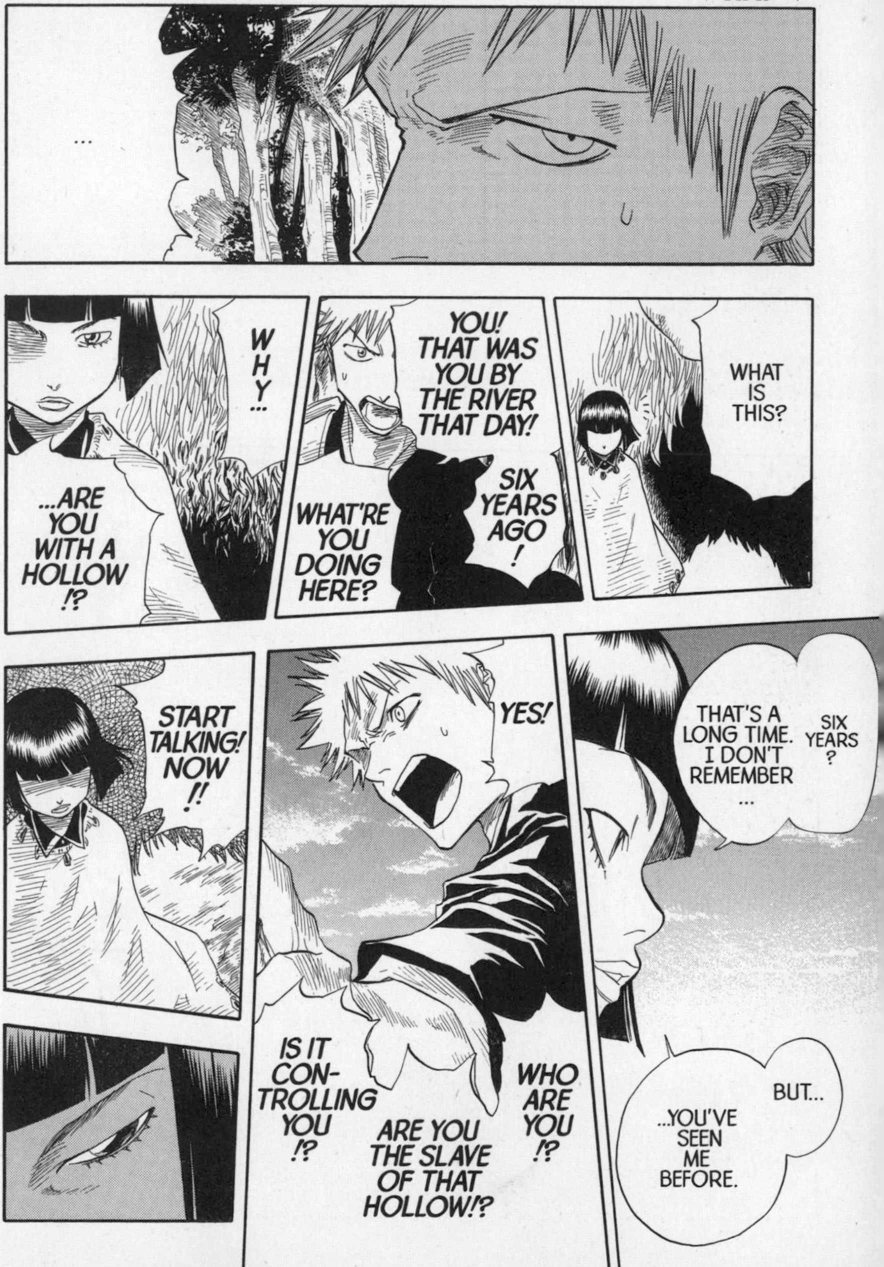
...
WHAT IS THIS?
YOU! THAT WAS YOU BY THE RIVER THAT DAY!
SIX YEARS AGO!
WHAT'RE YOU DOING HERE?
WHY...
...ARE YOU WITH A HOLLOW!?
SIX YEARS?
THAT'S A LONG TIME. I DON'T REMEMBER...
BUT...
...YOU'VE SEEN ME BEFORE.
YES!
WHO ARE YOU!?
ARE YOU THE SLAVE OF THAT HOLLOW!?
IS IT CONTROLLING YOU!?
START TALKING! NOW!!

READ THIS WAY

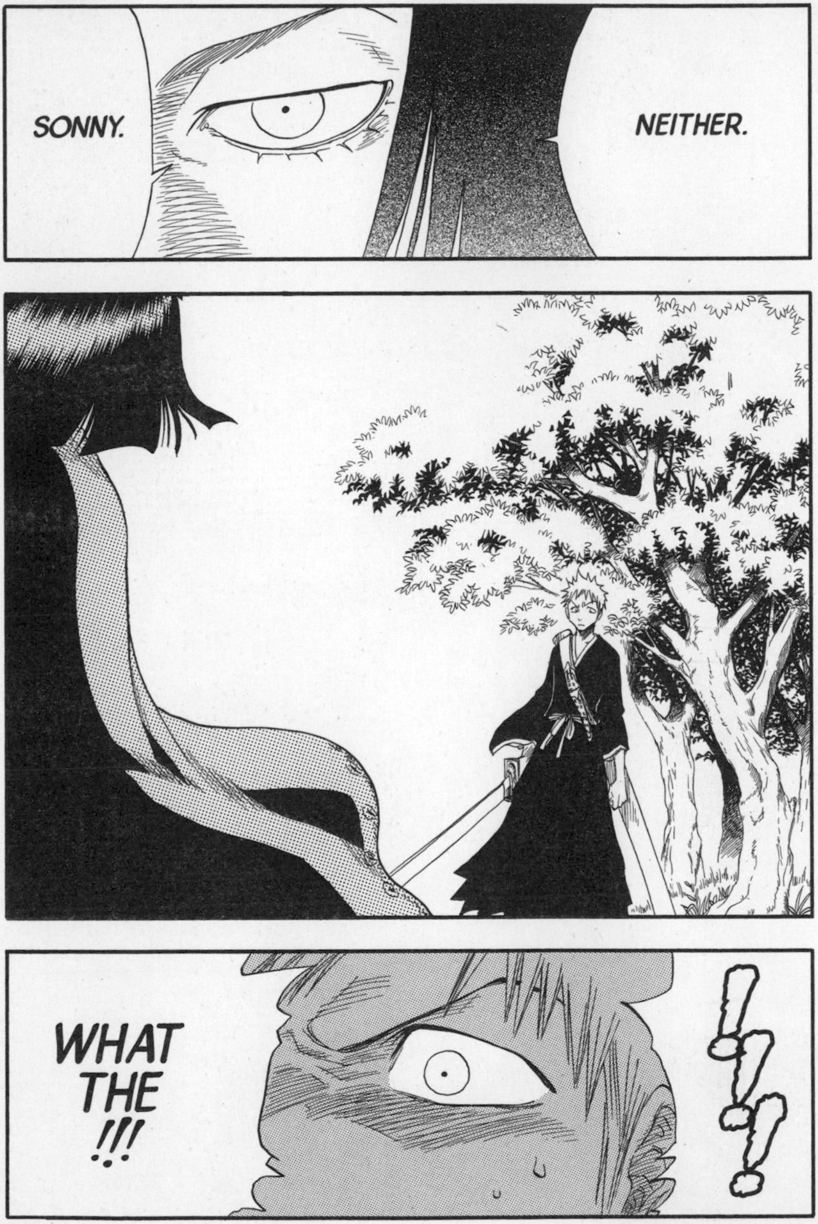

NEITHER.
SONNY.
!!
WHAT THE !!!

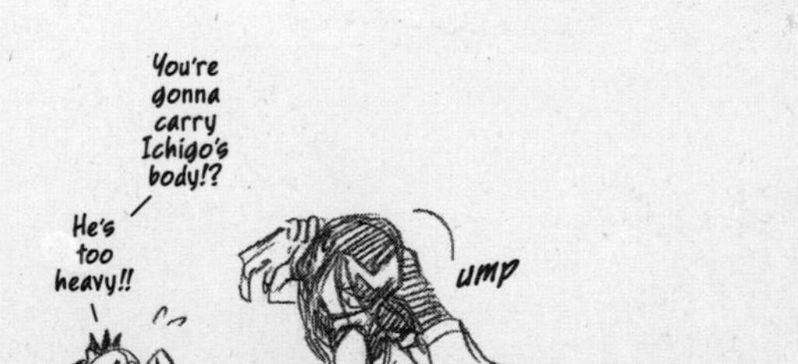
You're gonna carry Ichigo's body!?
He's too heavy!!
ump

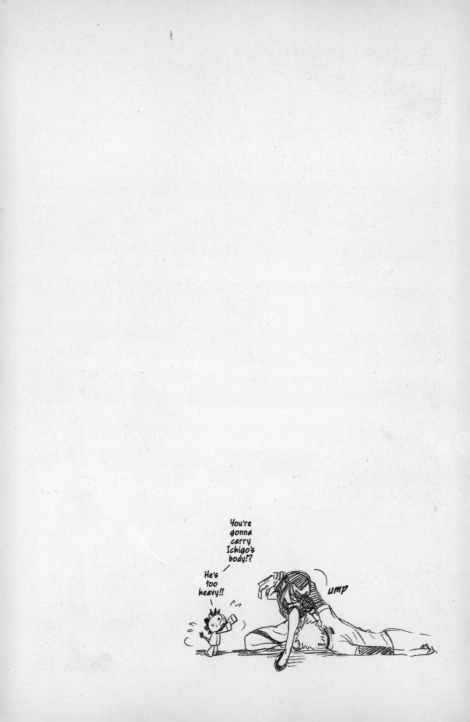

21. 6/17 op. 5 A Fighting Boy

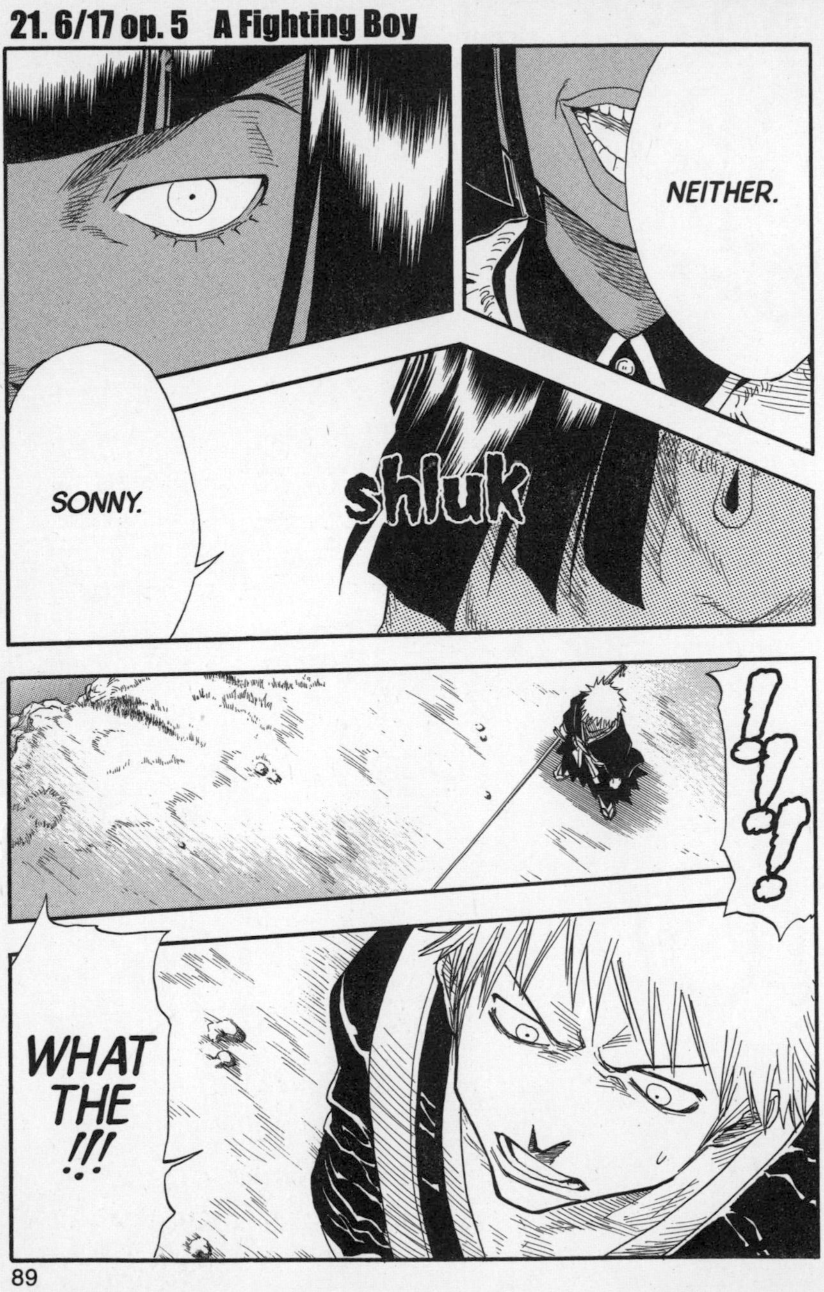
NEITHER.
SONNY.
shluk
!!!
WHAT THE !!!

21. 6/17 op. 5 A Fighting Boy

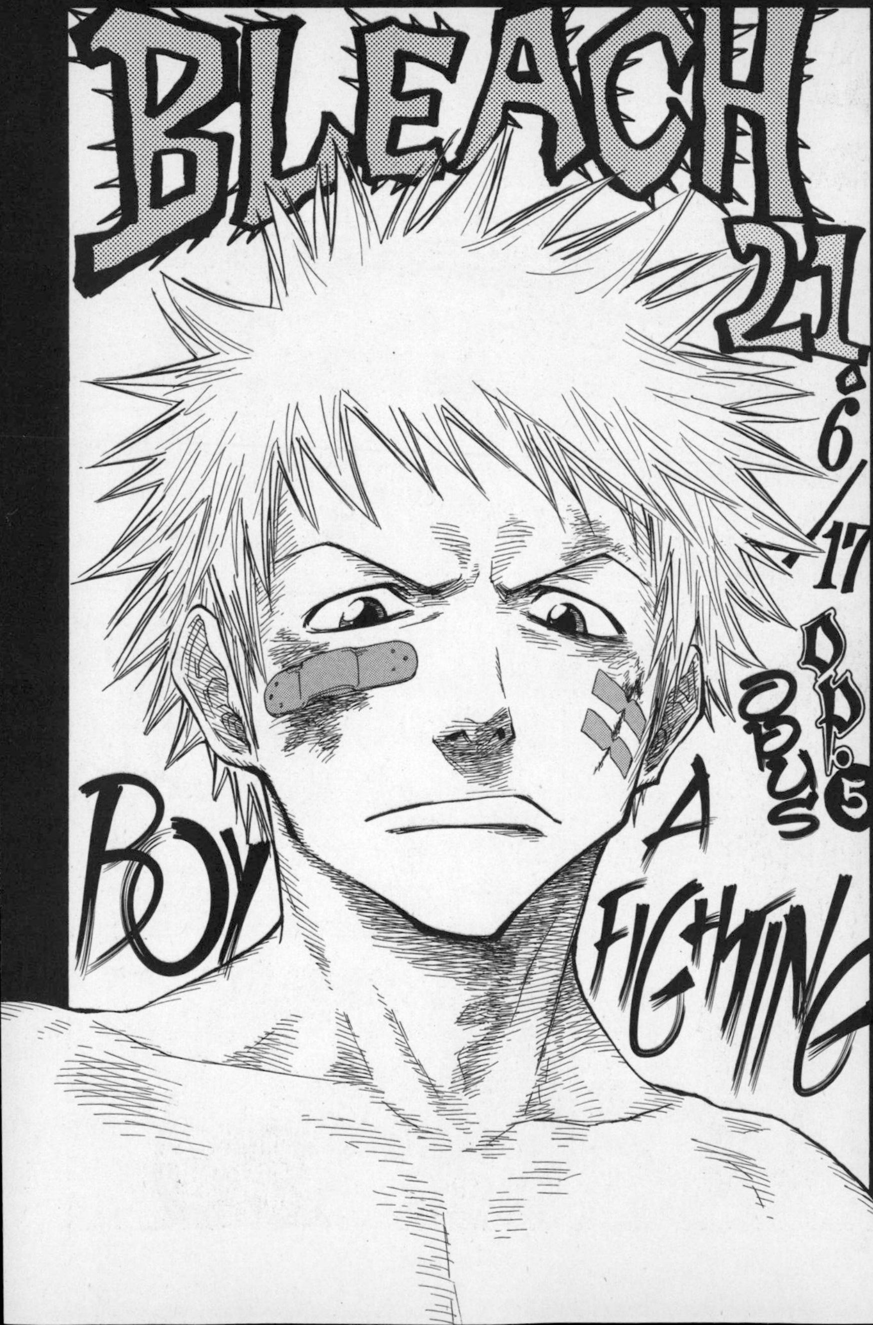
BLEACH
21. 6/17 op.5
OPUS
A FIGHTING
BOY

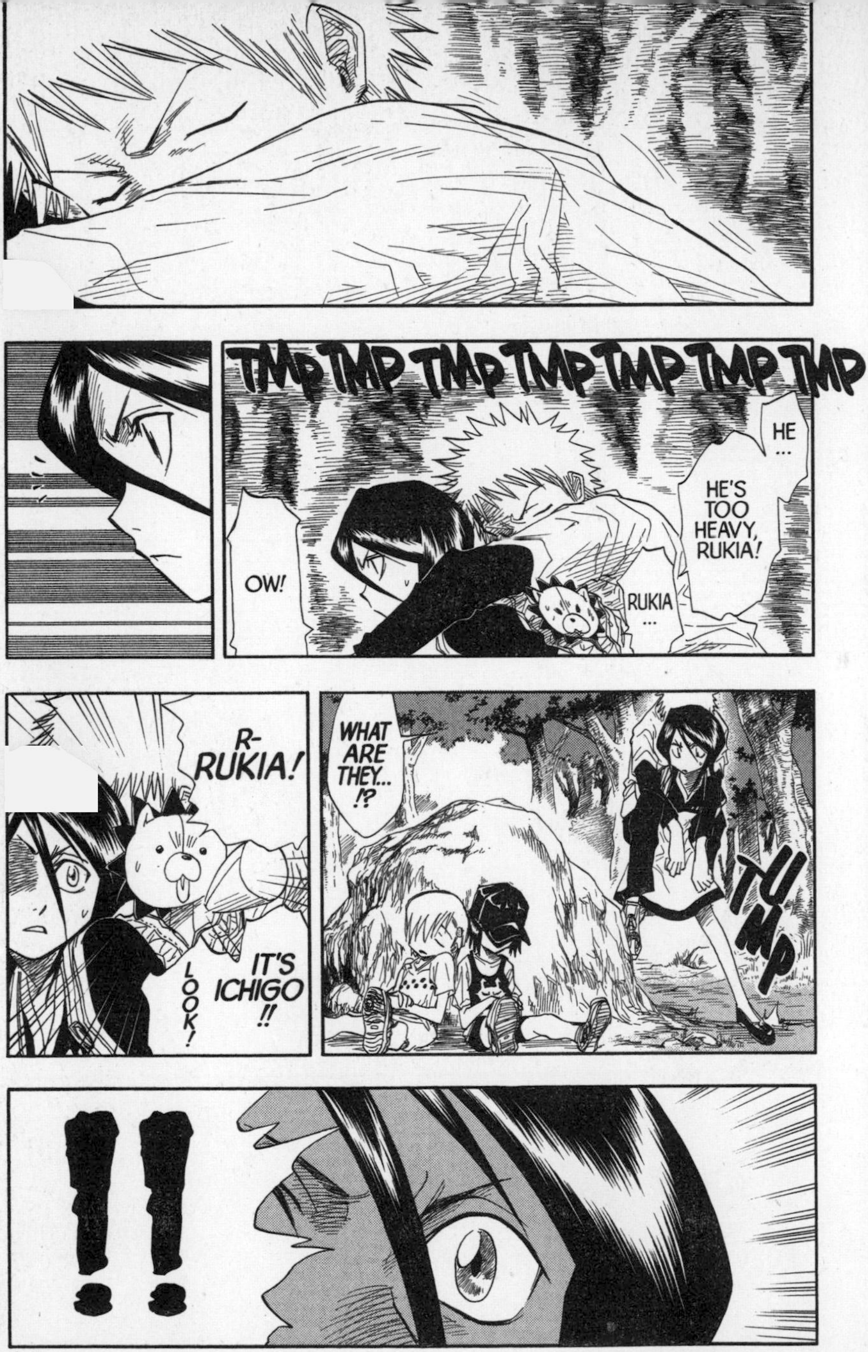
TMP TMP TMP TMP TMP TMP TMP
HE...
HE'S TOO HEAVY, RUKIA!
RUKIA...
OW!
WHAT ARE THEY...!?
TUMP
R-RUKIA!
IT'S ICHIGO!!
LOOK!
!!

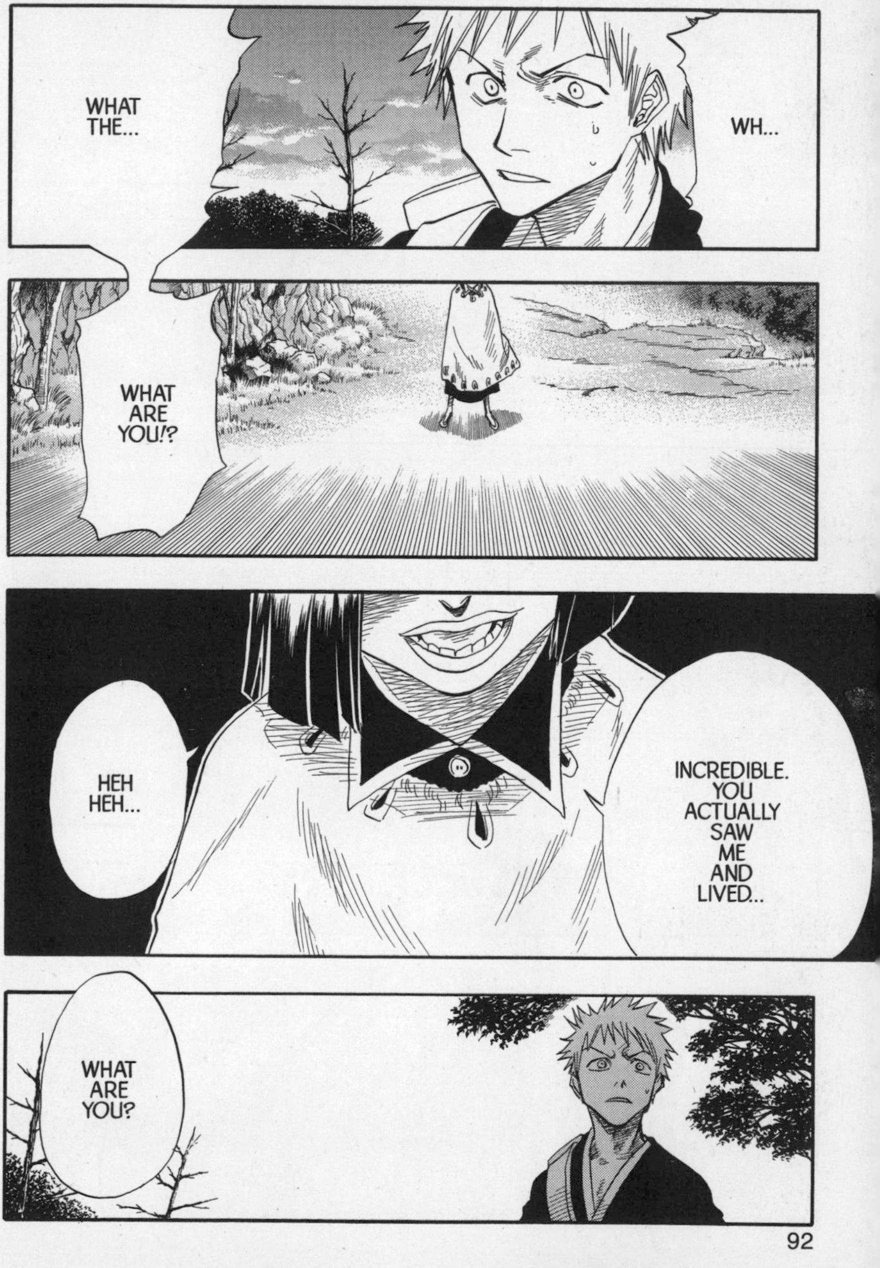
WH...
WHAT THE...
WHAT ARE YOU!?
INCREDIBLE. YOU ACTUALLY SAW ME AND LIVED...
HEH HEH...
WHAT ARE YOU?

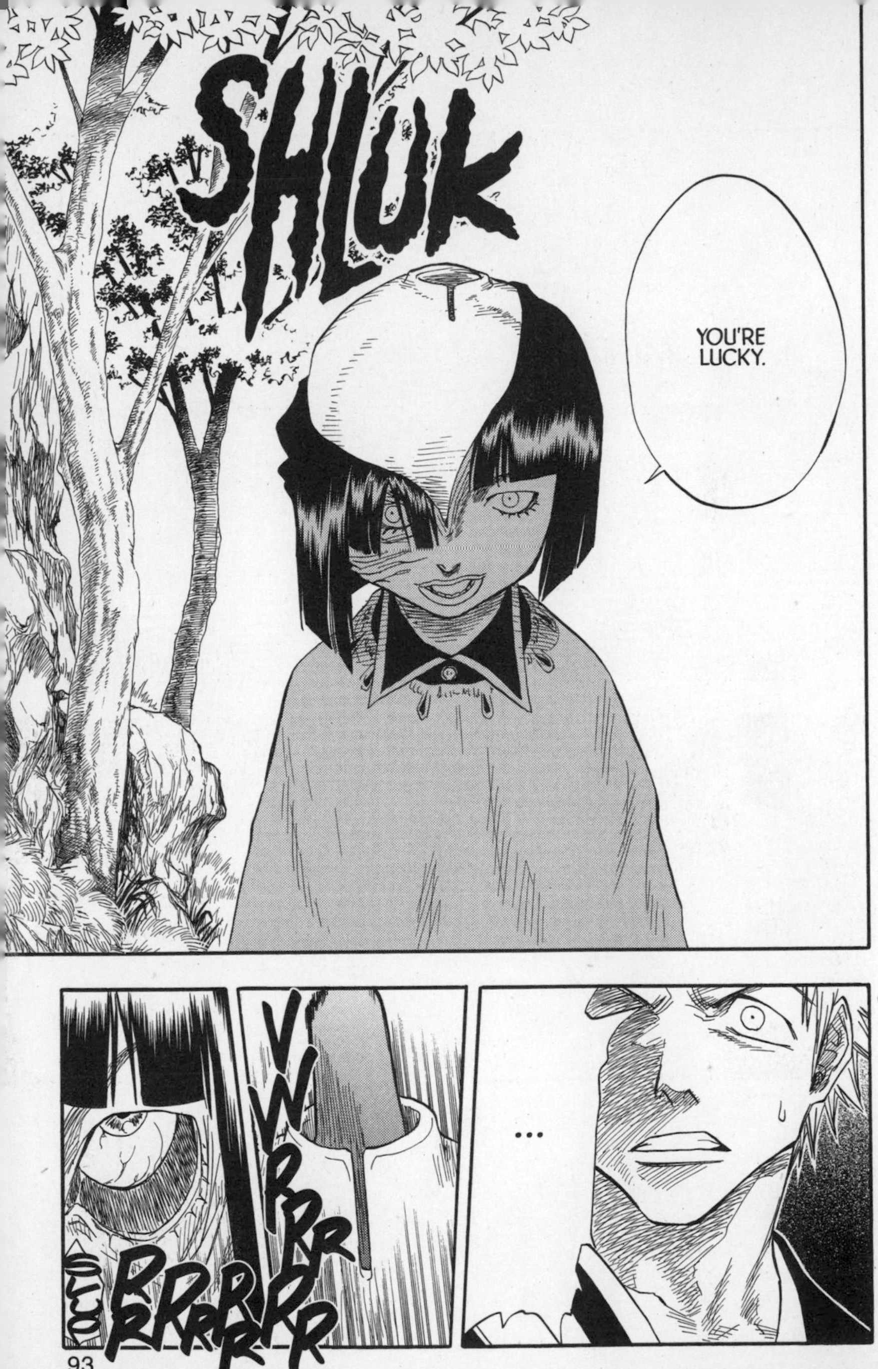
SHLUK
YOU'RE LUCKY.
...
VWRRRRR
RRRRRRR

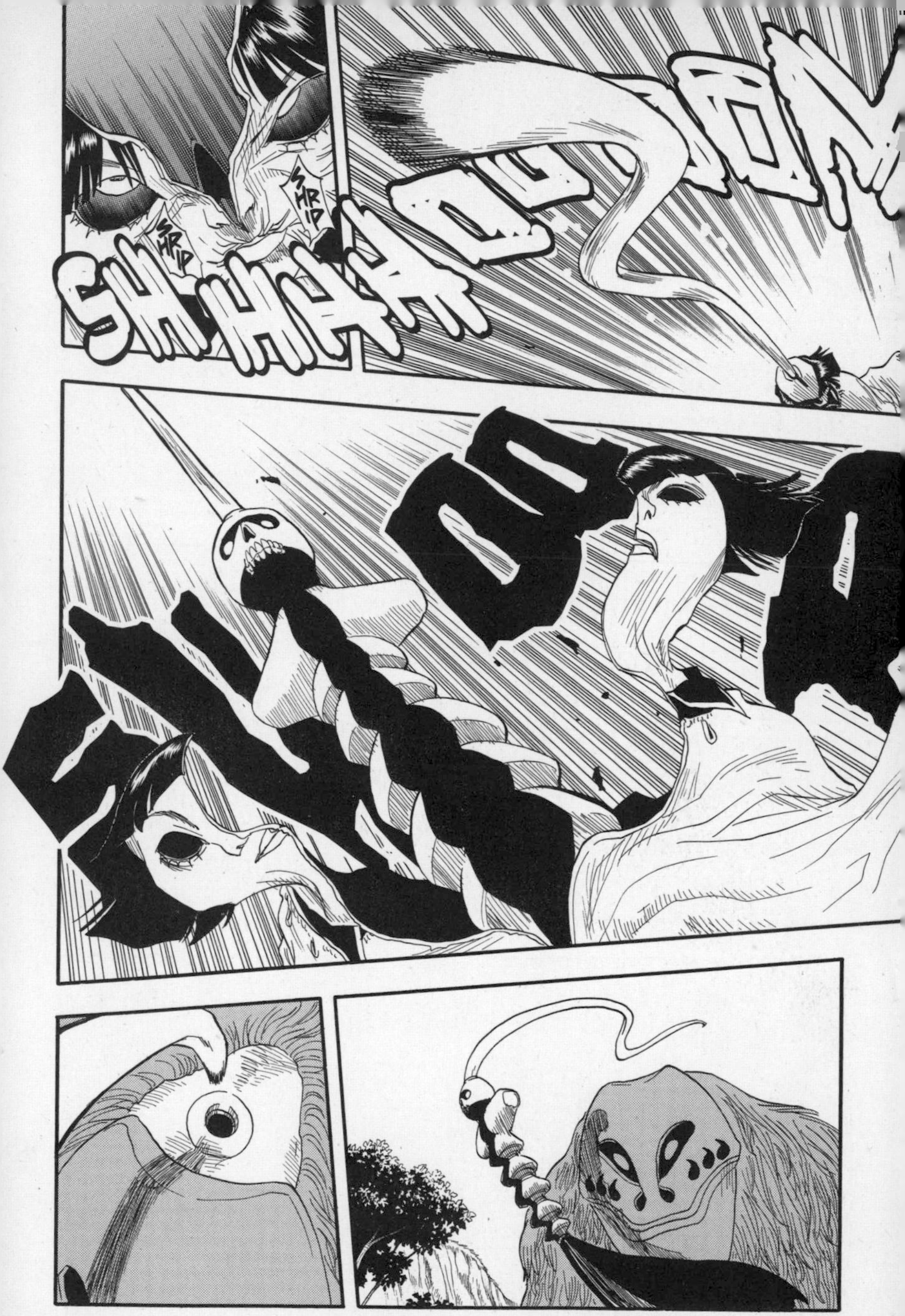
SHRIP
SHRIP

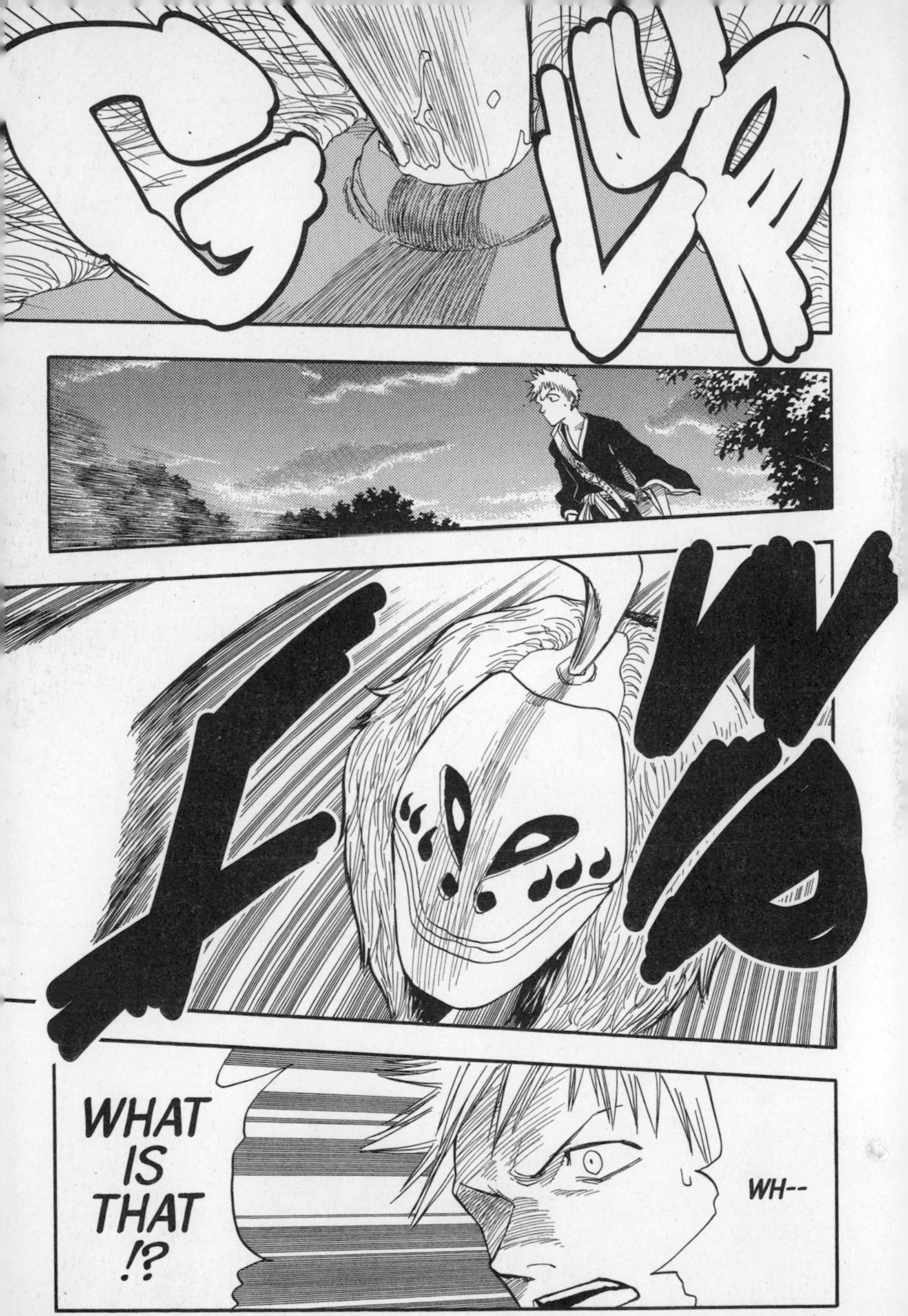
WH--
WHAT IS THAT!?

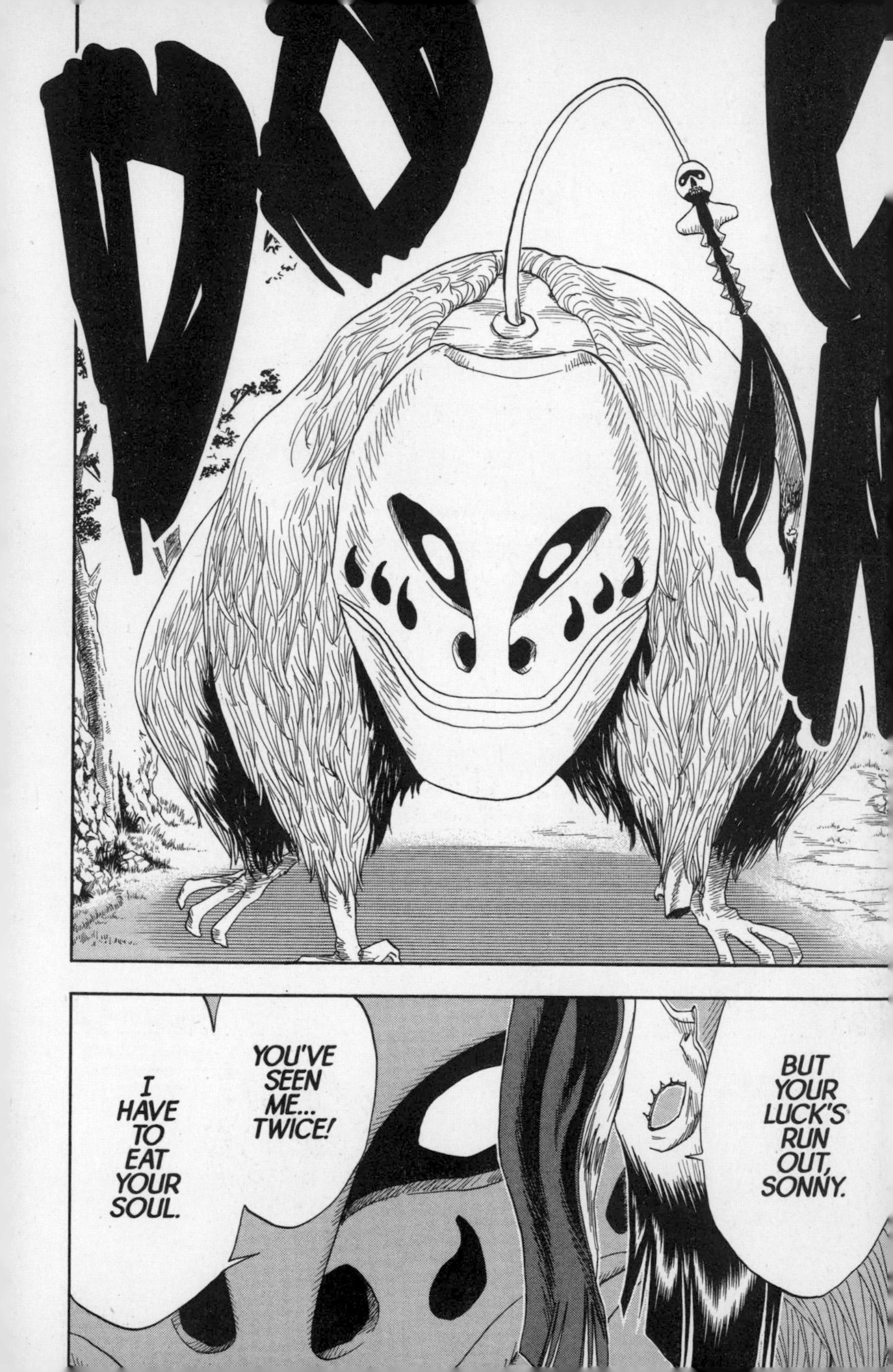
BUT YOUR LUCK'S RUN OUT, SONNY.
YOU'VE SEEN ME... TWICE!
I HAVE TO EAT YOUR SOUL.

READ THIS WAY

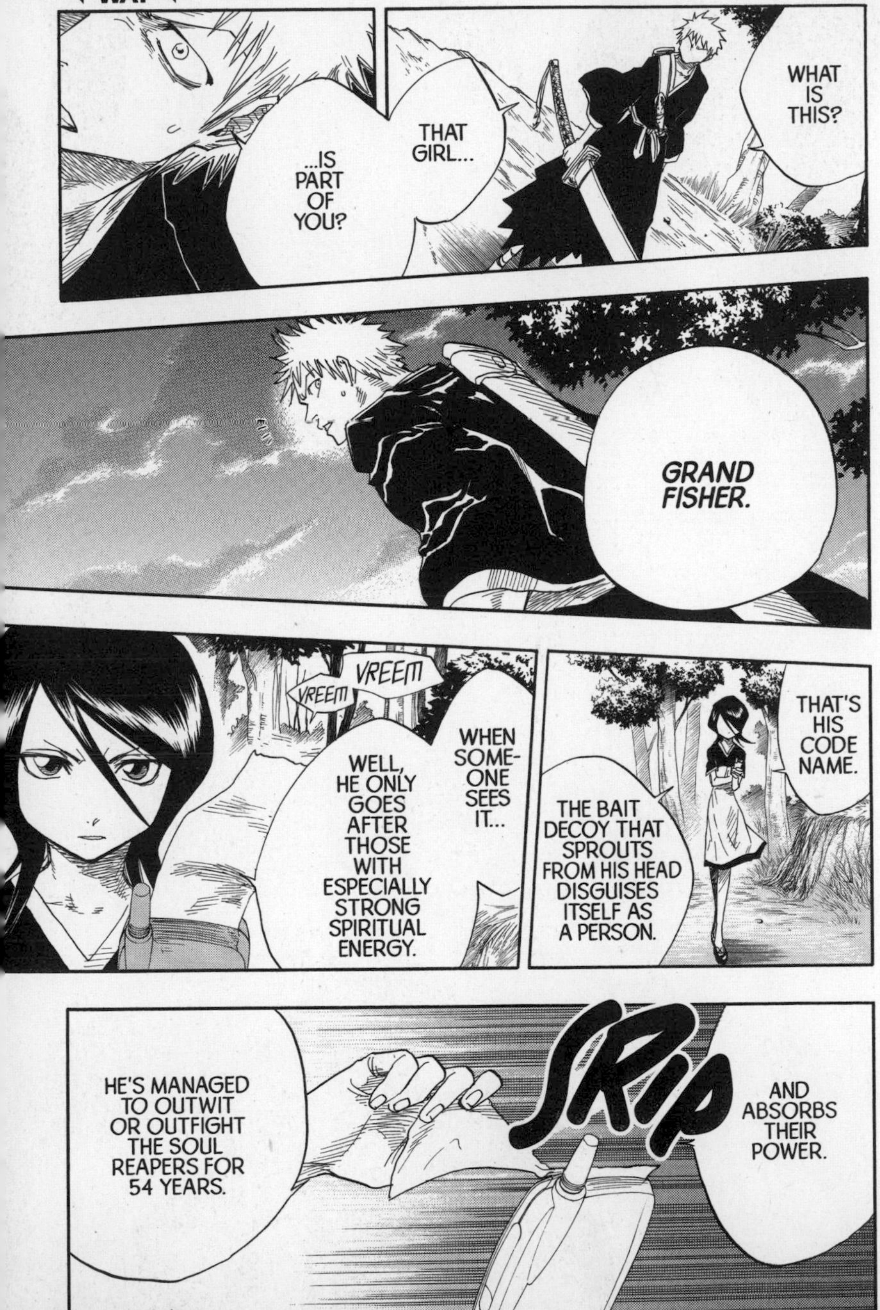
WHAT IS THIS?
THAT GIRL...
...IS PART OF YOU?
GRAND FISHER.
THAT'S HIS CODE NAME.
THE BAIT DECOY THAT SPROUTS FROM HIS HEAD DISGUISES ITSELF AS A PERSON.
VREEM
VREEM
WHEN SOME-ONE SEES IT...
WELL, HE ONLY GOES AFTER THOSE WITH ESPECIALLY STRONG SPIRITUAL ENERGY.
AND ABSORBS THEIR POWER.
SKRIP
HE'S MANAGED TO OUTWIT OR OUTFIGHT THE SOUL REAPERS FOR 54 YEARS.

READ THIS WAY

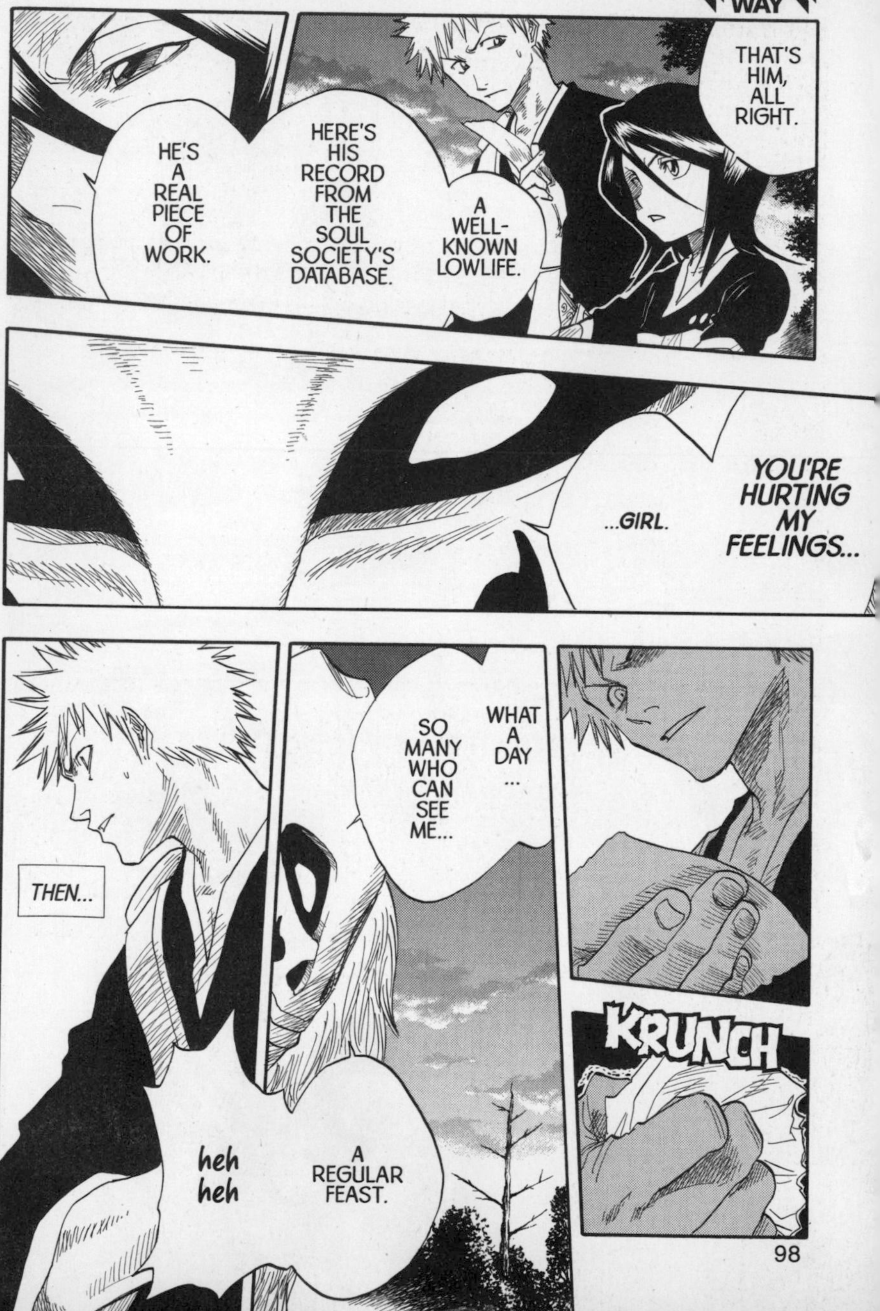
THAT'S HIM, ALL RIGHT.
A WELL-KNOWN LOWLIFE.
HERE'S HIS RECORD FROM THE SOUL SOCIETY'S DATABASE.
HE'S A REAL PIECE OF WORK.
YOU'RE HURTING MY FEELINGS...
...GIRL.
KRUNCH
WHAT A DAY...
SO MANY WHO CAN SEE ME...
A REGULAR FEAST.
heh heh
THEN...

READ THIS WAY

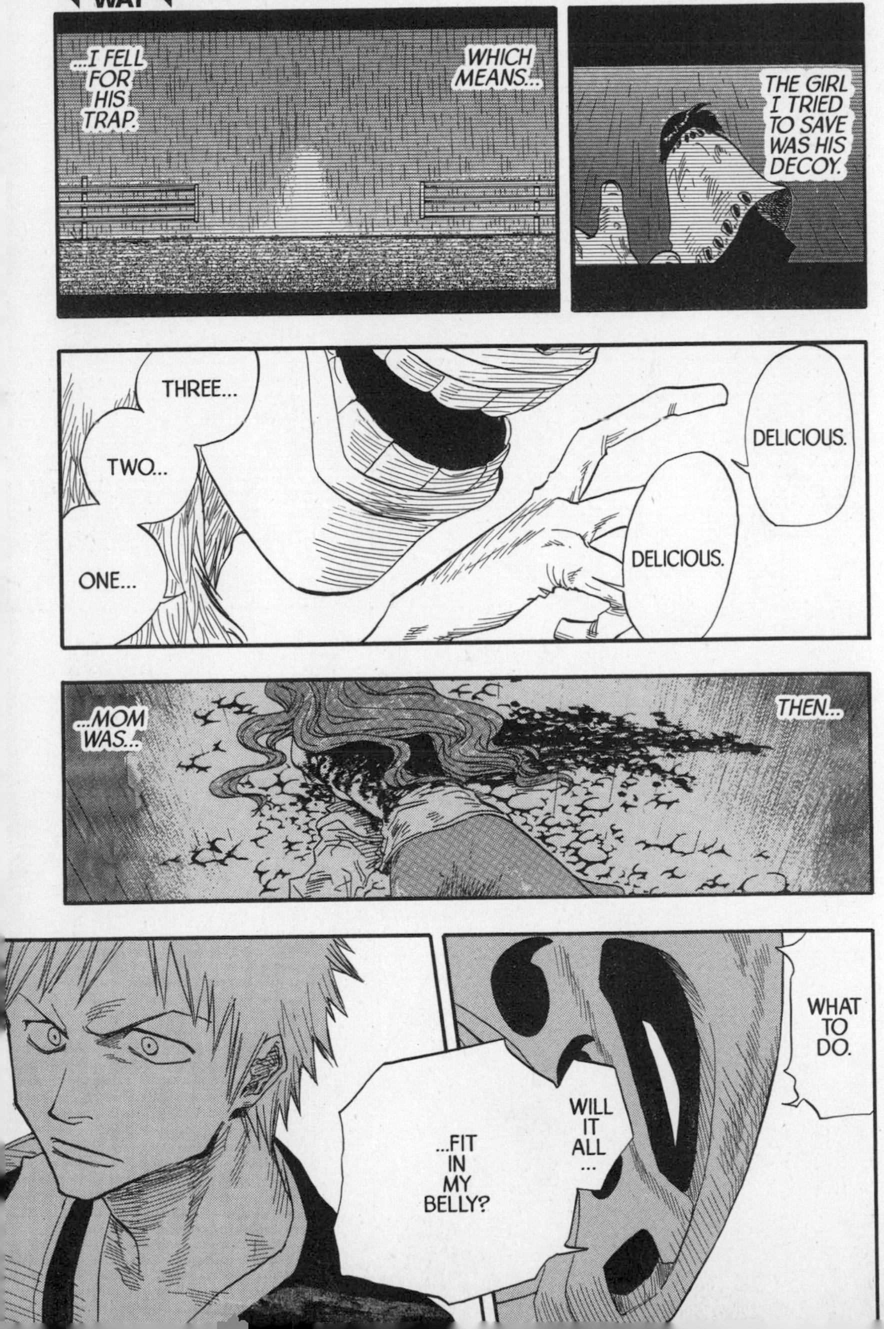
THE GIRL I TRIED TO SAVE WAS HIS DECOY.
WHICH MEANS...
...I FELL FOR HIS TRAP.
DELICIOUS.
DELICIOUS.
THREE...
TWO...
ONE...
THEN...
...MOM WAS...
WHAT TO DO.
WILL IT ALL...
...FIT IN MY BELLY?

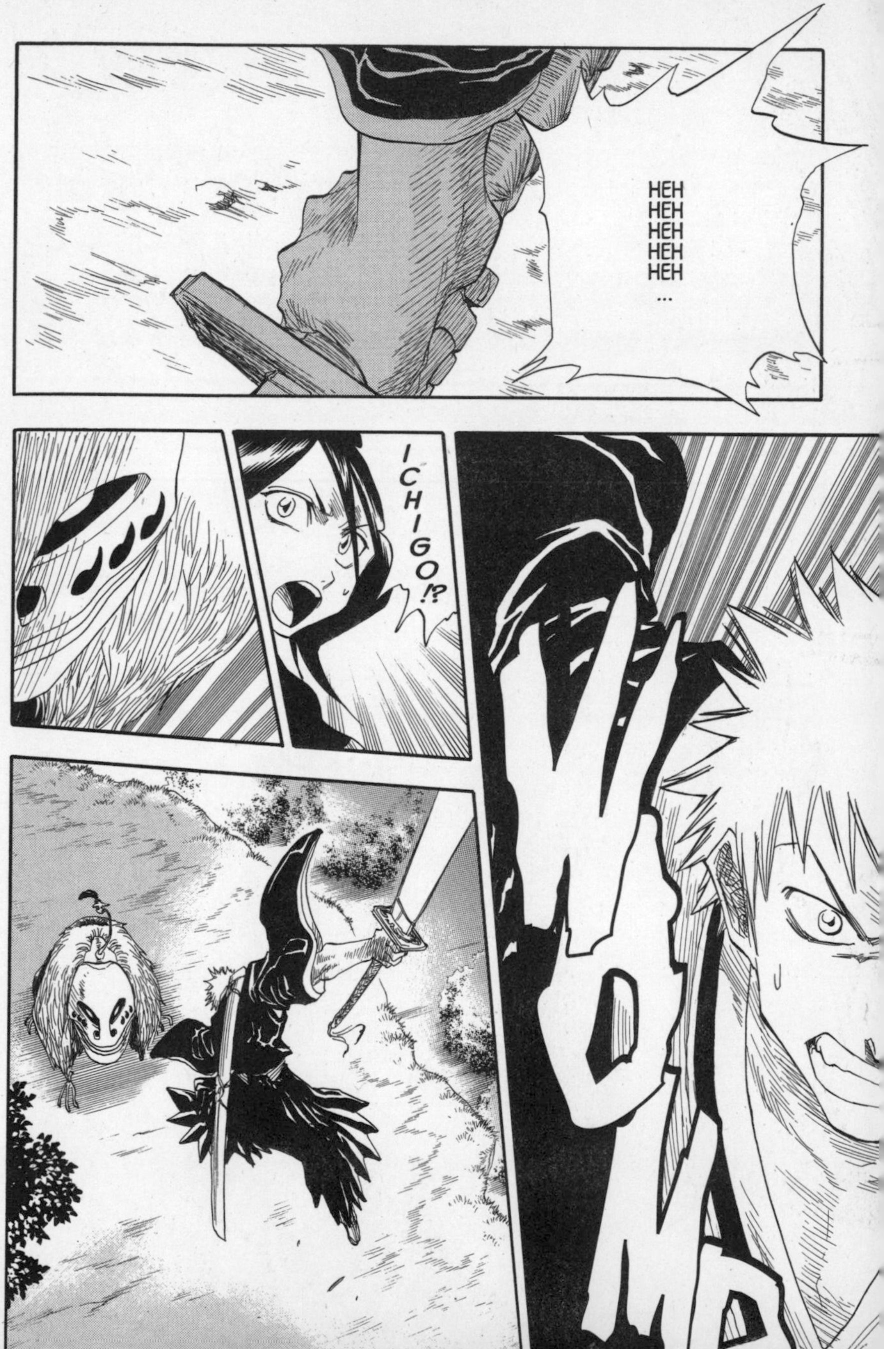
HEH
HEH
HEH
HEH
HEH
...
ICHIGO!?

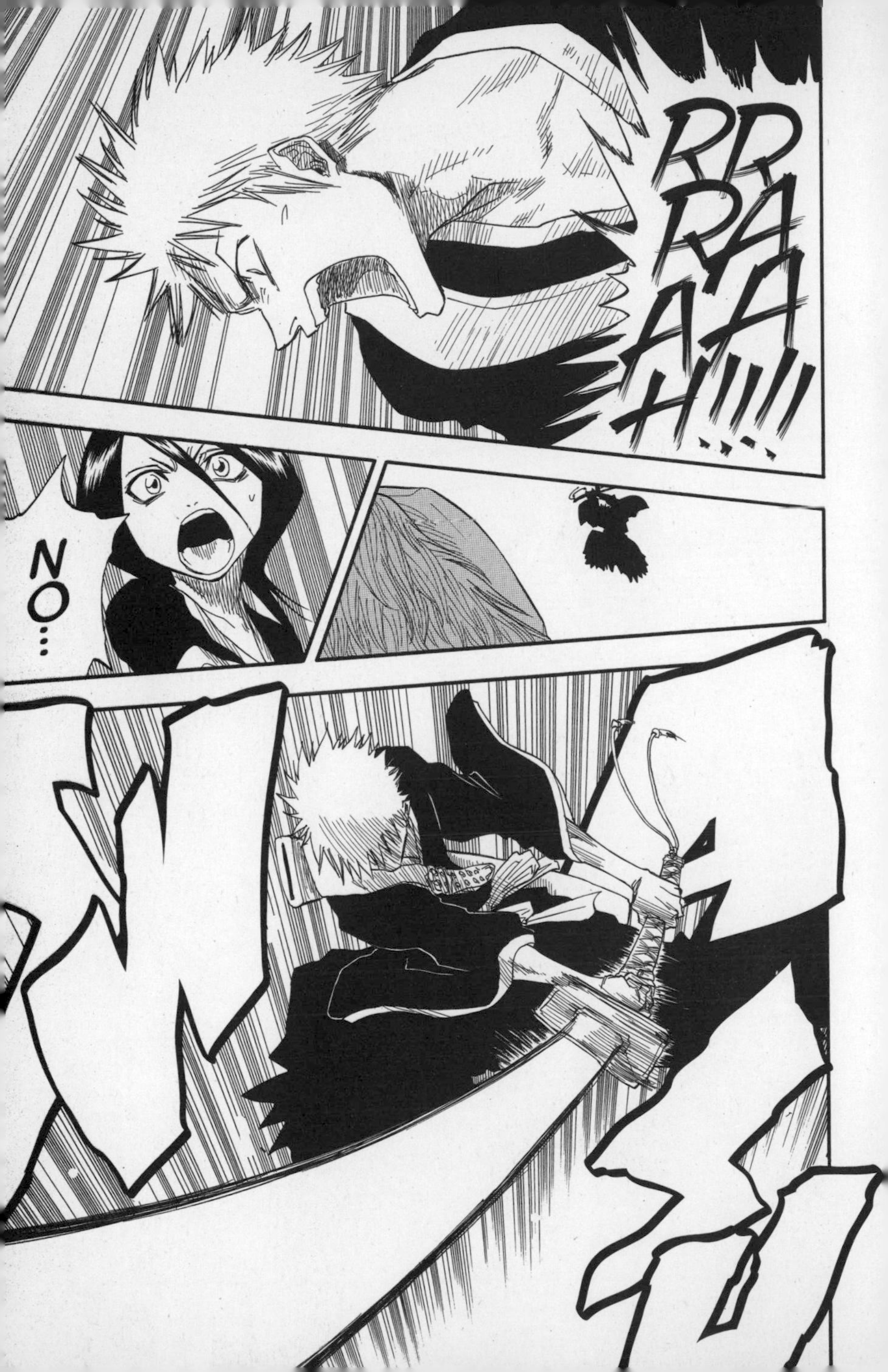
RRRAAH!!!!
NO...

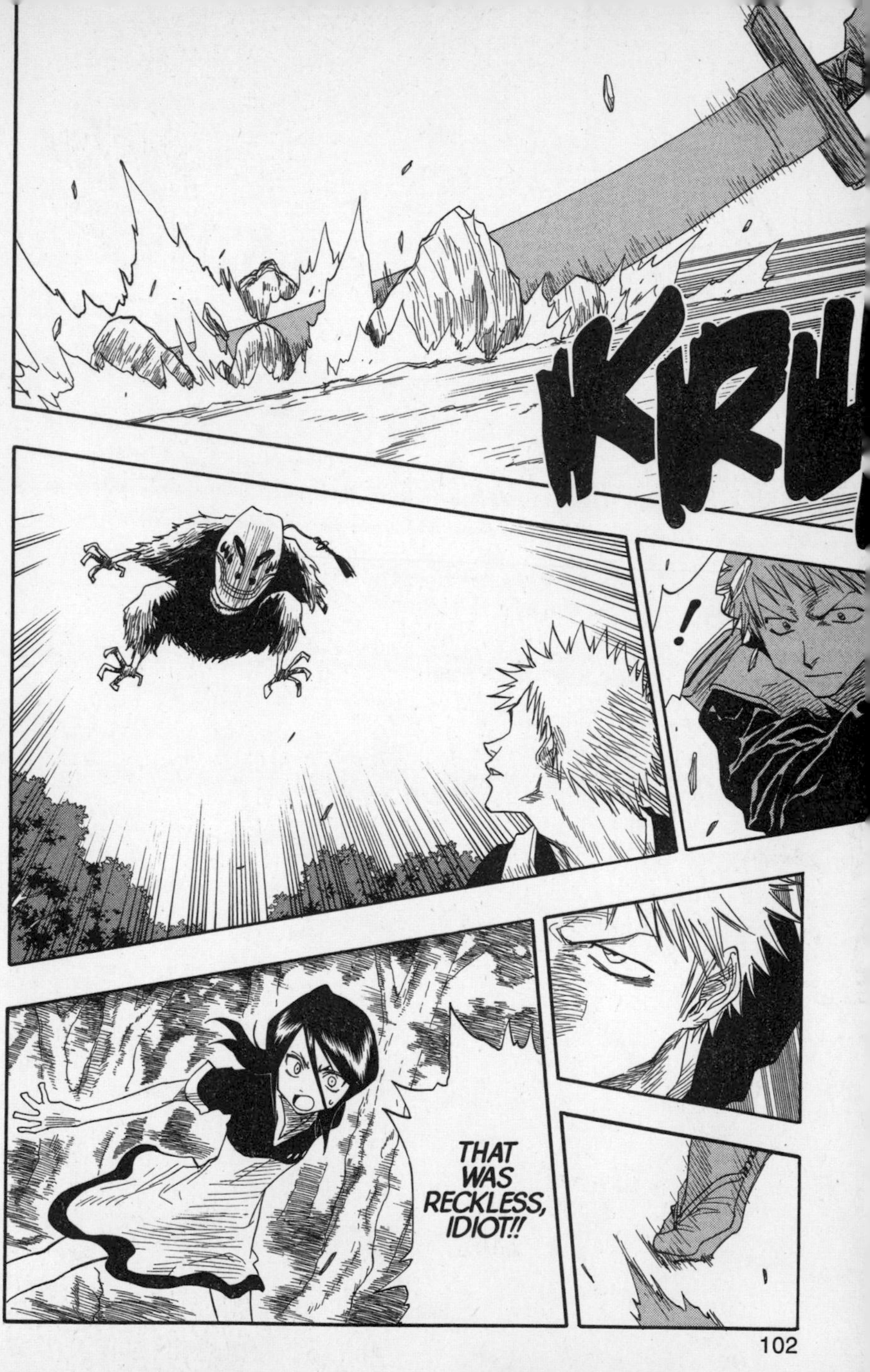
KRU
!
THAT WAS RECKLESS, IDIOT!!

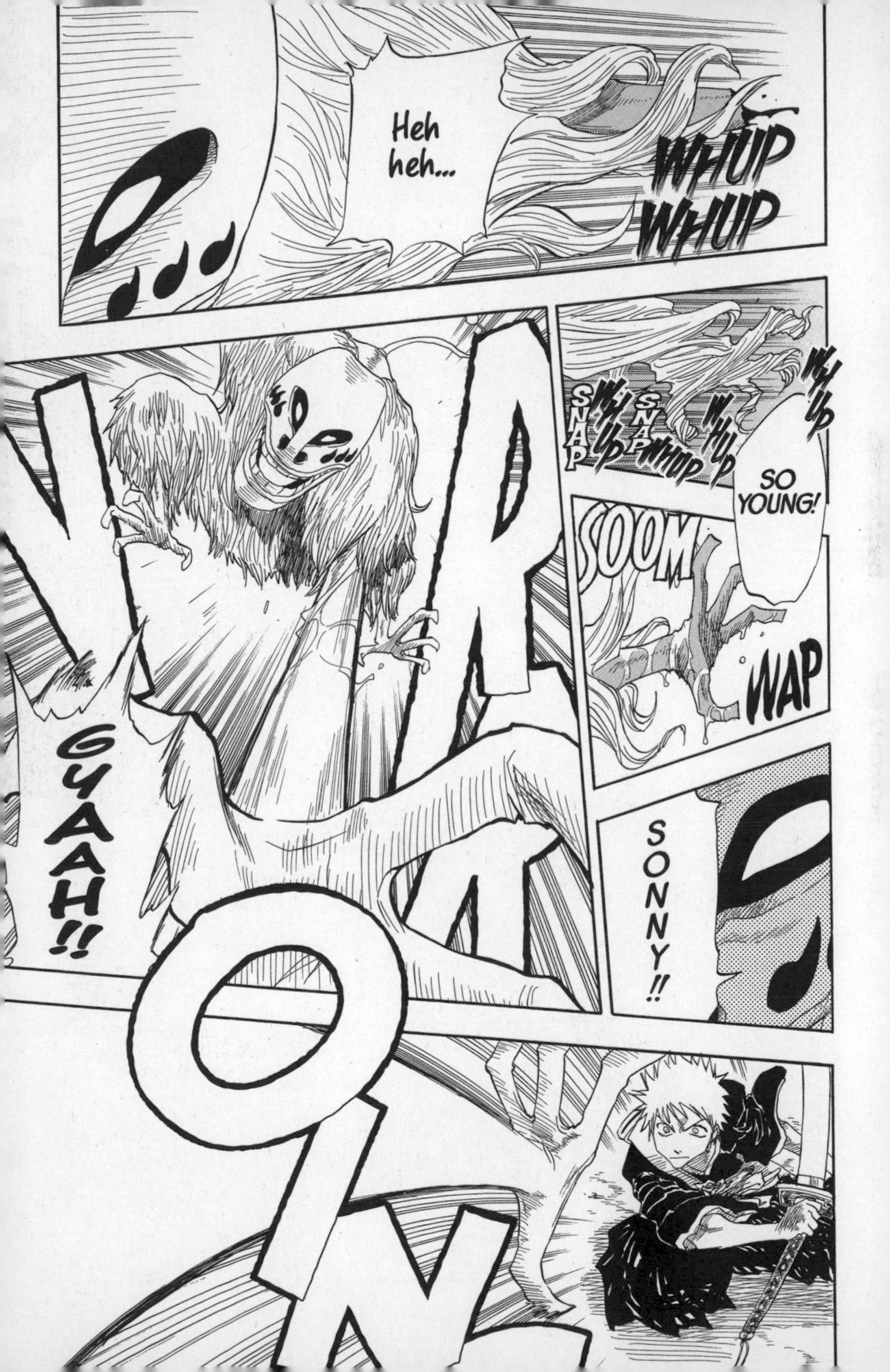
WHUP WHUP
Heh heh...
WHUP
WHUP
WHUP
SNAP
WHUP
SNAP
SO YOUNG!
SOOM
WAP
SONNY!!
WAP
GYAAH!!

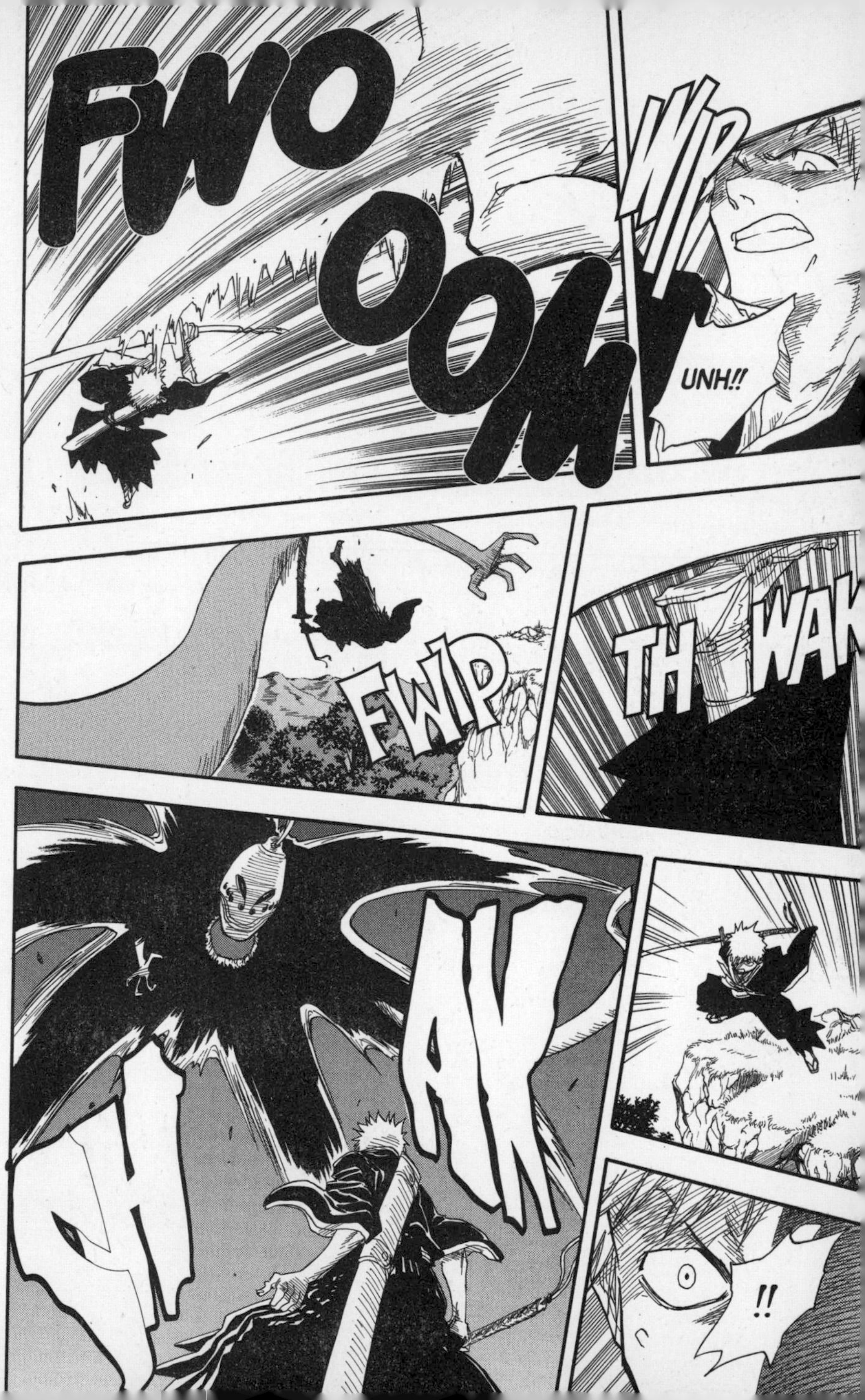
WHIP
UNH!!
FWOOOM
THWAK
FWIP
!!
CHAK

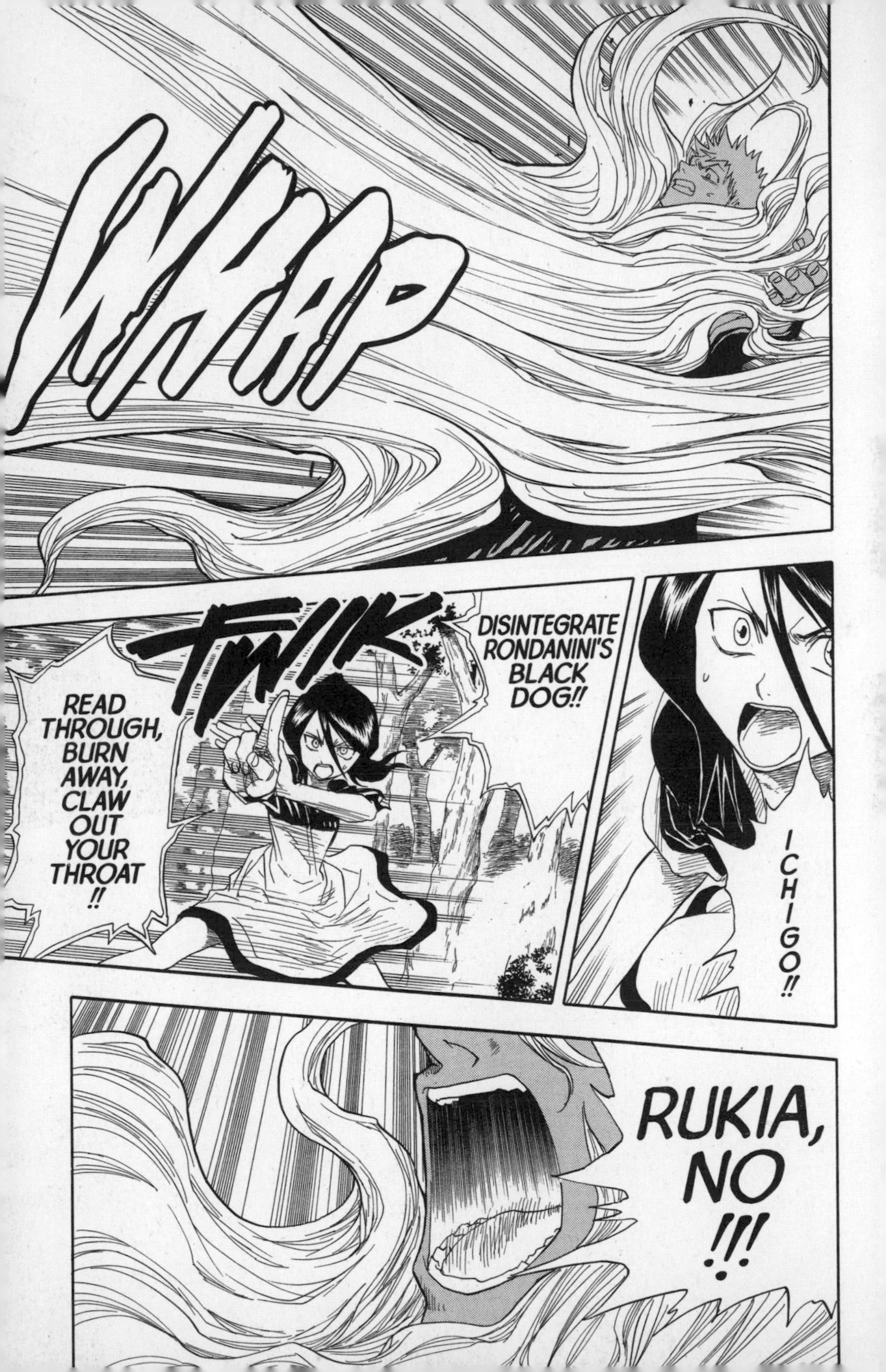
WHAP
ICHIGO!!
TWIK
DISINTEGRATE RONDANINI'S BLACK DOG!!
READ THROUGH, BURN AWAY, CLAW OUT YOUR THROAT!!
RUKIA, NO!!!

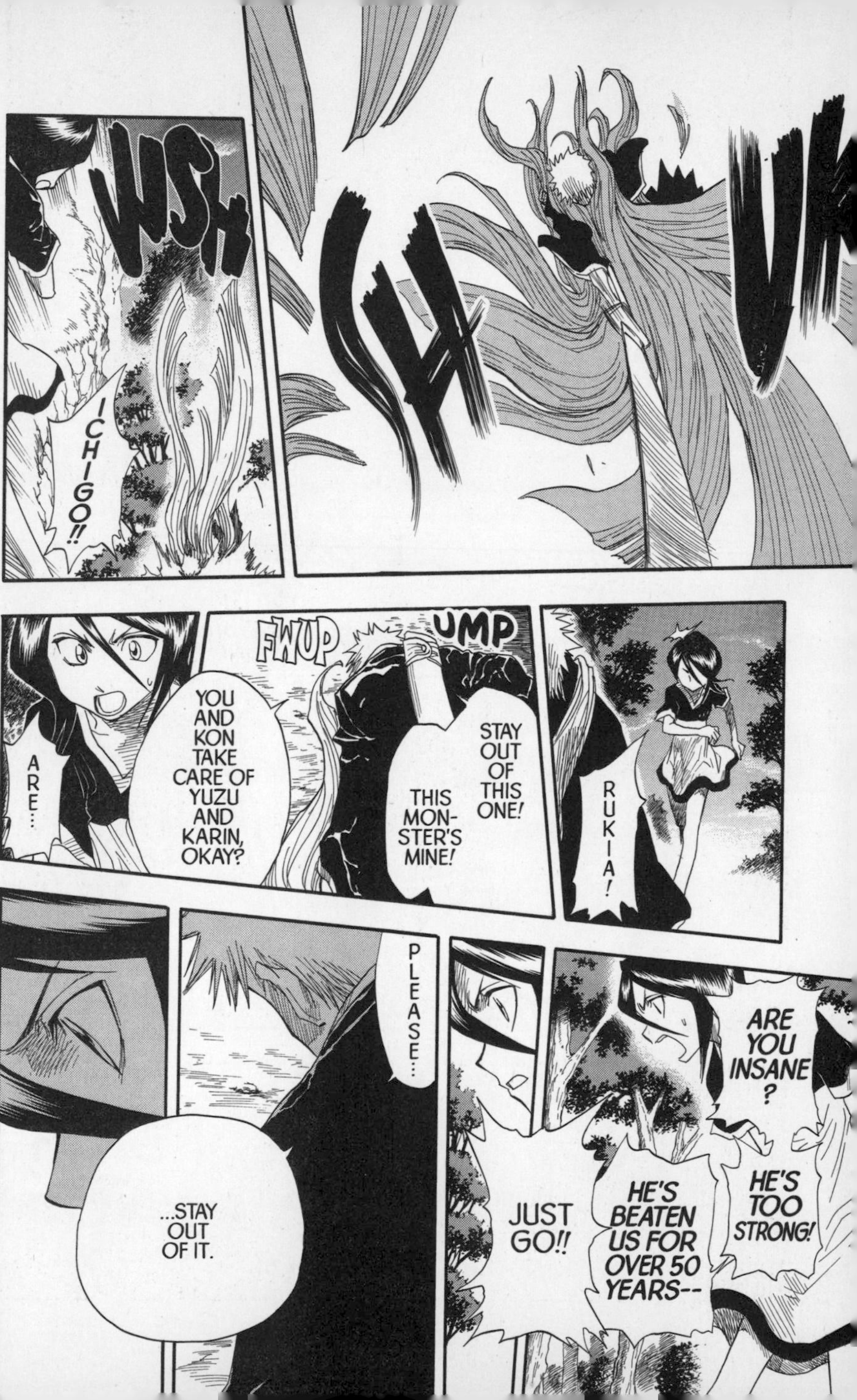
WSH
ICHIGO!!
RUKIA!
FWUP
UMP
STAY OUT OF THIS ONE!
THIS MONSTER'S MINE!
YOU AND KON TAKE CARE OF YUZU AND KARIN, OKAY?
ARE...
ARE YOU INSANE?
HE'S TOO STRONG!
HE'S BEATEN US FOR OVER 50 YEARS--
JUST GO!!
PLEASE...
...STAY OUT OF IT.

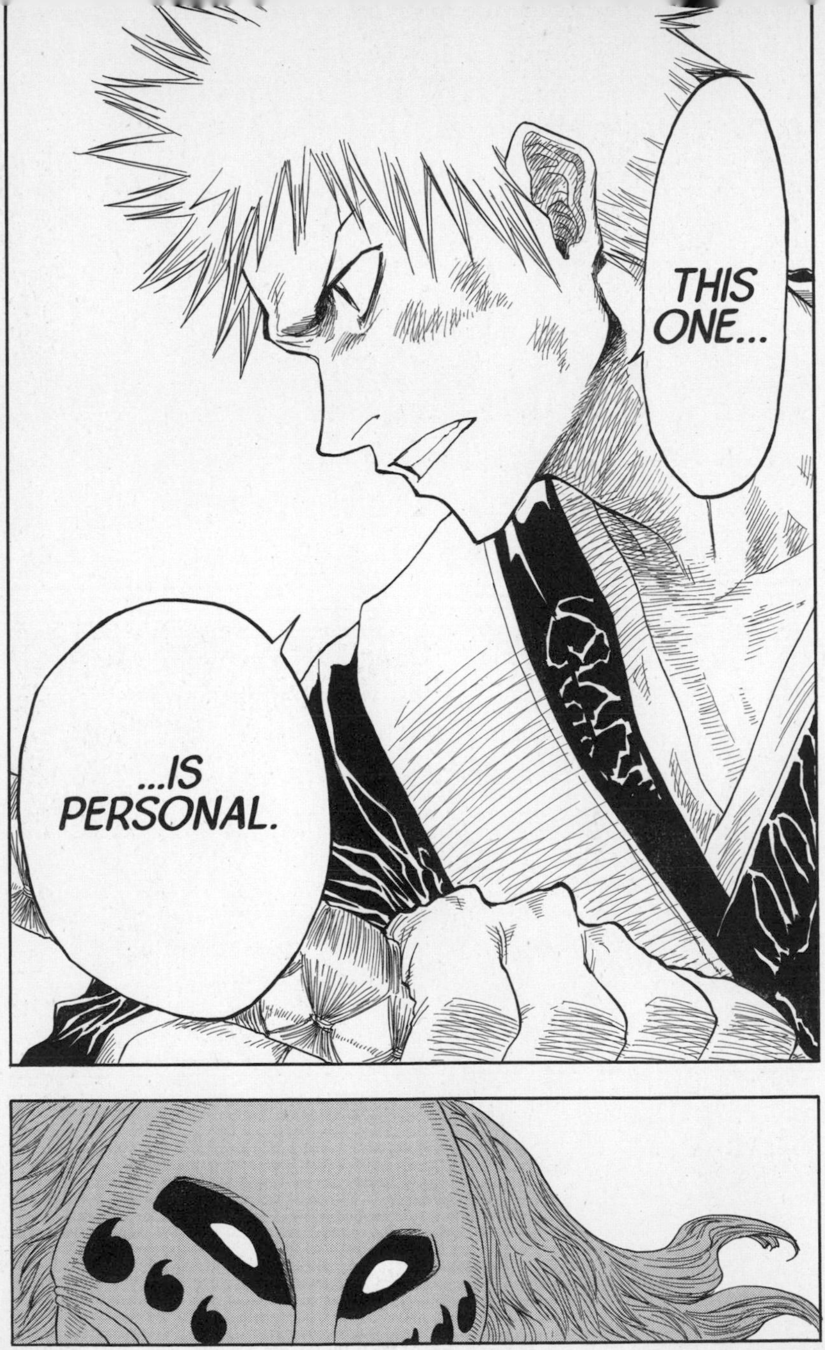
THIS ONE...
...IS PERSONAL.

RUKIA?
WHAT IS IT?
WHAT?
Backpack

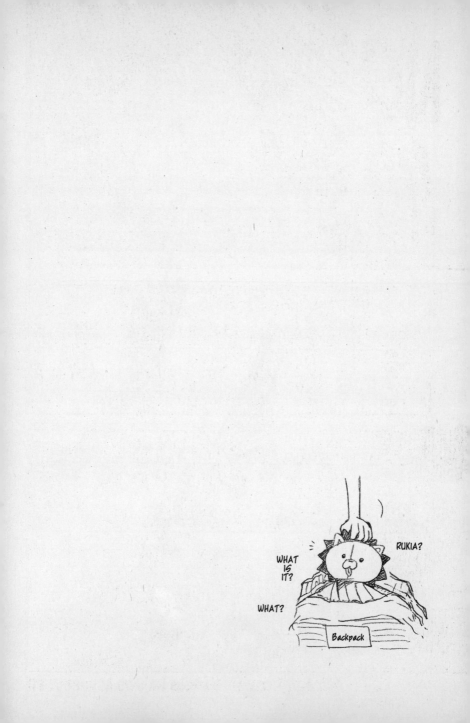

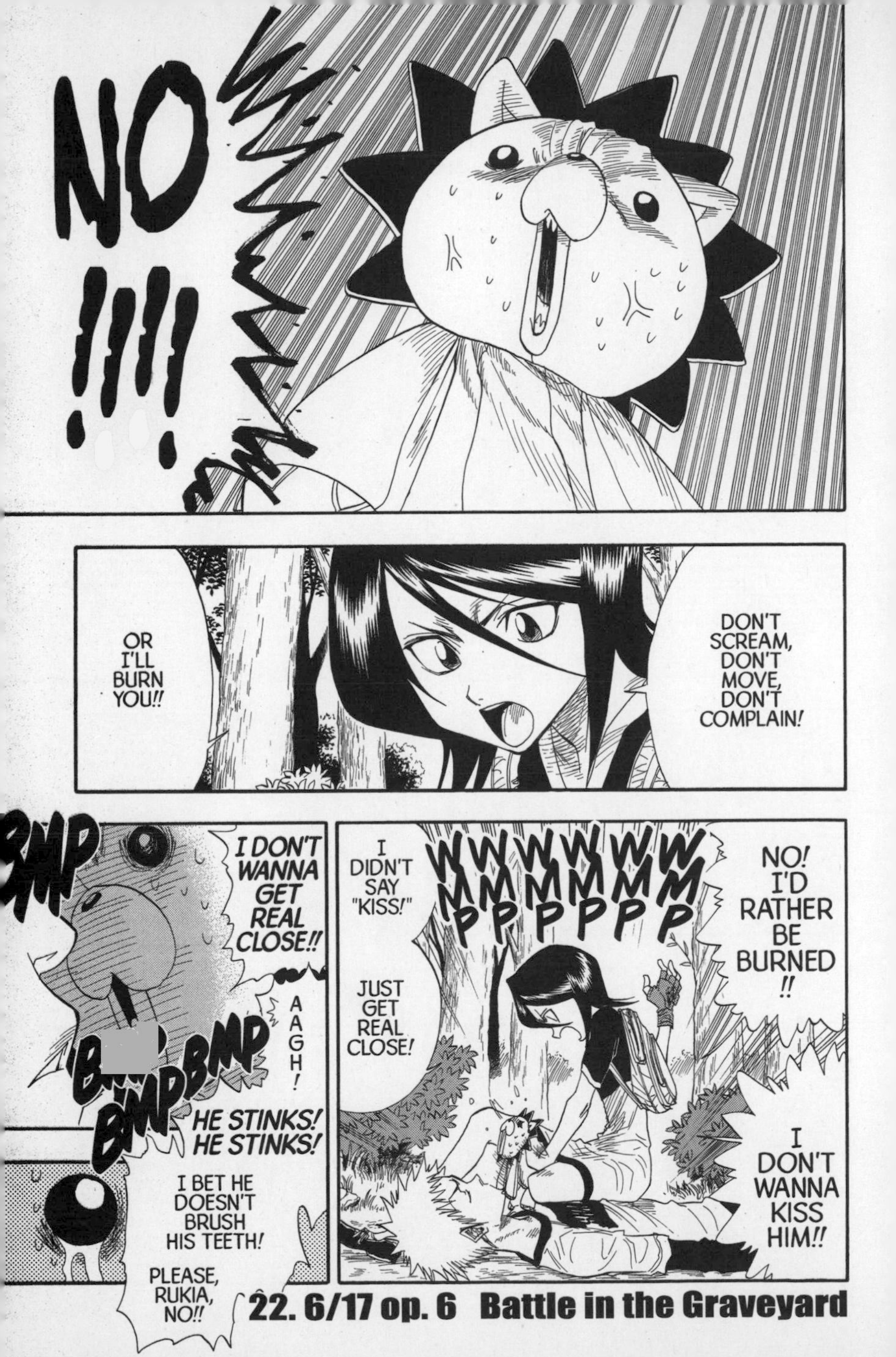
NO!!!!
DON'T SCREAM, DON'T MOVE, DON'T COMPLAIN!
OR I'LL BURN YOU!!
NO! I'D RATHER BE BURNED!!
I DON'T WANNA KISS HIM!!
WMP WMP WMP WMP WMP WMP
I DIDN'T SAY "KISS!"
JUST GET REAL CLOSE!
BMP
I DON'T WANNA GET REAL CLOSE!!
AAGH!
BMP BMP BMP
HE STINKS! HE STINKS!
I BET HE DOESN'T BRUSH HIS TEETH!
PLEASE, RUKIA, NO!!

22. 6/17 op. 6 Battle in the Graveyard

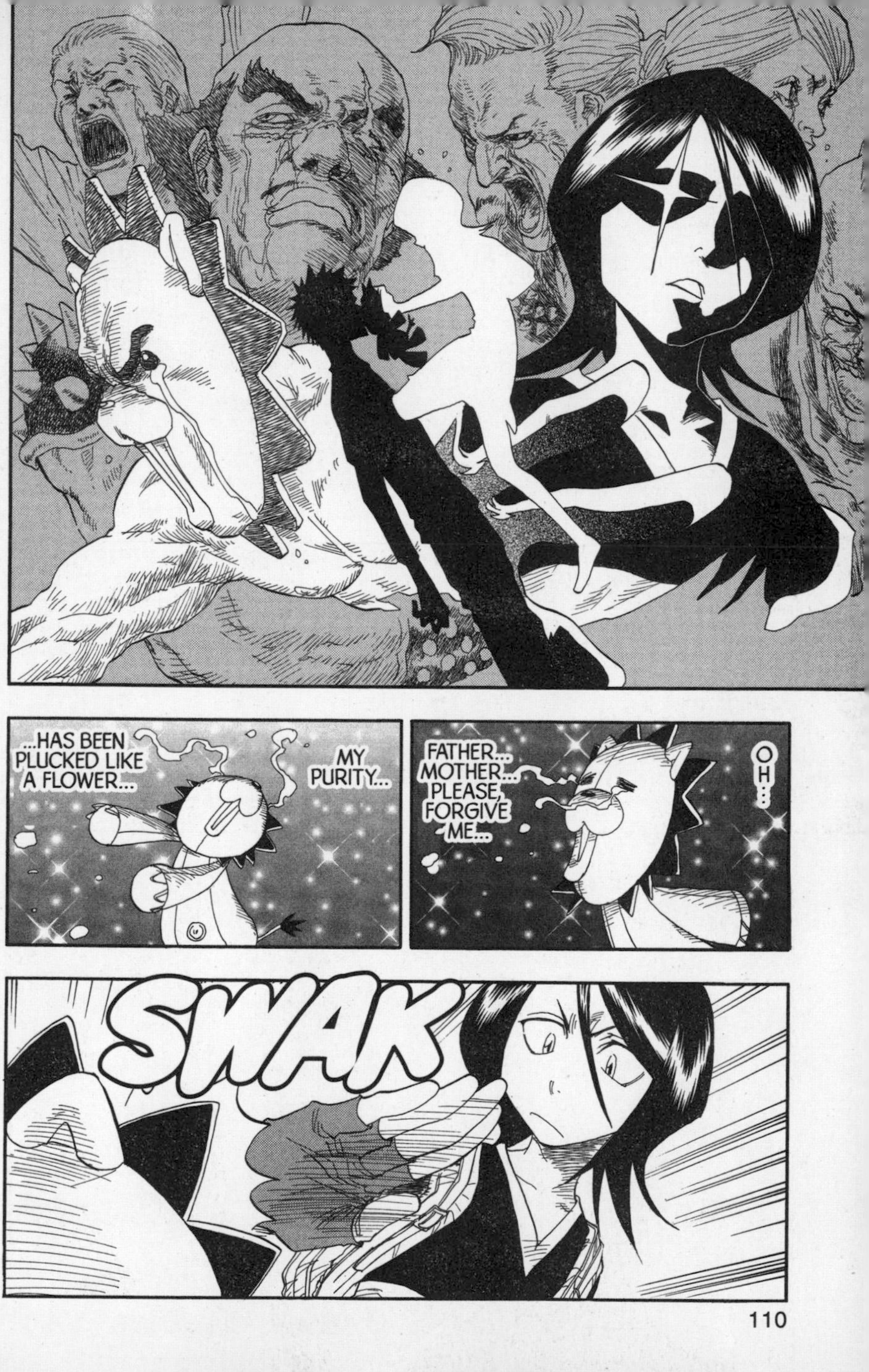
OH...
FATHER... MOTHER... PLEASE, FORGIVE ME...
MY PURITY...
...HAS BEEN PLUCKED LIKE A FLOWER...
SWAK

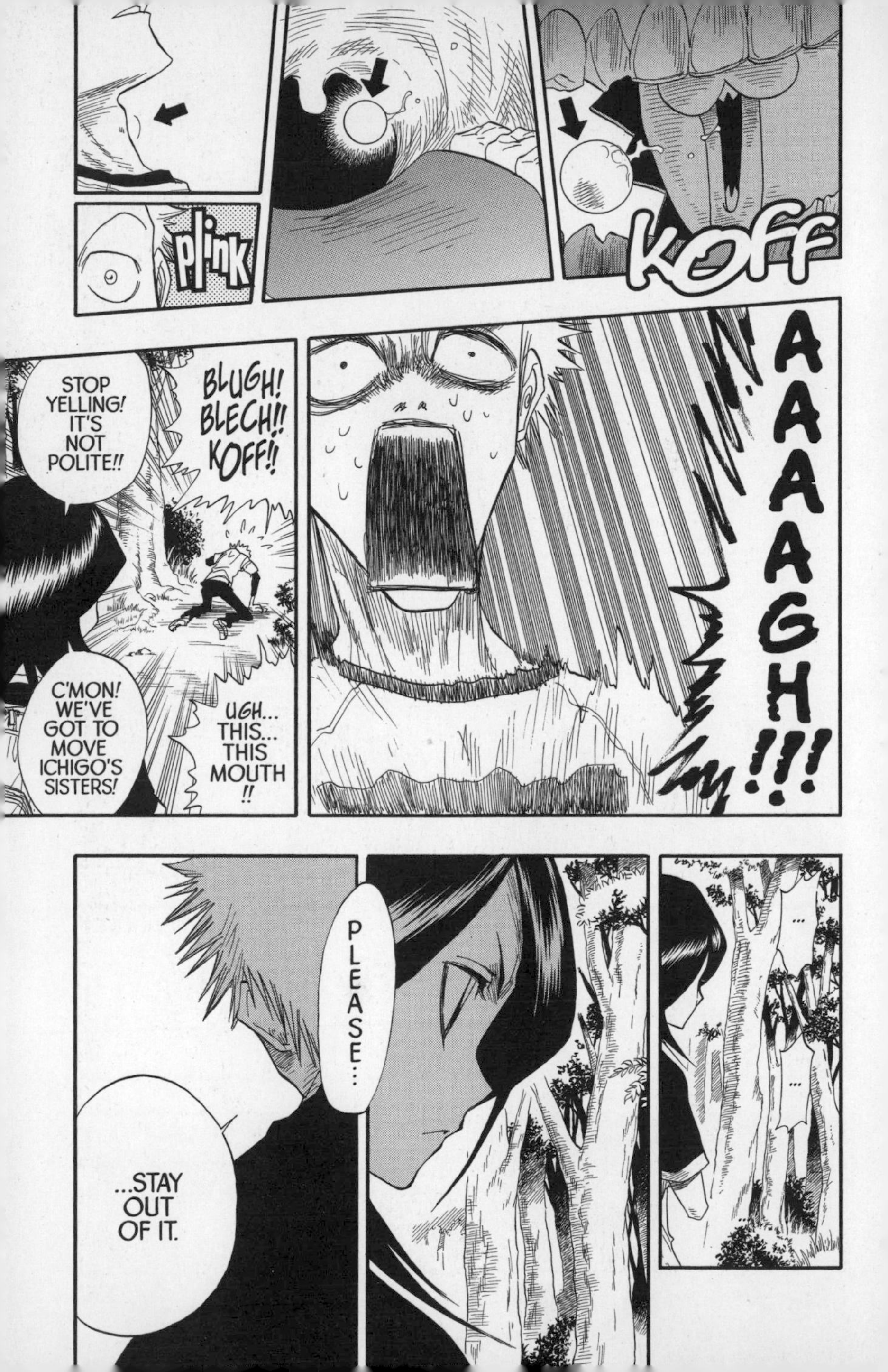
KOFF
plink
AAAAGH!!!
BLUGH! BLECH!! KOFF!!
STOP YELLING! IT'S NOT POLITE!!
UGH... THIS... THIS MOUTH!!
C'MON! WE'VE GOT TO MOVE ICHIGO'S SISTERS!
...
...
...
PLEASE...
...STAY OUT OF IT.

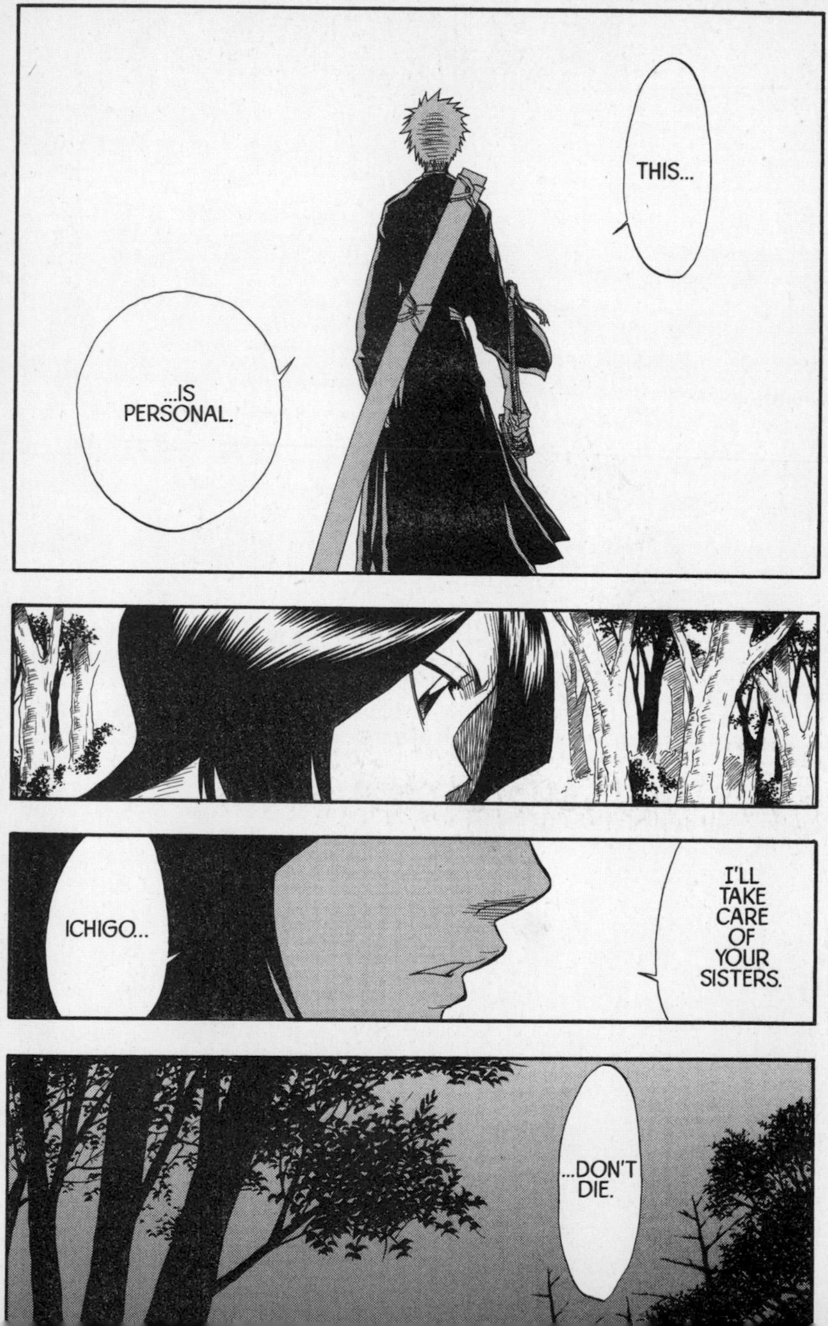
THIS...
...IS PERSONAL.
I'LL TAKE CARE OF YOUR SISTERS.
ICHIGO...
...DON'T DIE.

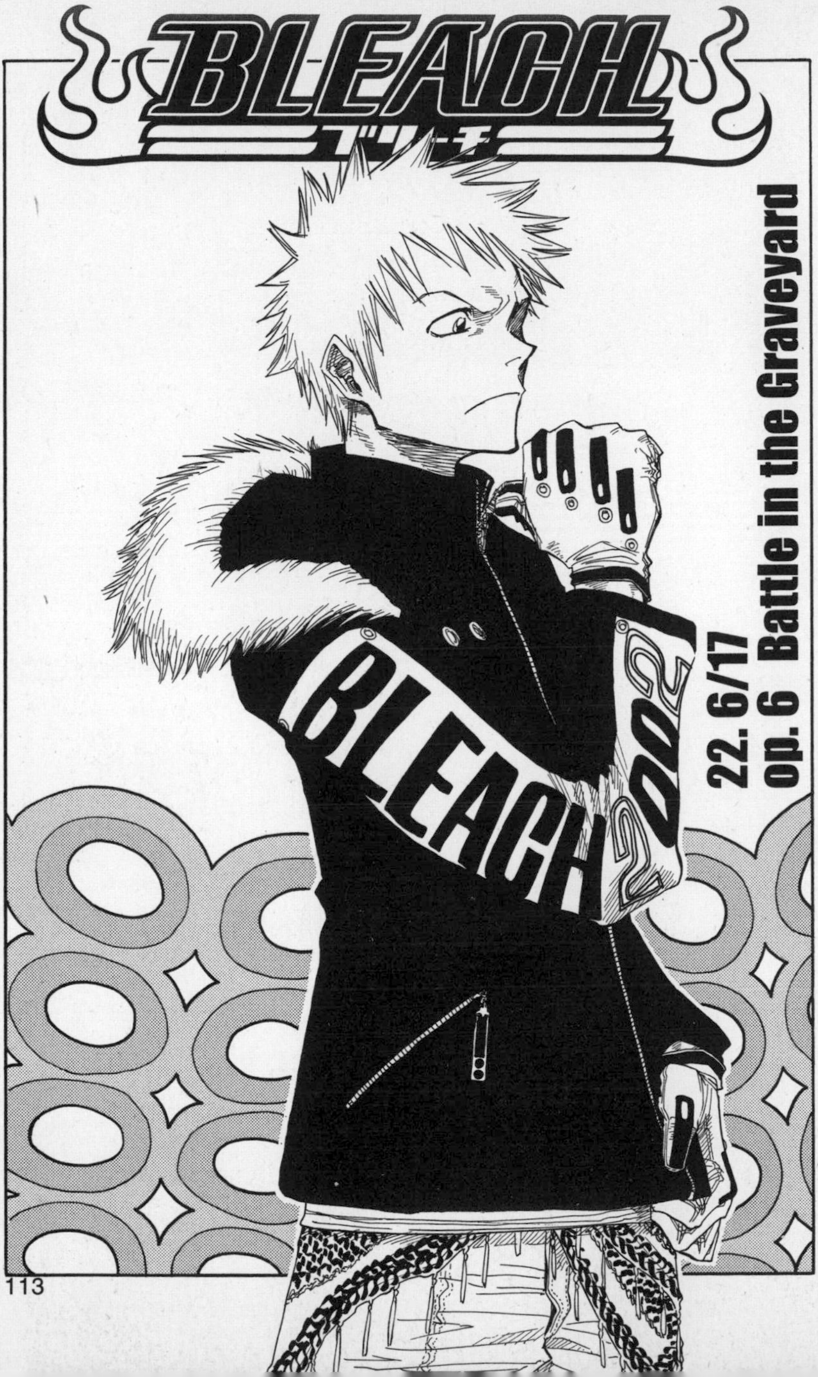

BLEACH
ブリーチ
BLEACH
2002

22. 6/17 op. 6 Battle in the Graveyard

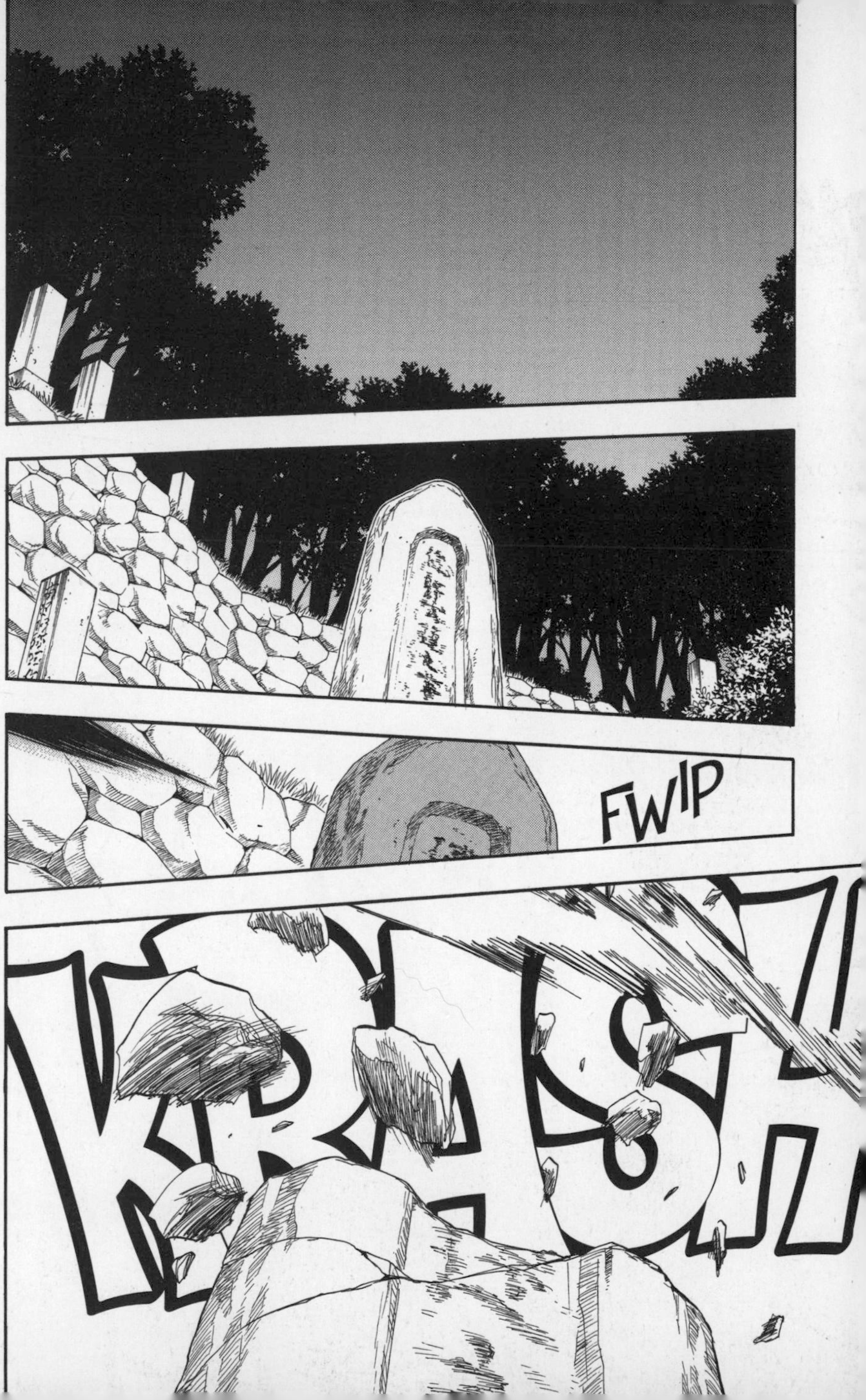
FWIP

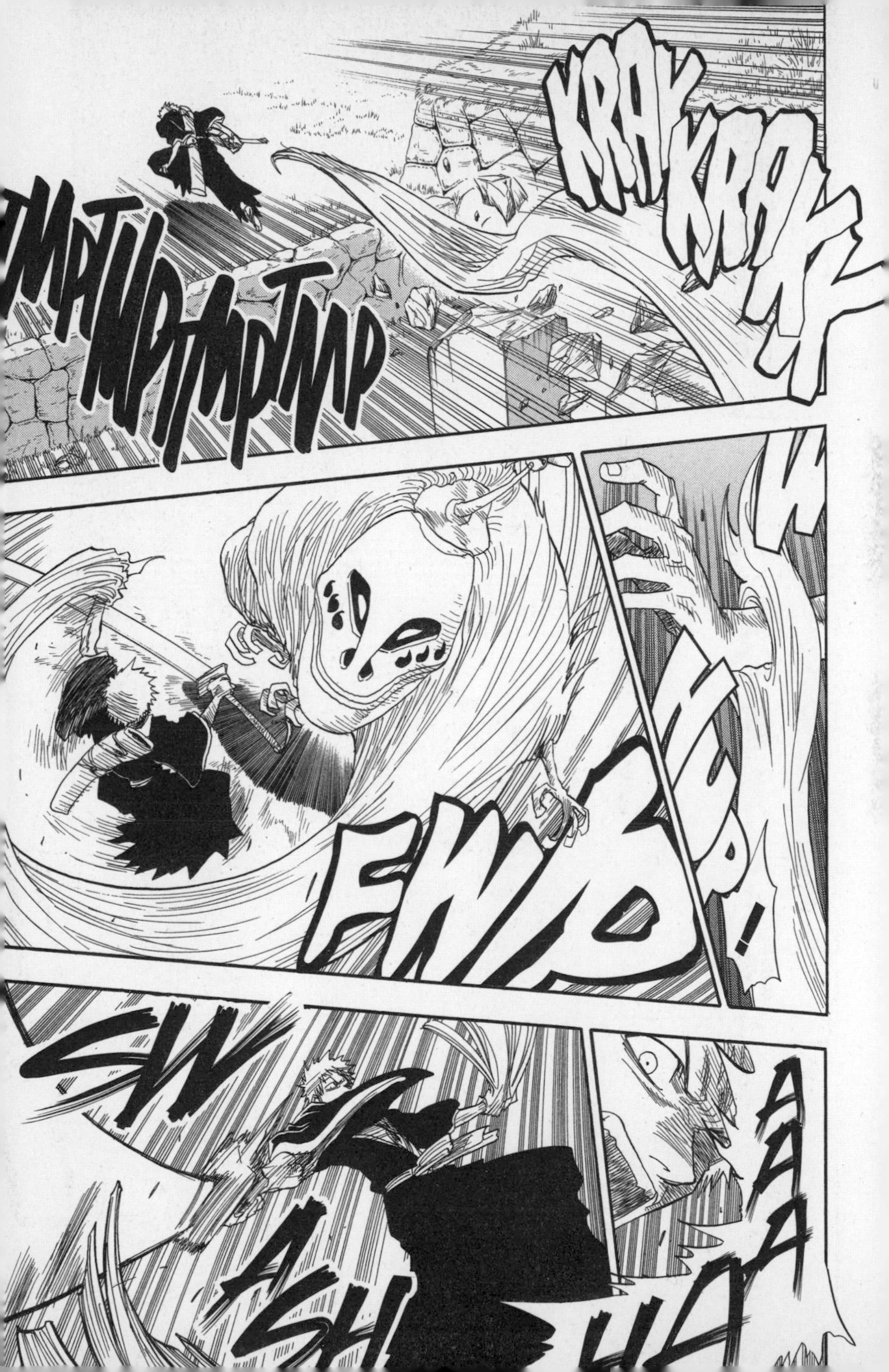
KRAK KRAK
TMP TMP TMP TMP TMP
WHUD!
FWD
SWASH

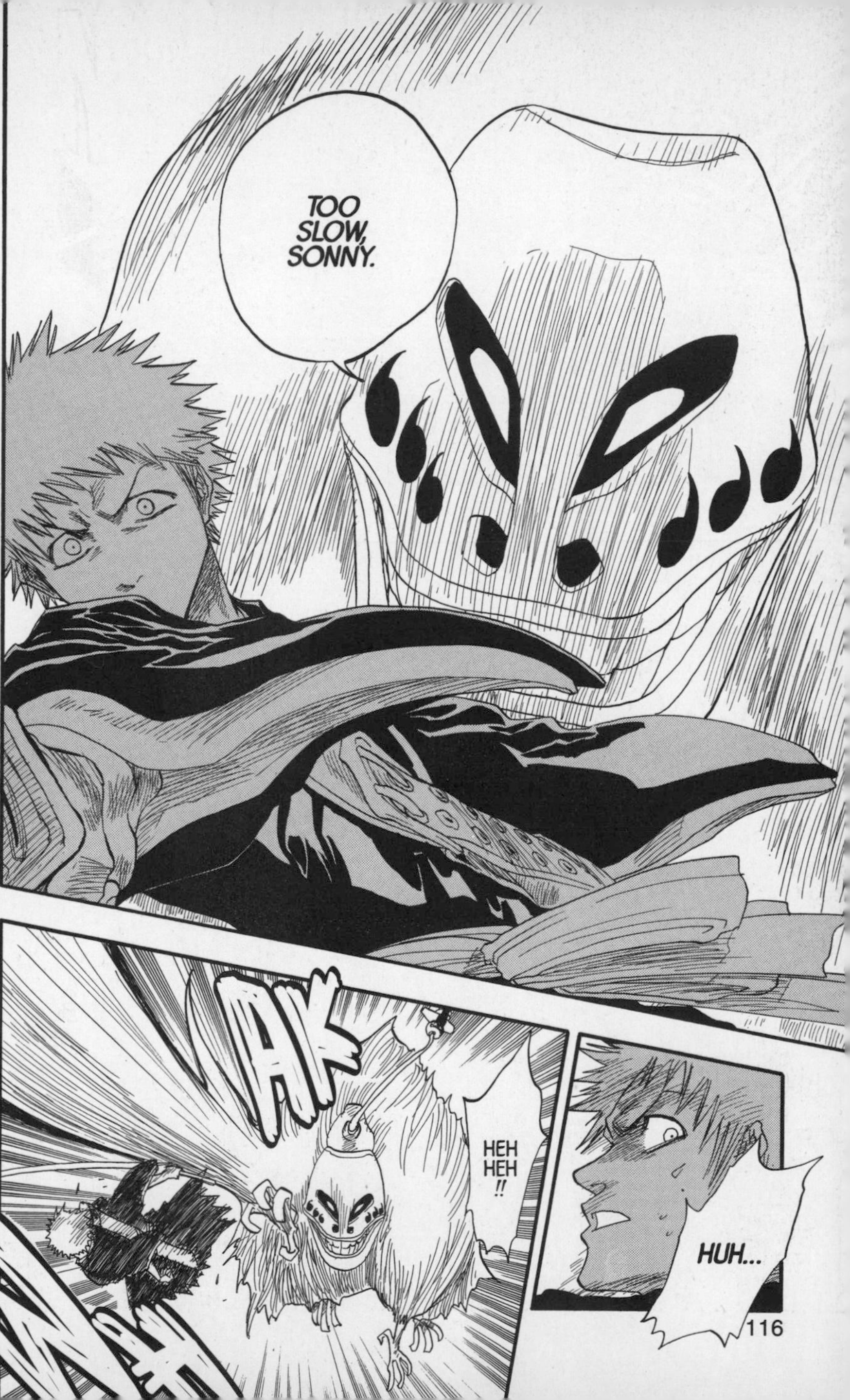
TOO SLOW, SONNY.
HUH...
AK
HEH HEH!!

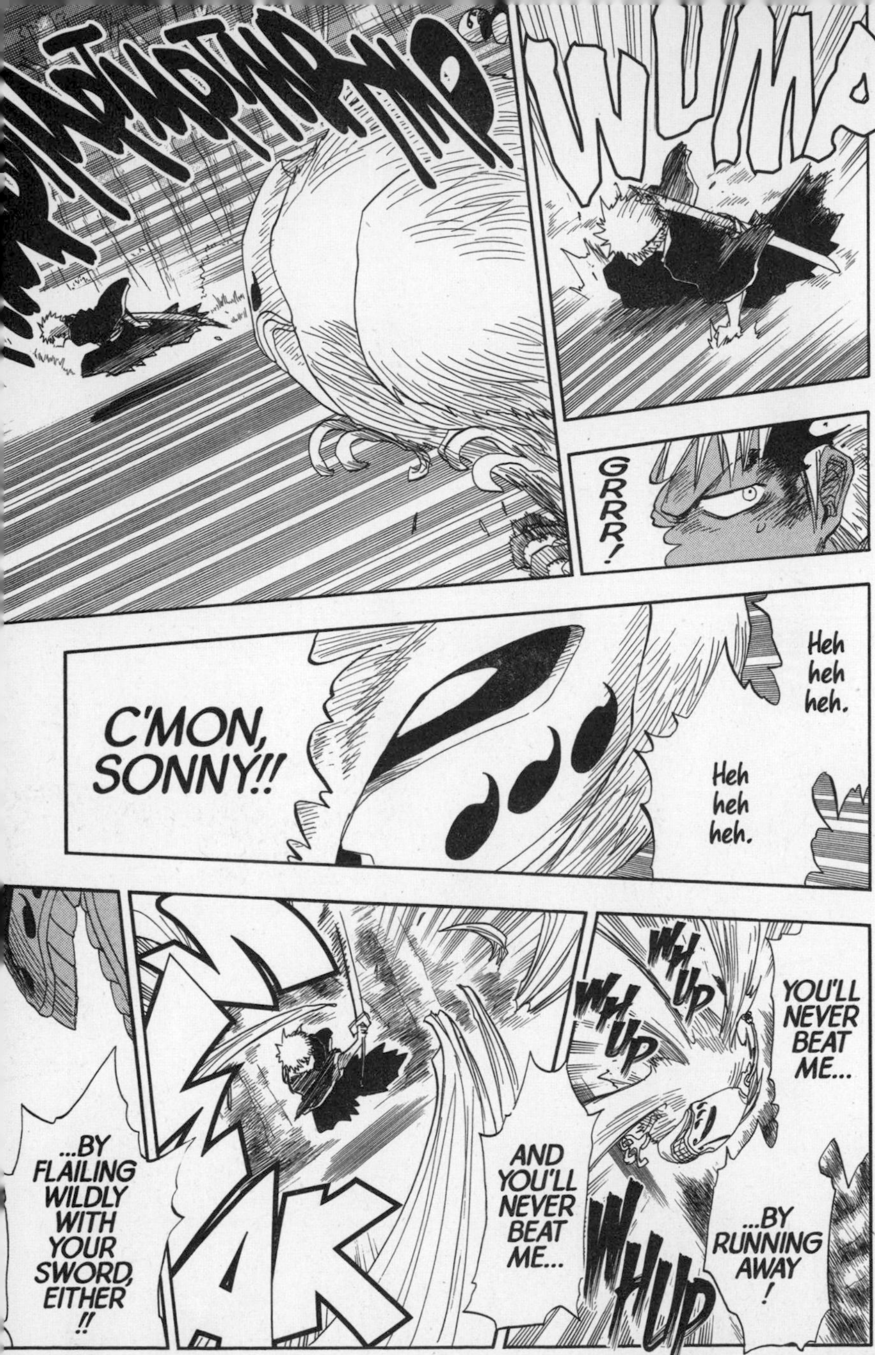

WUMP
GRRR!
THMPTHMPTHMP!!
Heh heh heh.
Heh heh heh.
C'MON, SONNY!!
WHUP
WHUP
YOU'LL NEVER BEAT ME...
...BY RUNNING AWAY!
WHUP
AND YOU'LL NEVER BEAT ME...
...BY FLAILING WILDLY WITH YOUR SWORD, EITHER!!

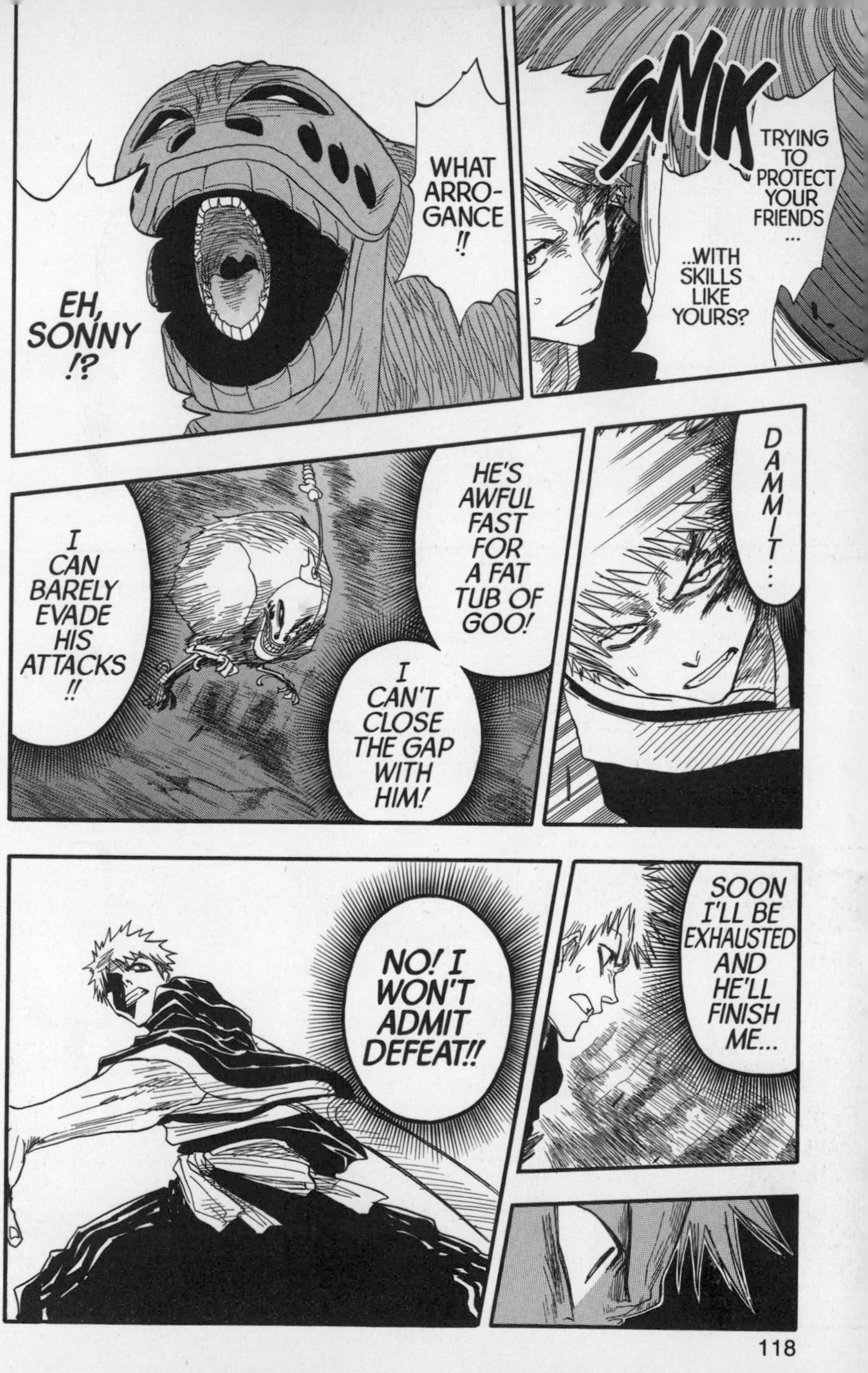
SNIK
TRYING TO PROTECT YOUR FRIENDS...
...WITH SKILLS LIKE YOURS?
WHAT ARRO-GANCE!!
EH, SONNY!?
DAMMIT...
HE'S AWFUL FAST FOR A FAT TUB OF GOO!
I CAN'T CLOSE THE GAP WITH HIM!
I CAN BARELY EVADE HIS ATTACKS!!
SOON I'LL BE EXHAUSTED AND HE'LL FINISH ME...
NO! I WON'T ADMIT DEFEAT!!

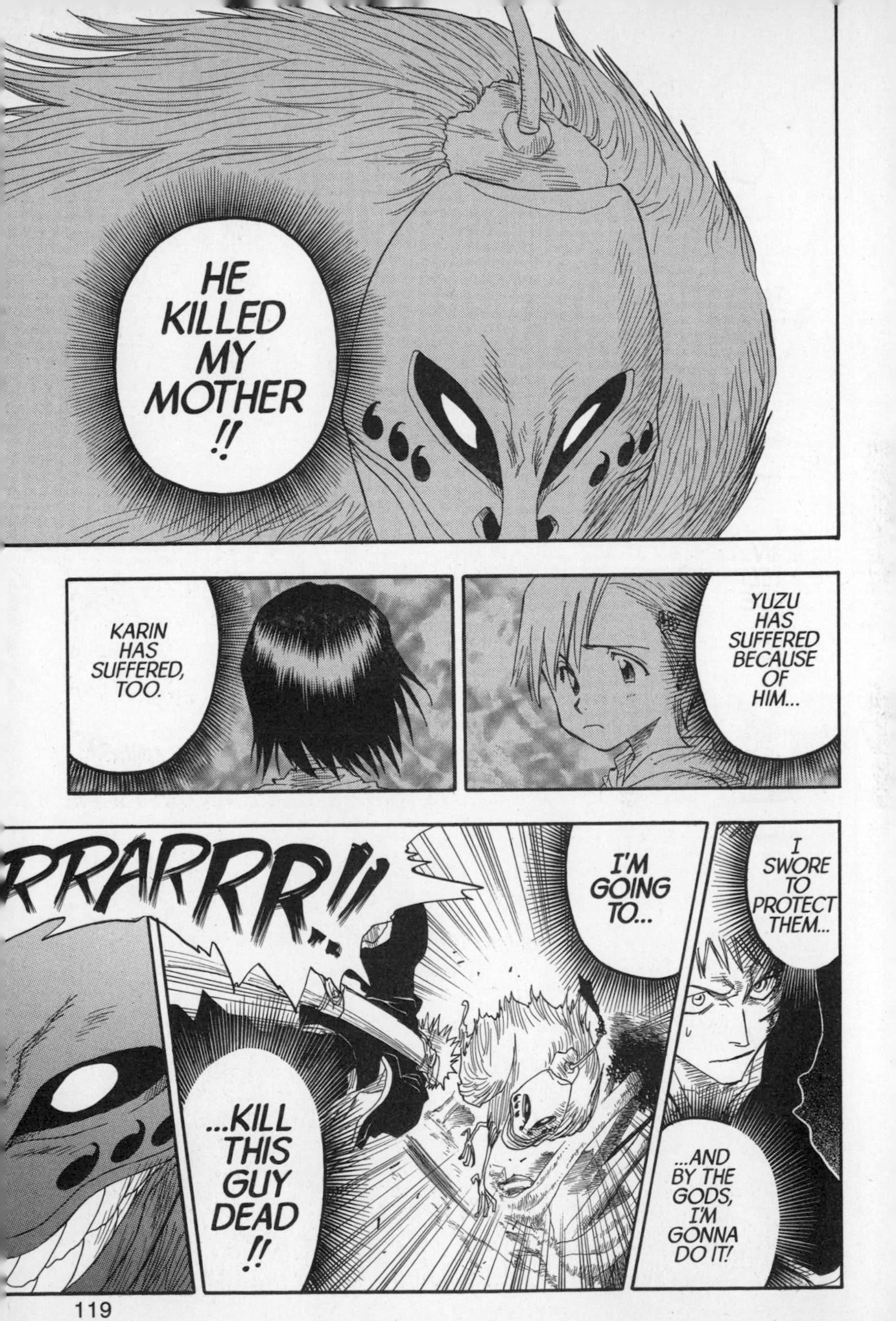
HE KILLED MY MOTHER!!
YUZU HAS SUFFERED BECAUSE OF HIM...
KARIN HAS SUFFERED, TOO.
I SWORE TO PROTECT THEM...
...AND BY THE GODS, I'M GONNA DO IT!
I'M GOING TO...
...KILL THIS GUY DEAD!!
RRARRRR!!

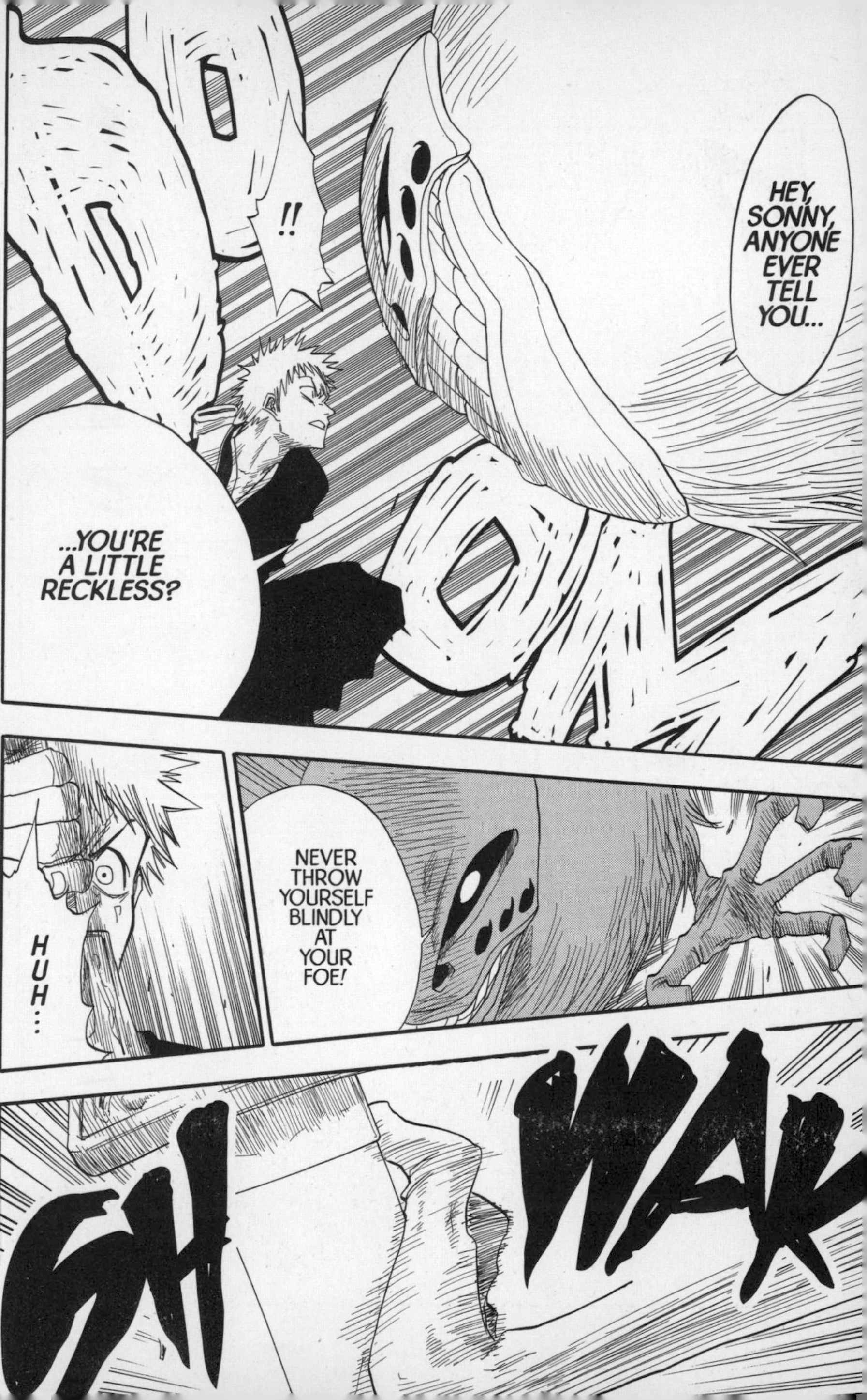
HEY, SONNY, ANYONE EVER TELL YOU...
!!
...YOU'RE A LITTLE RECKLESS?
NEVER THROW YOURSELF BLINDLY AT YOUR FOE!
HUH...
SH WAK

READ THIS WAY

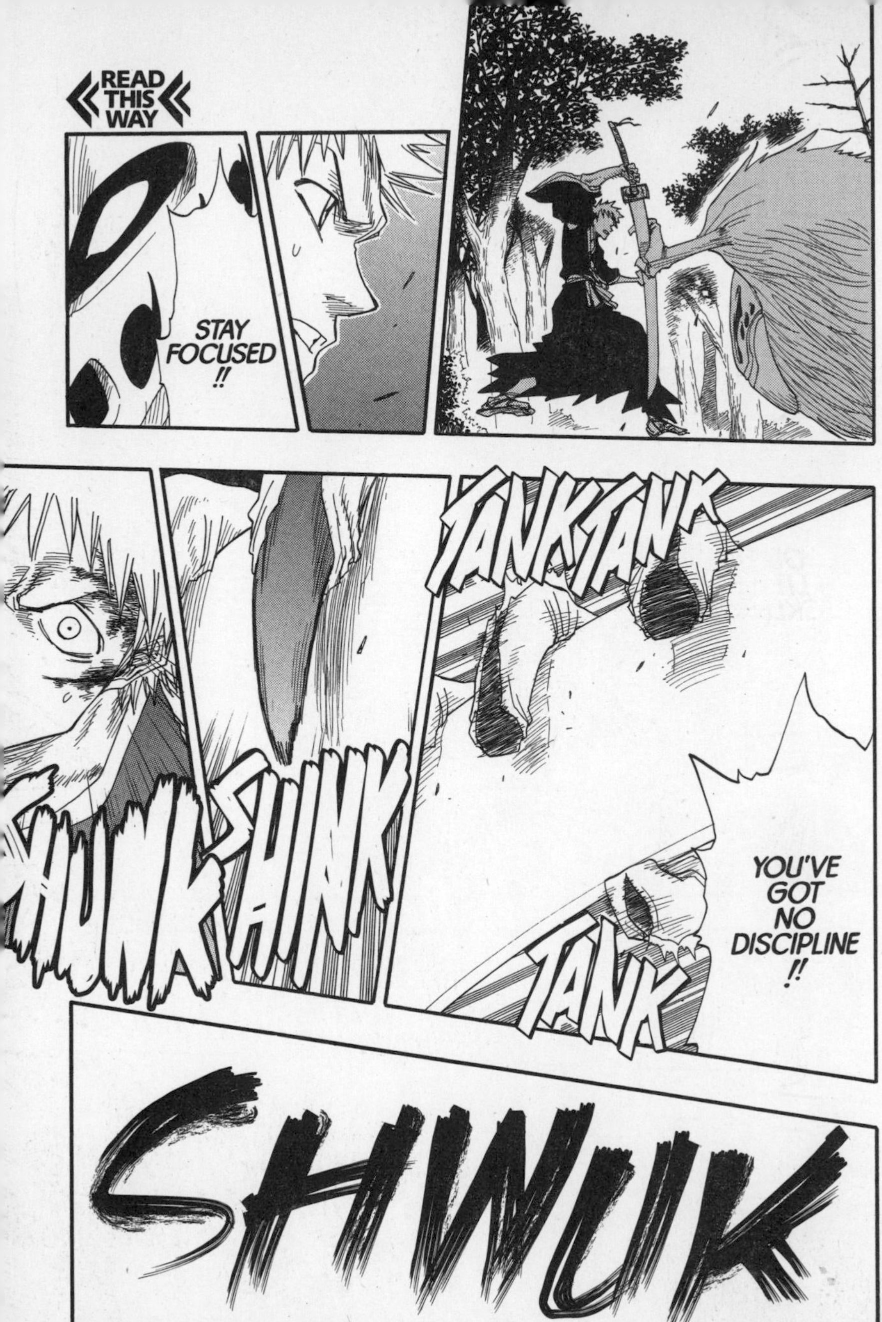
STAY FOCUSED !!
TANK TANK
YOU'VE GOT NO DISCIPLINE !!
TANK
SHINK
SHUNK
SHWUK

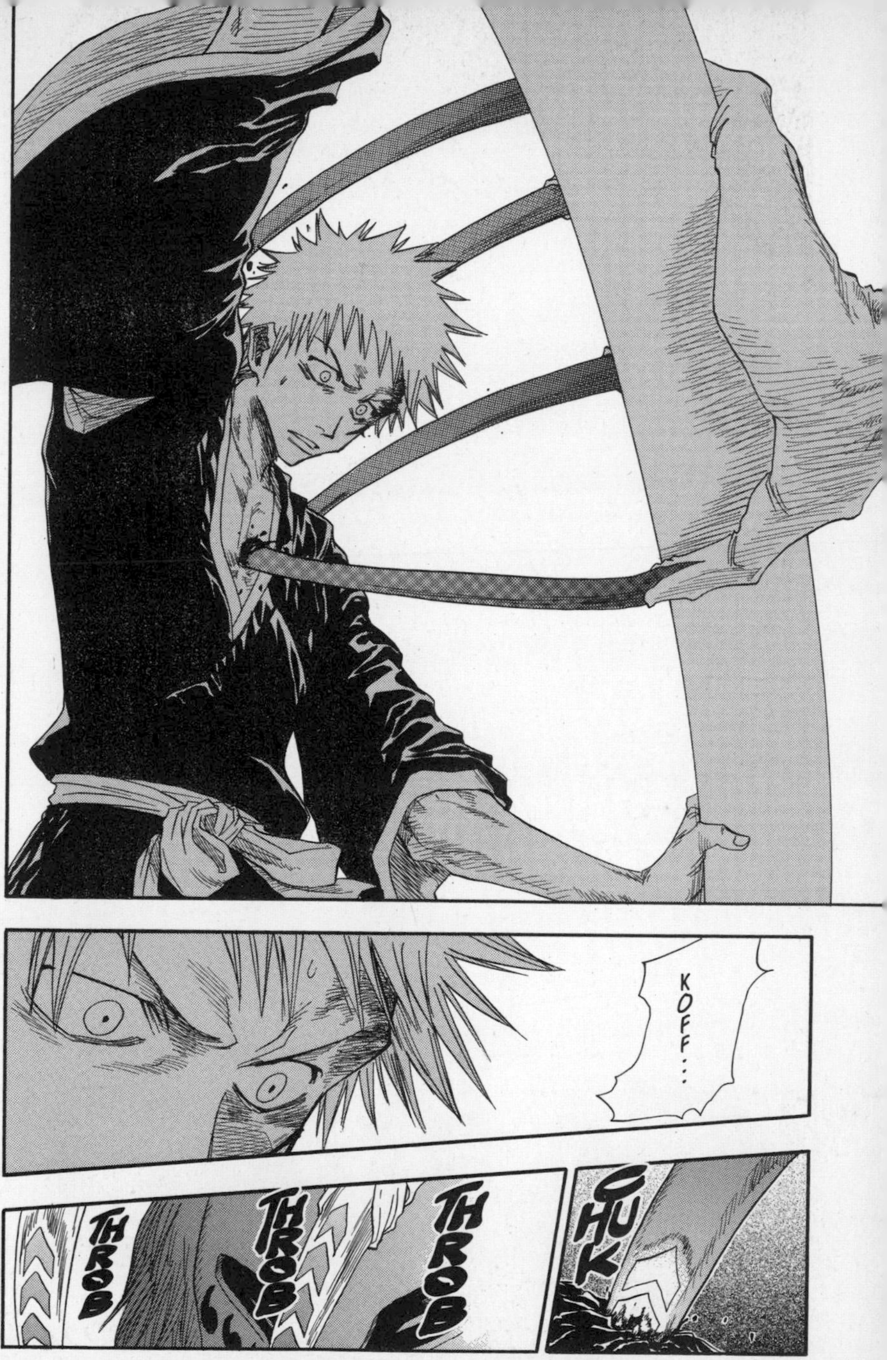
KOFF...
CHUK
THROB
THROB
THROB

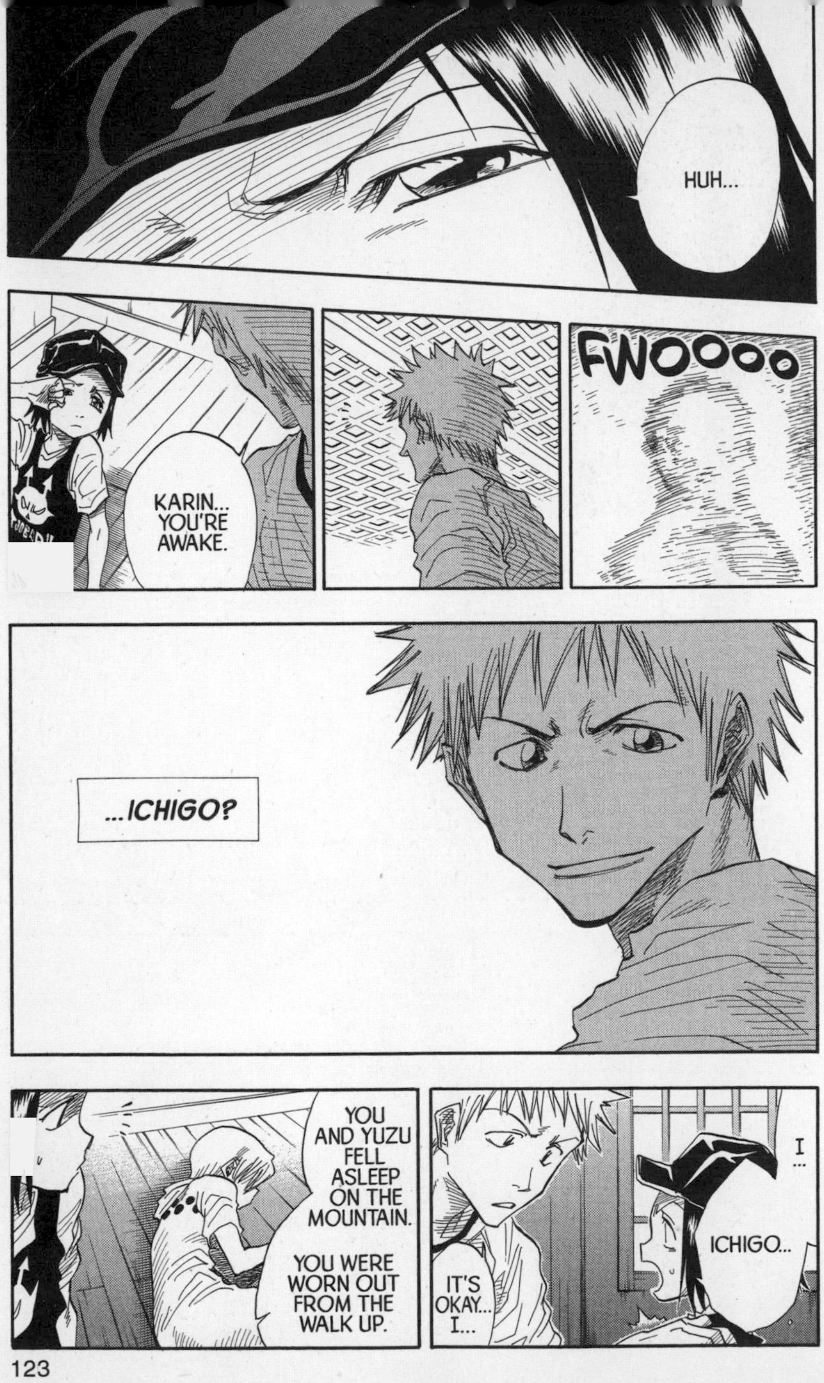
HUH...
FWOOOO
KARIN... YOU'RE AWAKE.
...ICHIGO?
I ...
ICHIGO...
IT'S OKAY... I...
YOU AND YUZU FELL ASLEEP ON THE MOUNTAIN.
YOU WERE WORN OUT FROM THE WALK UP.

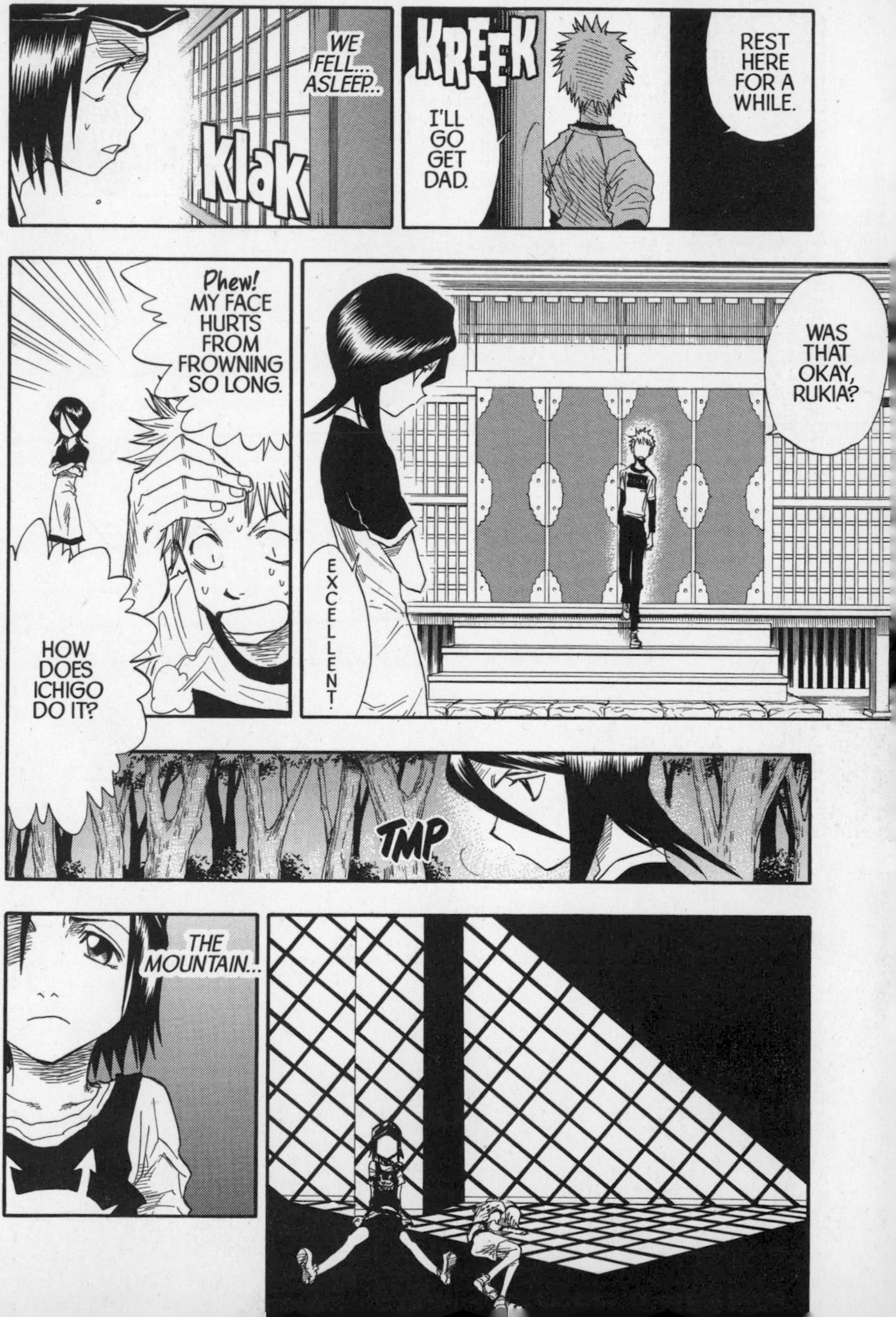
KREEK
REST HERE FOR A WHILE.
I'LL GO GET DAD.
WE FELL... ASLEEP...
Klak
WAS THAT OKAY, RUKIA?
EXCELLENT!
Phew! MY FACE HURTS FROM FROWNING SO LONG.
HOW DOES ICHIGO DO IT?
TMP
THE MOUNTAIN...

READ THIS WAY

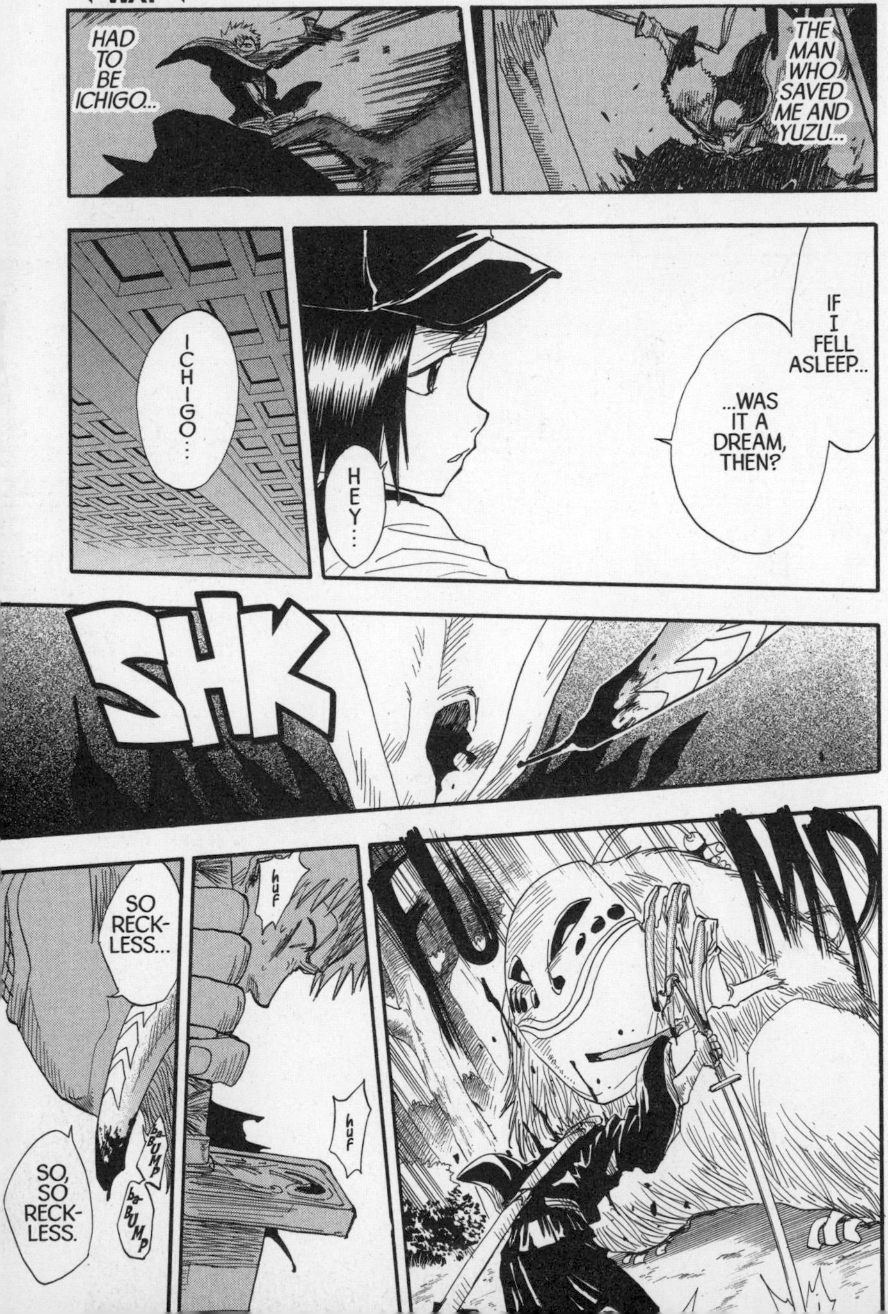
THE MAN WHO SAVED ME AND YUZU...
HAD TO BE ICHIGO...
IF I FELL ASLEEP...
...WAS IT A DREAM, THEN?
HEY...
ICHIGO...
SHK
FUMP
huf
huf
SO RECKLESS...
ba-BUMP
ba-BUMP
SO, SO RECKLESS.

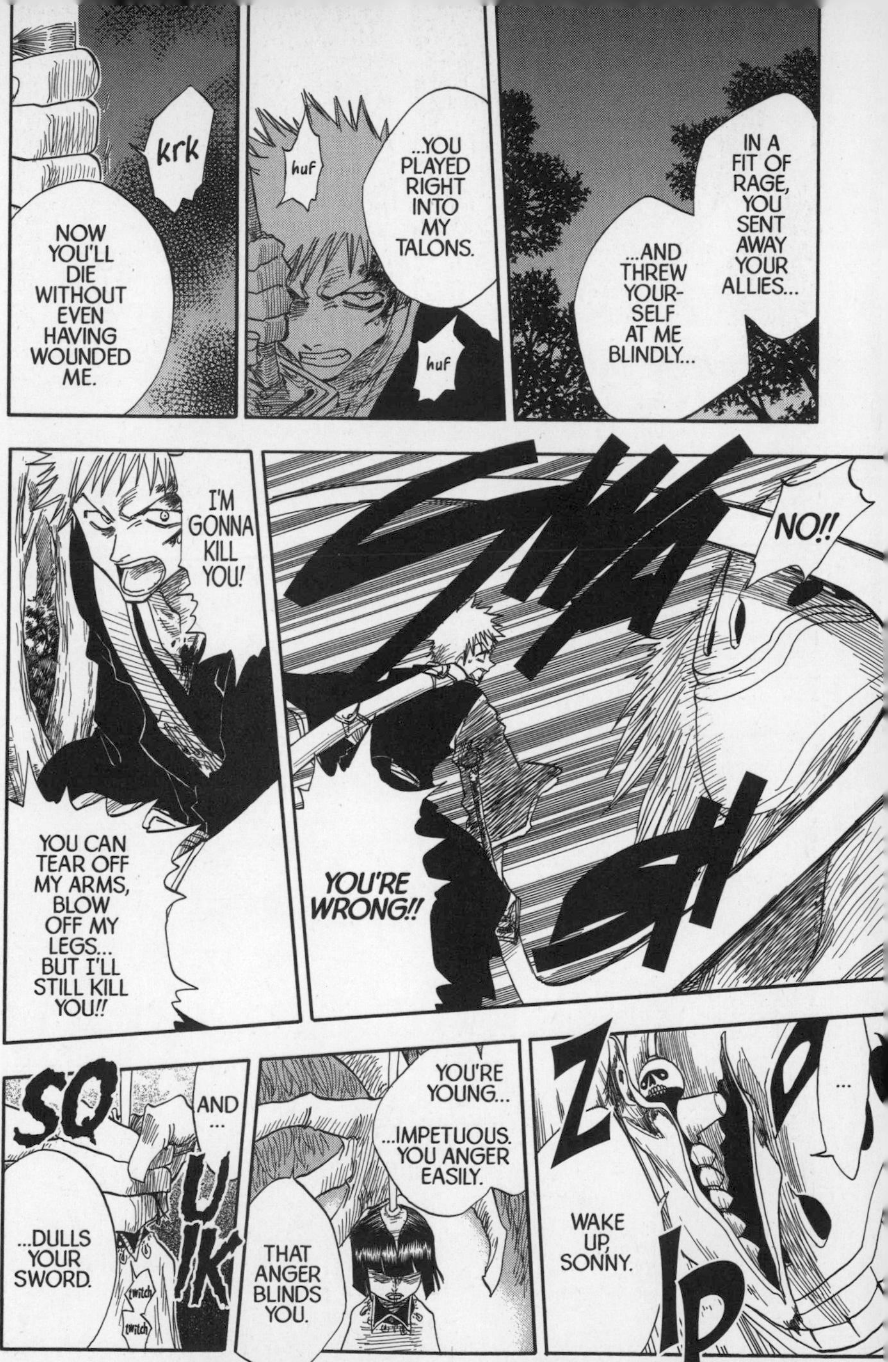
IN A FIT OF RAGE, YOU SENT AWAY YOUR ALLIES...
...AND THREW YOURSELF AT ME BLINDLY...
huf
...YOU PLAYED RIGHT INTO MY TALONS.
huf
krk
NOW YOU'LL DIE WITHOUT EVEN HAVING WOUNDED ME.
NO!!
YOU'RE WRONG!!
I'M GONNA KILL YOU!
YOU CAN TEAR OFF MY ARMS, BLOW OFF MY LEGS... BUT I'LL STILL KILL YOU!!
ZIP
...
WAKE UP, SONNY.
YOU'RE YOUNG...
...IMPETUOUS. YOU ANGER EASILY.
THAT ANGER BLINDS YOU.
AND...
SQUIK
...DULLS YOUR SWORD.
twitch
twitch

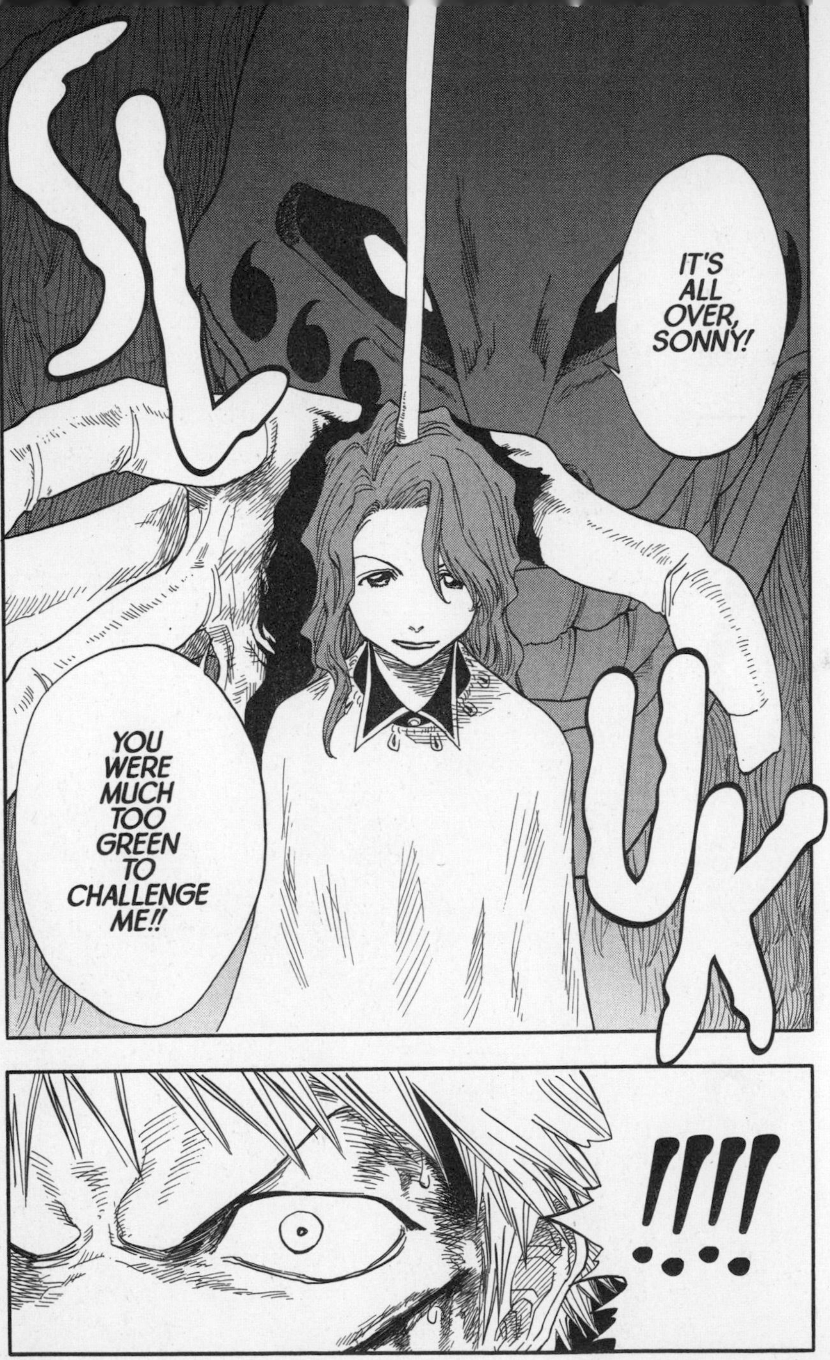
IT'S ALL OVER, SONNY!
SLUK
YOU WERE MUCH TOO GREEN TO CHALLENGE ME!!
!!!!

Q: Is it true that Ichigo doesn't brush his teeth?

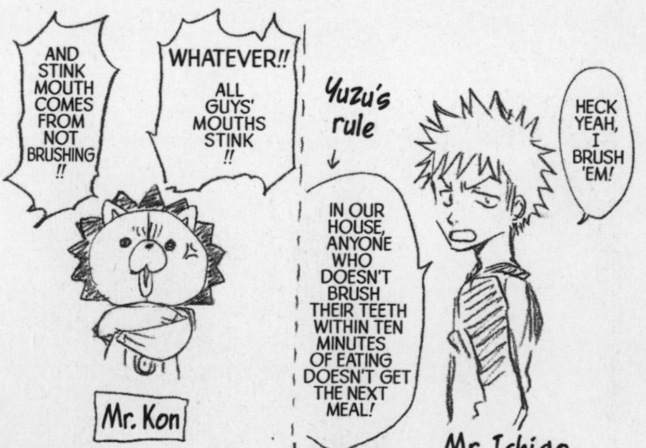
HECK YEAH, I BRUSH 'EM!
Mr. Ichigo
Yuzu's rule
IN OUR HOUSE, ANYONE WHO DOESN'T BRUSH THEIR TEETH WITHIN TEN MINUTES OF EATING DOESN'T GET THE NEXT MEAL!
WHATEVER!!
ALL GUYS' MOUTHS STINK!!
AND STINK MOUTH COMES FROM NOT BRUSHING!!
Mr. Kon

23. 6/17 op. 7 Sharp Will, Dull Blade

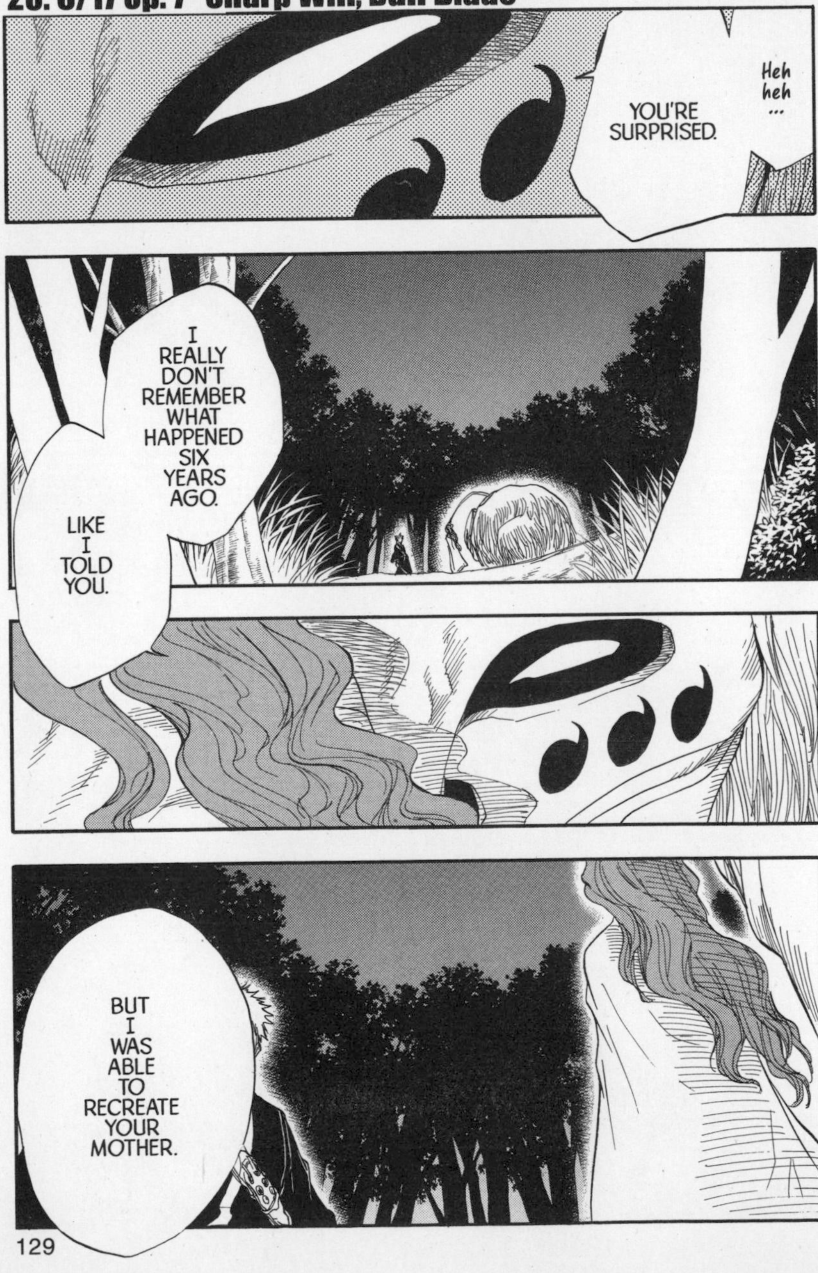
Heh heh ...
YOU'RE SURPRISED.
I REALLY DON'T REMEMBER WHAT HAPPENED SIX YEARS AGO.
LIKE I TOLD YOU.
BUT I WAS ABLE TO RECREATE YOUR MOTHER.

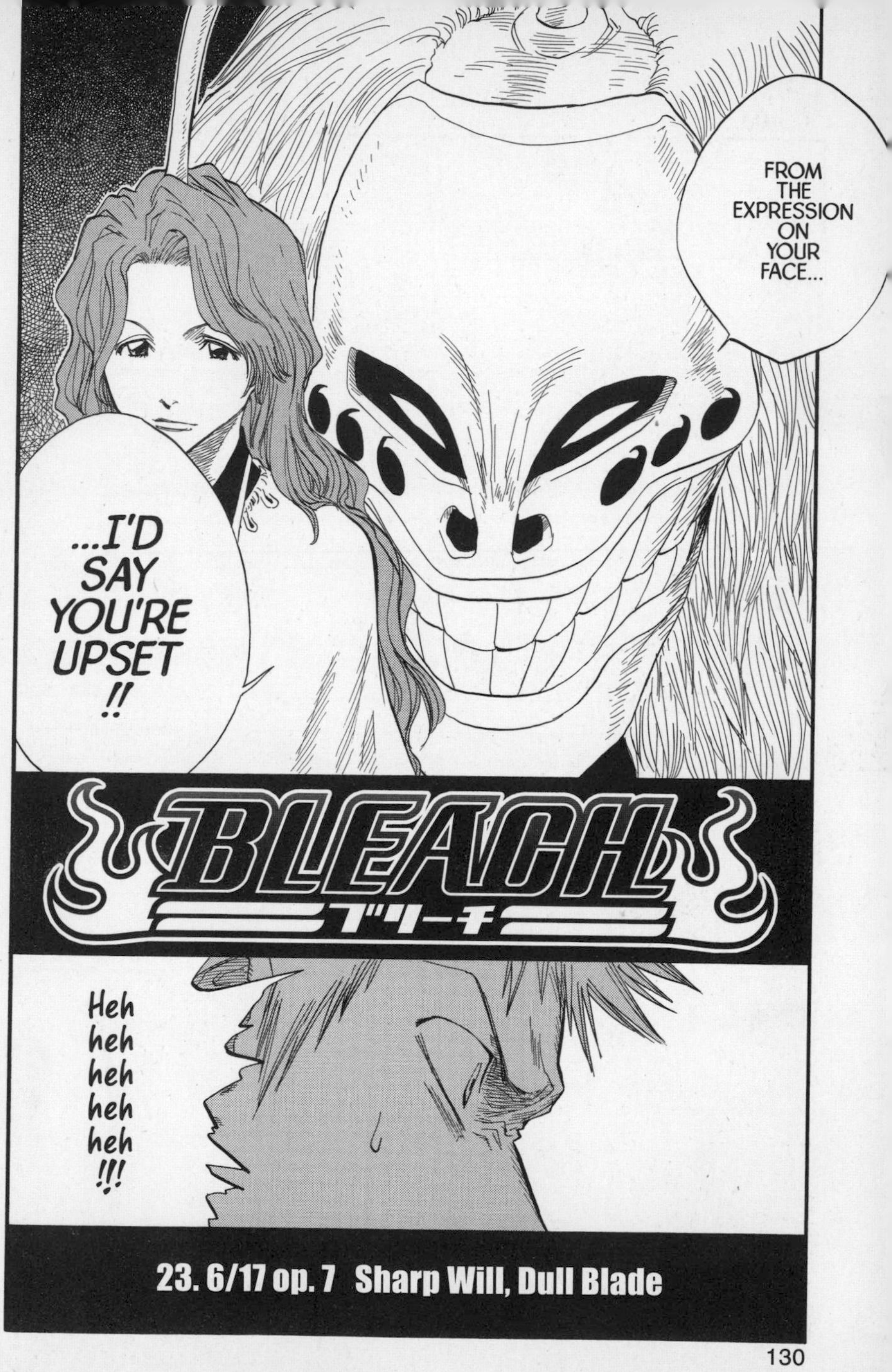
FROM THE EXPRESSION ON YOUR FACE...
...I'D SAY YOU'RE UPSET!!
BLEACH
ブリーチ
Heh heh heh heh heh heh!!!

23. 6/17 op. 7 Sharp Will, Dull Blade

READ THIS WAY

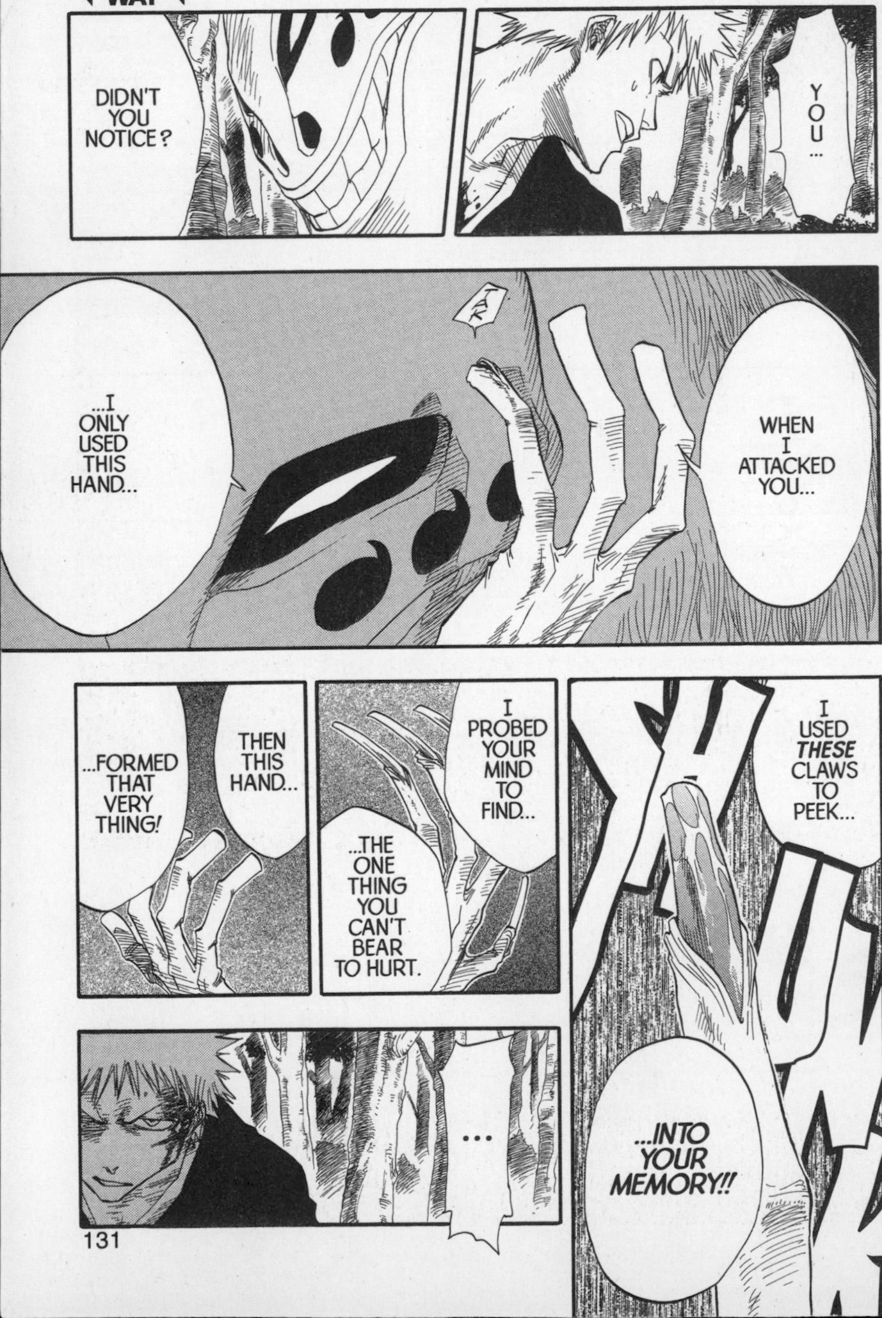

YOU...
DIDN'T YOU NOTICE?
WHEN I ATTACKED YOU...
...I ONLY USED THIS HAND...
I USED *THESE* CLAWS TO PEEK...
...INTO YOUR MEMORY!!
I PROBED YOUR MIND TO FIND...
...THE ONE THING YOU CAN'T BEAR TO HURT.
THEN THIS HAND...
...FORMED THAT VERY THING!
...

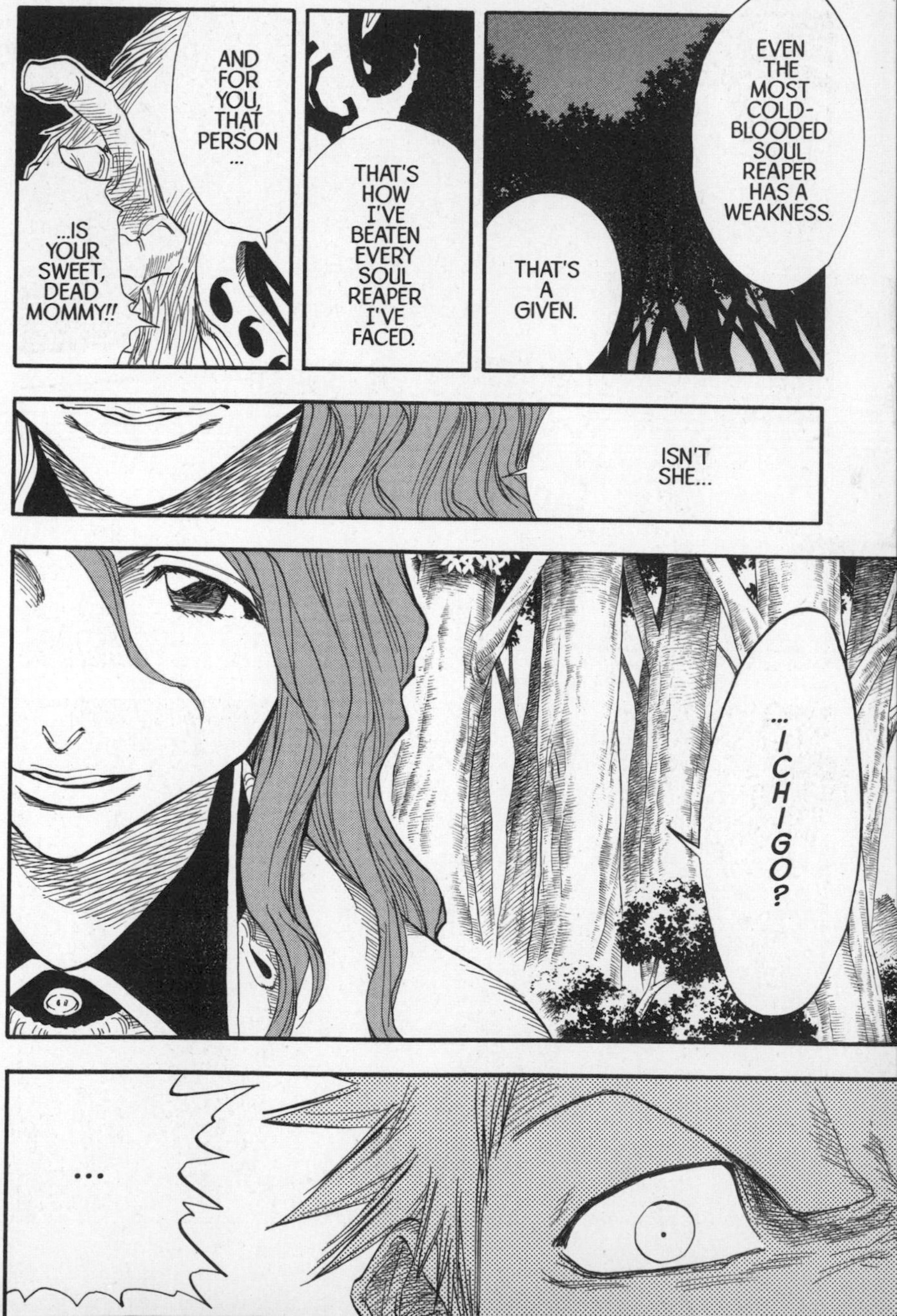
EVEN THE MOST COLD-BLOODED SOUL REAPER HAS A WEAKNESS.
THAT'S A GIVEN.
THAT'S HOW I'VE BEATEN EVERY SOUL REAPER I'VE FACED.
AND FOR YOU, THAT PERSON...
...IS YOUR SWEET, DEAD MOMMY!!
ISN'T SHE...
...ICHIGO?
...

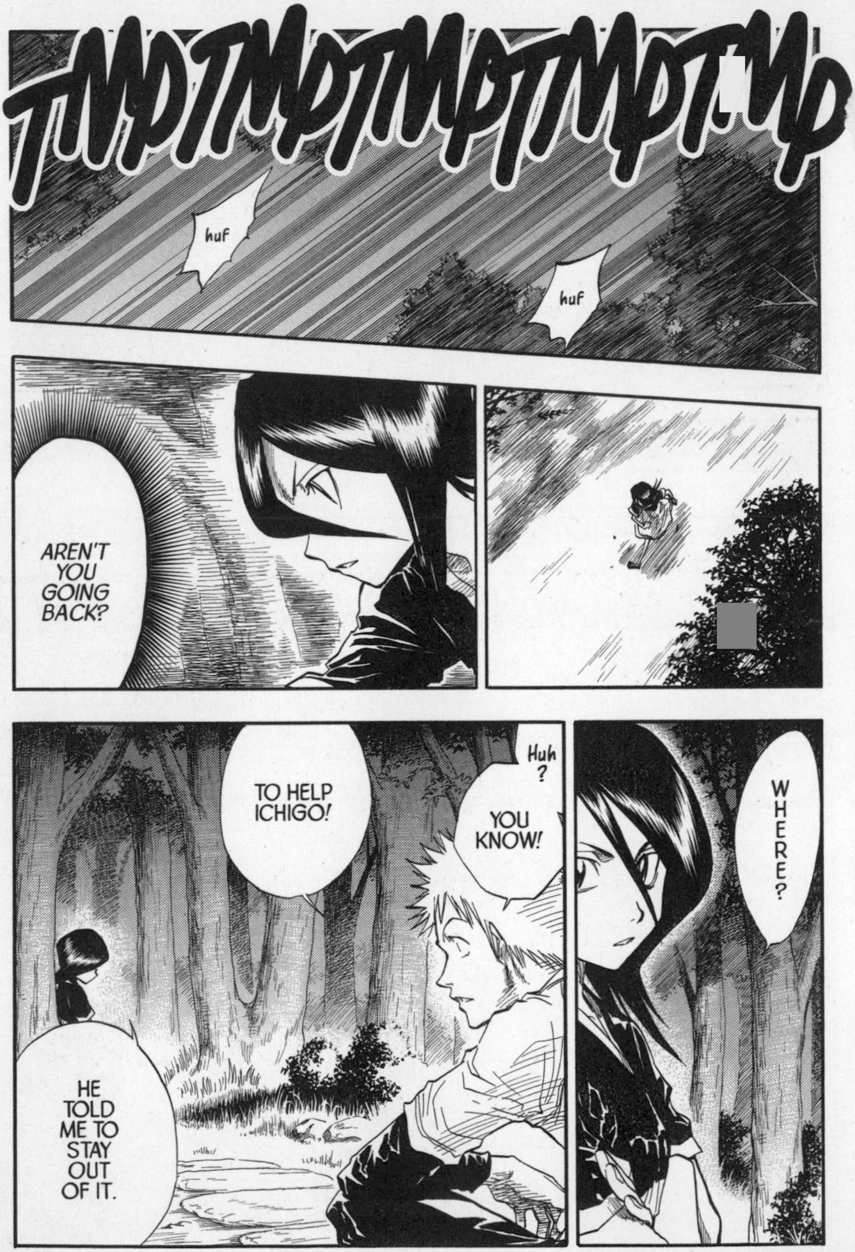
huf
huf
AREN'T YOU GOING BACK?
WHERE?
Huh?
YOU KNOW!
TO HELP ICHIGO!
HE TOLD ME TO STAY OUT OF IT.

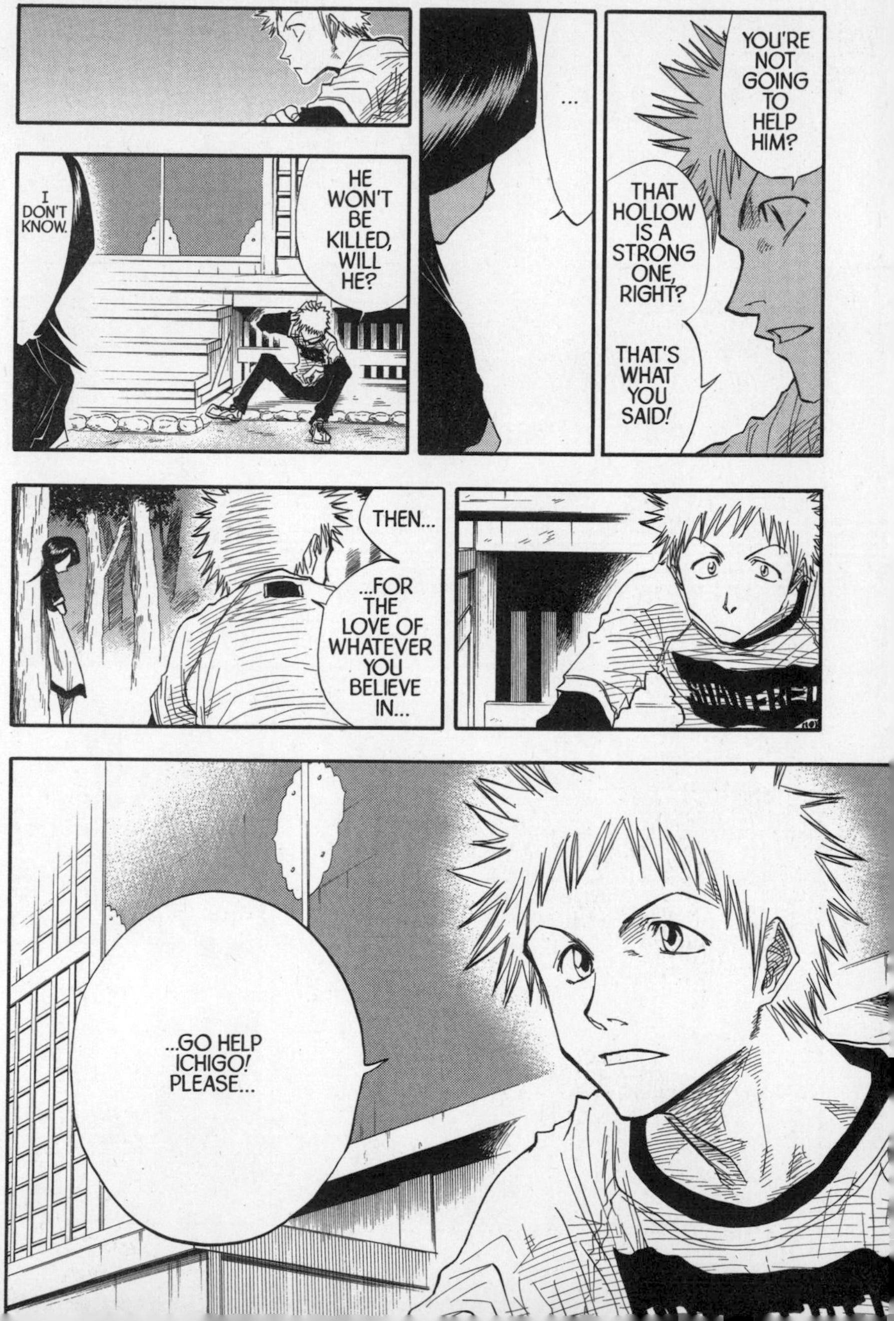
YOU'RE NOT GOING TO HELP HIM?
THAT HOLLOW IS A STRONG ONE, RIGHT?
THAT'S WHAT YOU SAID!
...
HE WON'T BE KILLED, WILL HE?
I DON'T KNOW.
THEN...
...FOR THE LOVE OF WHATEVER YOU BELIEVE IN...
...GO HELP ICHIGO! PLEASE...

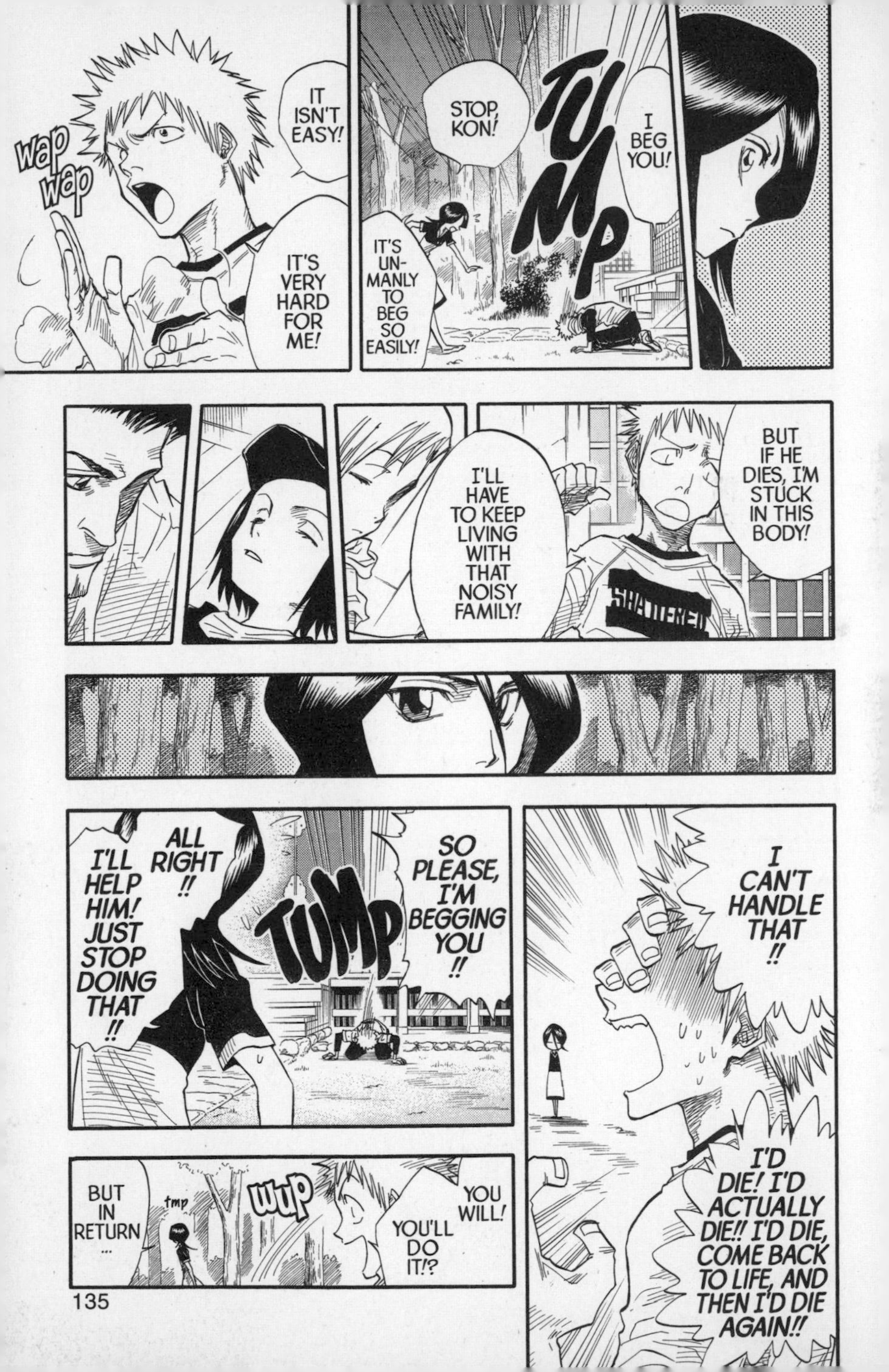
I BEG YOU!
TUMP
STOP, KON!
IT'S UN-MANLY TO BEG SO EASILY!
IT ISN'T EASY!
wap wap
IT'S VERY HARD FOR ME!
BUT IF HE DIES, I'M STUCK IN THIS BODY!
SHATTERED
I'LL HAVE TO KEEP LIVING WITH THAT NOISY FAMILY!
I CAN'T HANDLE THAT!!
I'D DIE! I'D ACTUALLY DIE!! I'D DIE, COME BACK TO LIFE, AND THEN I'D DIE AGAIN!!
SO PLEASE, I'M BEGGING YOU!!
TUMP
ALL RIGHT!!
I'LL HELP HIM! JUST STOP DOING THAT!!
YOU WILL!
YOU'LL DO IT!?
wup
tmp
BUT IN RETURN ...

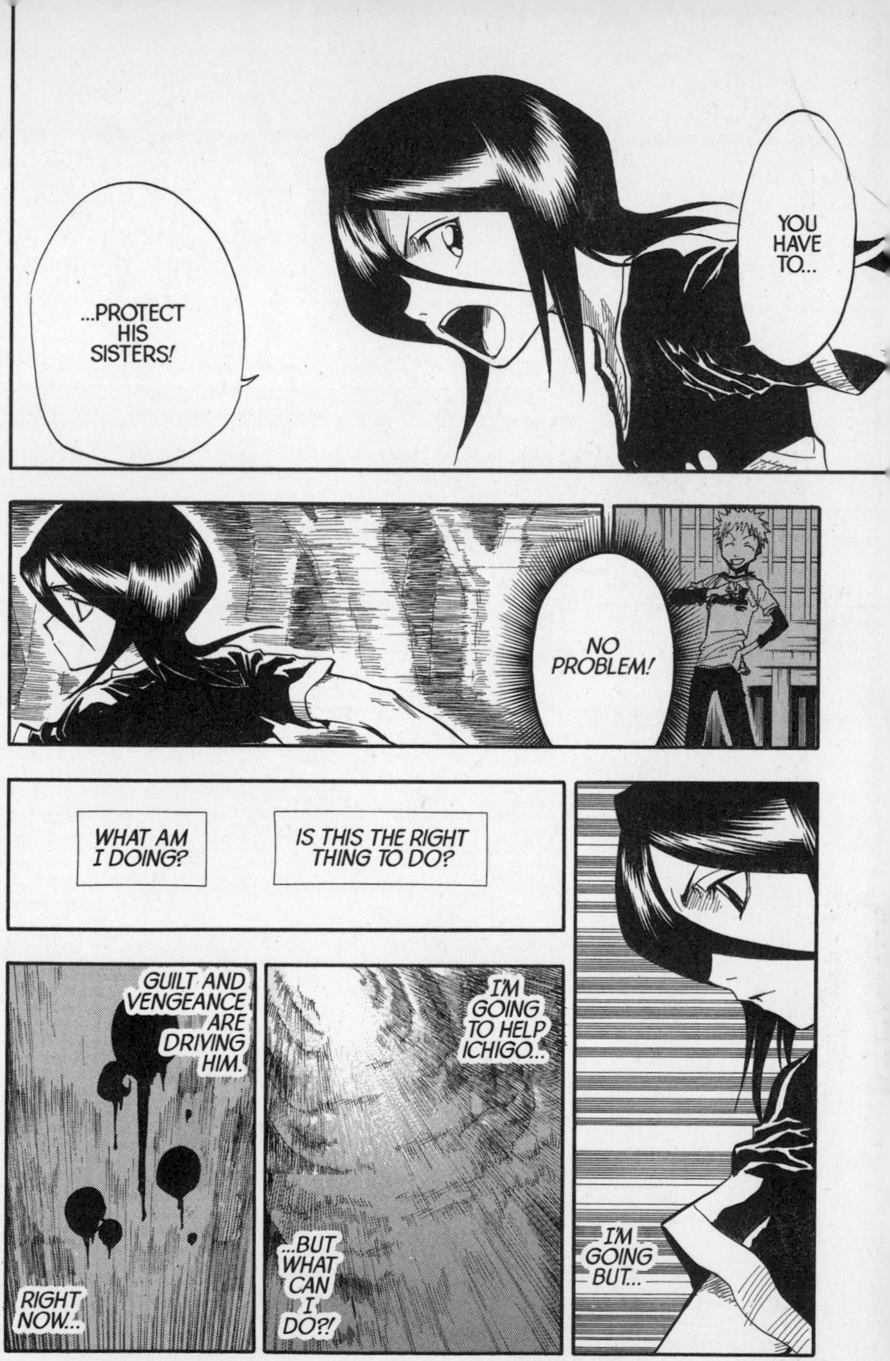
YOU HAVE TO...
...PROTECT HIS SISTERS!
NO PROBLEM!
I'M GOING BUT...
IS THIS THE RIGHT THING TO DO?
WHAT AM I DOING?
I'M GOING TO HELP ICHIGO...
...BUT WHAT CAN I DO?!
GUILT AND VENGEANCE ARE DRIVING HIM.
RIGHT NOW...

READ THIS WAY

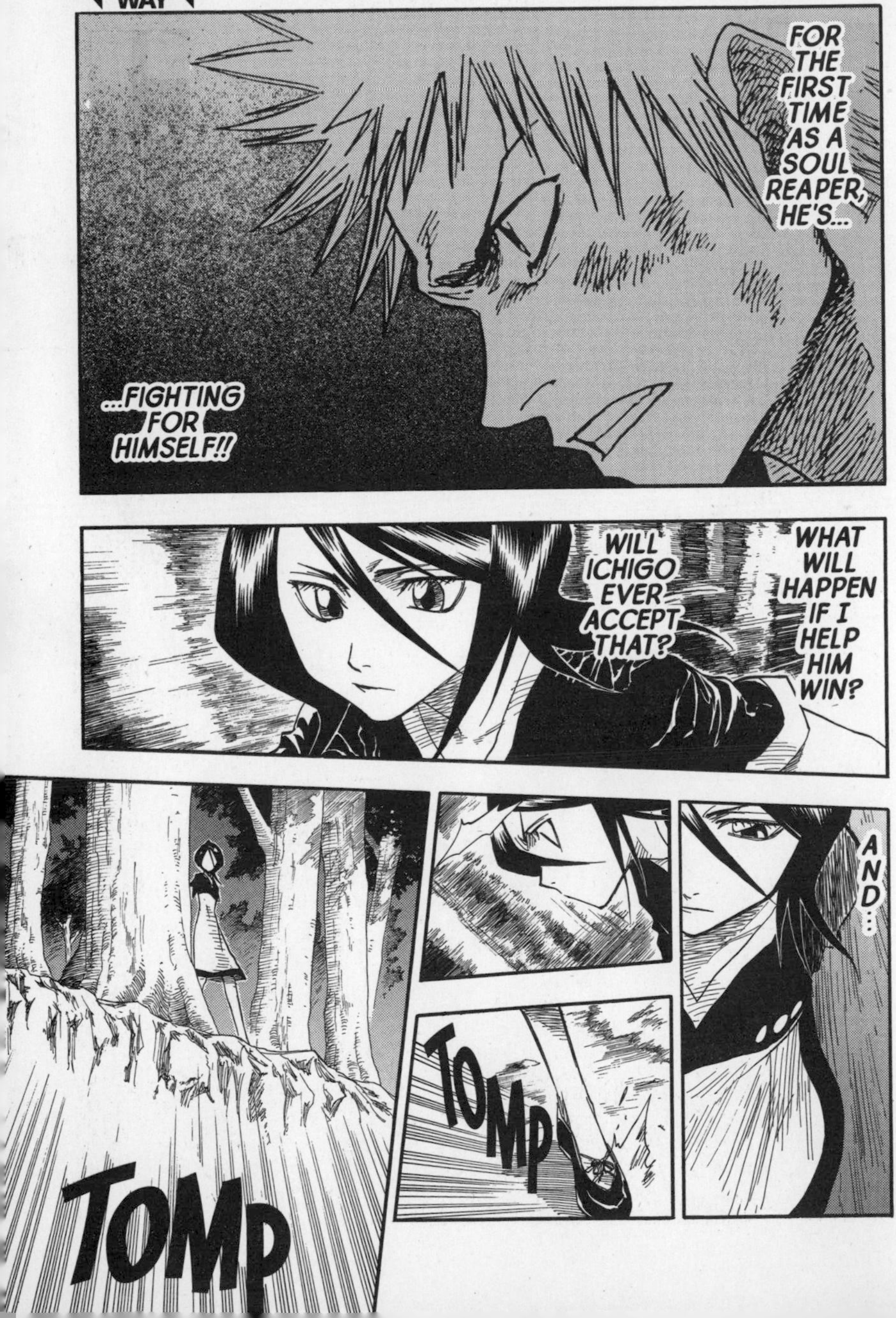
FOR THE FIRST TIME AS A SOUL REAPER, HE'S...
...FIGHTING FOR HIMSELF!!
WHAT WILL HAPPEN IF I HELP HIM WIN?
WILL ICHIGO EVER ACCEPT THAT?
AND...
TOMP
TOMP

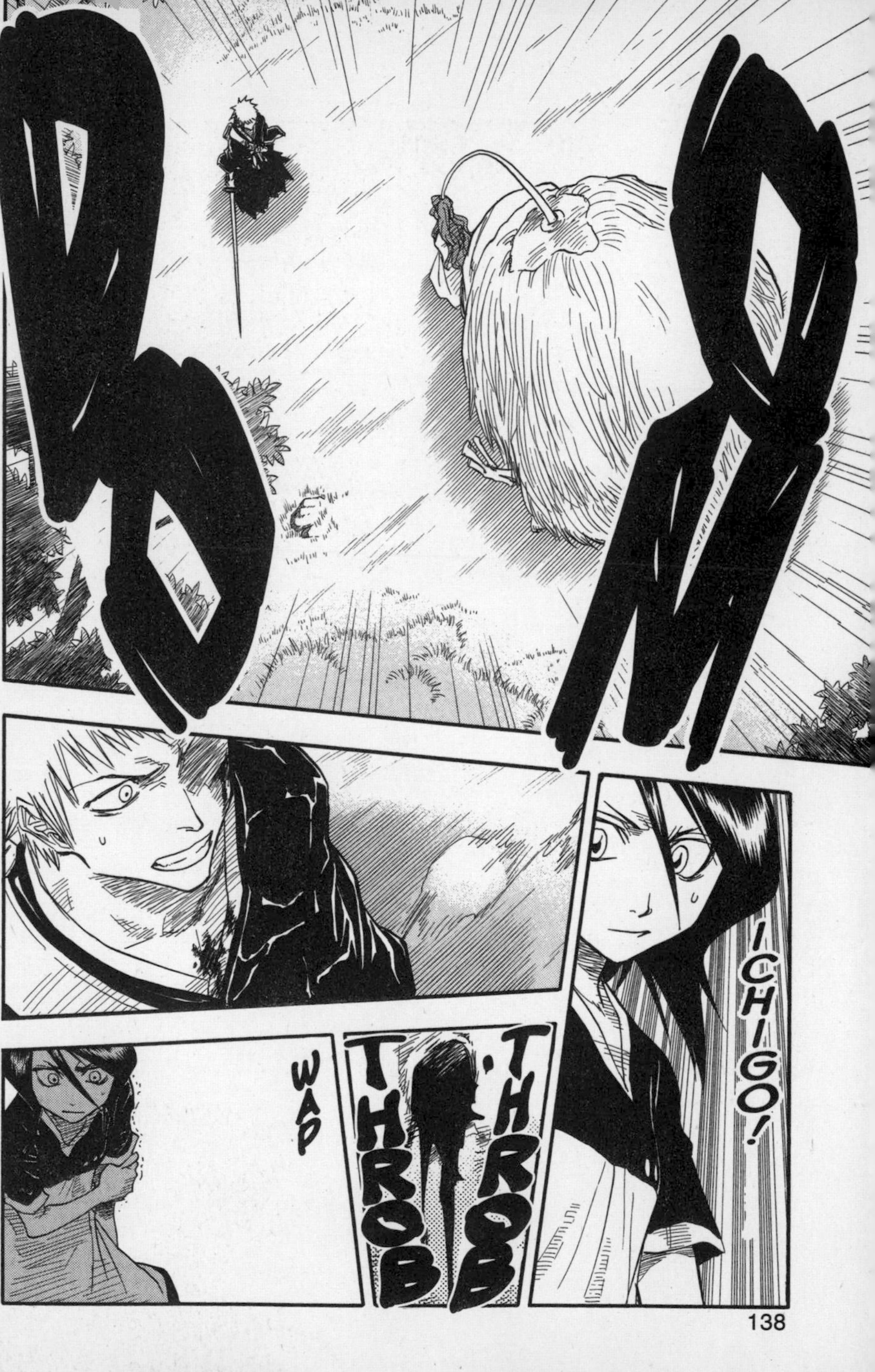
DOOM
ICHIGO!
THROB THROB
WAP

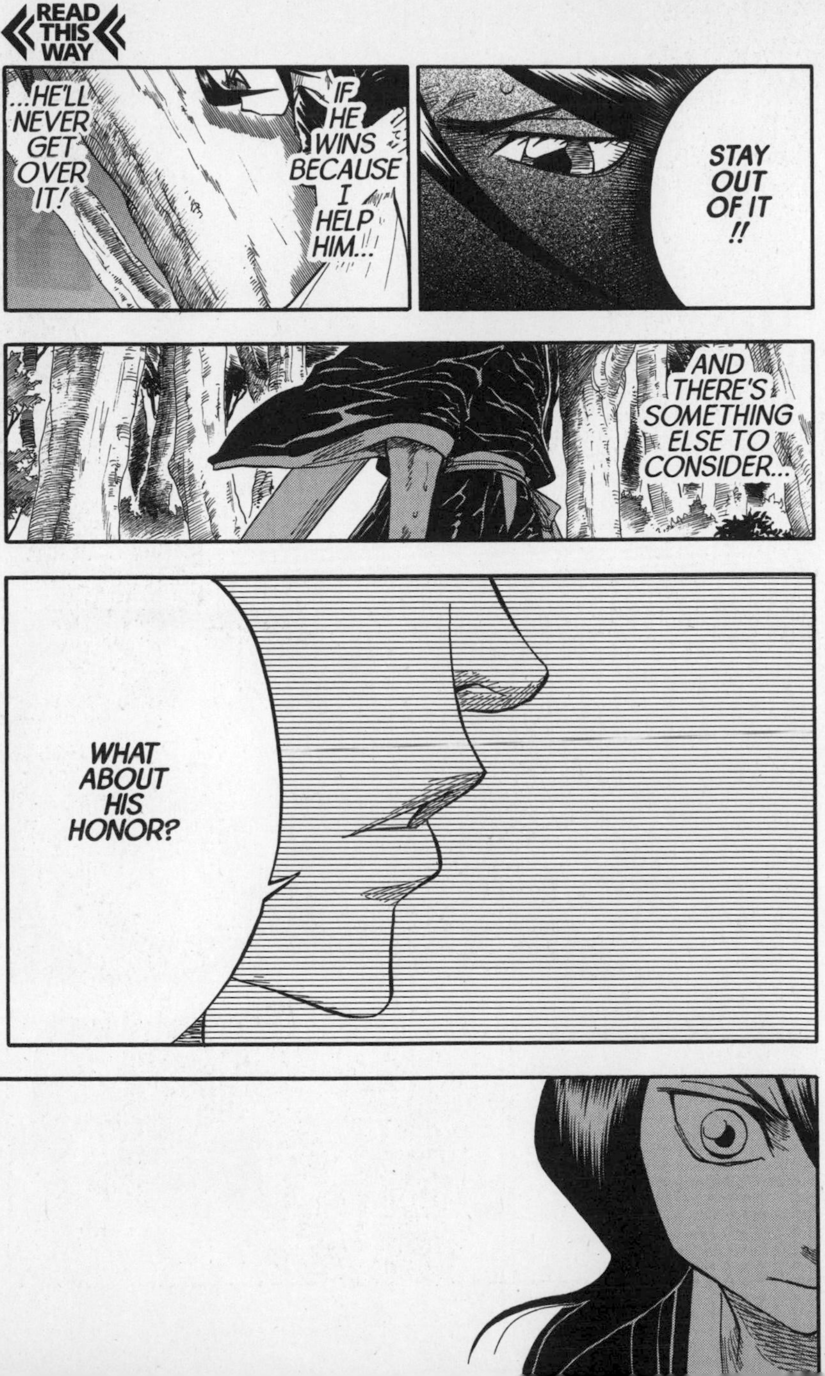
READ THIS WAY
STAY OUT OF IT !!
IF HE WINS BECAUSE I HELP HIM...
...HE'LL NEVER GET OVER IT!
AND THERE'S SOMETHING ELSE TO CONSIDER...
WHAT ABOUT HIS HONOR?

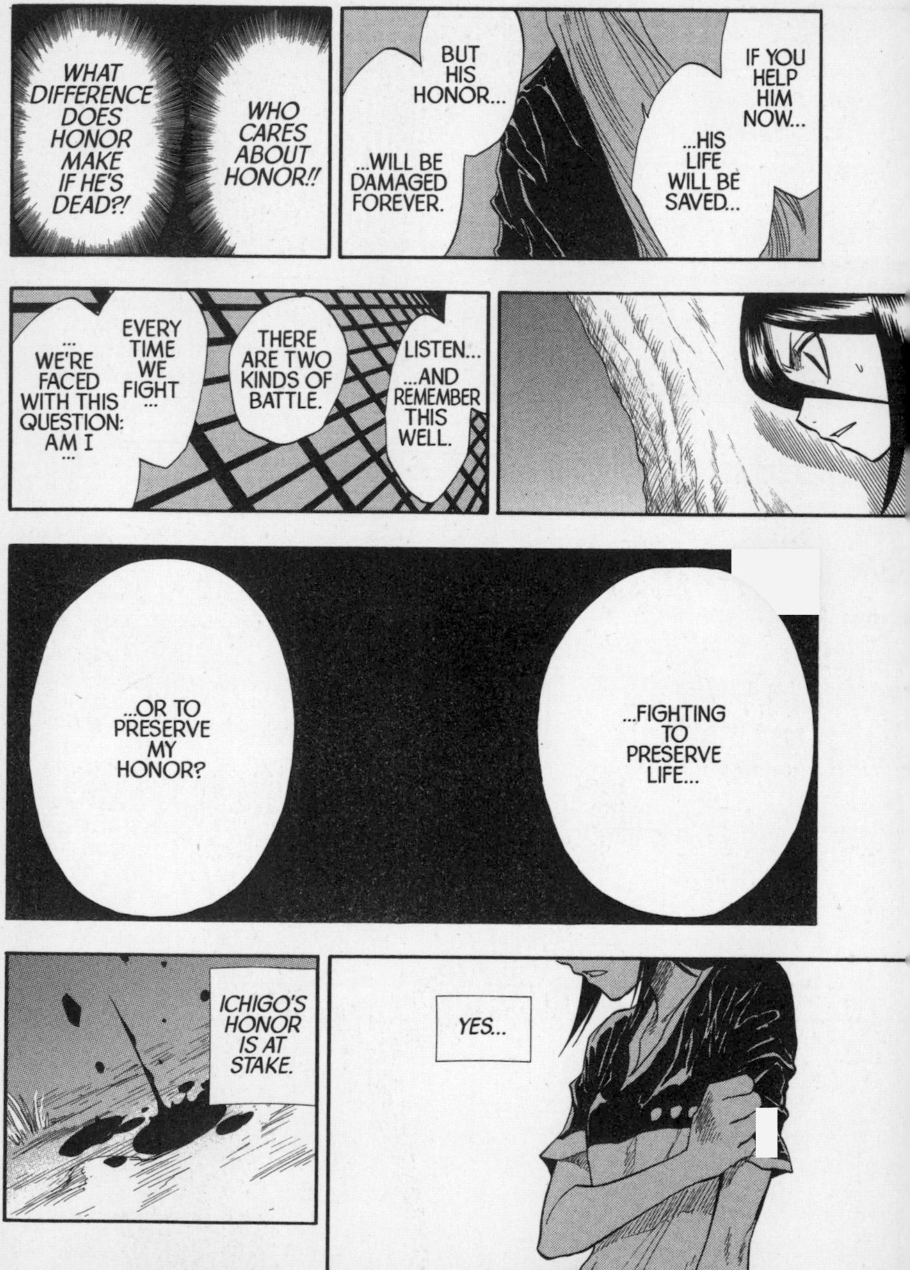
IF YOU HELP HIM NOW...
...HIS LIFE WILL BE SAVED...
BUT HIS HONOR...
...WILL BE DAMAGED FOREVER.
WHO CARES ABOUT HONOR!!
WHAT DIFFERENCE DOES HONOR MAKE IF HE'S DEAD?!
LISTEN...
...AND REMEMBER THIS WELL.
THERE ARE TWO KINDS OF BATTLE.
EVERY TIME WE FIGHT ...
... WE'RE FACED WITH THIS QUESTION: AM I ...
...FIGHTING TO PRESERVE LIFE...
...OR TO PRESERVE MY HONOR?
YES...
ICHIGO'S HONOR IS AT STAKE.

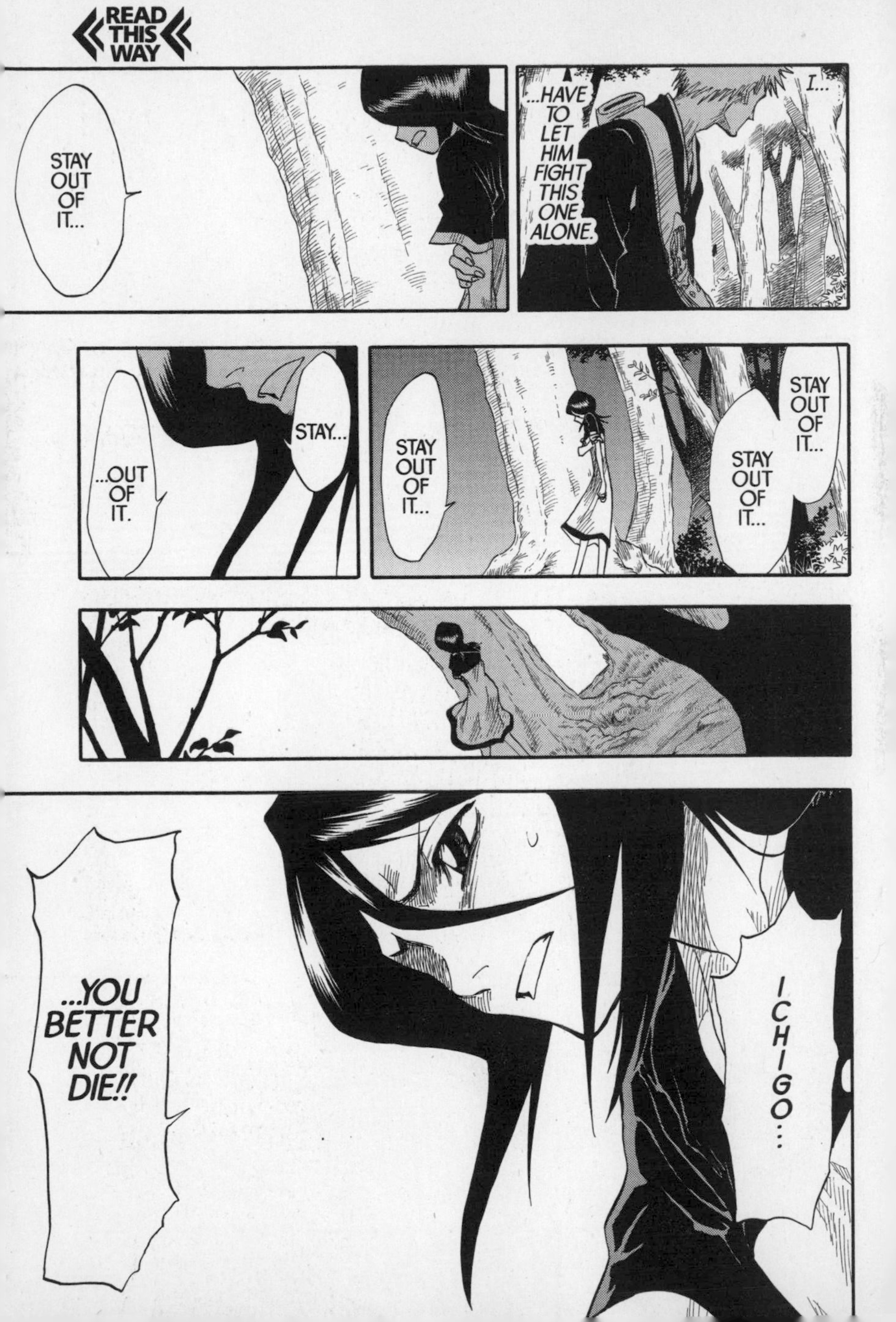
READ THIS WAY
I...
...HAVE TO LET HIM FIGHT THIS ONE ALONE.
STAY OUT OF IT...
STAY OUT OF IT...
STAY OUT OF IT...
STAY OUT OF IT...
STAY...
...OUT OF IT.
ICHIGO...
...YOU BETTER NOT DIE!!

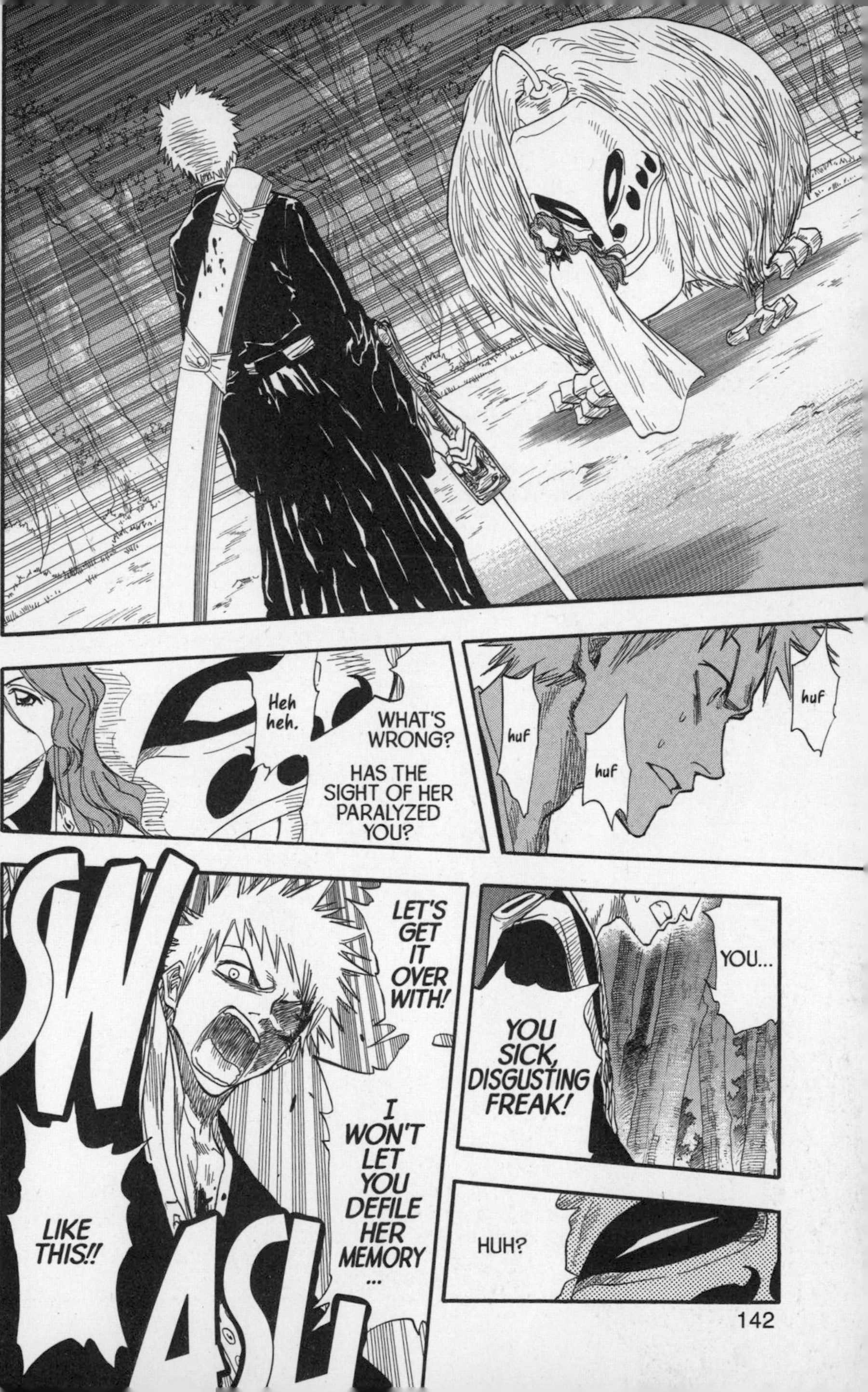
huf
huf
huf
Heh heh.
WHAT'S WRONG?
HAS THE SIGHT OF HER PARALYZED YOU?
YOU...
YOU SICK, DISGUSTING FREAK!
HUH?
LET'S GET IT OVER WITH!
I WON'T LET YOU DEFILE HER MEMORY...
LIKE THIS!!
SWASH

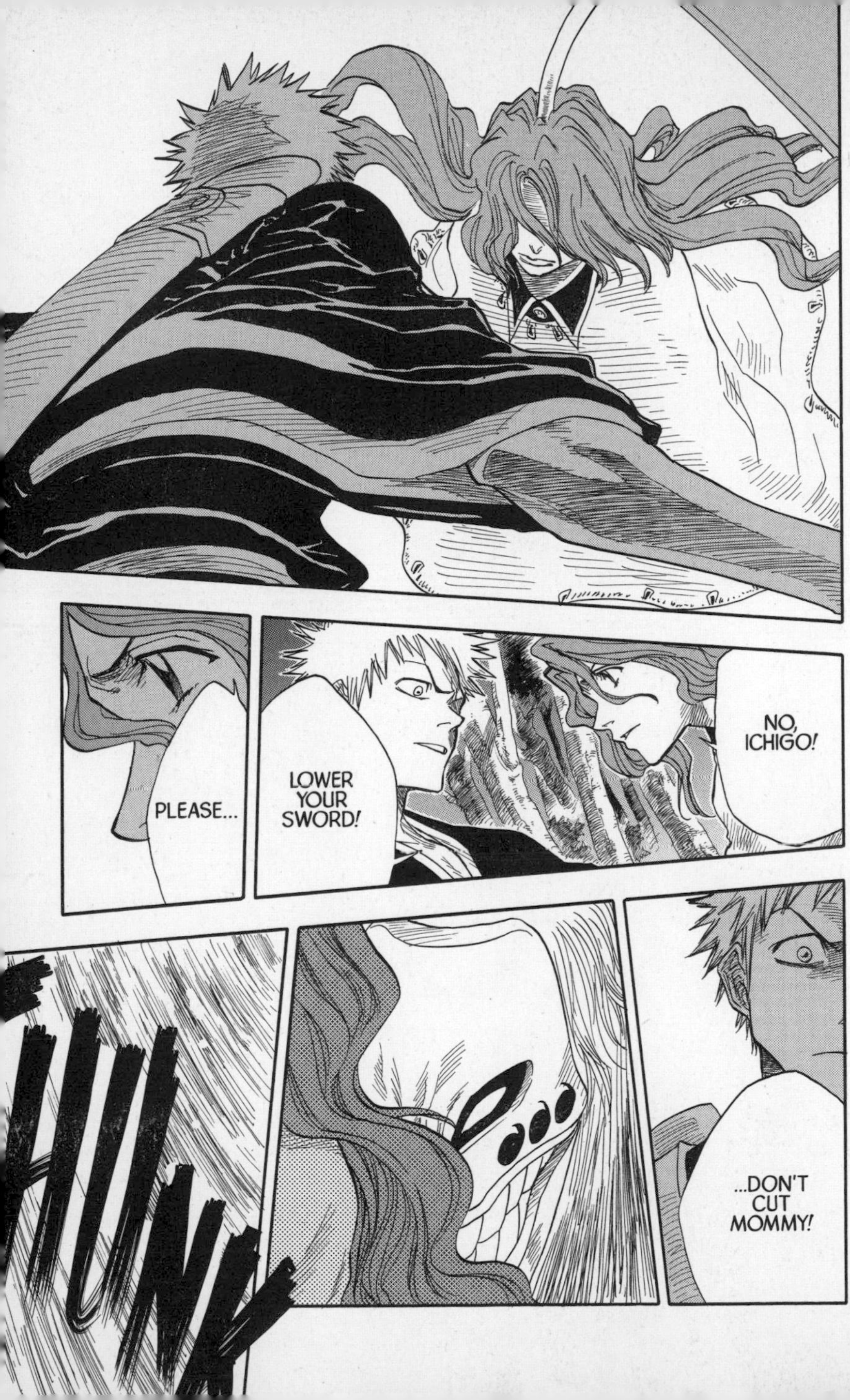
NO, ICHIGO!
LOWER YOUR SWORD!
PLEASE...
...DON'T CUT MOMMY!

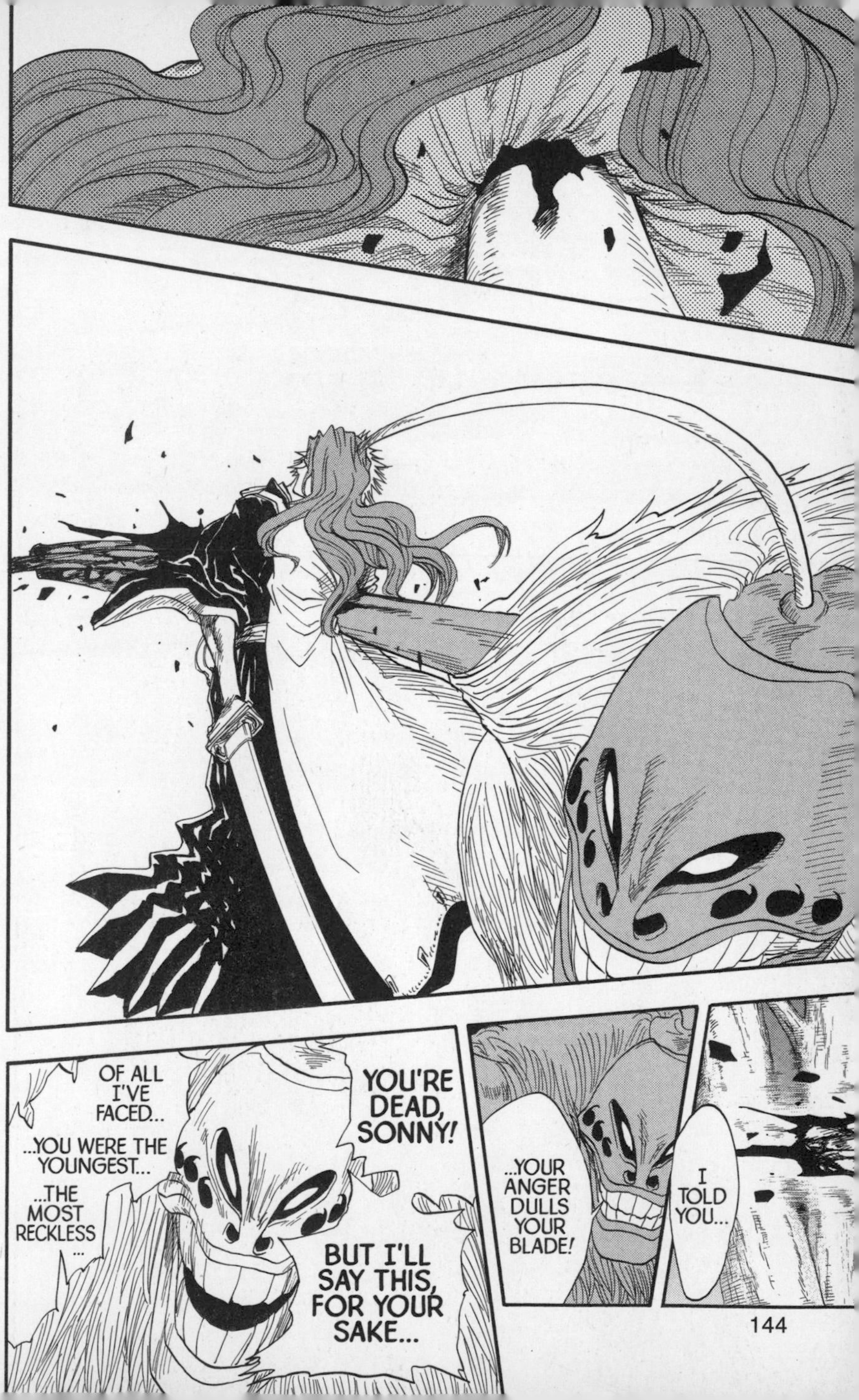
I TOLD YOU...
...YOUR ANGER DULLS YOUR BLADE!
YOU'RE DEAD, SONNY!
OF ALL I'VE FACED...
...YOU WERE THE YOUNGEST...
...THE MOST RECKLESS...
BUT I'LL SAY THIS, FOR YOUR SAKE...

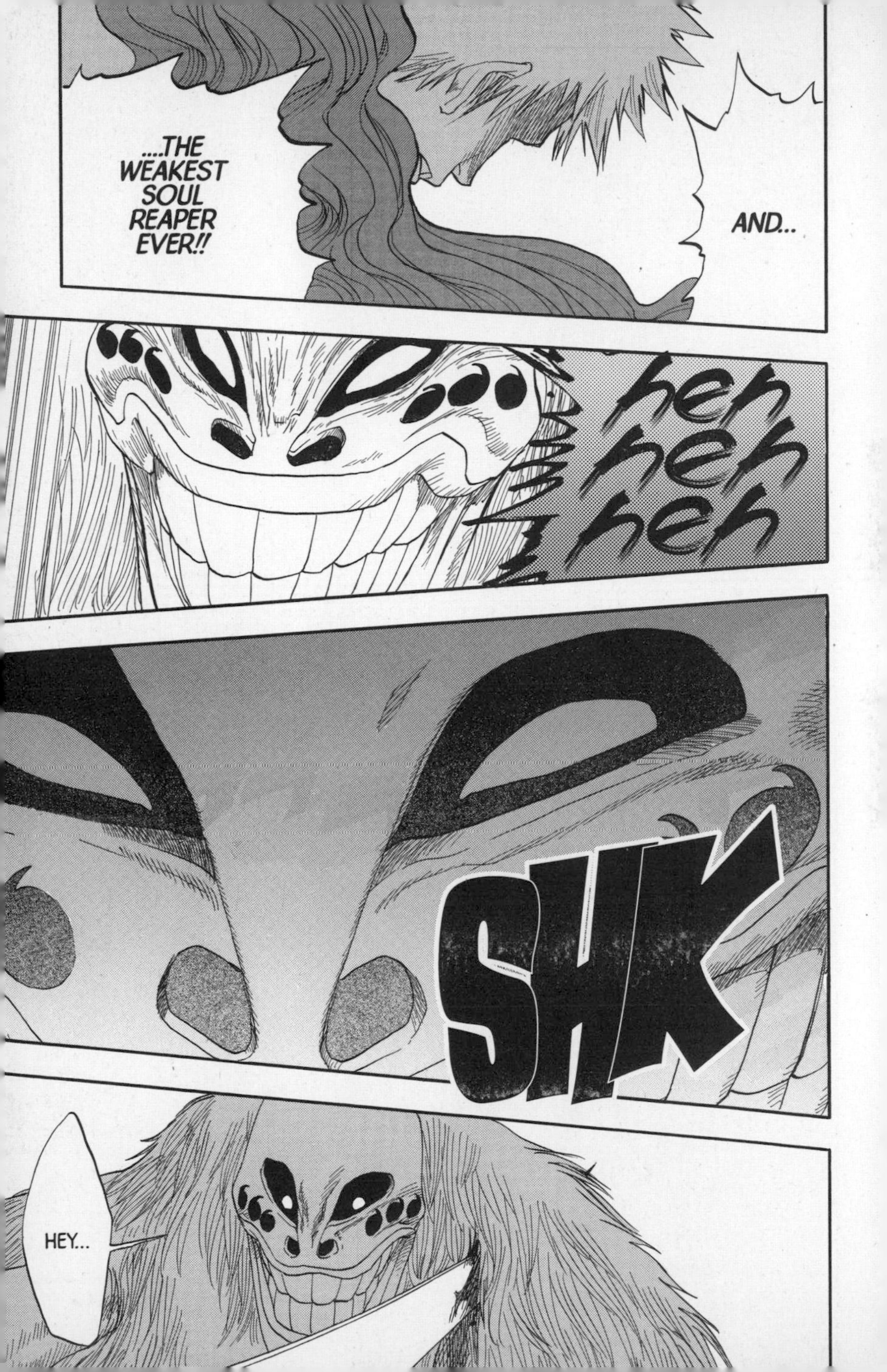
AND...
....THE WEAKEST SOUL REAPER EVER!!
heh heh heh
SHK
HEY...

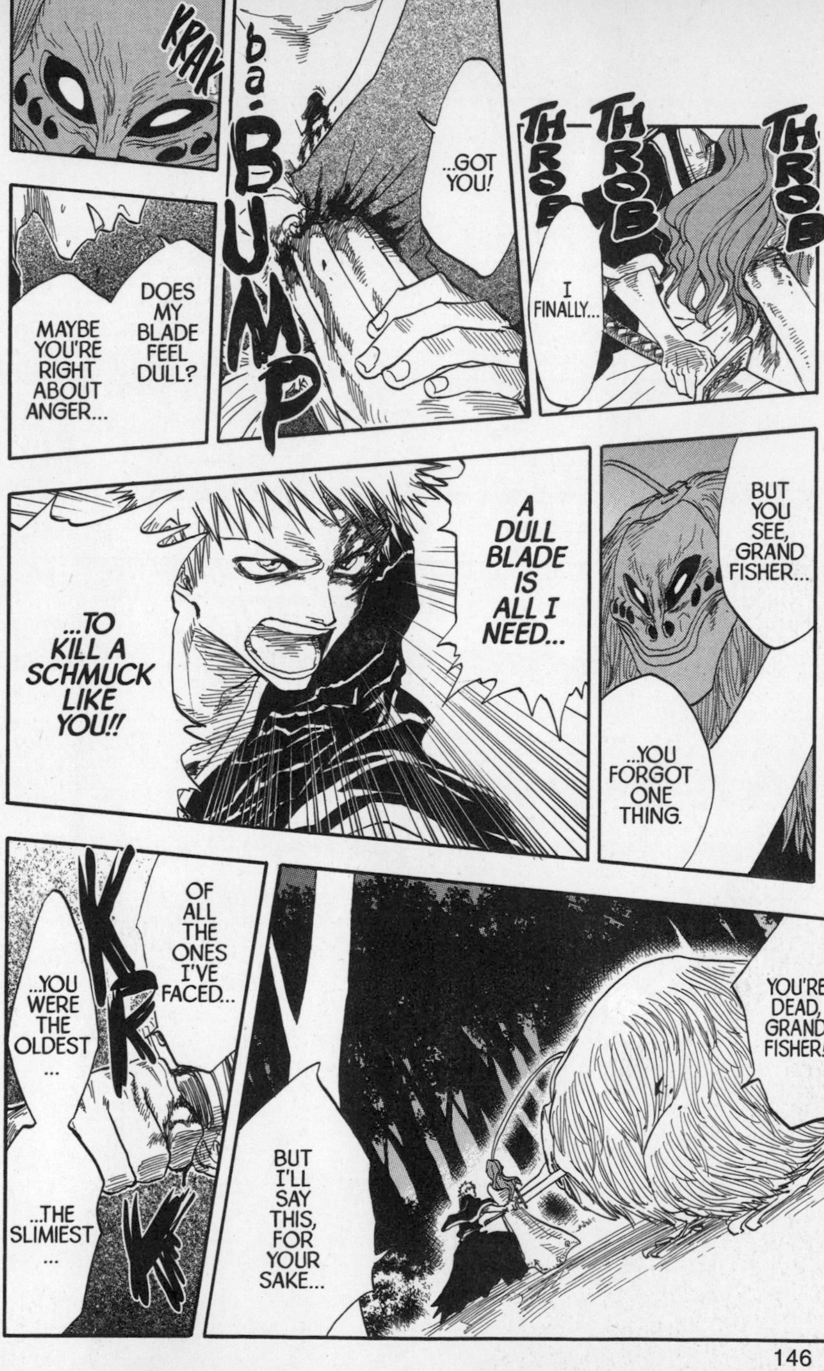
THROB THROB THROB
I FINALLY...
ba-BUMP
...GOT YOU!
KRAK
DOES MY BLADE FEEL DULL?
MAYBE YOU'RE RIGHT ABOUT ANGER...
BUT YOU SEE, GRAND FISHER...
...YOU FORGOT ONE THING.
A DULL BLADE IS ALL I NEED...
...TO KILL A SCHMUCK LIKE YOU!!
YOU'RE DEAD, GRAND FISHER!
BUT I'LL SAY THIS, FOR YOUR SAKE...
OF ALL THE ONES I'VE FACED...
...YOU WERE THE OLDEST...
...THE SLIMIEST...

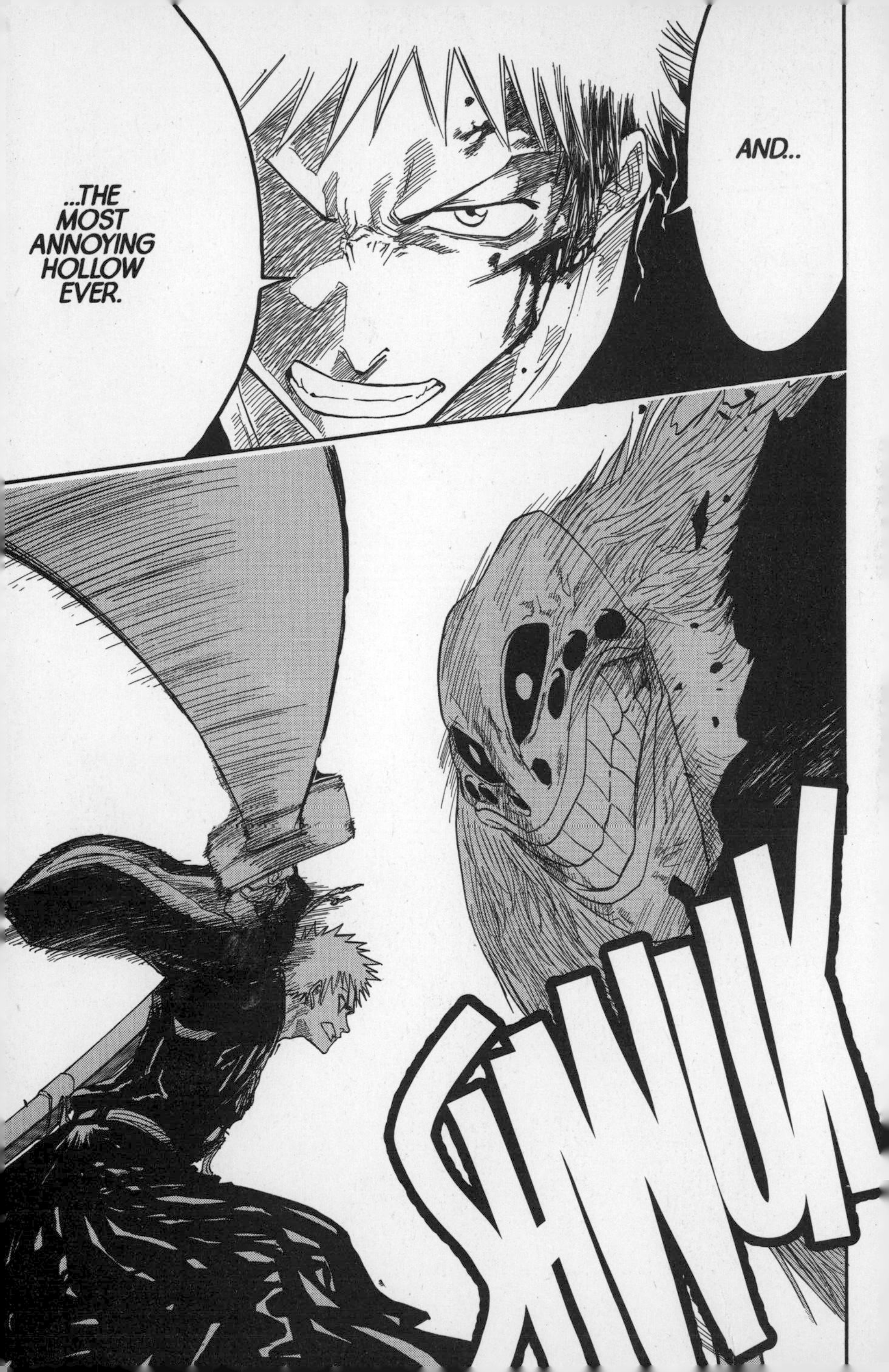
AND...
...THE MOST ANNOYING HOLLOW EVER.

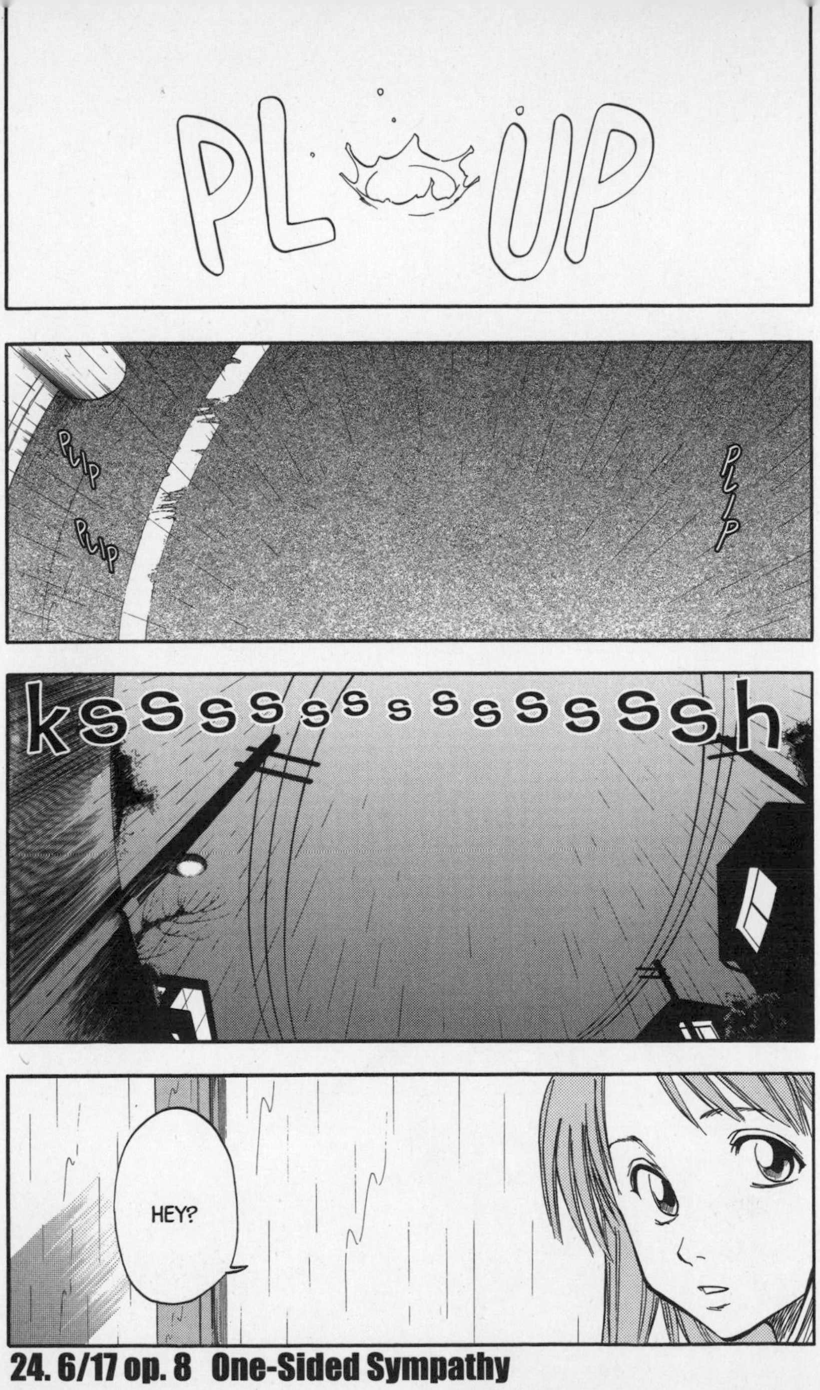
PLUP
PLIP
PLIP
PLIP
kssssssssssssssh
HEY?

24. 6/17 op. 8 One-Sided Sympathy

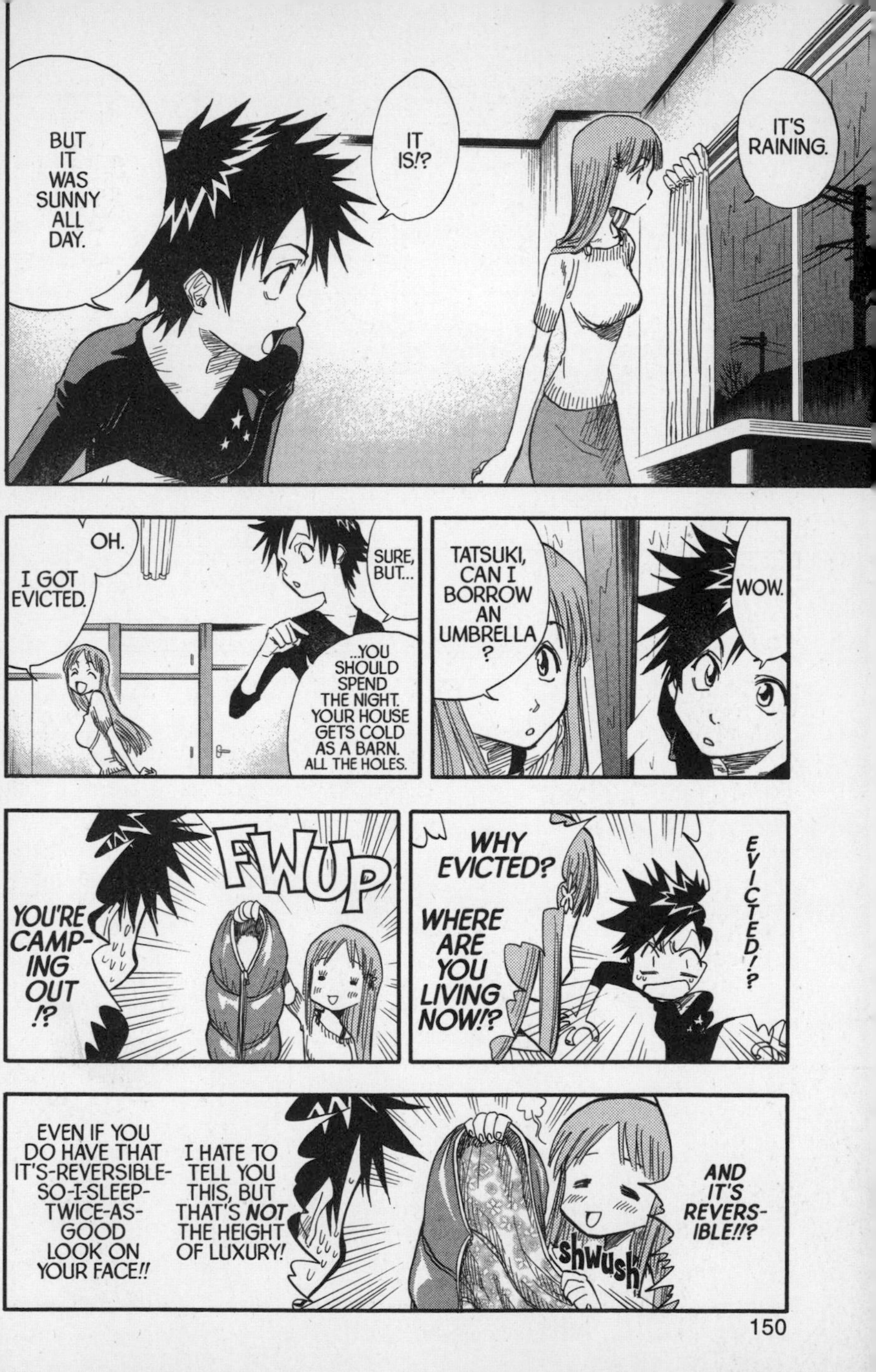
IT'S RAINING.
IT IS!?
BUT IT WAS SUNNY ALL DAY.
WOW.
TATSUKI, CAN I BORROW AN UMBRELLA?
SURE, BUT...
...YOU SHOULD SPEND THE NIGHT. YOUR HOUSE GETS COLD AS A BARN. ALL THE HOLES.
OH.
I GOT EVICTED.
EVICTED!?
WHY EVICTED?
WHERE ARE YOU LIVING NOW!?
FWUP
YOU'RE CAMP-ING OUT!?
AND IT'S REVERS-IBLE!!?
shwush!
I HATE TO TELL YOU THIS, BUT THAT'S *NOT* THE HEIGHT OF LUXURY!
EVEN IF YOU DO HAVE THAT IT'S-REVERSIBLE-SO-I-SLEEP-TWICE-AS-GOOD LOOK ON YOUR FACE!!

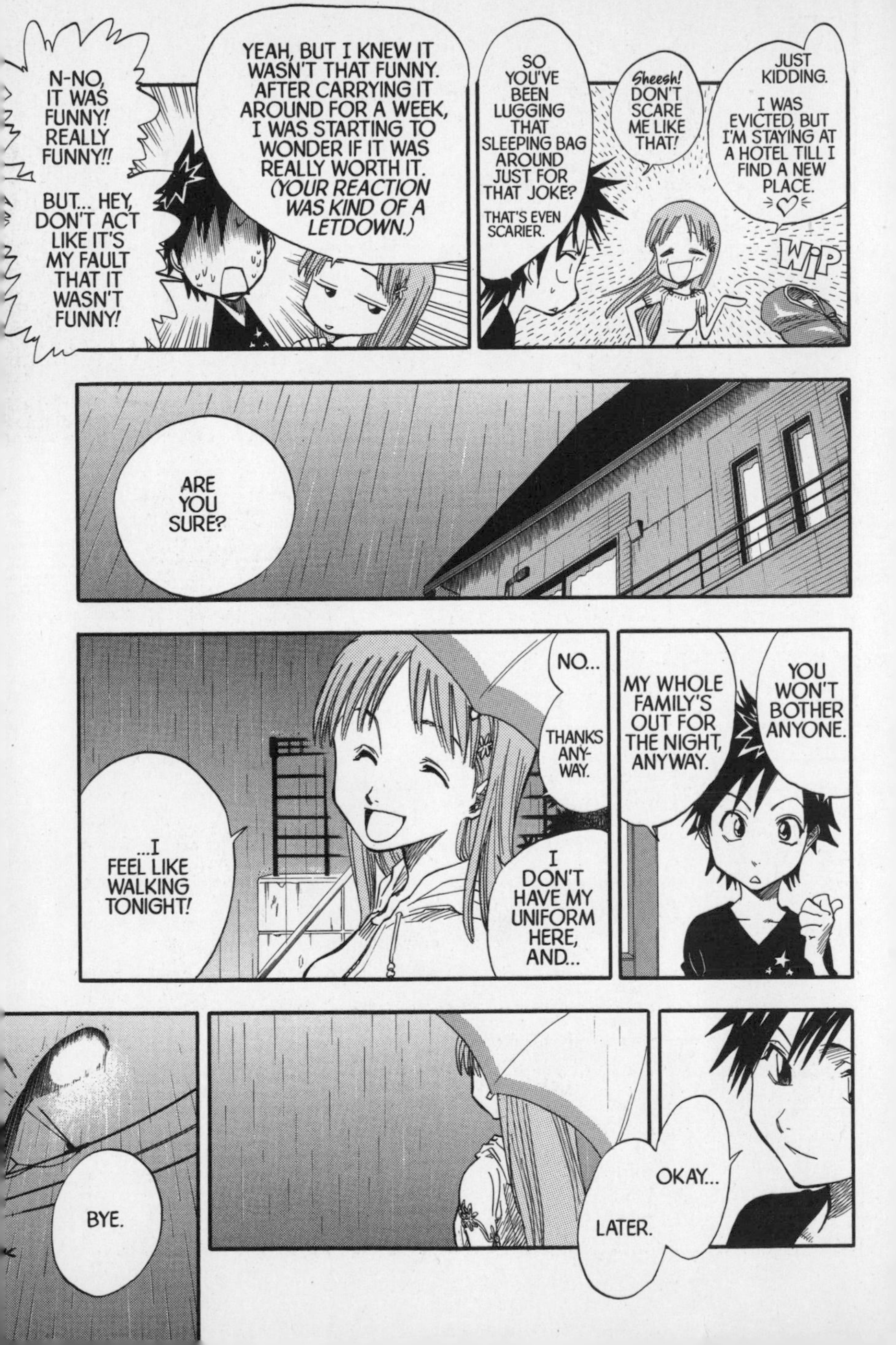
JUST KIDDING.
I WAS EVICTED, BUT I'M STAYING AT A HOTEL TILL I FIND A NEW PLACE.
Sheesh! DON'T SCARE ME LIKE THAT!
WIP
SO YOU'VE BEEN LUGGING THAT SLEEPING BAG AROUND JUST FOR THAT JOKE?
THAT'S EVEN SCARIER.
YEAH, BUT I KNEW IT WASN'T THAT FUNNY. AFTER CARRYING IT AROUND FOR A WEEK, I WAS STARTING TO WONDER IF IT WAS REALLY WORTH IT. (YOUR REACTION WAS KIND OF A LETDOWN.)
N-NO, IT WAS FUNNY! REALLY FUNNY!!
BUT... HEY, DON'T ACT LIKE IT'S MY FAULT THAT IT WASN'T FUNNY!
ARE YOU SURE?
YOU WON'T BOTHER ANYONE.
MY WHOLE FAMILY'S OUT FOR THE NIGHT, ANYWAY.
NO...
THANKS ANYWAY.
I DON'T HAVE MY UNIFORM HERE, AND...
...I FEEL LIKE WALKING TONIGHT!
OKAY...
LATER.
BYE.

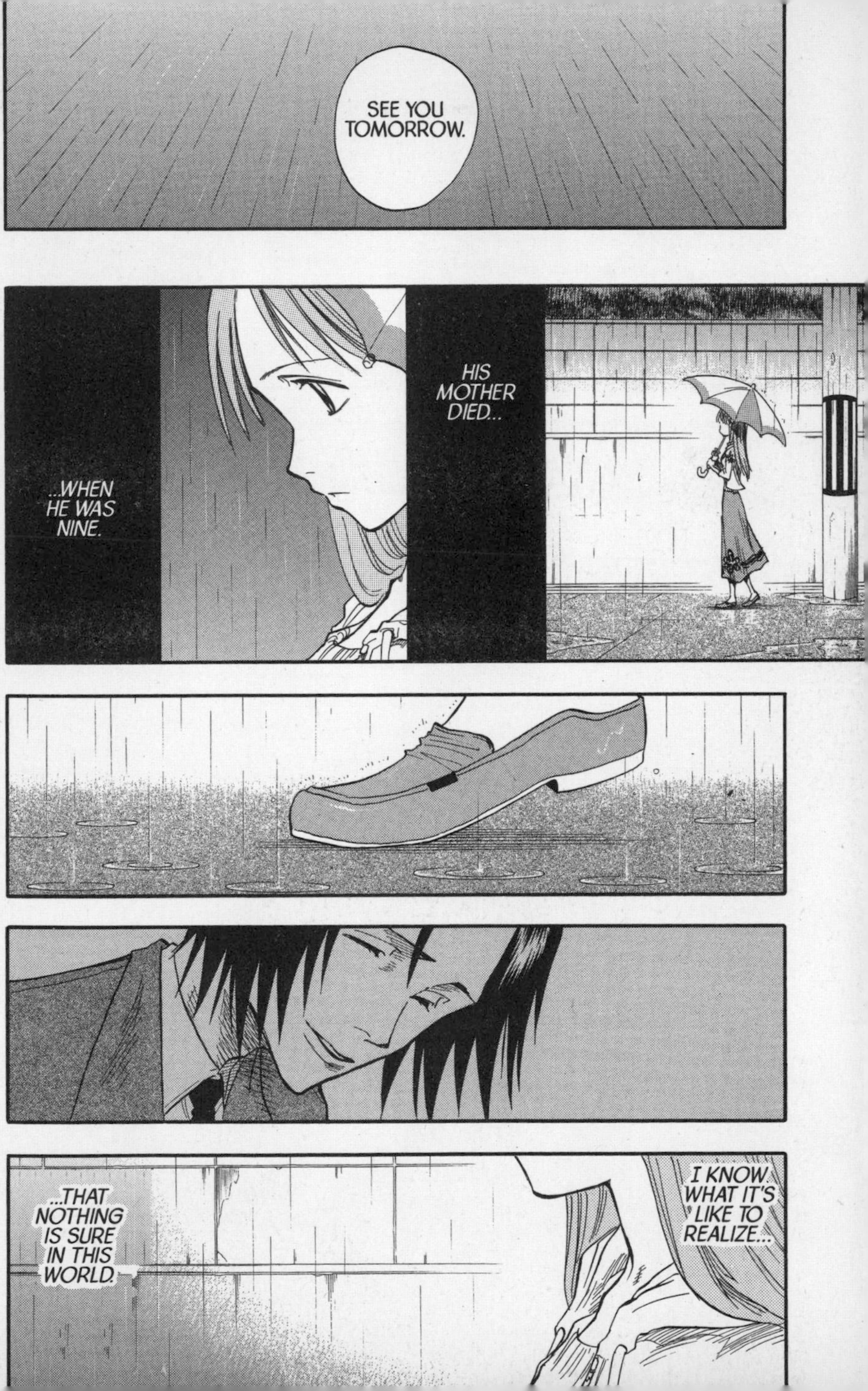
SEE YOU TOMORROW.
HIS MOTHER DIED...
...WHEN HE WAS NINE.
I KNOW WHAT IT'S LIKE TO REALIZE...
...THAT NOTHING IS SURE IN THIS WORLD.

READ THIS WAY

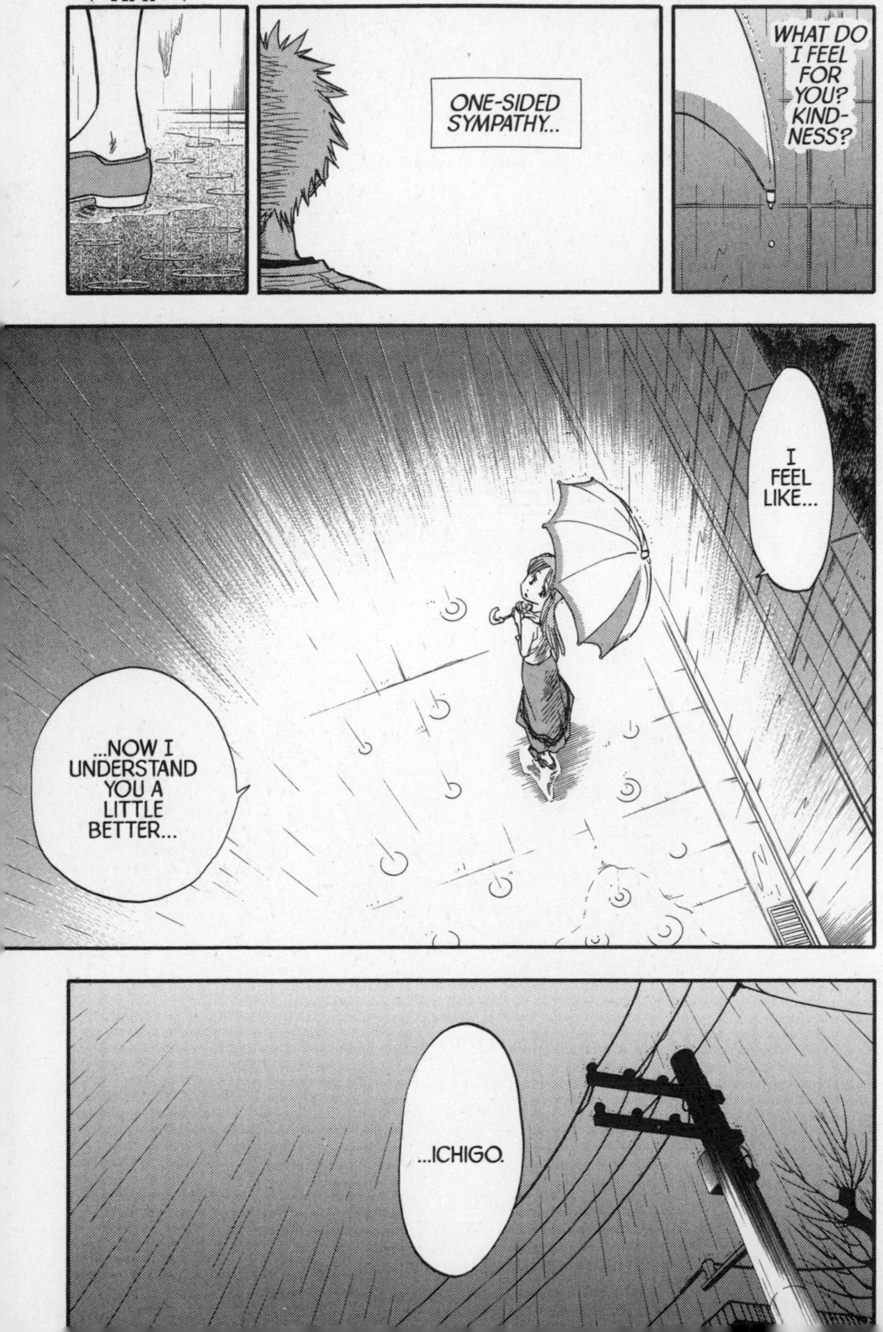
WHAT DO I FEEL FOR YOU? KINDNESS?
ONE-SIDED SYMPATHY...
I FEEL LIKE...
...NOW I UNDERSTAND YOU A LITTLE BETTER...
...ICHIGO.

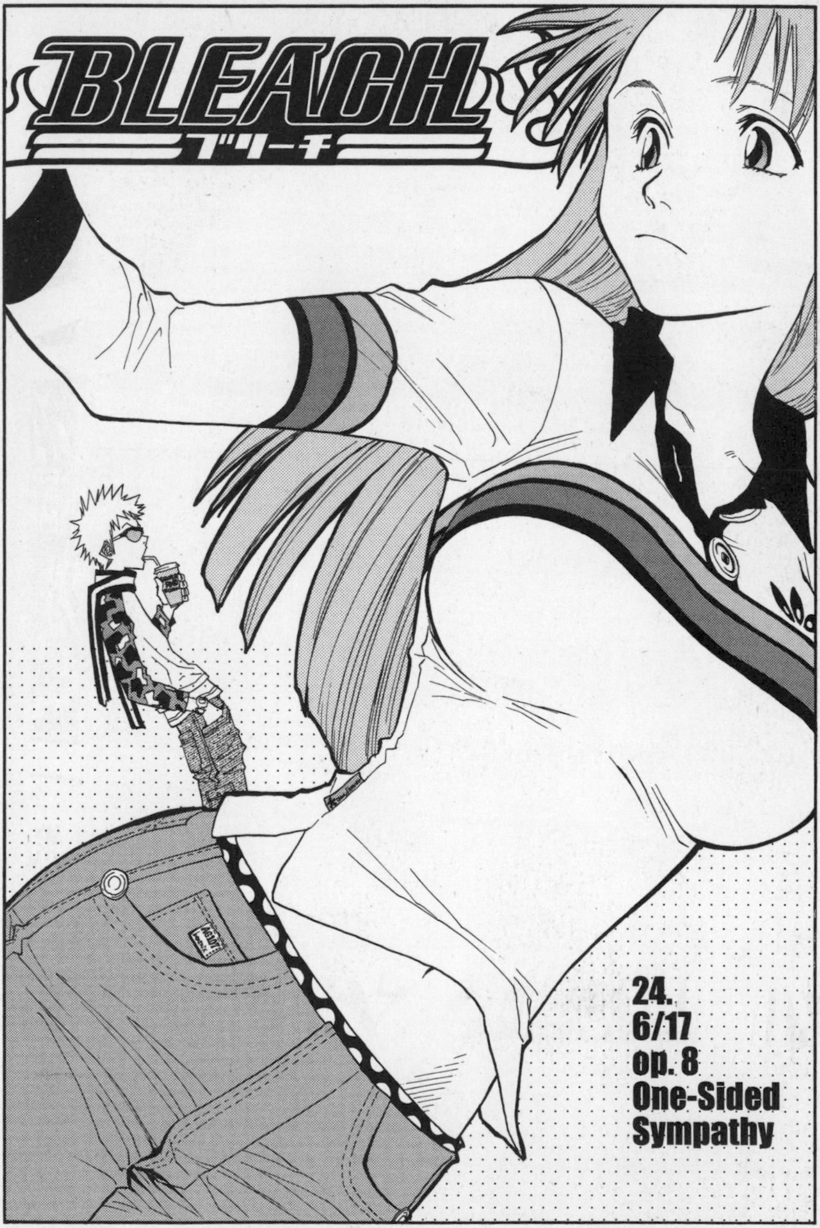
BLEACH
ブリーチ
24.
6/17
op. 8
One-Sided
Sympathy

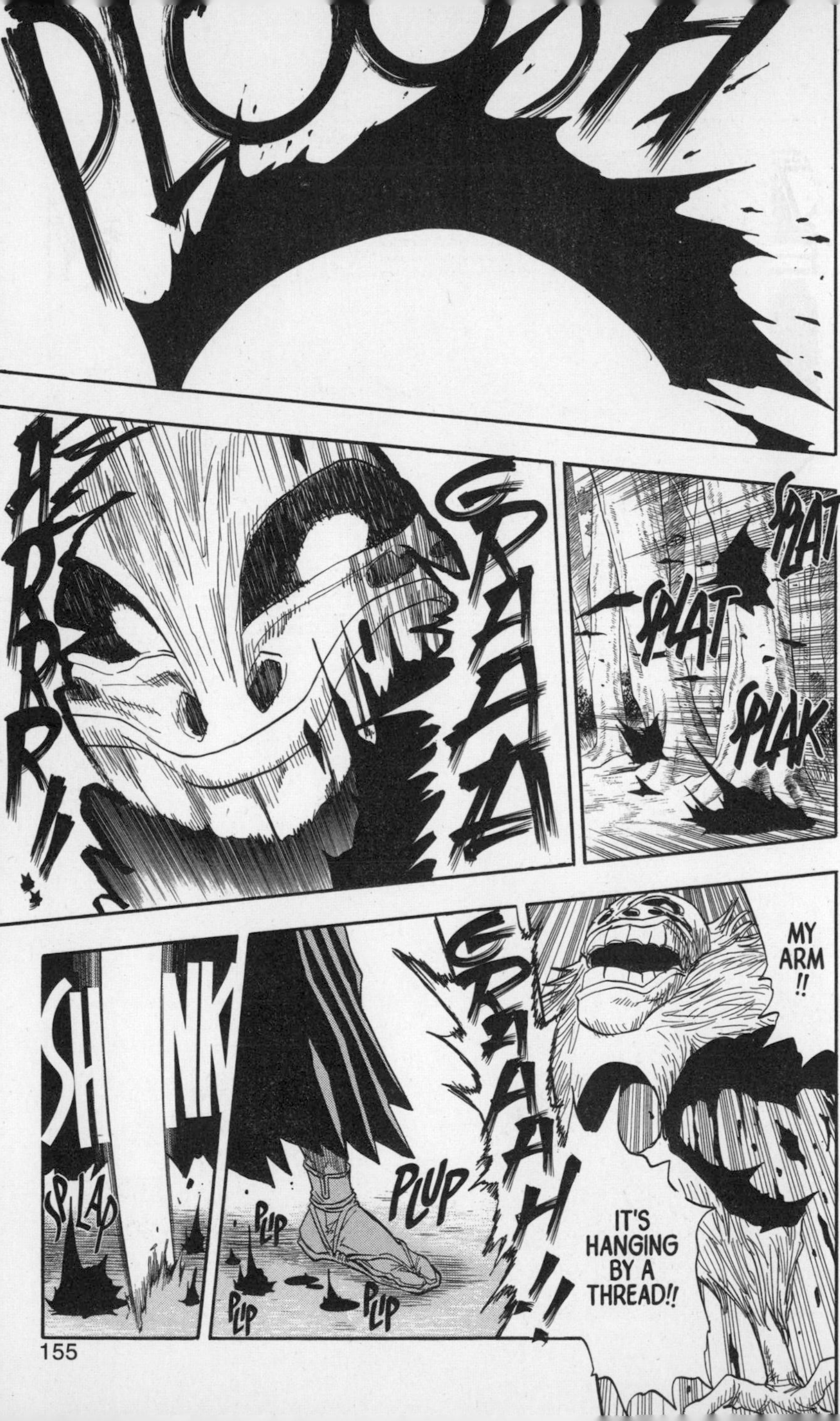
SPLAT
SPLAT
SPLAK
MY ARM!!
IT'S HANGING BY A THREAD!!
PLUP
PLUP
PLUP
PLUP
SHINK
SPLAP

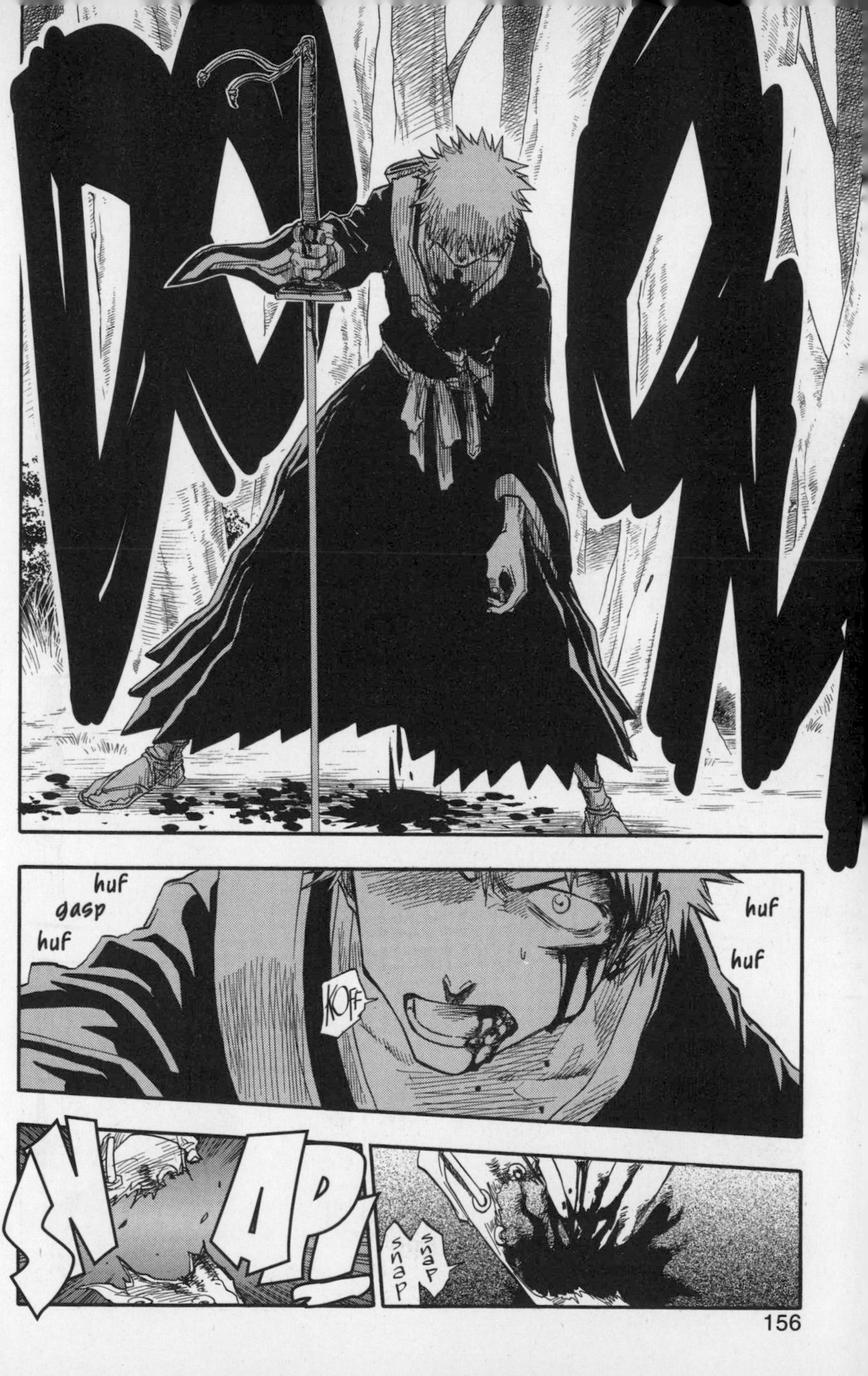
huf
huf
huf
gasp
huf
KOFF
snap
snap
SNAP!

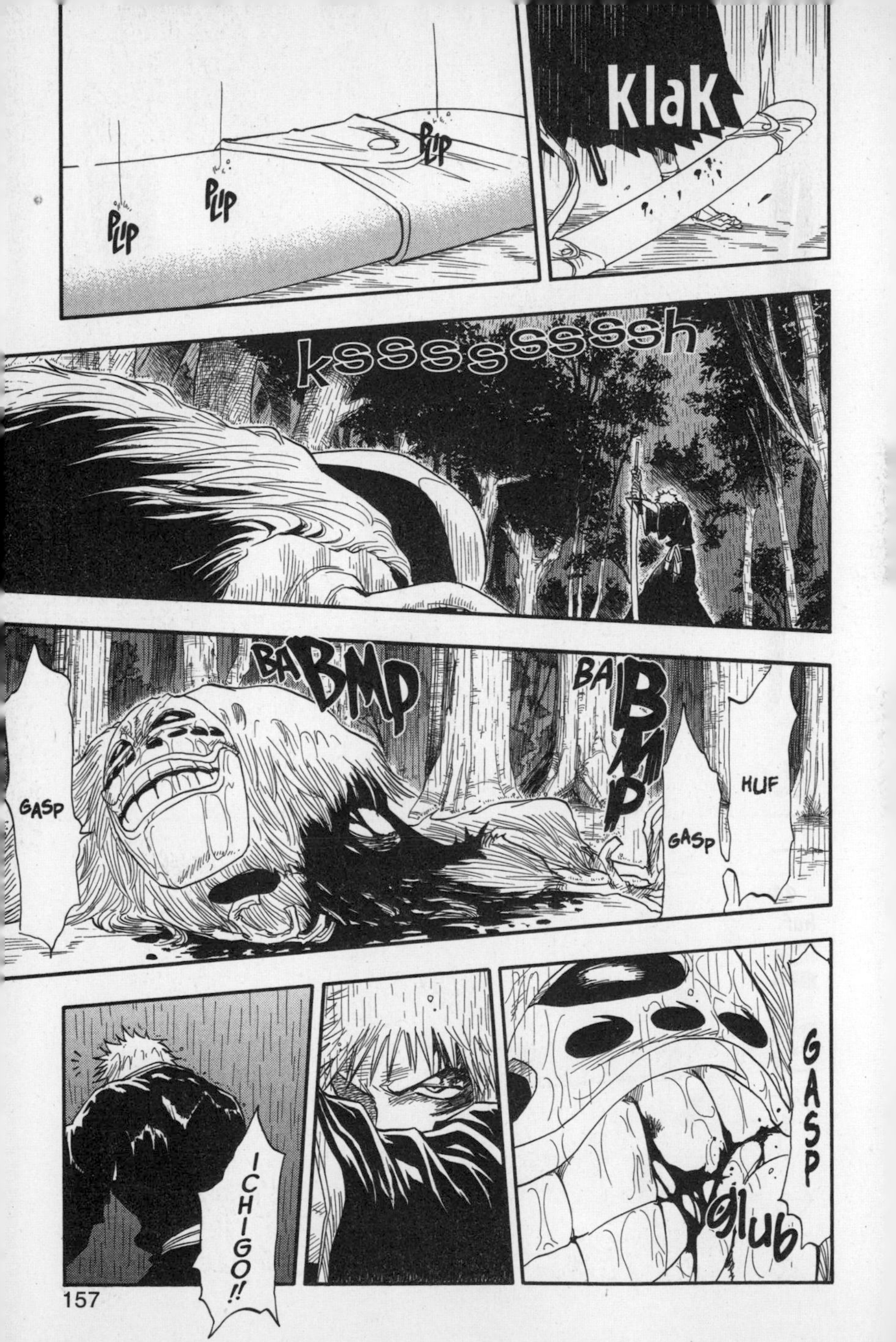
klak
PLIP
PLIP
PLIP
ksssssssh
HUF
GASP
BABMP
BABMP
GASP
GASP
glub
ICHIGO!!

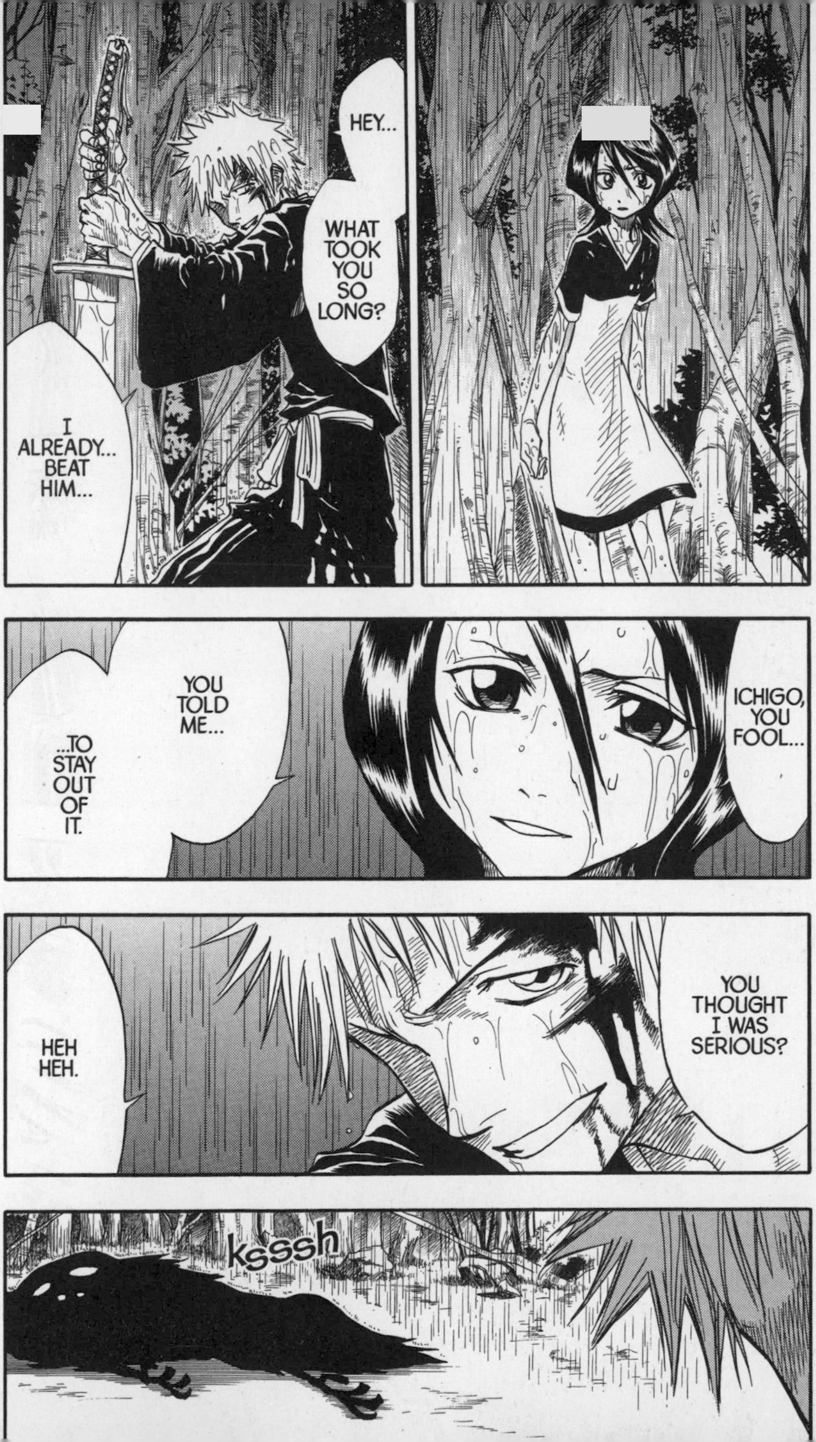
HEY...
WHAT TOOK YOU SO LONG?
I ALREADY... BEAT HIM...
ICHIGO, YOU FOOL...
YOU TOLD ME...
...TO STAY OUT OF IT.
YOU THOUGHT I WAS SERIOUS?
HEH HEH.
ksssh

READ THIS WAY

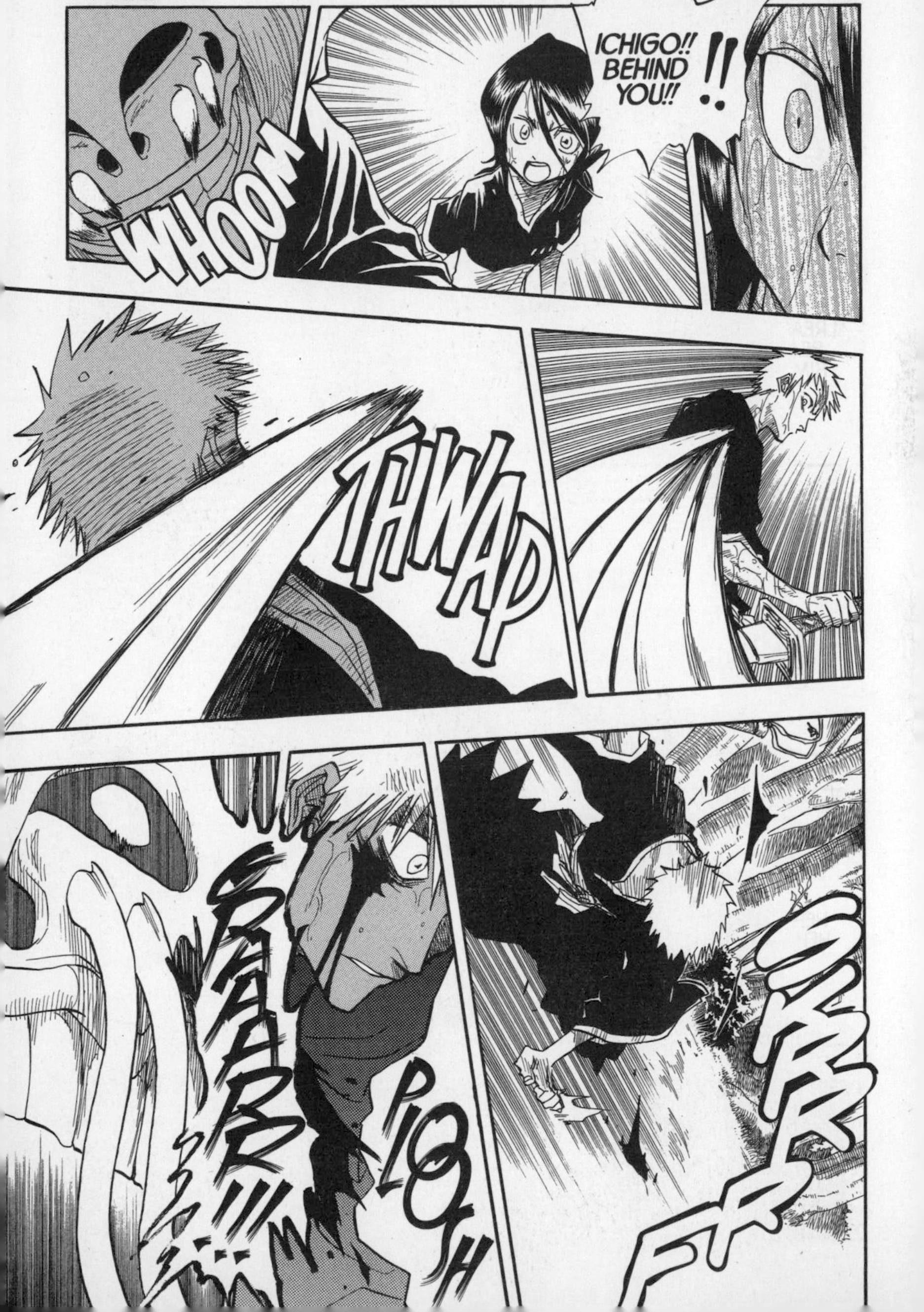
!!
ICHIGO!! BEHIND YOU!!
WHOOM
THWAP
PLOSH

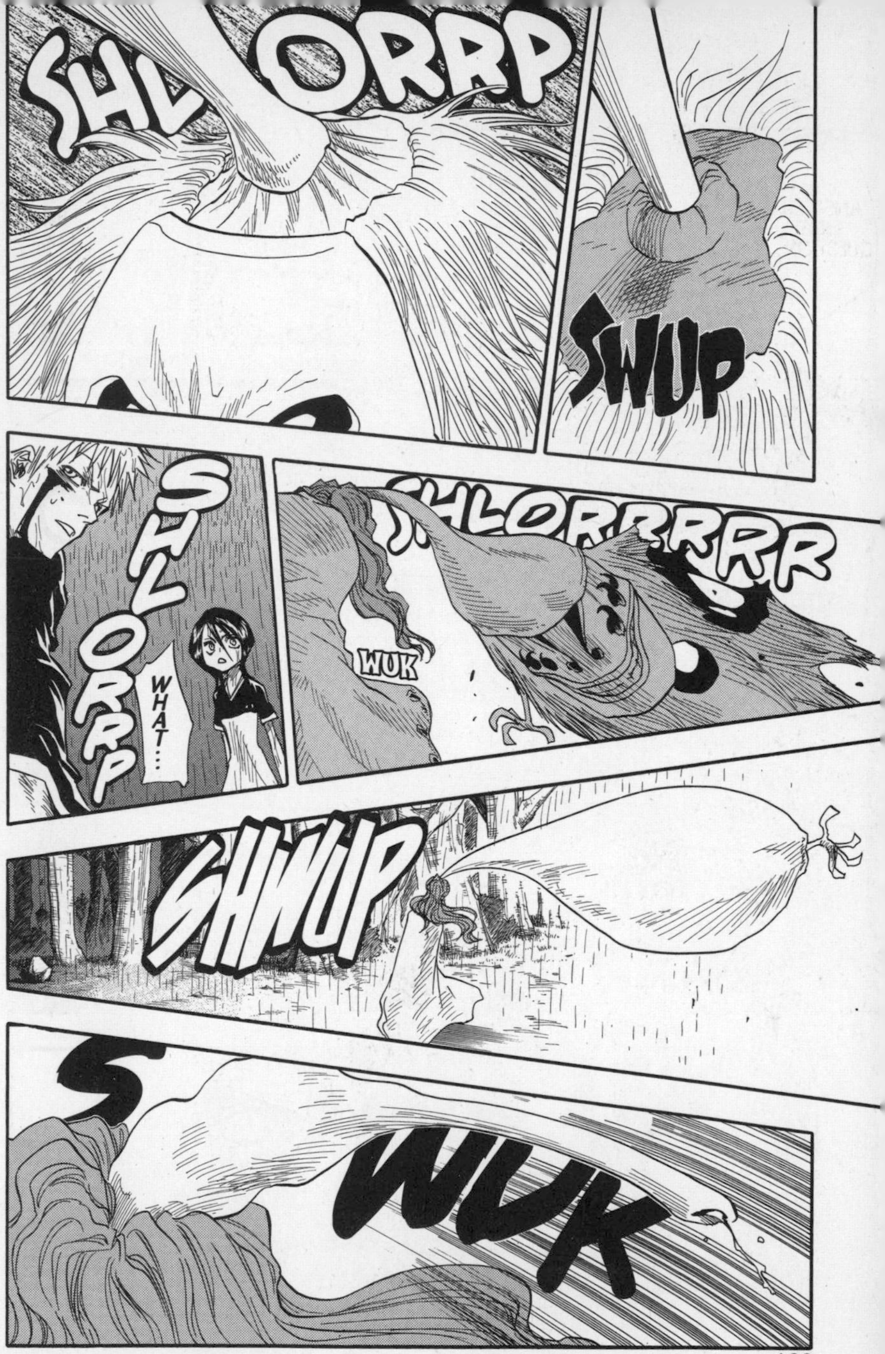
SWUP
SHLORRP
SHLORRRRR
WUK
SHLORRP
WHAT...
SHWUP
SWUK

READ THIS WAY

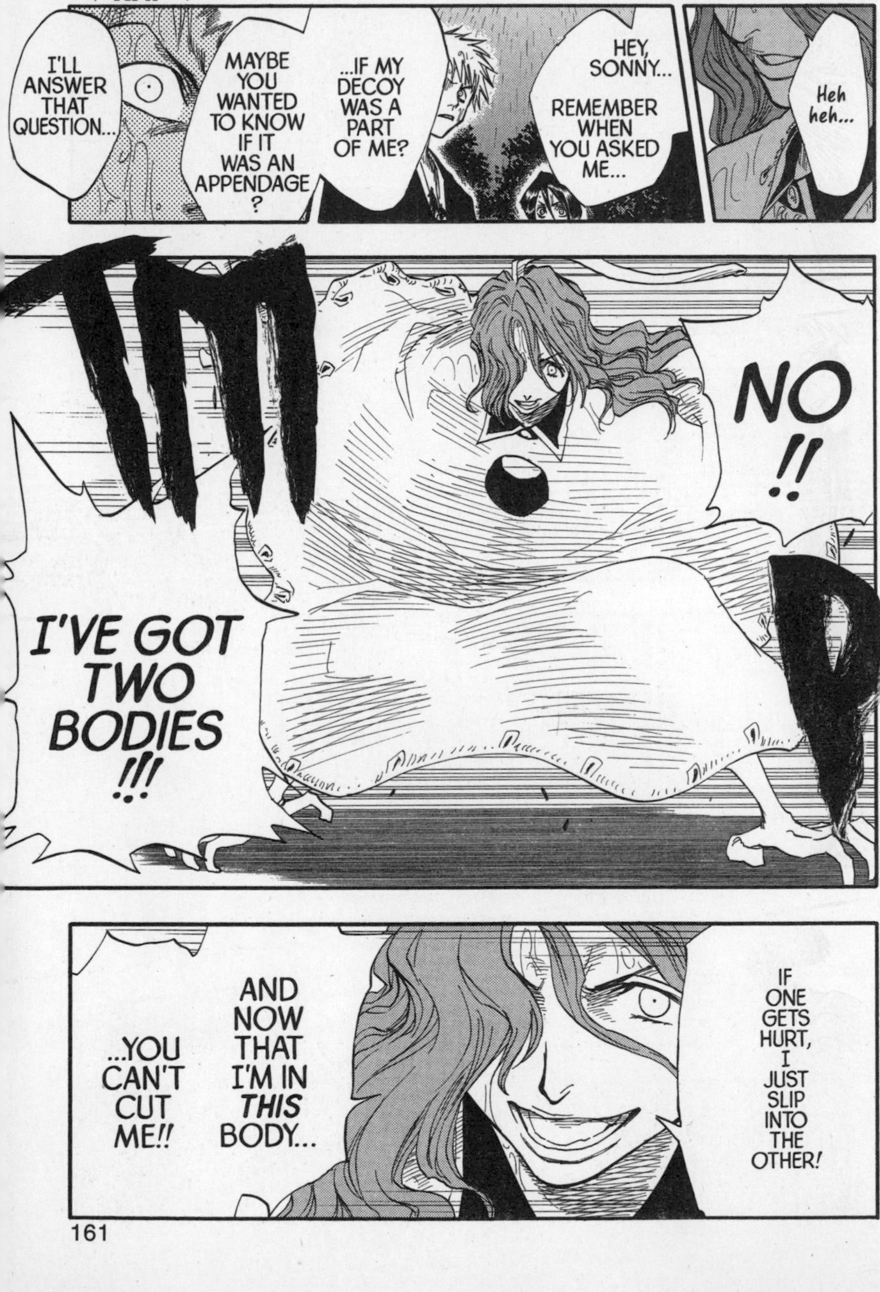
Heh heh...
HEY, SONNY...
REMEMBER WHEN YOU ASKED ME...
...IF MY DECOY WAS A PART OF ME?
MAYBE YOU WANTED TO KNOW IF IT WAS AN APPENDAGE?
I'LL ANSWER THAT QUESTION...
NO!!
I'VE GOT TWO BODIES!!!
IF ONE GETS HURT, I JUST SLIP INTO THE OTHER!
AND NOW THAT I'M IN *THIS* BODY...
...YOU CAN'T CUT ME!!

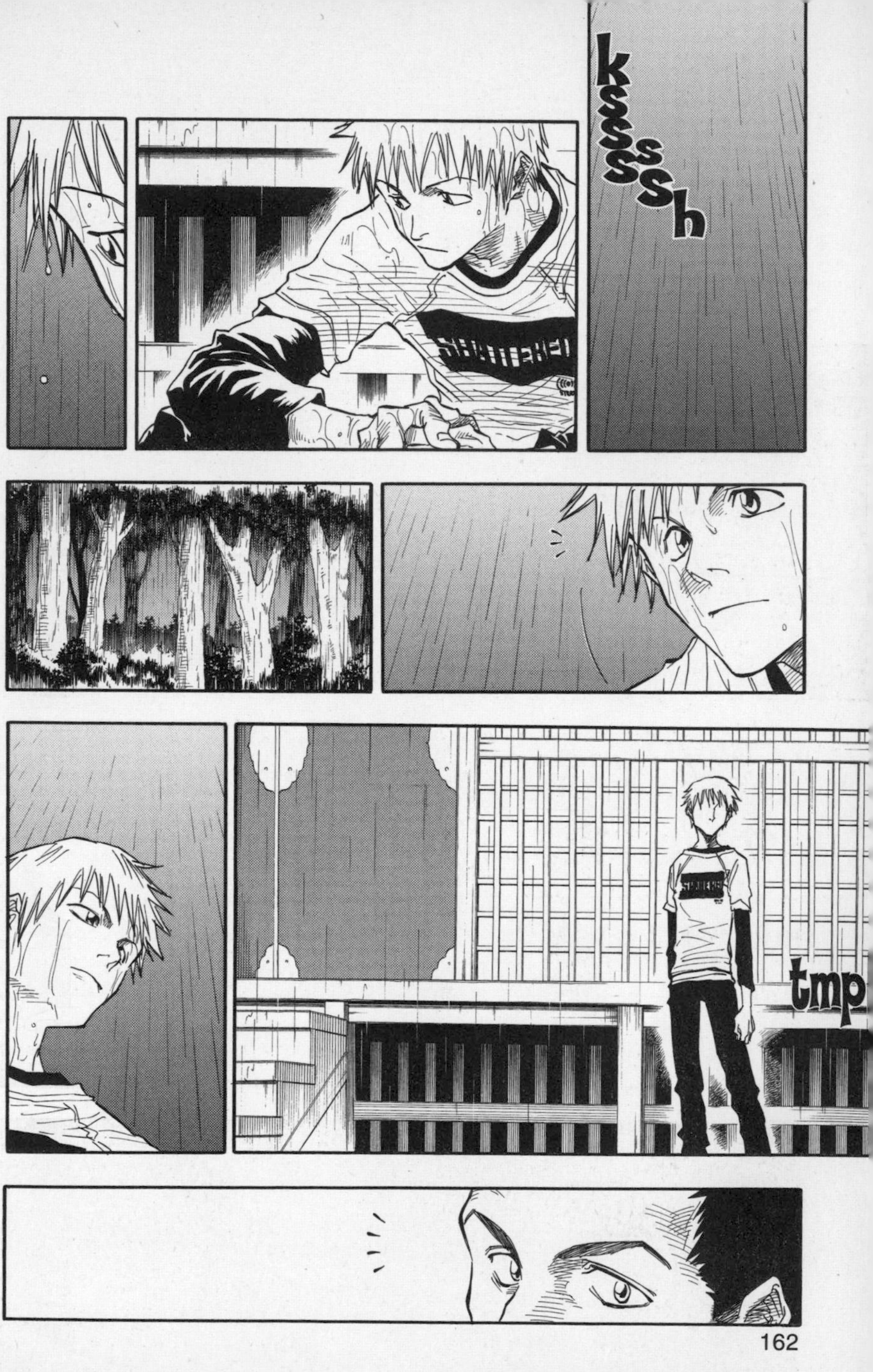
kssssh
tmp

READ THIS WAY

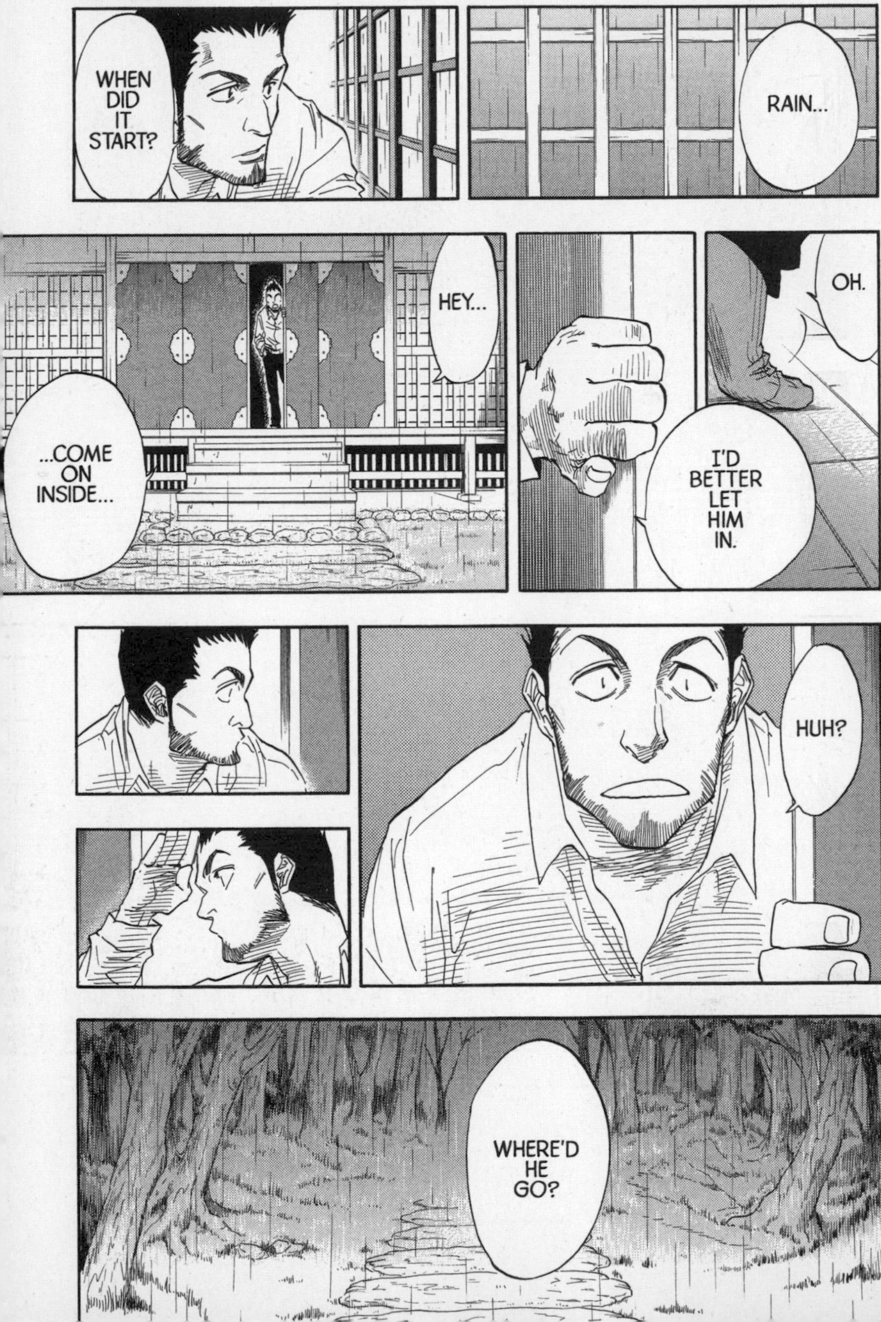
RAIN...
WHEN DID IT START?
OH.
I'D BETTER LET HIM IN.
HEY...
...COME ON INSIDE...
HUH?
WHERE'D HE GO?

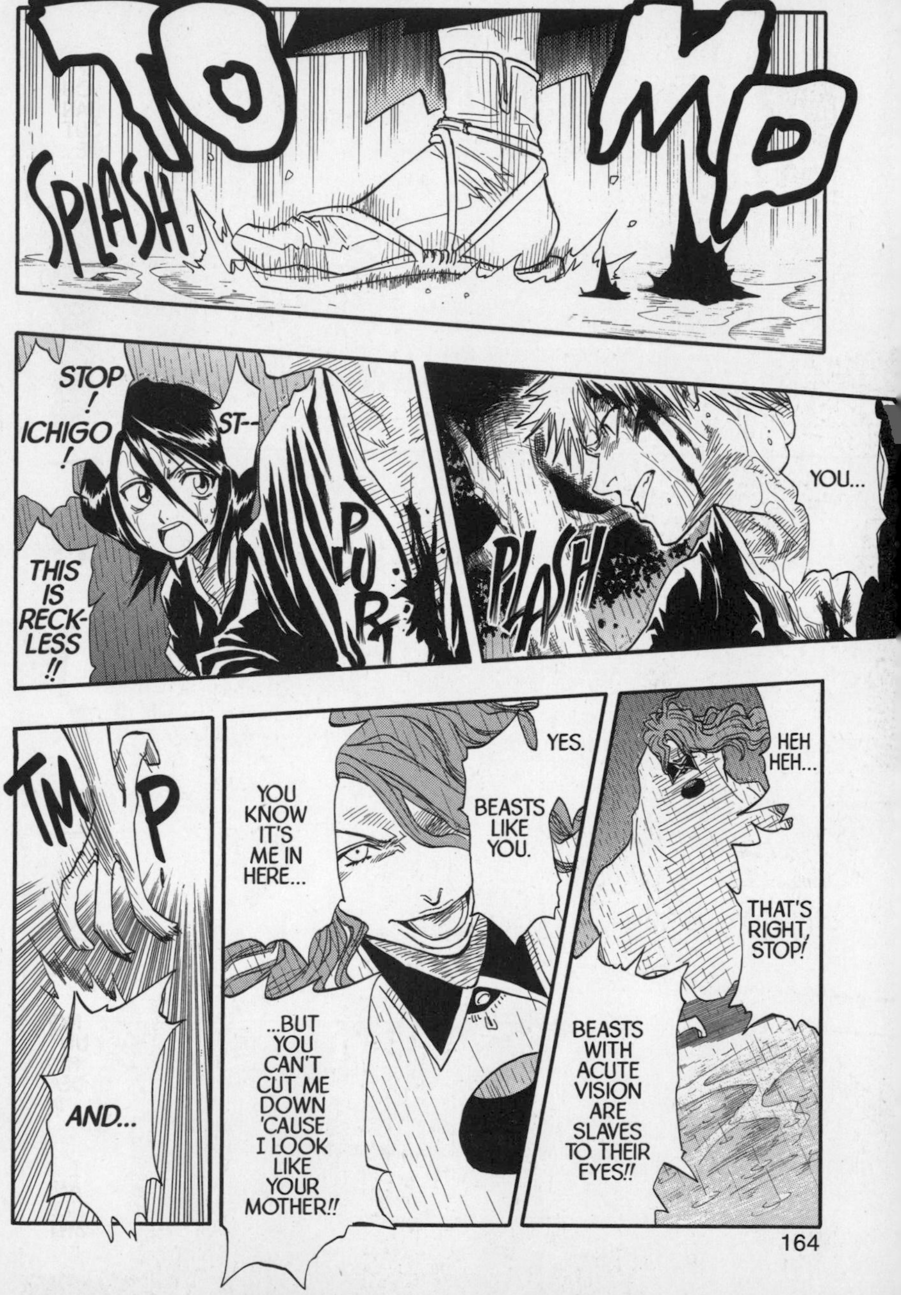
TOMP
SPLASH
YOU...
PLASH
ST--
STOP! ICHIGO!
PLURT
THIS IS RECKLESS!!
HEH HEH...
THAT'S RIGHT, STOP!
BEASTS WITH ACUTE VISION ARE SLAVES TO THEIR EYES!!
YES.
BEASTS LIKE YOU.
YOU KNOW IT'S ME IN HERE...
...BUT YOU CAN'T CUT ME DOWN 'CAUSE I LOOK LIKE YOUR MOTHER!!
TMP
AND...

READ THIS WAY

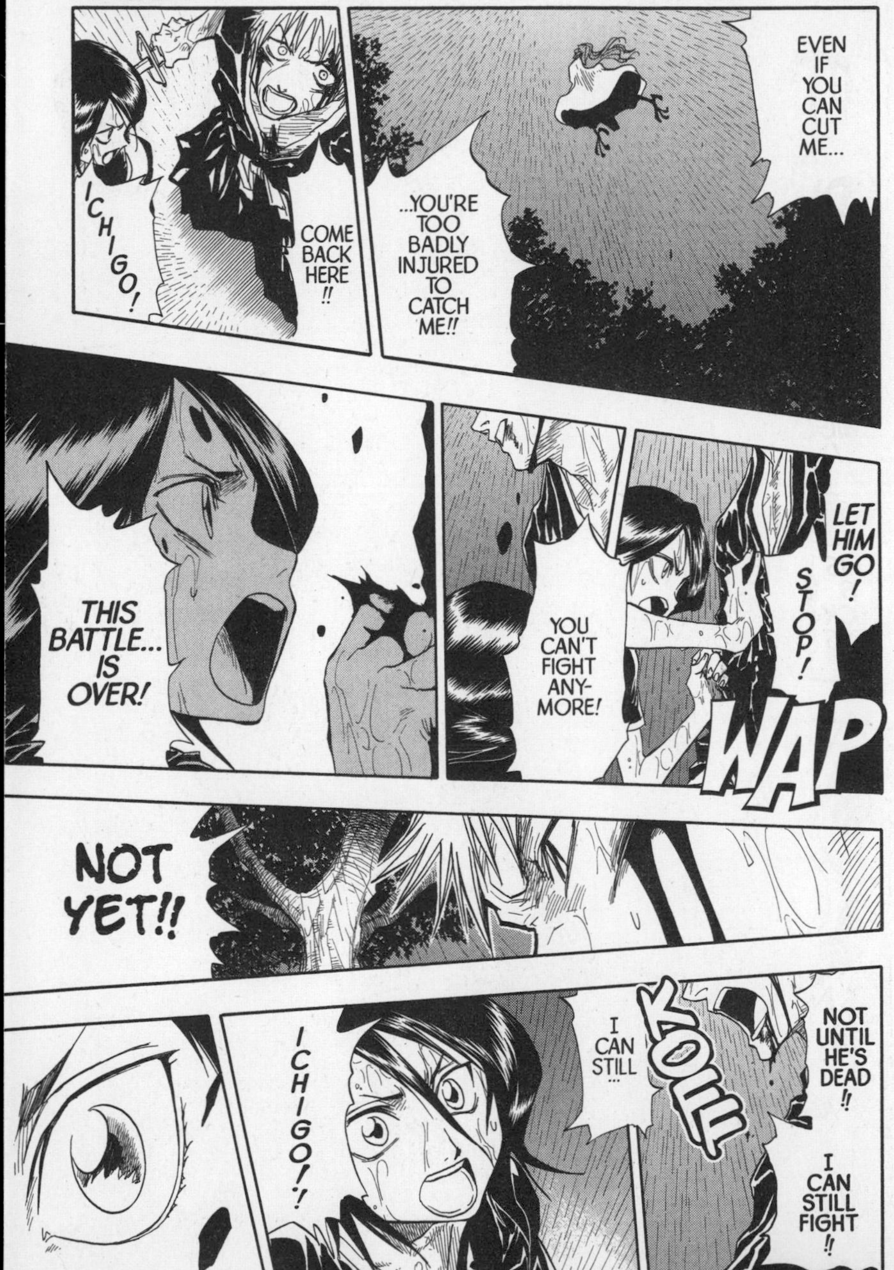
EVEN IF YOU CAN CUT ME...
...YOU'RE TOO BADLY INJURED TO CATCH ME!!
COME BACK HERE!!
ICHIGO!
LET HIM GO!
STOP!
WAP
YOU CAN'T FIGHT ANY-MORE!
THIS BATTLE... IS OVER!
NOT YET!!
NOT UNTIL HE'S DEAD!!
I CAN STILL FIGHT!!
KOFF
I CAN STILL...
ICHIGO!!

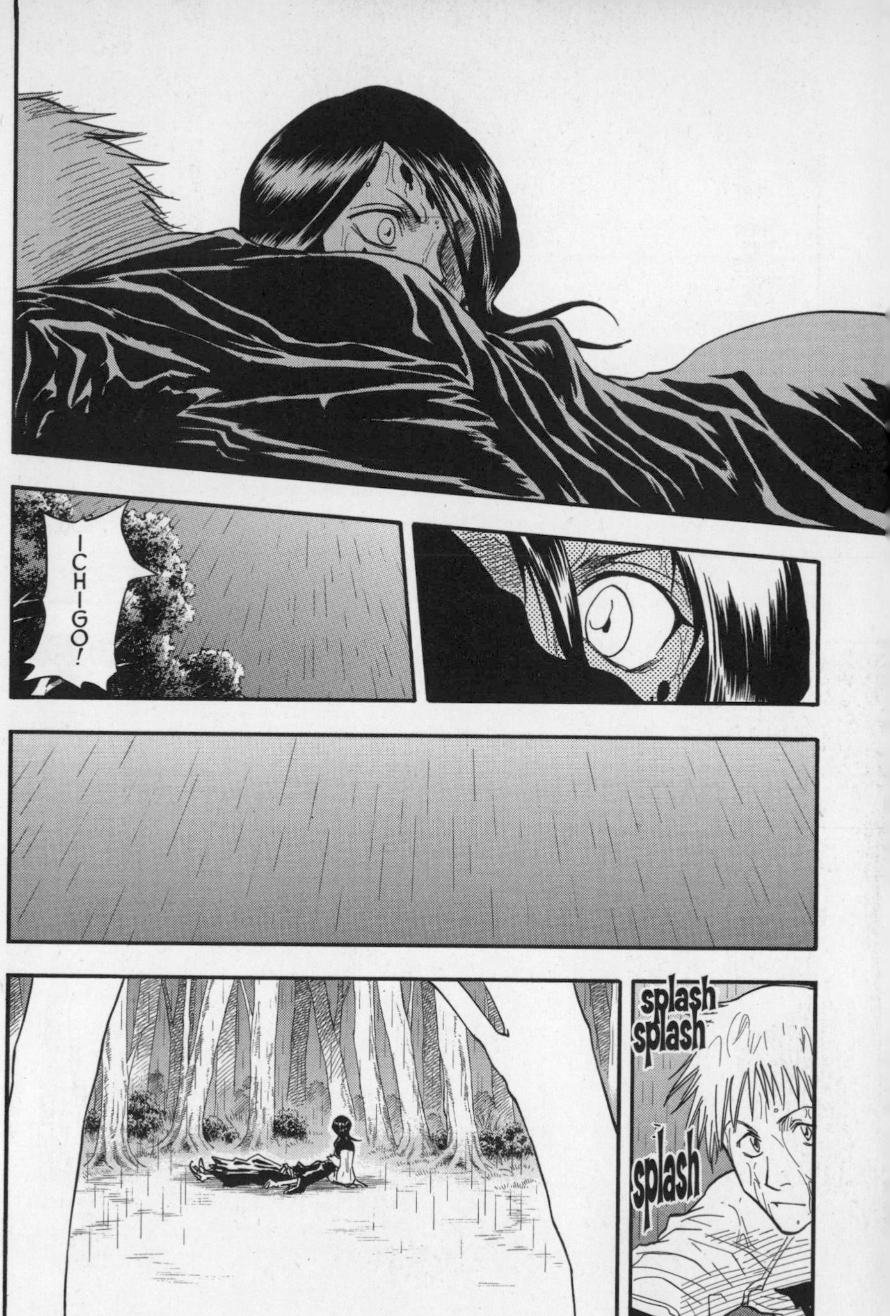
ICHIGO!
splash
splash
splash

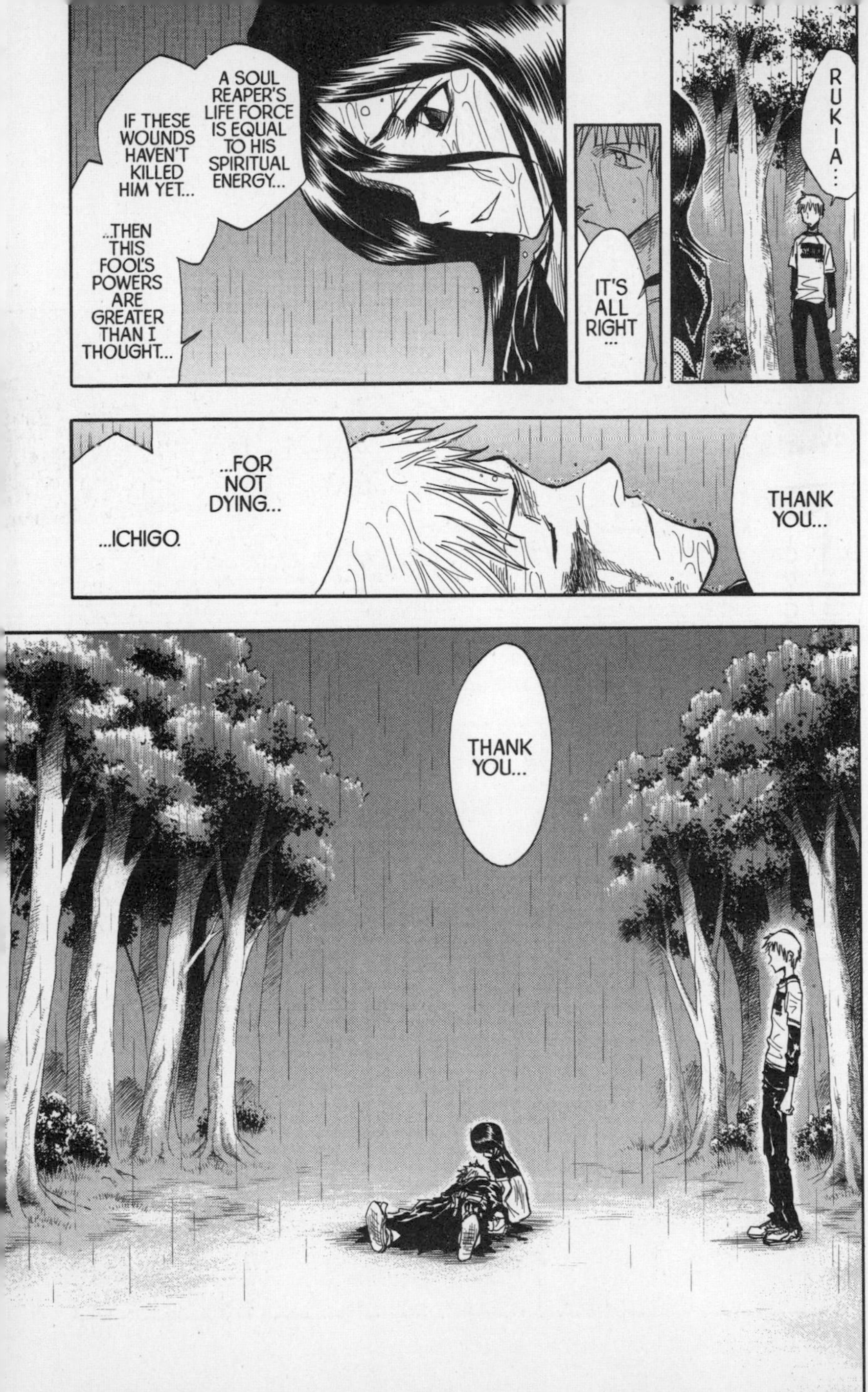
RUKIA...
IT'S ALL RIGHT...
A SOUL REAPER'S LIFE FORCE IS EQUAL TO HIS SPIRITUAL ENERGY...
IF THESE WOUNDS HAVEN'T KILLED HIM YET...
...THEN THIS FOOL'S POWERS ARE GREATER THAN I THOUGHT...
THANK YOU...
...FOR NOT DYING...
...ICHIGO.
THANK YOU...

25. 6/17 op. 9 A Fighting Boy 2 (The Cigarette Blues Mix)

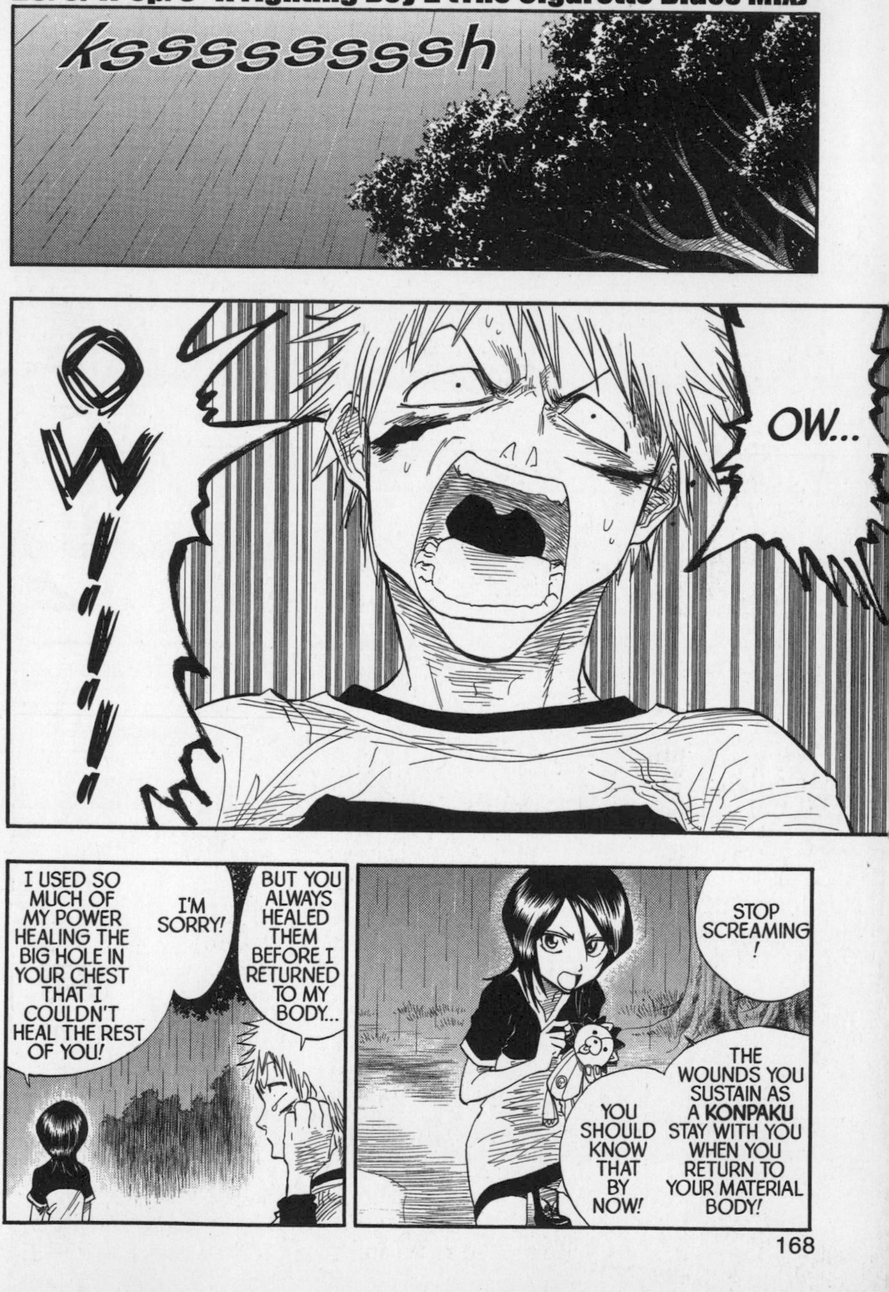
ksssssssh
OW...
OW!!!!
STOP SCREAMING!
THE WOUNDS YOU SUSTAIN AS A KONPAKU STAY WITH YOU WHEN YOU RETURN TO YOUR MATERIAL BODY!
YOU SHOULD KNOW THAT BY NOW!
BUT YOU ALWAYS HEALED THEM BEFORE I RETURNED TO MY BODY...
I'M SORRY!
I USED SO MUCH OF MY POWER HEALING THE BIG HOLE IN YOUR CHEST THAT I COULDN'T HEAL THE REST OF YOU!

READ THIS WAY

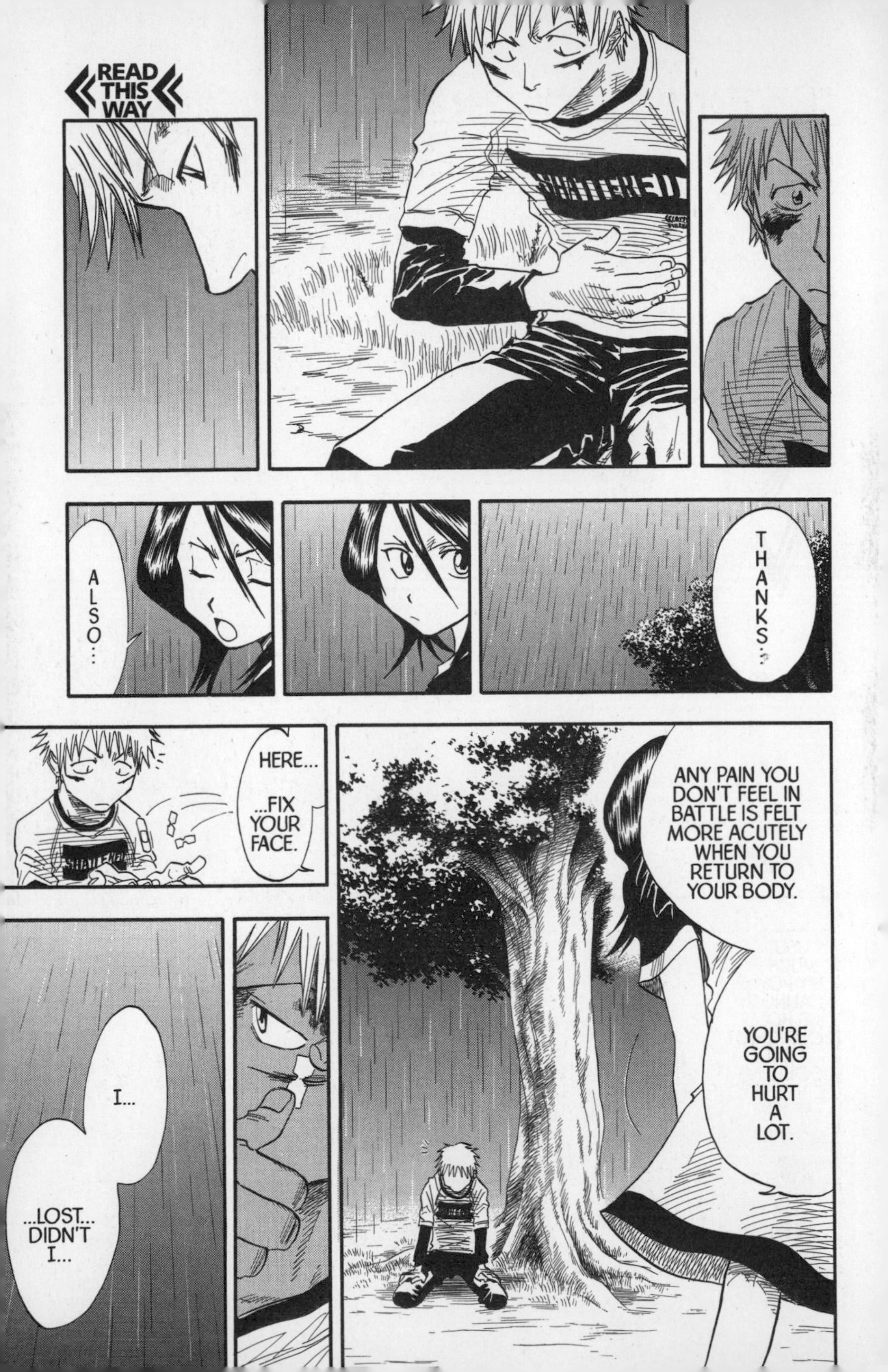
THANKS...
ALSO...
ANY PAIN YOU DON'T FEEL IN BATTLE IS FELT MORE ACUTELY WHEN YOU RETURN TO YOUR BODY.
YOU'RE GOING TO HURT A LOT.
HERE...
...FIX YOUR FACE.
I...
...LOST... DIDN'T I...

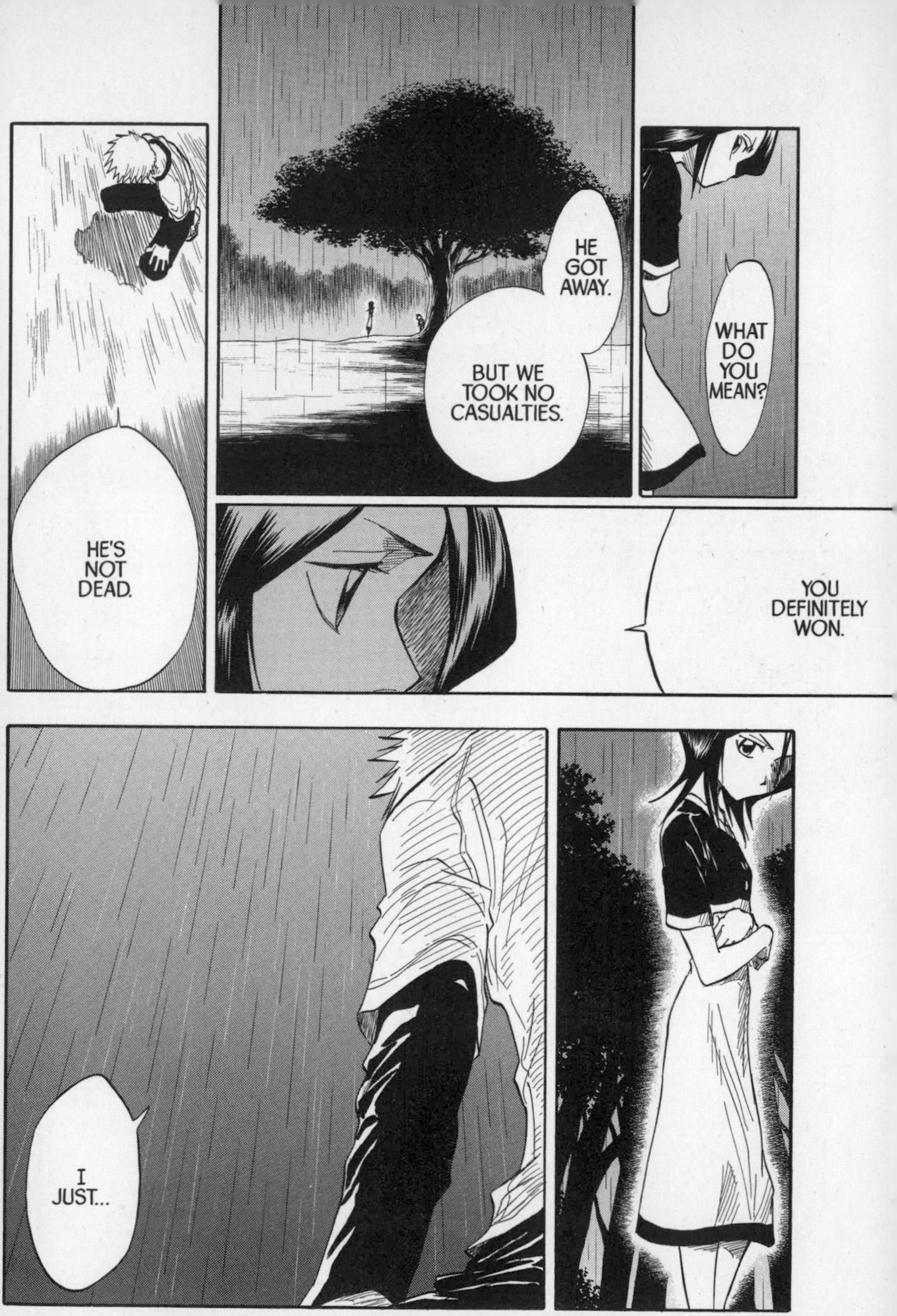
WHAT DO YOU MEAN?
HE GOT AWAY.
BUT WE TOOK NO CASUALTIES.
YOU DEFINITELY WON.
HE'S NOT DEAD.
I JUST...

READ THIS WAY

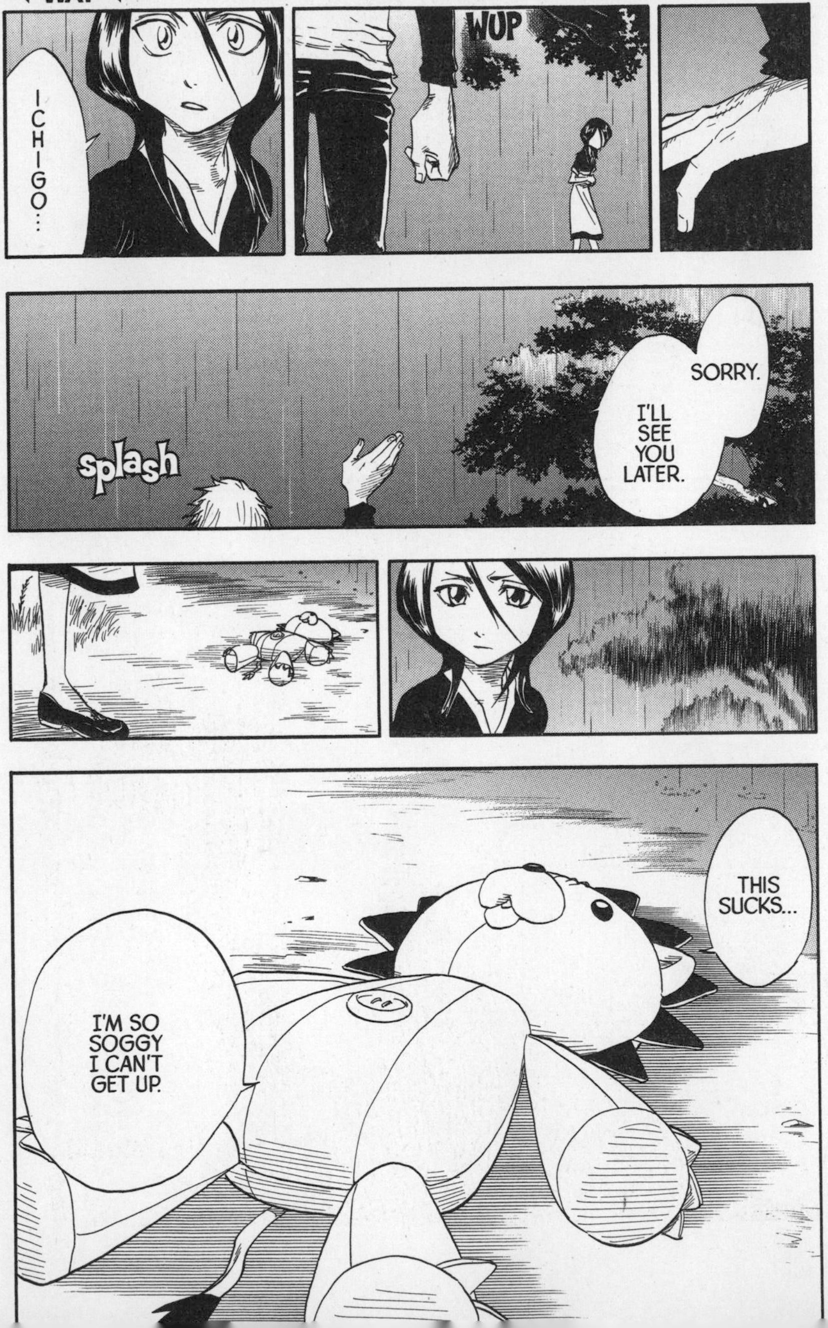
WUP
ICHIGO...
SORRY.
I'LL SEE YOU LATER.
splash
THIS SUCKS...
I'M SO SOGGY I CAN'T GET UP.

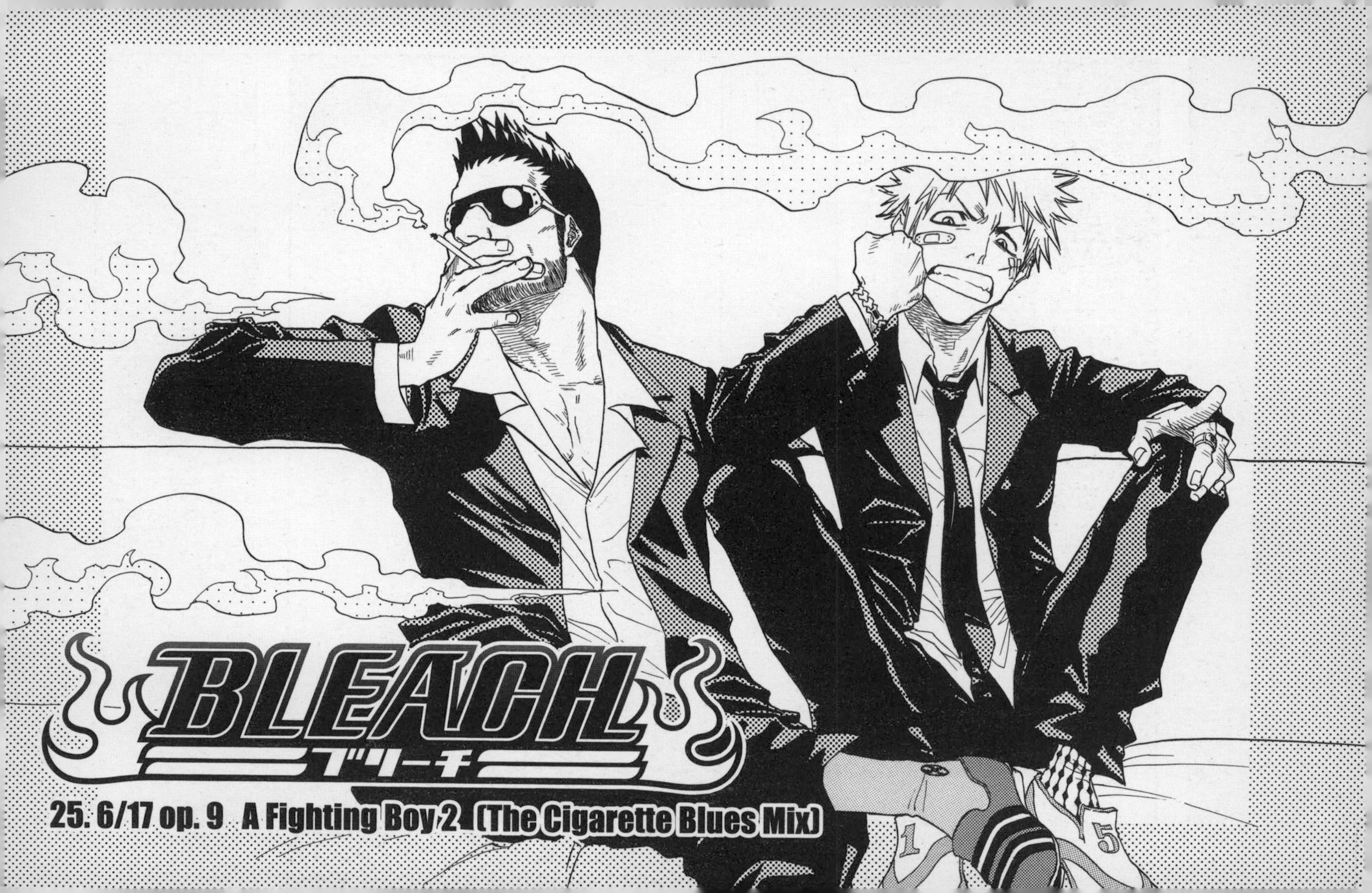
BLEACH
ブリーチ
25. 6/17 op. 9 A Fighting Boy 2 (The Cigarette Blues Mix)

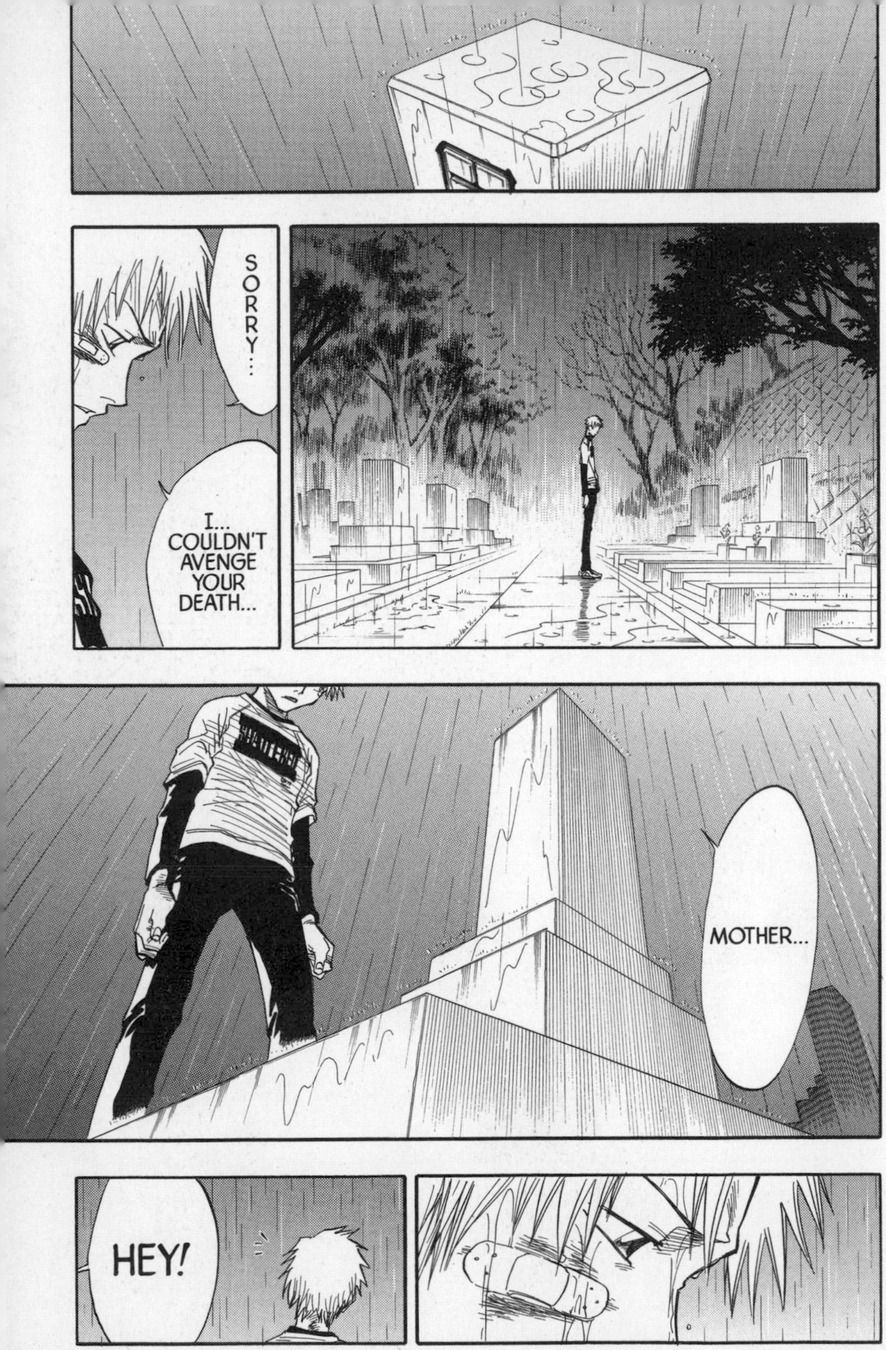
SORRY...
I... COULDN'T AVENGE YOUR DEATH...
MOTHER...
HEY!

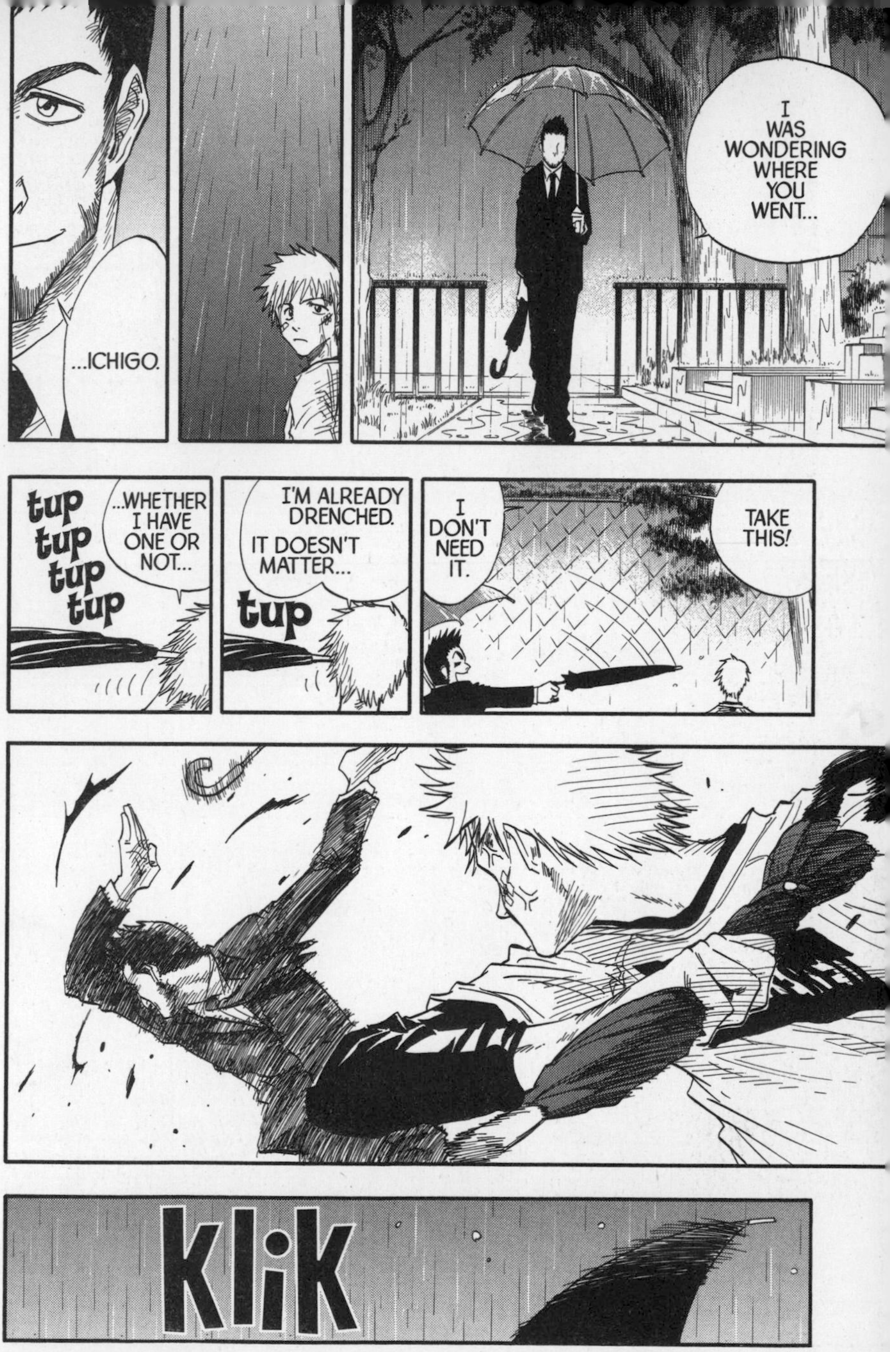
I WAS WONDERING WHERE YOU WENT...
...ICHIGO.
TAKE THIS!
I DON'T NEED IT.
I'M ALREADY DRENCHED.
IT DOESN'T MATTER...
tup
...WHETHER I HAVE ONE OR NOT...
tup tup tup tup
Klik

READ THIS WAY

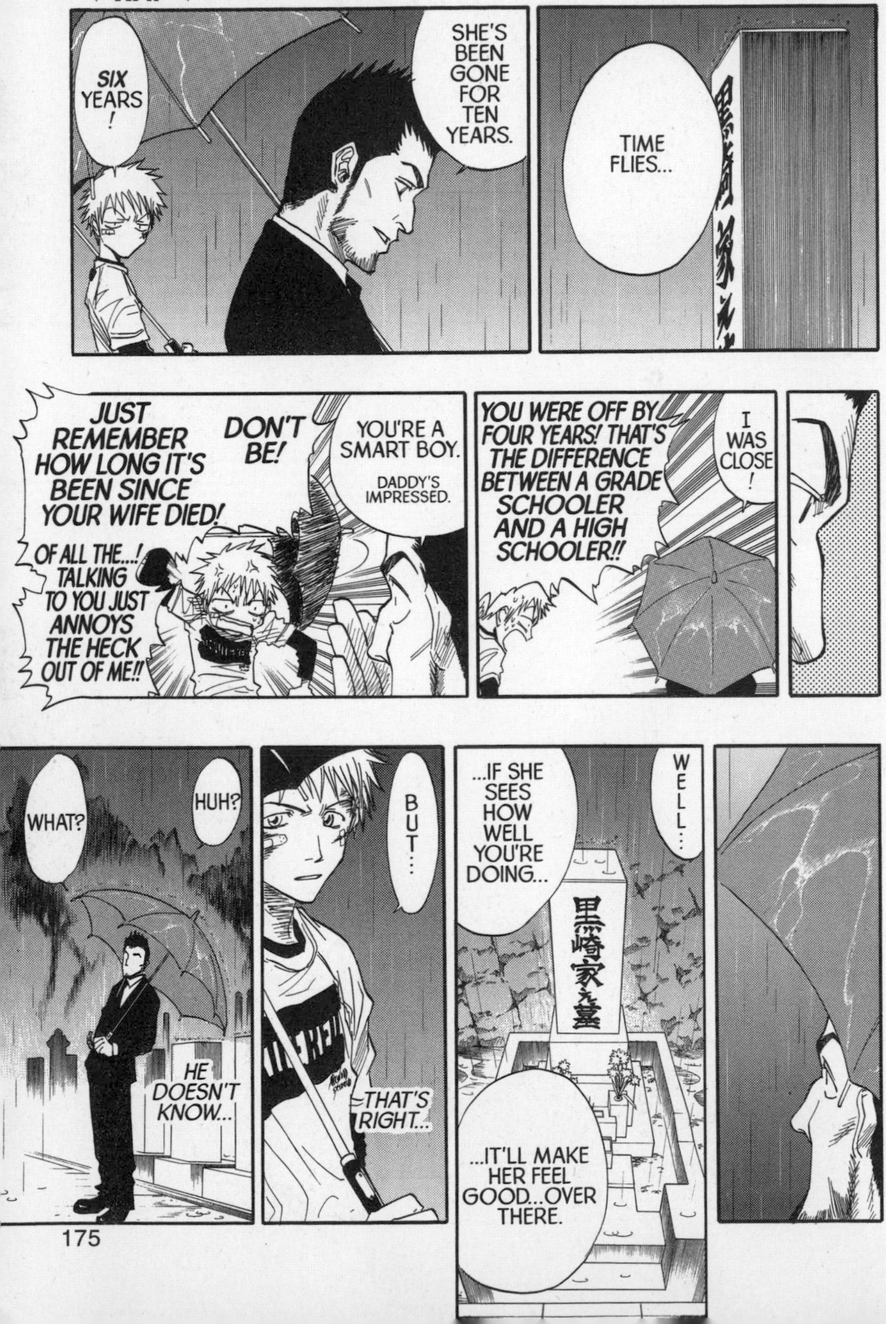

TIME FLIES...
SHE'S BEEN GONE FOR TEN YEARS.
SIX YEARS!
I WAS CLOSE!
YOU WERE OFF BY FOUR YEARS! THAT'S THE DIFFERENCE BETWEEN A GRADE SCHOOLER AND A HIGH SCHOOLER!!
YOU'RE A SMART BOY.
DADDY'S IMPRESSED.
DON'T BE!
JUST REMEMBER HOW LONG IT'S BEEN SINCE YOUR WIFE DIED!
OF ALL THE...! TALKING TO YOU JUST ANNOYS THE HECK OUT OF ME!!
WELL...
...IF SHE SEES HOW WELL YOU'RE DOING...
黒崎家之墓
...IT'LL MAKE HER FEEL GOOD...OVER THERE.
BUT...
THAT'S RIGHT...
HUH?
WHAT?
HE DOESN'T KNOW...

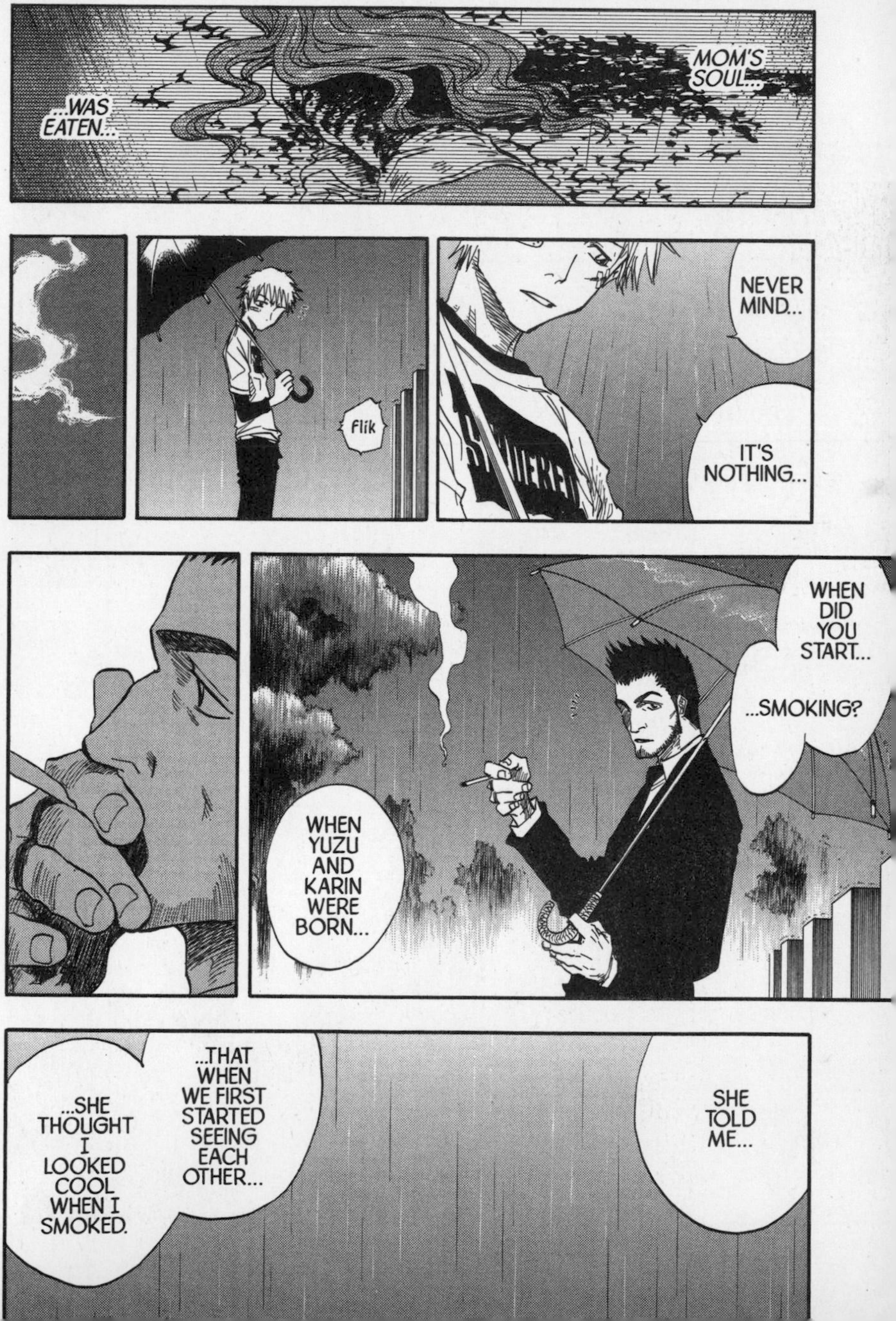
MOM'S SOUL...
...WAS EATEN...
NEVER MIND...
IT'S NOTHING...
Flik
WHEN DID YOU START...
...SMOKING?
WHEN YUZU AND KARIN WERE BORN...
SHE TOLD ME...
...THAT WHEN WE FIRST STARTED SEEING EACH OTHER...
...SHE THOUGHT I LOOKED COOL WHEN I SMOKED.

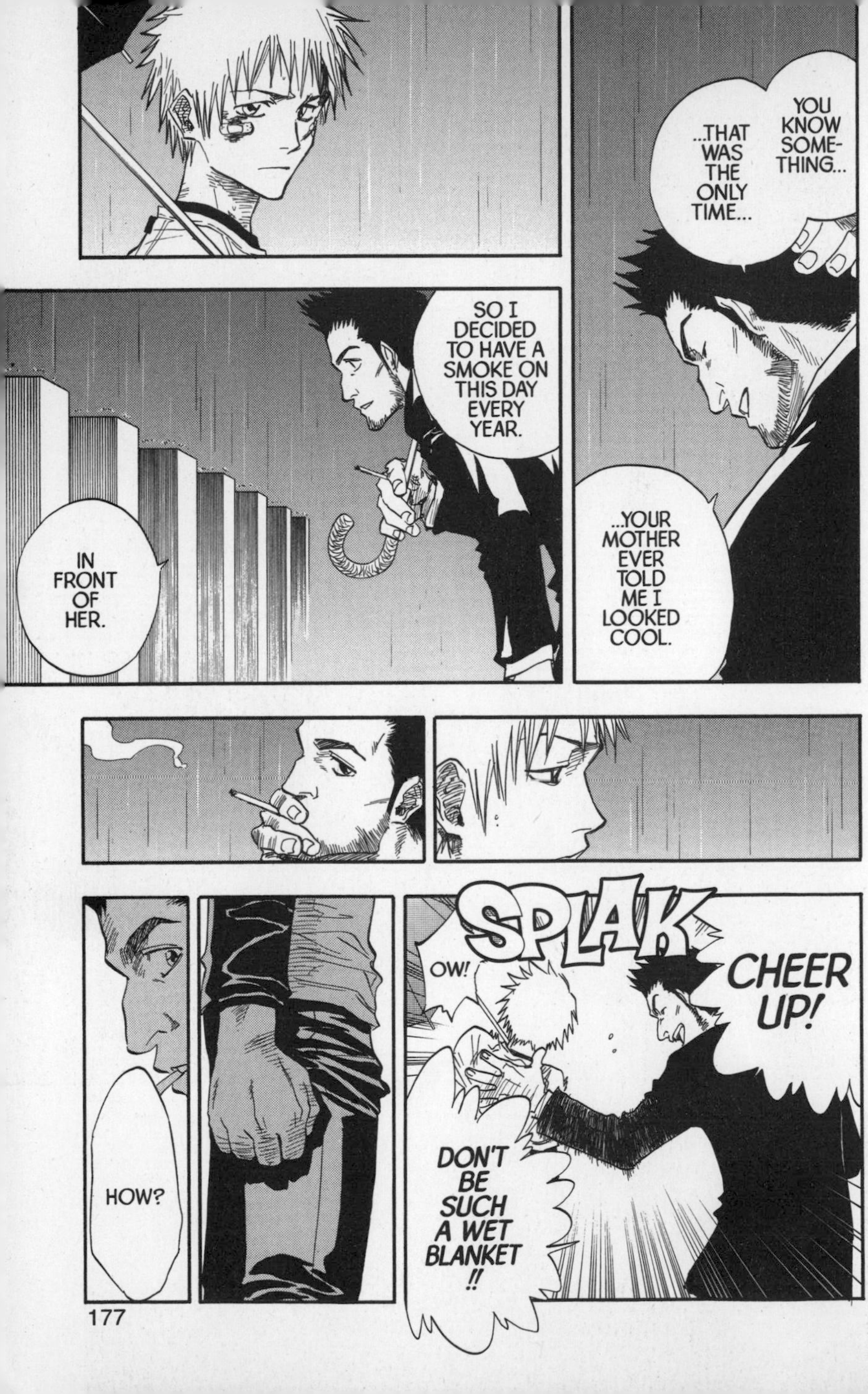
YOU KNOW SOME-THING...
...THAT WAS THE ONLY TIME...
...YOUR MOTHER EVER TOLD ME I LOOKED COOL.
SO I DECIDED TO HAVE A SMOKE ON THIS DAY EVERY YEAR.
IN FRONT OF HER.
SPLAK
CHEER UP!
OW!
DON'T BE SUCH A WET BLANKET !!
HOW?

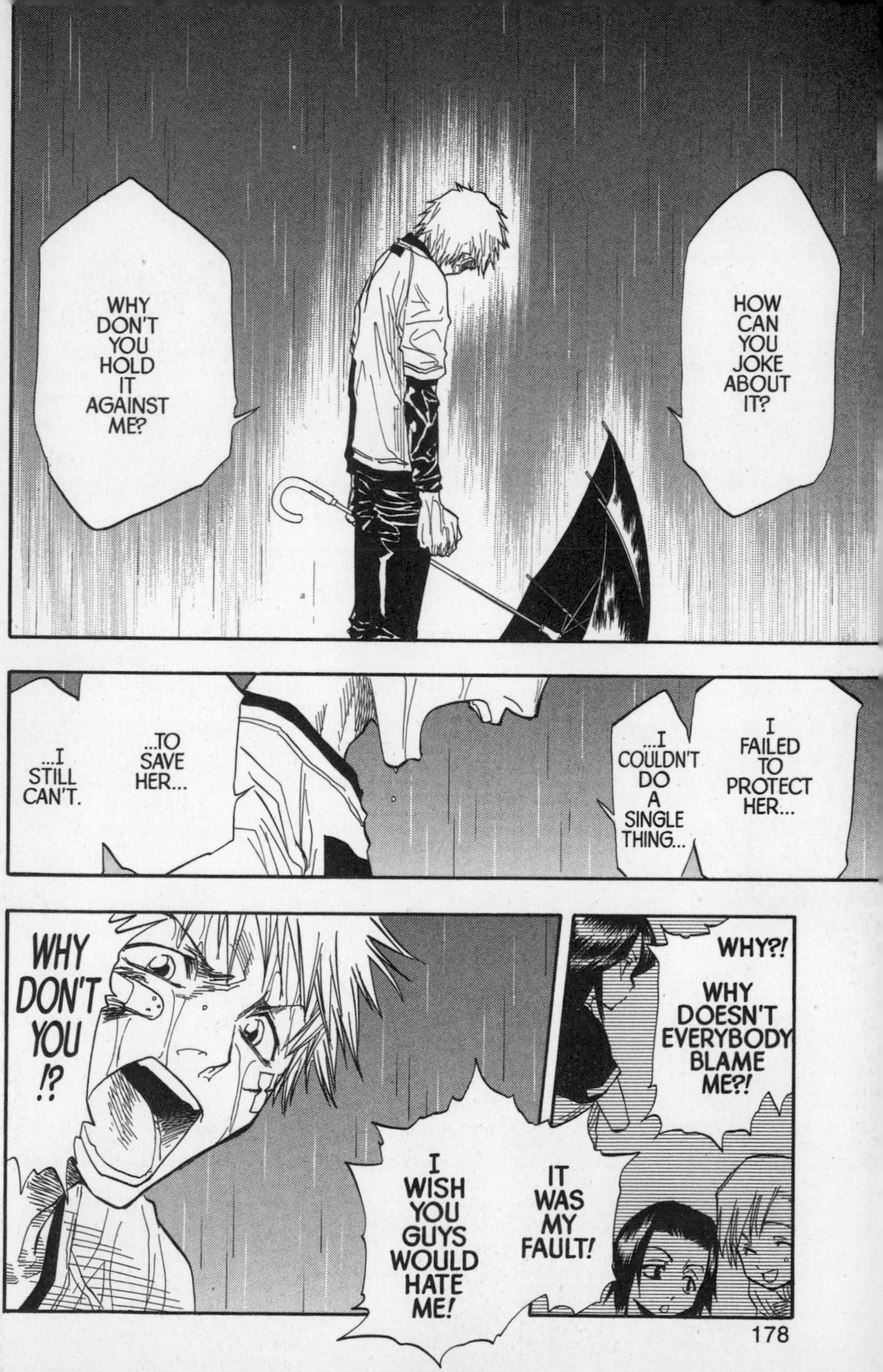
HOW CAN YOU JOKE ABOUT IT?
WHY DON'T YOU HOLD IT AGAINST ME?
I FAILED TO PROTECT HER...
...I COULDN'T DO A SINGLE THING...
...TO SAVE HER...
...I STILL CAN'T.
WHY?!
WHY DOESN'T EVERYBODY BLAME ME?!
IT WAS MY FAULT!
I WISH YOU GUYS WOULD HATE ME!
WHY DON'T YOU !?

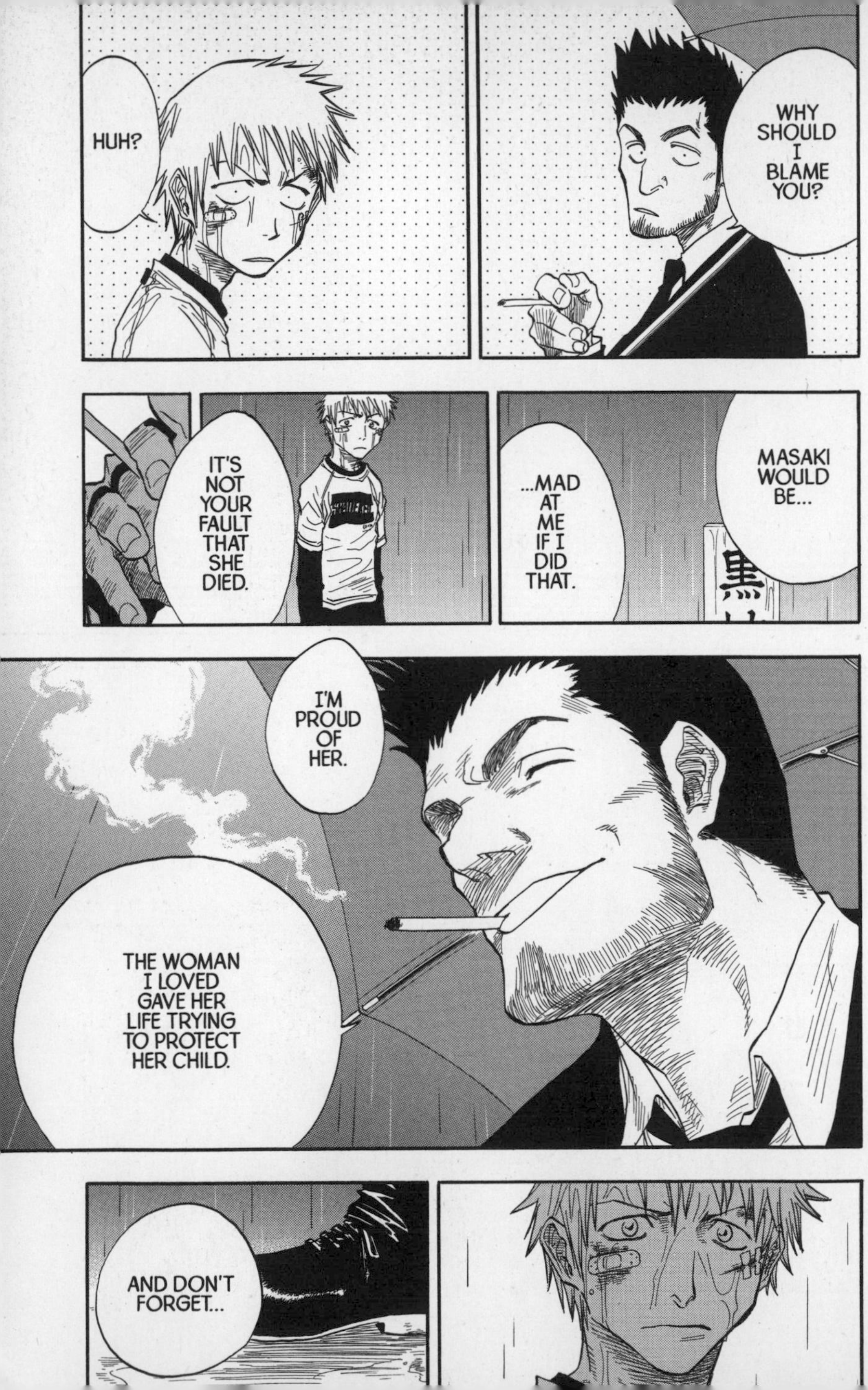
WHY SHOULD I BLAME YOU?
HUH?
MASAKI WOULD BE...
...MAD AT ME IF I DID THAT.
IT'S NOT YOUR FAULT THAT SHE DIED.
I'M PROUD OF HER.
THE WOMAN I LOVED GAVE HER LIFE TRYING TO PROTECT HER CHILD.
AND DON'T FORGET...

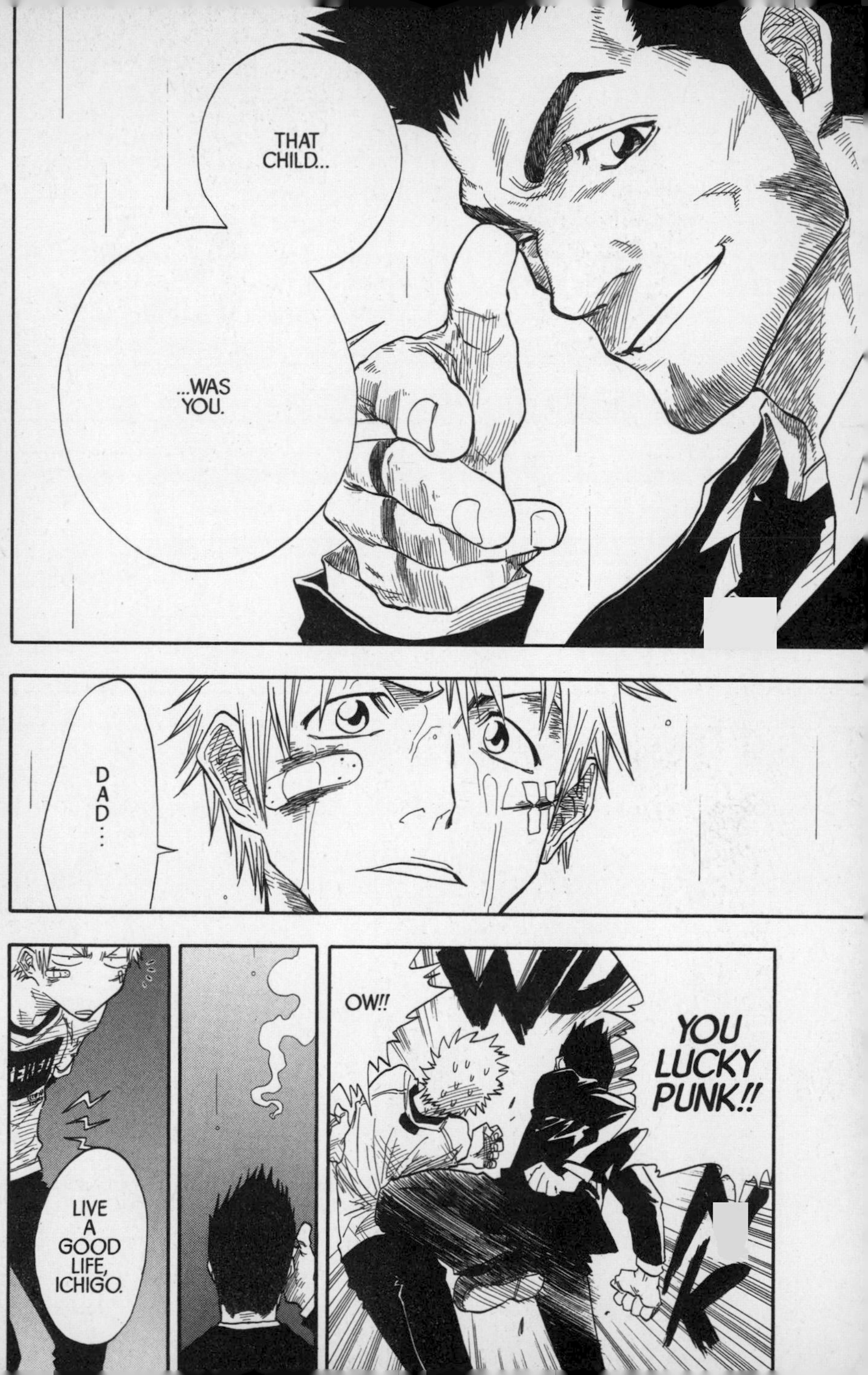
THAT CHILD...
...WAS YOU.
DAD...
YOU LUCKY PUNK!!
OW!!
LIVE A GOOD LIFE, ICHIGO.

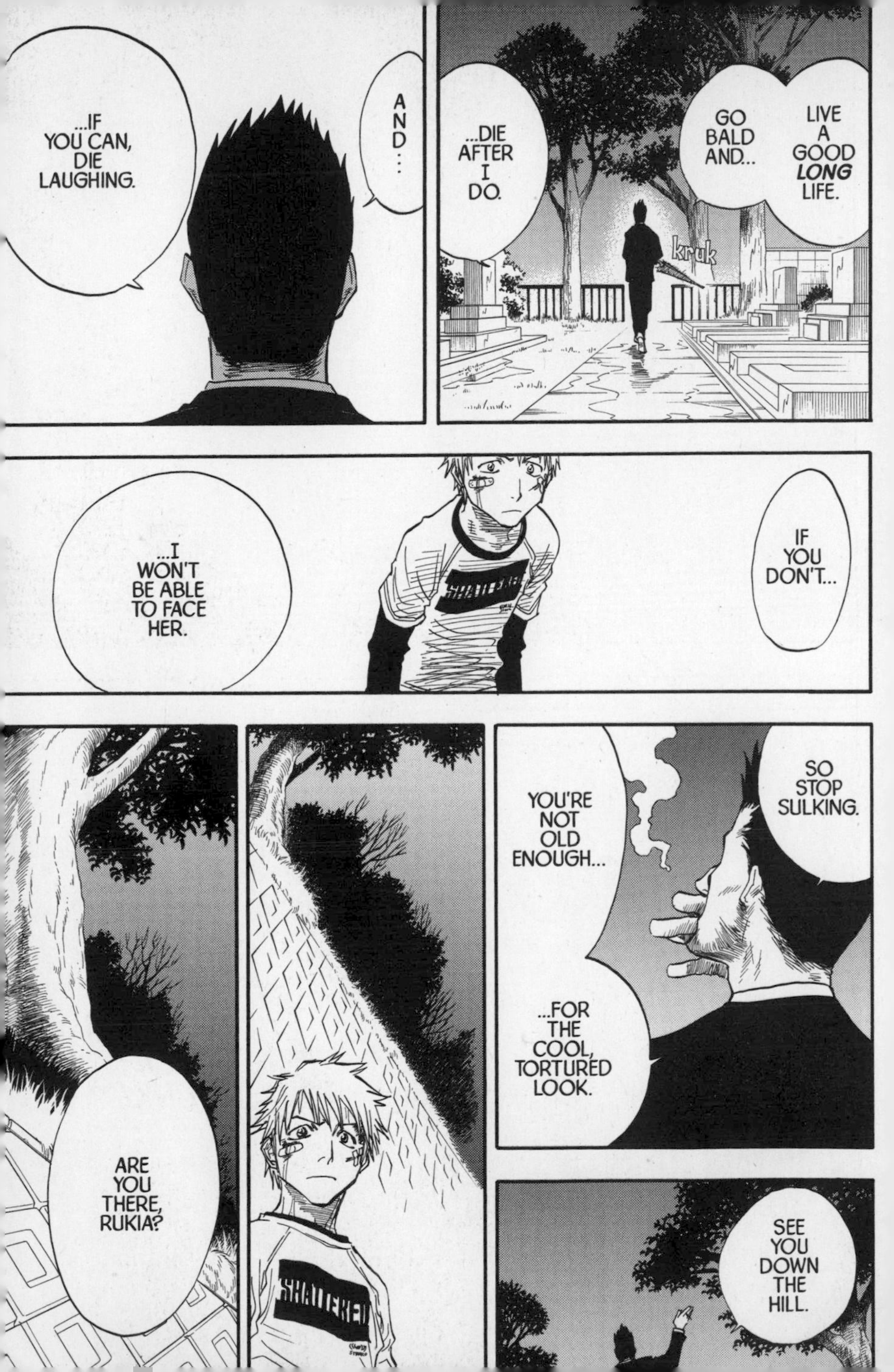
LIVE A GOOD **LONG** LIFE.
GO BALD AND...
kruk
...DIE AFTER I DO.
AND...
...IF YOU CAN, DIE LAUGHING.
IF YOU DON'T...
...I WON'T BE ABLE TO FACE HER.
SO STOP SULKING.
YOU'RE NOT OLD ENOUGH...
...FOR THE COOL, TORTURED LOOK.
SEE YOU DOWN THE HILL.
ARE YOU THERE, RUKIA?

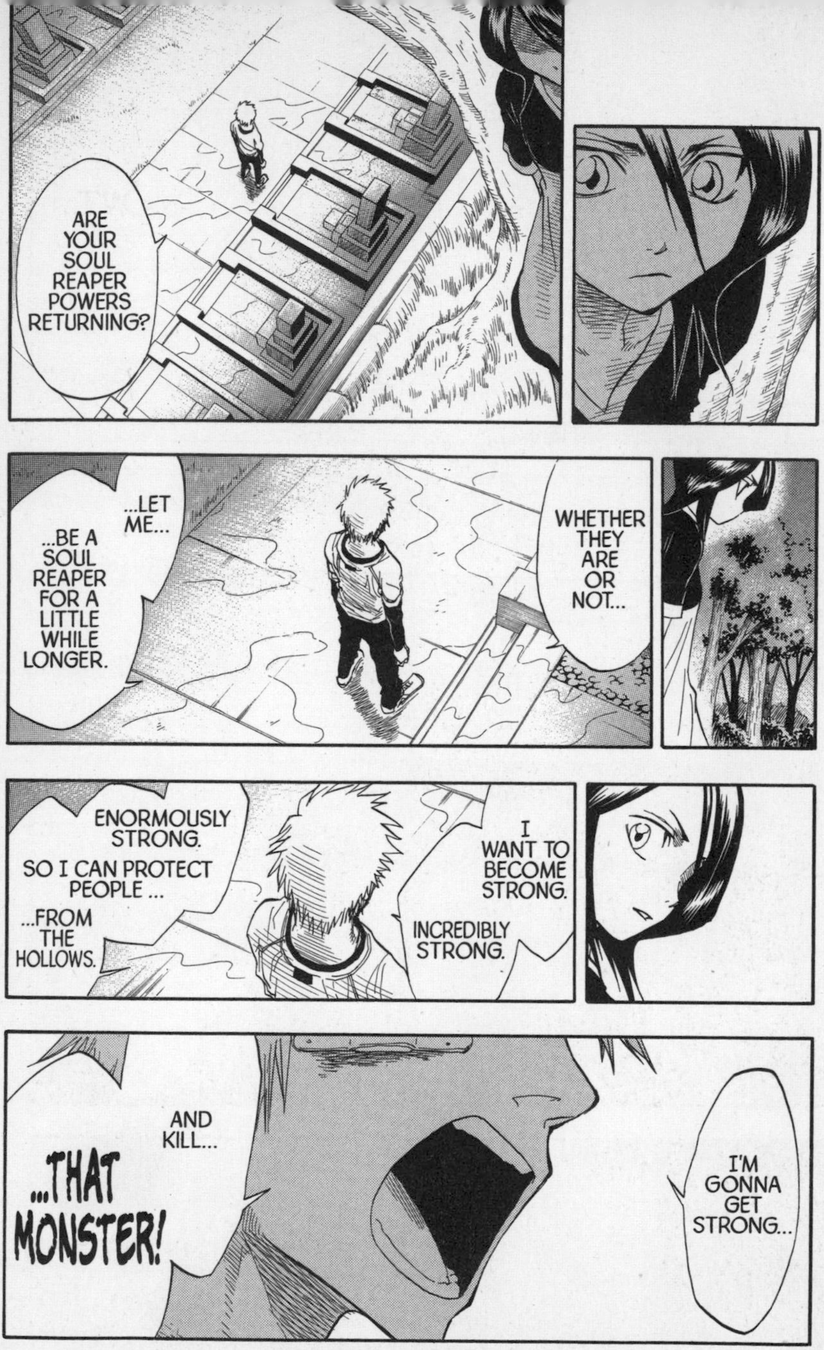
ARE YOUR SOUL REAPER POWERS RETURNING?
WHETHER THEY ARE OR NOT...
...LET ME...
...BE A SOUL REAPER FOR A LITTLE WHILE LONGER.
I WANT TO BECOME STRONG.
INCREDIBLY STRONG.
ENORMOUSLY STRONG.
SO I CAN PROTECT PEOPLE ...
...FROM THE HOLLOWS.
I'M GONNA GET STRONG...
AND KILL...
...THAT MONSTER!

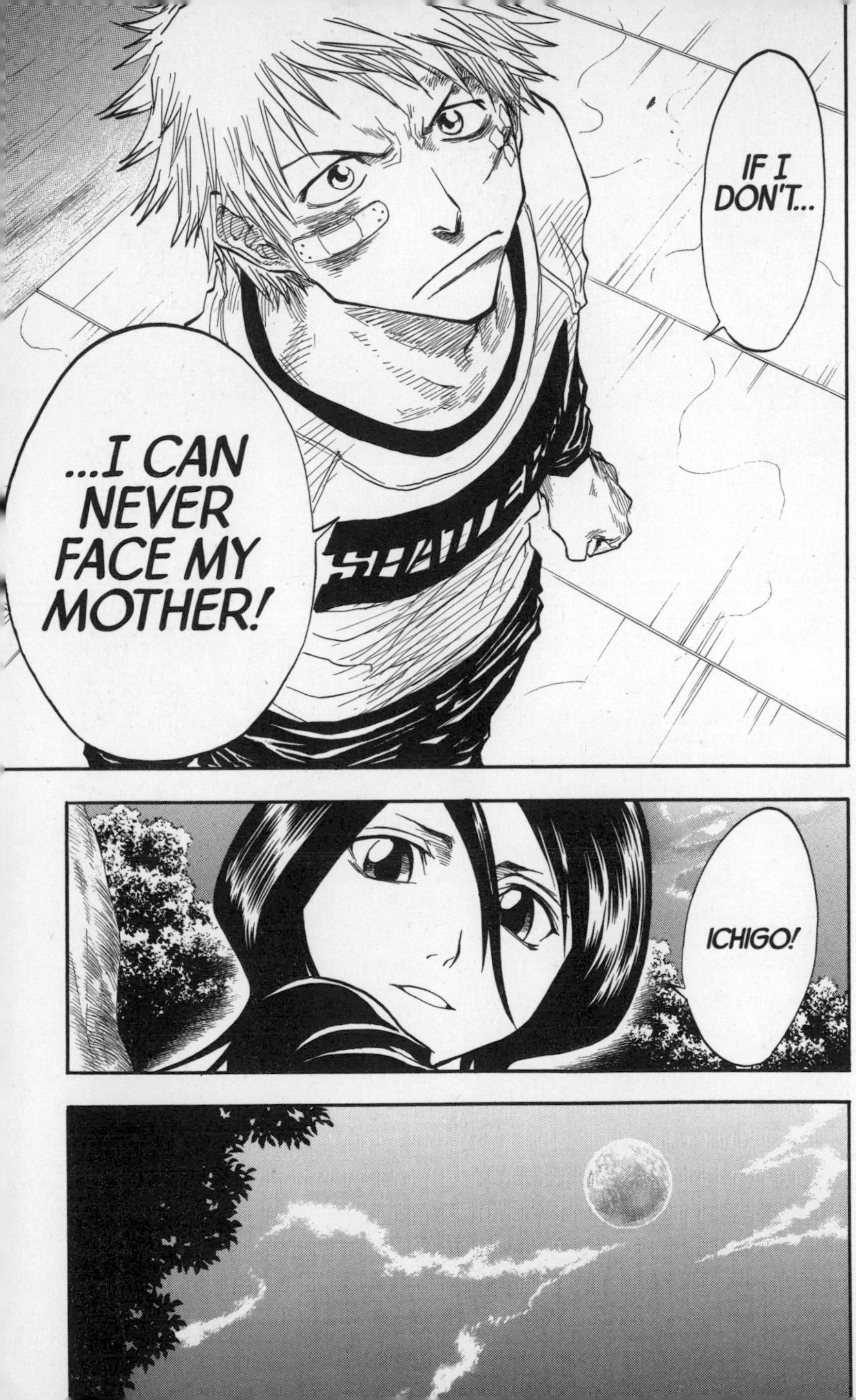
IF I DON'T...
...I CAN NEVER FACE MY MOTHER!
ICHIGO!

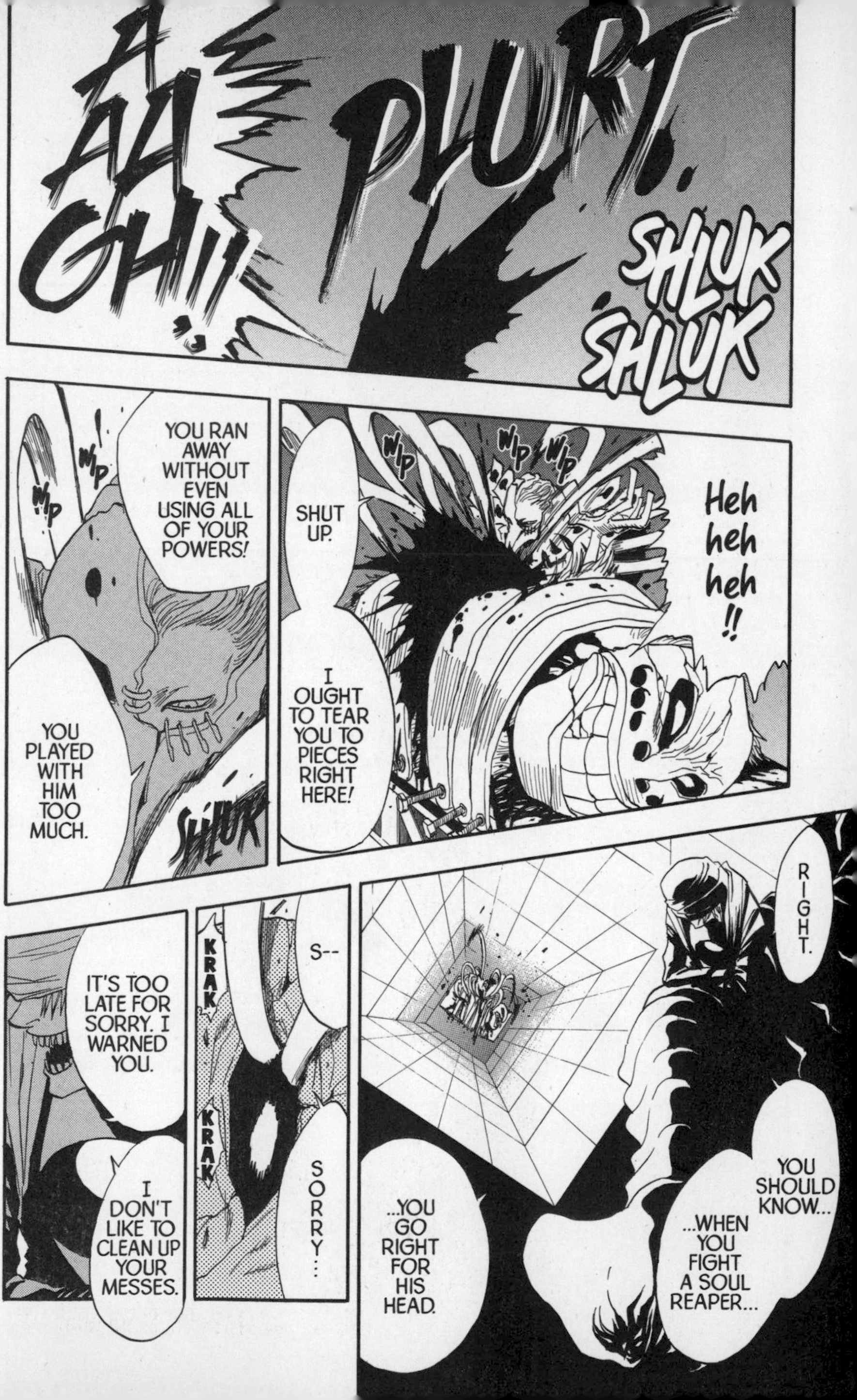
SHLUK SHLUK
PLURT.
AAACHI!!
Heh heh heh!!
WIP WIP WIP
SHUT UP.
I OUGHT TO TEAR YOU TO PIECES RIGHT HERE!
YOU RAN AWAY WITHOUT EVEN USING ALL OF YOUR POWERS!
WIP WIP
YOU PLAYED WITH HIM TOO MUCH.
SHLUK
RIGHT.
YOU SHOULD KNOW...
...WHEN YOU FIGHT A SOUL REAPER...
...YOU GO RIGHT FOR HIS HEAD.
S--
KRAK
KRAK
SORRY...
IT'S TOO LATE FOR SORRY. I WARNED YOU.
I DON'T LIKE TO CLEAN UP YOUR MESSES.

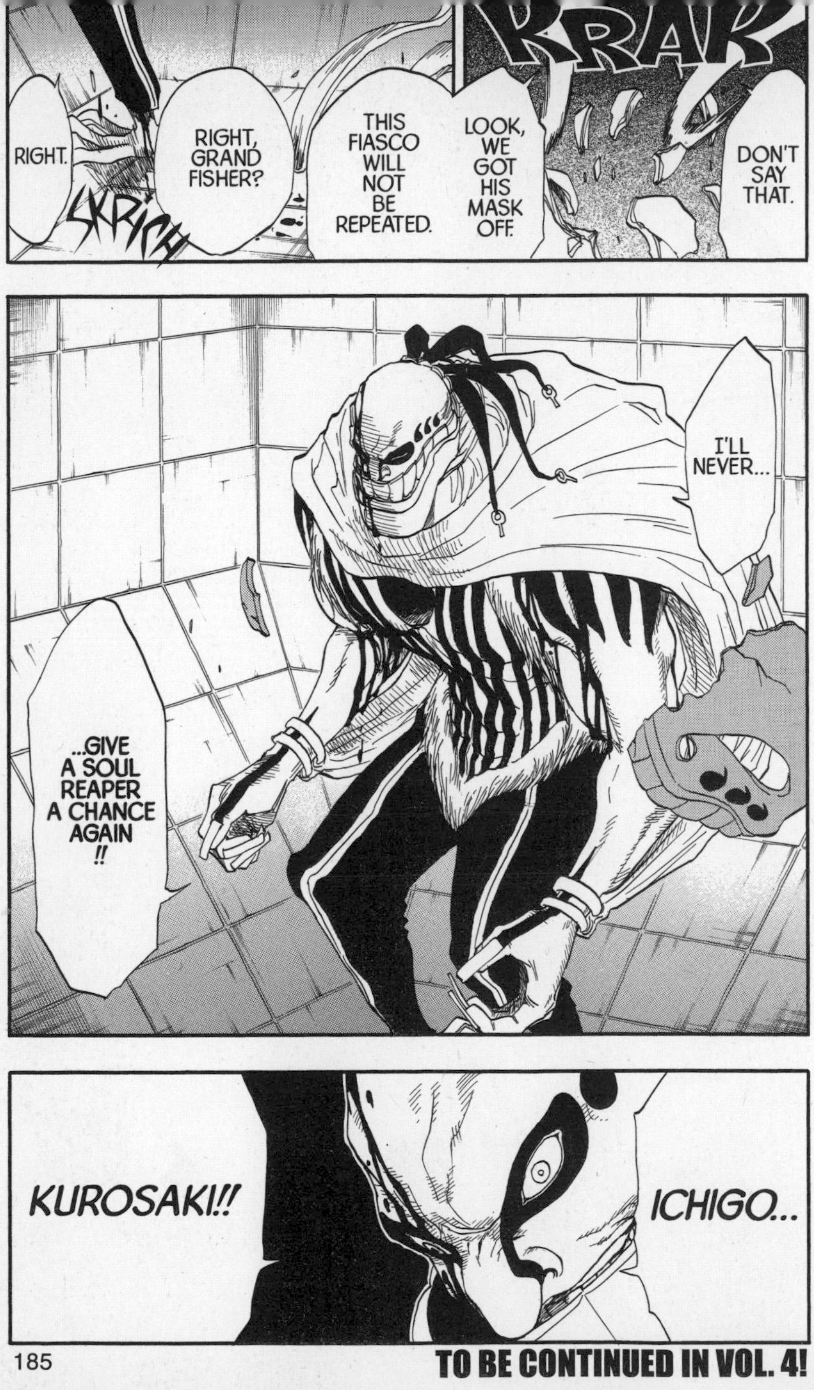

DON'T SAY THAT.
KRAK
LOOK, WE GOT HIS MASK OFF.
THIS FIASCO WILL NOT BE REPEATED.
RIGHT, GRAND FISHER?
SKRICH
RIGHT.
I'LL NEVER...
...GIVE A SOUL REAPER A CHANCE AGAIN !!
ICHIGO...
KUROSAKI!!

TO BE CONTINUED IN VOL. 4!

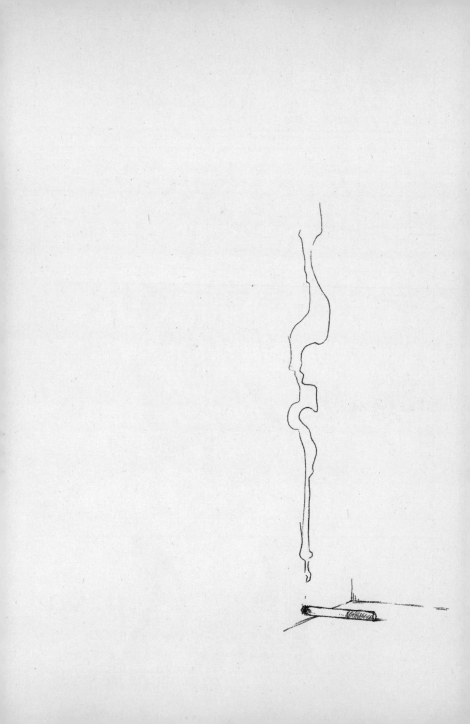

★ here is the data of **BLEACH.!!**

OVERALL ATTENDANCE NUMBER: 3	**TATSUKI ARISAWA**	アリサワ・タツキ
FEMALE STUDENT NUMBER: 1		

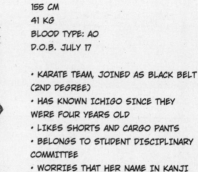

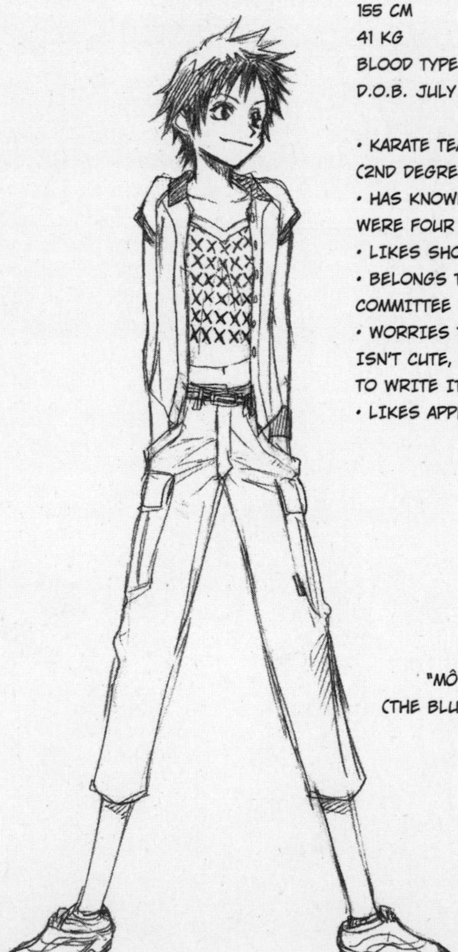

155 CM
41 KG
BLOOD TYPE: AO
D.O.B. JULY 17

- KARATE TEAM, JOINED AS BLACK BELT (2ND DEGREE)
- HAS KNOWN ICHIGO SINCE THEY WERE FOUR YEARS OLD
- LIKES SHORTS AND CARGO PANTS
- BELONGS TO STUDENT DISCIPLINARY COMMITTEE
- WORRIES THAT HER NAME IN KANJI ISN'T CUTE, SO SHE MAKES IT A POINT TO WRITE IT IN HIRAGANA
- LIKES APPLE PIE

THEME SONG

HÀI
"MÔ AOI TORI WA TOBANAI"
(THE BLUEBIRDS DON'T FLY ANYMORE)

RECORDED IN
"LOVE LETTER"

ISSHIN KUROSAKI

クロサキ・イッシン

186 CM
80 KG
BLOOD TYPE: AB
D.O.B. DECEMBER 10

• HEAD OF KUROSAKI FAMILY
• LOCAL DOCTOR. CAN DO
ANYTHING EXCEPT MAJOR SURGERY
• LIKES POTATO BEAN PASTE CAKES
• HE WAS ACTUALLY SUPPOSED TO BE
A MORTICIAN INSTEAD OF A DOCTOR
UNTIL THE VERY LAST MINUTE THIS
MANGA WAS PUBLISHED, SO HE
LOOKS BETTER IN A BLACK SUIT
THAN A WHITE LAB COAT.

THEME SONG

SOCIAL DISTORTION

"DON'T DRAG ME DOWN

RECORDED IN
"WHITE LIGHT,
WHITE HEAT,
WHITE TRASH"

Next Volume Preview

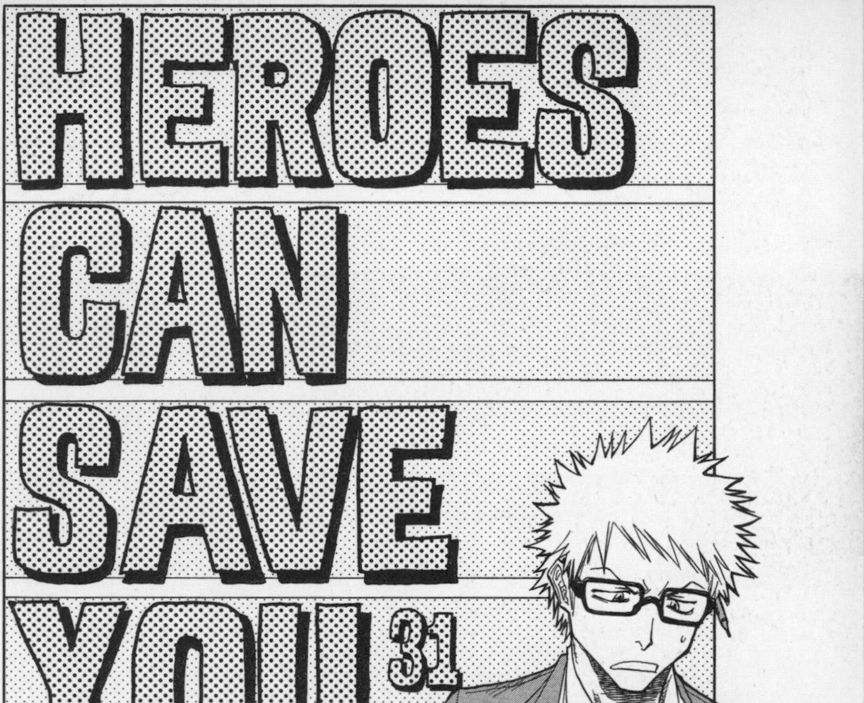
HEROES CAN SAVE YOU
31
15

Japan's most popular reality show stars a media-savvy spiritualist named Don Kanonji who dazzles audiences with his on-air exorcisms… and his TV show is headed straight for Ichigo's neighborhood! With a hardcore fan following (comprised mostly of teenage girls), Don prepares to wow the audience with his prime-time mysticism, but Ichigo remains skeptical. Might all this hustle and bustle only make the spirit world unstable? All this and more, on sale in December of 2004!

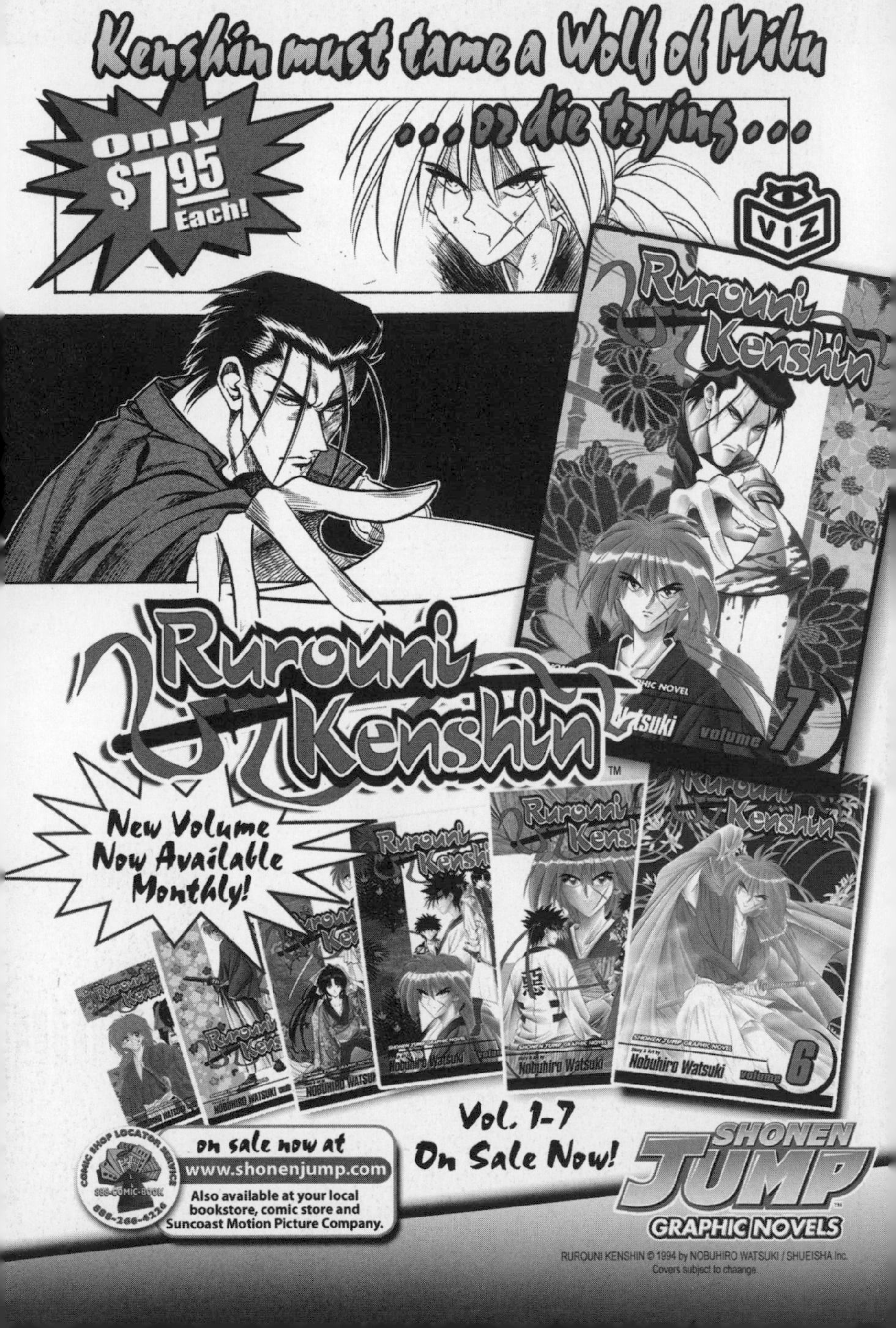
Kenshin must tame a Wolf of Mibu
...or die trying...
Only $7.95 Each!
VIZ
Rurouni Kenshin
Rurouni Kenshin™
New Volume Now Available Monthly!
Nobuhiro Watsuki
volume 6
Vol. 1-7 On Sale Now!
on sale now at
www.shonenjump.com
Also available at your local bookstore, comic store and Suncoast Motion Picture Company.
COMIC SHOP LOCATOR SERVICE
888-COMIC-BOOK
888-266-4226
SHONEN JUMP™
GRAPHIC NOVELS
RUROUNI KENSHIN © 1994 by NOBUHIRO WATSUKI / SHUEISHA Inc.
Covers subject to chaange.

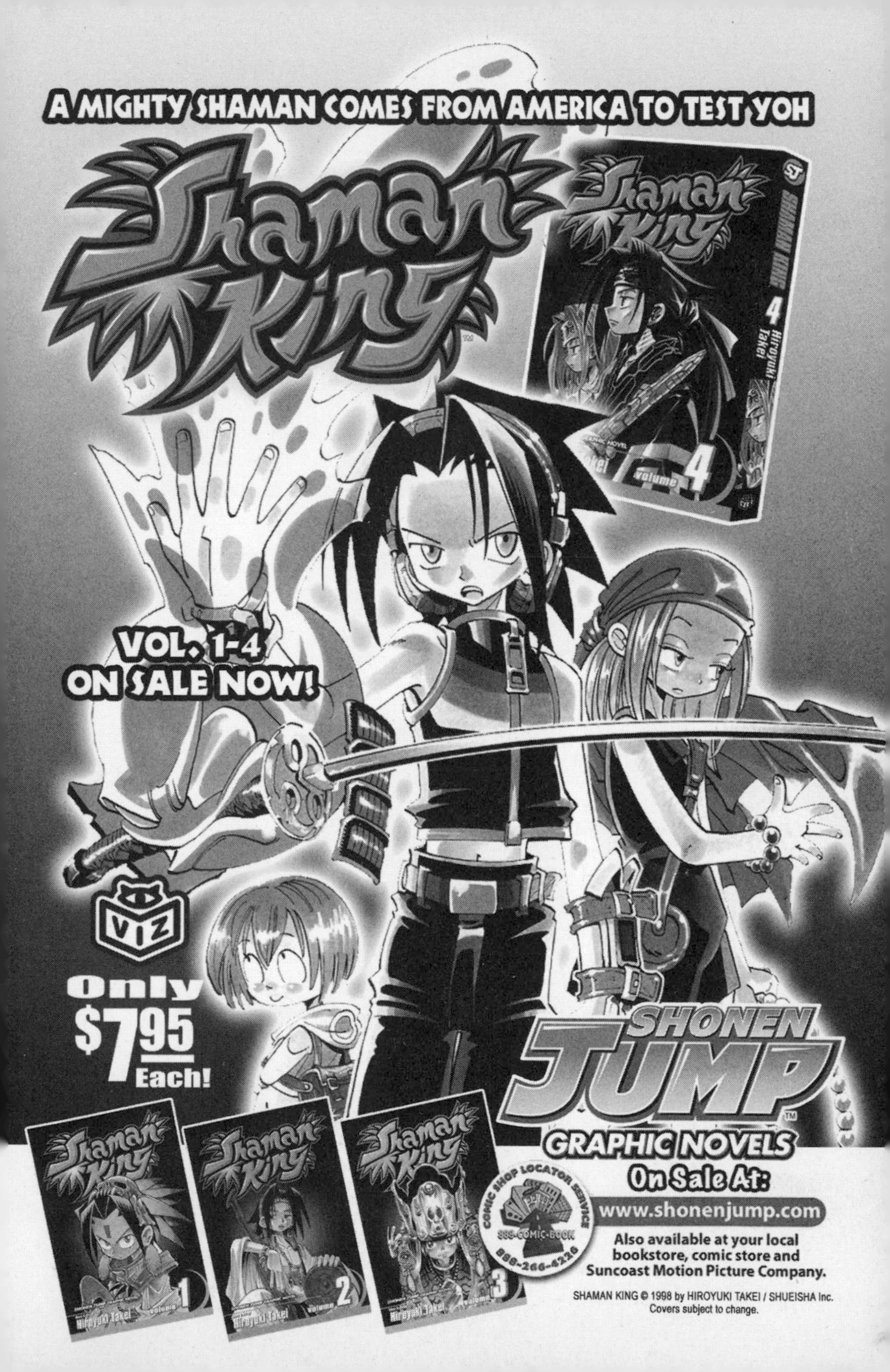
A MIGHTY SHAMAN COMES FROM AMERICA TO TEST YOH
Shaman King
VOL. 1-4
ON SALE NOW!
VIZ
Only
$7.95
Each!
SHONEN JUMP
GRAPHIC NOVELS
On Sale At:
www.shonenjump.com
COMIC SHOP LOCATOR SERVICE
888-COMIC-BOOK
888-266-4226
Also available at your local bookstore, comic store and Suncoast Motion Picture Company.
SHAMAN KING © 1998 by HIROYUKI TAKEI / SHUEISHA Inc.
Covers subject to change.